SUPERNATURAL GODS

SPIRITUAL MYSTERIES, PSYCHIC EXPERIENCES AND SCIENTIFIC TRUTHS

About the Author

Having earned his master's degree in theology from Andover Newton Theological School, **Jim Willis** has been an ordained minister for over forty years. He has also taught college courses in comparative religion and cross-cultural studies. In addition, Willis has been a professional musician, high school orchestra and band teacher, arts council director, and even a drive-time radio show host. His background in theology and education led to his writings on religion, the apocalypse, cross-cultural spirituality, and the mysteries of the unknown. His books include Visible Ink Press' *The Religion Book, Armageddon Now: The End of the World A to Z*, and *Ancient Gods: Lost Histories, Ancient Truths, and the Conspiracy of Silence*. He also published *Faith, Trust & Belief: A Trilogy of the Spirit*. Willis resides in the woods of South Carolina with his wife, Barbara, and their dog, Rocky.

SUPERNATURAL
GODS

SPIRITUAL MYSTERIES,
PSYCHIC EXPERIENCES
AND SCIENTIFIC TRUTHS

Jim Willis

VISIBLE
INK
PRESS

Detroit

Also from Visible Ink Press

Alien Mysteries, Conspiracies, and Cover-Ups
by Kevin D. Randle
ISBN: 978-1-57859-418-4

Ancient Gods: Lost Histories, Ancient Truths, and the Conspiracy of Silence
by Jim Willis
ISBN: 978-1-57859-614-0

Angels A to Z, 2nd edition
by Evelyn Dorothy Oliver, Ph.D., and James R Lewis, Ph.D.
ISBN: 978-1-57859-212-8

Armageddon Now: The End of the World A to Z
by Jim Willis and Barbara Willis
ISBN: 978-1-57859-168-8

The Astrology Book: The Encyclopedia of Heavenly Influences, 2nd edition
by James R. Lewis
ISBN: 978-1-57859-144-2

The Bigfoot Book: The Encyclopedia of Sasquatch, Yeti, and Cryptid Primates
by Nick Redfern
ISBN: 978-1-57859-561-7

Conspiracies and Secret Societies: The Complete Dossier, 2nd edition
by Brad Steiger and Sherry Hansen Steiger
ISBN: 978-1-57859-368-2

Demons, the Devil, and Fallen Angels
by Marie D. Jones and Larry Flaxman
ISBN: 978-1-57859-613-3

The Dream Encyclopedia, 2nd edition
by James R Lewis, Ph.D., and Evelyn Dorothy Oliver, Ph.D.
ISBN: 978-1-57859-216-6

The Dream Interpretation Dictionary: Symbols, Signs, and Meanings
By J. M. DeBord
ISBN: 978-1-57859-637-9

The Encyclopedia of Religious Phenomena
by J. Gordon Melton, Ph.D.
ISBN: 978-1-57859-209-8

The Fortune-Telling Book: The Encyclopedia of Divination and Soothsaying
by Raymond Buckland
ISBN: 978-1-57859-147-3

The Government UFO Files: The Conspiracy of Cover-Up
By Kevin D. Randle
ISBN: 978-1-57859-477-1

Hidden Realms, Lost Civilizations, and Beings from Other Worlds
by Jerome Clark
ISBN: 978-1-57859-175-6

The Horror Show Guide: The Ultimate Frightfest of Movies
By Mike May
ISBN: 978-1-57859-420-7

The Illuminati: The Secret Society That Hijacked the World
By Jim Marrs
ISBN: 978-1-57859-619-5

The Monster Book: Creatures, Beasts, and Fiends of Nature
By Nick Redfern
ISBN: 978-1-57859-575-4

The New World Order Book
by Nick Redfern
ISBN: 978-1-57859-615-7

Real Aliens, Space Beings, and Creatures from Other Worlds,
by Brad Steiger and Sherry Hansen Steiger
ISBN: 978-1-57859-333-0

Real Encounters, Different Dimensions, and Otherworldly Beings
by Brad Steiger with Sherry Hansen Steiger
ISBN: 978-1-57859-455-9

Real Ghosts, Restless Spirits, and Haunted Places, 2nd edition
by Brad Steiger
ISBN: 978-1-57859-401-6

Real Miracles, Divine Intervention, and Feats of Incredible Survival
by Brad Steiger and Sherry Hansen Steiger
ISBN: 978-1-57859-214-2

Real Monsters, Gruesome Critters, and Beasts from the Darkside
by Brad Steiger
ISBN: 978-1-57859-220-3

Real Vampires, Night Stalkers, and Creatures from the Darkside
by Brad Steiger
ISBN: 978-1-57859-255-5

Real Visitors, Voices from Beyond, and Parallel Dimensions
By Brad Steiger and Sherry Hansen Steiger
ISBN: 978-1-57859-541-9

Real Zombies, the Living Dead, and Creatures of the Apocalypse
by Brad Steiger
ISBN: 978-1-57859-296-8

The Religion Book: Places, Prophets, Saints, and Seers
by Jim Willis
ISBN: 978-1-57859-151-0

The Sci-Fi Movie Guide: The Universe of Film from Alien to Zardoz
By Chris Barsanti
ISBN: 978-1-57859-503-7

Secret History: Conspiracies from Ancient Aliens to the New World Order
By Nick Redfern
ISBN: 978-1-57859-479-5

Secret Societies: The Complete Guide to Histories, Rites, and Rituals
by Nick Redfern
ISBN: 978-1-57859-483-2

The Spirit Book: The Encyclopedia of Clairvoyance, Channeling, and Spirit Communication
by Raymond Buckland
ISBN: 978-1-57859-172-5

Supernatural Gods: Spiritual Mysteries, Psychic Experiences, and Scientific Truths
by Jim Willis
ISBN: 978-1-57859-660-7

UFO Dossier: 100 Years of Government Secrets, Conspiracies, and Cover-Ups
By Kevin D. Randle
ISBN: 978-1-57859-564-8

Unexplained! Strange Sightings, Incredible Occurrences, and Puzzling Physical Phenomena, 3rd edition
by Jerome Clark
ISBN: 978-1-57859-344-6

The Vampire Book: The Encyclopedia of the Undead, 3rd edition
by J. Gordon Melton, Ph.D.
ISBN: 978-1-57859-281-4

The Werewolf Book: The Encyclopedia of Shape-Shifting Beings, 2nd edition
by Brad Steiger
ISBN: 978-1-57859-367-5

The Witch Book: The Encyclopedia of Witchcraft, Wicca, and Neo-Paganism
by Raymond Buckland
ISBN: 978-1-57859-114-5

The Zombie Book: The Encyclopedia of the Living Dead
by Nick Redfern and Brad Steiger
ISBN: 978-1-57859-504-4

"REAL NIGHTMARES" E-BOOKS BY BRAD STEIGER

Book 1: *True and Truly Scary Unexplained Phenomenon*

Book 2: *The Unexplained Phenomena and Tales of the Unknown*

Book 3: *Things That Go Bump in the Night*

Book 4: *Things That Prowl and Growl in the Night*

Book 5: *Fiends That Want Your Blood*

Book 6: *Unexpected Visitors and Unwanted Guests*

Book 7: *Dark and Deadly Demons*

Book 8: *Phantoms, Apparitions, and Ghosts*

Book 9: *Alien Strangers and Foreign Worlds*

Book 10: *Ghastly and Grisly Spooks*

Book 11: *Secret Schemes and Conspiring Cabals*

Book 12: *Freaks, Fiends, and Evil Spirits*

PLEASE VISIT US AT VISIBLEINKPRESS.COM

**SUPERNATURAL GODS:
SPIRITUAL MYSTERIES,
PSYCHIC EXPERIENCES, AND
SCIENTIFIC TRUTHS**

Visible Ink Press®
43311 Joy Rd., #414
Canton, MI 48187-2075

Visible Ink Press is a registered trademark of Visible Ink Press LLC.

Most Visible Ink Press books are available at special quantity discounts when purchased in bulk by corporations, organizations, or groups. Customized printings, special imprints, messages, and excerpts can be produced to meet your needs. For more information, contact Special Markets Director, Visible Ink Press, www.visibleink.com, or 734-667-3211.

Managing Editor: Kevin S. Hile
Art Director: Mary Claire Krzewinski
Typesetting: Marco Divita
Proofreaders: Larry Baker and Aarti Stephens
Indexer: Shoshana Hurwitz
Cover images: Shutterstock.

Cataloging-in-Publicatiion Data is on file at the Library of Congress.

ISBN: 978-1-57859-660-7

Printed in the United States of America.

10 9 8 7 6 5 4 3 2 1

TABLE OF CONTENTS

PART I: THE OBJECT OF THE QUEST

PART II: THE METHOD OF THE QUEST

PART III: THE END OF THE QUEST AND BEYOND

Acknowledgments

A number of years ago, when we finally arrived at a time of life when we no longer had to rush off to work, my wife, Barbara, and I began what has proved to be an enduring and very pleasant custom. Every day, after breakfast on the porch, we read aloud for a few minutes before setting off to do whatever we're going to do for the day. We usually read challenging nonfiction, but often take a break to peruse fun stuff, as well. It leads to some great conversations and exchanges of ideas and concepts. It's amazing how serendipitous the habit has proved to be. It's no longer a surprise when the day's reading covers exactly what we need to hear for that particular day. When daughter Jan joins us from her home in Florida, she sits in. As it so happens, she was visiting for a week shortly after I completed the opening chapters of this book, and again for a week right after I finished Part III. On both occasions, I took the opportunity to spend a few days reading these sections to them. The ensuing exchange was very valuable and resulted in changes of both style and content. Barbara, of course, reads every word I write, and a few selected chapters were emailed to Jan for her feedback. To both Barb and Jan goes a heartfelt thank you for their encouragement and their input!

I've never met Dr. Dean Radin of the Institute of Noetic Sciences in California, but I've read all his books and shared a few email conversations with him. He has become another mentor whom I have never met. His work is important, and I encourage everyone to familiarize themselves with it. Besides being an important author, researcher, and contributor to Noetic science, he is (or, as he would say, was) a bluegrass aficionado like me. He tells me that his skills have rusted a bit due to his heavy workload, but that "in his mind he can still play like the wind!" As a former musician myself, I can only say, "Amen!"

Julie Soskin is another favorite of mine whom I have never met in person. We email from time to time, though, read each other's books, and have carried on some Skype conversations. I first met her through a wonderful DVD produced and directed by her husband, Rupert Soskin, called *The Spirit and the Serpent*. I have to follow her work from afar because she lives and works in France and England, but she is a gifted sensitive/teacher with penetrating insight. Thank you, Julie, for having come into my life.

This is my fourth book working with Roger Jänecke, Kevin Hile, and the talented group of editors and production folks at Visible Ink Press. It's been fun! I hope we can do some more. VIP still appreciates the spiritual and tactile experience of holding a real book in your hands. May they continue to spread that joy to future generations!

Photo Sources

1999shadow (Wikicommons): p. 116.

Zenobia Barlow: p. 255.

Bridgeman Art Library: p. 322.

J y Lewis-Williams Clottes: p. 30.

Sophie Delar: p. 90.

John Anster Fitzgerald: p. 35.

H. J. Ford: p. 102.

Ricard André Frantz: p. 60.

Lörincz Gabriella: p. 257

Genvessel (Wikicommons): p. 200.

Stephen Jay Gould: p. 49.

Kevin Hile: pp. 56, 319.

Kyle Hoobin: p. 199.

International Institute of Social History, Amsterdam: p. 177.

Internet Archive Book Images: p. 114.

J-Wiki (Wikicommons): p. 142.

Phil Konstantin: p. 213.

Kris Krüg: p. 185.

Lamorak (Wikicommons): p. 104.

Library of Congress: pp. 4, 244.

Marc Lieberman: p. 110.

Metonyme (Wikicommons): p. 167.

Myths of the Hindus & Buddhists (1914): p. 85.

Michael Persinger: p. 149.

Playing Futures: Applied Nomadology: p. 317.

Andrew Pontzen and Fabio Governato: p. 372 (left).

Shutterstock: pp. 4, 13, 21, 28, 37, 42, 43, 48, 58, 62, 67, 70, 73, 75, 78, 81, 83, 87, 88, 109, 123, 124, 130, 132, 134, 136, 140, 146, 150, 154, 158, 161, 169, 171, 183, 190, 192, 194, 204, 207, 211, 217, 218, 223, 228, 230, 233, 237, 248, 253, 258, 269, 272, 275, 277, 284, 289, 293, 298, 301, 303, 312, 315, 324, 326, 332, 338, 340, 344, 346, 353, 359, 364, 366, 369, 372 (right).

Pete Souza: p. 328.

Claire Taylor: p. 107.

Terpischore (Wikicommons): p. 240.

Tamiko Thiel: p. 68.

INTRODUCTION:
MAGIC AND THE QUEST FOR THE SUPERNATURAL

Perceptions and Realities

In my previous book, *Ancient Gods,* we speculated that many of the ancient gods of our ancestors were, in fact, real, live people, who, after the destruction of their advanced civilization, brought ideas and technologies to our ancestors. Some of these visitors were remembered so vividly—and their existence passed on so powerfully over generations—that legends and myths grew up about them until they were eventually deified and remembered as gods.

But that doesn't explain everything about early spirituality. The prevalence and importance of religion from our earliest days on Earth right down through to the present-day force us to ask another question: Are there such things as supernatural gods?

Perhaps we should phrase it another way: Is there such a thing as magic?

We're not talking about stage illusions, sleight of hand, or card tricks, neither are we referring to displays that keep us occupied *here* so that a magician can manipulate something over *there,* where we're not looking.

No, we mean honest-to-god, defy-the-senses, real-time, unexplainable *Magic* with a capital "M." The kind that cannot be predicted within the parameters of the scientific method. The kind that defies interpretation. The kind that breaks the rules. The kind that leaves us filled with a sense of awe and wonder.

Sir Arthur C. Clark once said that any sufficiently advanced technology is indistinguishable from magic.

As was often the case, he was right. Electricity would have appeared magical a few hundred years ago. Flicking a switch and flooding a room with light would once have gotten you burned at the stake. Only a god could do that, or a devil, depending on your theological bent.

Given Sir Arthur's definition, magic could simply be described as any spectacular, mind-bending result that stems from natural laws we don't yet understand. Most of us—maybe even all of us—who have been subjected to a typical modern education would probably feel quite comfortable with this explanation.

In our day and age, the microscopic world of quantum physics, a field only about a hundred years old, is revealing rules that govern phenomena that our ancestors would have called magical. They define the realm of the supernatural.

Take the newly discovered Higgs Field, for instance. Most theoretical physicists believe it to be an energy field that exists everywhere, permeating the realm of the reality we perceive. When Peter Higgs first predicted the existence of such a field, he based his conclusions solely on mathematical predictions. He never thought it might be proven by experimental methods during his lifetime. But it appears he was wrong. Scientists at the CERN particle accelerator complex in Switzerland now think they have provided sufficient results to prove the existence of the Higgs Field—the field that provides the means for energy to be converted into mass—the process described by Einstein's famous $E=mc^2$ equation (energy equals mass times the speed of light squared). If their discovery holds up, as it appears it may, it might be said that physicists are dabbling in magic.

The Higgs Field is most often described as resembling molasses ("treacle" in the United Kingdom) through which energy flows from "somewhere" to here. The field "slows down" the energy particle, "giving it" mass because it no longer travels at a speed sufficient to retain its original identity. In short, the "E" of Einstein's equation no longer maintains its velocity and "becomes" denser. In other words, it forms the "mass" we call "matter," the substance that is perceived by our senses. In order to convert mass back into energy it needs to attain not just the speed of light but the speed of light squared.

The chair upon which you sit is "slowed down" energy that appears solid enough to hold your weight. In slowing down it became subject to the laws of gravity. The view out your window is "solidified" energy, molded by its trip through the Higgs Field and transformed by your senses, which perceive it to be something real. The original particles, formerly massless energy, have been slowed down because they have become heavier, or bulkier. Were it not for this field, particles would not have enough mass to attract each other through the laws of gravity. They would not "clump" together to form what we call "real" objects. They would just zip around, oblivious to one another.

Understand, now, that the Higgs Field doesn't *generate* mass. It doesn't create the particles in the first place. According to accepted laws of conservation, that's impossible. All it does is slow particles down so laws of physics on this side of the field can take over and work their magic.

This "magic" is called the *Higgs Effect*. Particles that pass though the field gain mass because they slow down, clump together through gravitational force, and form measurable objects.

"But what about light itself?" you ask. "Light travels, obviously, at the speed of light. Why doesn't it slow down and become something quite different than that which we experience?"

That is where the magic comes in. Light is not just a particle. It is also a wave. As such, it gains energy, not mass. We can measure its wavelength property and discover its speed. But as soon as we stop it long enough to try and figure out where it is, light becomes a particle.

"So where does the original energy come from?" you ask. "What's on the other side of the Higgs Field?"

No one knows. That's where Arthur C. Clark's definition of magic kicks in. It's unexplored territory. "Here there be dragons!" Because it is *above* the natural world, we call it *super*natural. This is the domain of the gods.

Brian Greene, as he does as well or better than anybody, tried to explain this magical landscape in an article he wrote for *Smithsonian* magazine:

> Physicists tell a parable about fish investigating the laws of physics but are so habituated to their watery world they fail to consider its influence. The fish struggle mightily to explain the gentle swaying of plants as well as their own locomotion. The laws they ultimately find are complex and unwieldy. Then one brilliant fish has a breakthrough. Maybe the complexity reflects simple fundamental laws acting themselves out in a complex environment—one that's filled with a viscous, incompressible and pervasive fluid: the ocean. At first, the insightful fish is ignored, even ridiculed. But slowly, the others, too, realize that their environment, its familiarity notwithstanding, has a significant impact on everything they observe.
>
> —Brian Greene, *Smithsonian*, magazine, July 2013

In short, what was once "magic," the work of the gods, is really just the result of previously undiscovered rules acting within a heretofore unseen field. There is nothing "magic" about it at all. It is what Clark called "sufficiently advanced technology."

But let's be honest. Does this explanation make the whole thing less "magical"? If massless energy particles over on the other side of the Higgs Field suddenly appear as a solid rock here in our world, isn't that magical? If the perception realm we inhabit over here consists of energy particles from somewhere outside our world that magically acquired mass as they traveled through a field we can't observe, let alone adequately describe, isn't that a good trick?

Doesn't it make you wonder about what we call magic? Doesn't it make you question whether or not we indeed know anything about what we swear is reality? Doesn't it make you suspect that we might be living in a dream world that is really nothing at all as it appears to be when we experience it through our meager senses of taste, sight, smell, touch, and hearing? Doesn't it make you wonder about the *super*natural?

"But this is real!" you scream. "If I kick a rock with my foot, it hurts!"

Well, maybe so. But science assures us that the pain itself is only an illusion produced by electromagnetic impulses coursing through what amounts to a chemical soup and a neurological network.

I know that doesn't make it hurt any less. But science is science, so there you go. Embrace it. Live with it. That's the way it is.

A Cultural Adaption

There are many who will read these words and scoff, saying, "I know what I see!" No one will ever convince them that they have bought into the illusion. Such is its power over us. How strange it is that truth itself appears as an illusion.

A wonderful cultural adaptation of the paradox that juxtaposes reality with illusion was captured in an episode of the television series *Northern Exposure*. The series is set in the fictional town of Cicely, Alaska. A traveling carnival finds itself stranded for a few days, awaiting the repair of its bus. The owner of the traveling circus is a physicist-turned-magician who quickly finds a kindred soul in the self-taught mystic who is also the town's radio announcer.

The announcer capitalizes on the performer's presence to attempt to get his own personal handle on some of the truths that underlie existence. He decides to ask the carnival physicist-turned-magician why he changed jobs. What he learns is that "On the subatomic level everything is so bizarre, so unfathomable. With magic, you have some control."

This prompts the announcer to later reflect to his audience:

When we think of a magician, the image that comes to mind is Merlin. Long white beard, cone-shaped hat, right? You know. Well, in one version of this Arthurian legend, the archetypal sorcerer retires. Checks out of the conjuring biz. His reason? The rationalists are taking over. The time for magic is coming to an end. Well, ol' Merlin should have stuck around because those same rationalists trying to put a rope around reality suddenly found themselves in the psychedelic land of physics. A land of quarks, gluons, and neutrinos. A place that refuses to play by Newtonian rules. A place that refuses to play by any rules. A place better suited for the Merlins of the world.

Eventually, the two have a follow-up conversation that runs something like this:

> *Announcer:* This has been bugging me for a long time. I was doing some reading on superstring atomic theory. I was having a hard time … because my math is weak … but it seems to me that when you get into the onion of an atom and you get to the smaller and smaller particles you find that you really don't have any particles at all.
>
> *Carni:* Yeah.
>
> *Announcer:* So subatomic particles might just really be vibrating waves of energy?
>
> *Carni:* Correct. Right. Listen. No mass, no "thing."
>
> *Announcer:* The essential building block of everything is nothing?
>
> *Carni:* All is an illusion. That's what I hated about the (physics) business. What are you supposed to do with information like that?

The announcer again muses to his radio audience about what he discovered from the conversation:

> If there is nothing of substance in the world; if the ground we walk on is just a mirage; if reality itself really isn't real—what are we left with? What do we hang our hat on? Magic! The stuff not ruled by rational law.

Magical Realms

If all this is true—and the best scientists of our day insist it is—it opens up a whole new way of thinking about what is real and what is not. After all, if a massless realm exists out there on the other side of the Higgs Field, a world of energy consisting of forms we simply cannot understand, a *super*natural world in which even our most sophisticated measuring devices are not only crude but insufficient, a world totally outside our realm of perception, we have to wonder about other possible worlds, as well.

What about parallel universes or dimensions of time? What about so-called "spiritual" habitations such as Heaven? How do we understand such things as déjà vu and shamanic "journeying" to other realms? How do we explain common testimonies about near death experiences or out-of-body travel? What do we do with the vast evidence of religious texts that have made similar claims for thousands of years? Have all these people, numbering at least in the millions, been deceived? Can we confidently sit back in our armchairs and declare them all delusional? Are we so sure of ourselves?

Don't forget that when quantum physics was new, even Albert Einstein didn't believe it. What is accepted truth today was fantastic speculation a century ago. People once declared to be impossible things we now take for granted. They ridiculed pioneers of science, many of whom went to their graves wondering if they were, indeed, crazy for suggesting such nonsense as space travel and higher dimensions.

George and Ira Gershwin once wrote a prophetic song called "They All Laughed" that went like this, in part:

They all laughed at Christopher Columbus when he said the world was round.

They all laughed when Edison recorded sound.

They all laughed at Wilbur and his brother when they said that man could fly.

They told Marconi wireless was a phony.

It's the same old cry ...

Who's got the last laugh now?

This song reminds us that many "moderns" have laughed at the testimony of people through the ages who claimed to have somehow experienced supernatural worlds of perception that exist beyond the range of our senses. Maybe the discoveries of a previously unknown world now called quantum reality, a realm thought to undergird and support what we have traditionally called the world of the "real," have proven to be, in the words of Arthur C. Clark, a "sufficiently advanced technology." In other words, maybe supernatural "magic" really exists.

Where Some Have Gone Before

Now we come to the crux of the issue. We know that consciousness exists on this side of the Higgs field. After all, even though we can't explain it, even though we argue about what it is, we know we are conscious beings. Some of us even know what it is to be knocked *un*conscious. We know consciousness has something to do with our brains, which are either *generators of* or *receptors for* consciousness. (For now, we'll accept an either/or for that argument.)

Here's the point. If consciousness exists on this side of the Higgs field, sustained by intelligent beings like us, who is to say that consciousness doesn't also exist on the *other* side of the Higgs field, possessed by equally intelligent beings who project themselves into our perception realm by means of the extension of what might be called *universal* consciousness? As we shall soon see, for at least the last 40,000 years a small but influential number of practitioners have lived who claim to have experienced the presence of these beings in various ways.

Call them what you will—gods, angels, fairies, elves, jinns, leprechauns, demons, spirit guides, or helpers—there is simply no rational reason to assume that beings who can experience rational consciousness exist only on our side of the fence—the material universe. We now know, through tried and true scientific and mathematical processes, that whole universes exist outside our perception realm. And if you consider the number of people who, down through the entire history of humankind, have claimed a belief in God or other beings who presumably are not made up of matter, the evidence becomes overwhelming that we can no longer honestly hold a rational position that says we are the only conscious beings in an infinite multiverse. Those who do so simply demonstrate a closed mind.

This begs the question: If such intelligent beings and an environment that supports them exist, if what have been traditionally called supernatural "gods" are real and can, under certain conditions, project themselves into our world, is it not possible that many millions of people, either by accident or on purpose, have found a way to bridge the gap and perceive those beings?

In this book we're going to explore the claims of people who seem to have broken free of the perception realm bound by our five senses. In many different ways, they have experienced something unique before returning to our "real" world with some pretty fantastic stories. Be they biblical prophets or Native American shamans, ancient Druids or New Age mystics, they all claim that our world is a lot grander than we might like to think. The supernatural is real. The "Powers That Be" are real. The ancient gods are real. The European traditions of mystical encounters are real.

All these people struggled with language, of course. Words are, after all, metaphors based on the experience we all share every day. How can language, developed within the "box" of the senses in order to describe what is found there, possibly suffice to describe something totally outside that reality? It might be said that when you experience a supernatural realm, you travel to a place where words are insufficient, and then you have to attempt to describe what you saw using words that are inadequate.

Some say it feels like alien abduction; others claim the experience consists of dreams, miracles, out-of-body trips, or shamanic journeying. Biblical prophets such as Ezekiel claim they "saw" the Lord or were "caught up" to Heaven. When you read their words without the lens of modern religion getting in the way, their testimonies sound very similar to the universal shamanic experience.

Ancient spiritual traditions such as *animism* and *shamanism* have long insisted that unseen realities lie outside the range of our physical senses. These traditions are found in every major world religion practiced today. Religious *afterlife* concepts, such as heaven and hell, which exist in a reality beyond our earthly perceptions, may be quietly considered outmoded by many modern-day parishioners who sit in antiseptic, technologically driven sanctuaries, but they are still a standard of all church, synagogue, and mosque curricula in today's world.

Putting aside arguments concerning the literal truth of such teachings, which presuppose a personally experienced eternal life but ground that belief in terms familiar to a modern, scientific, linear-time mindset, is there evidence that unseen worlds, hidden from the perception of reality we inhabit in our day-to-day life, actually exist? Are these parallel worlds invisible to us because they lie outside our senses' ability to perceive them? Are we a small part of a much larger picture?

Modern academics argue that reality consists of that which we can see, touch, smell, taste, and hear. It is measurable, logical, and provable. It is explained through mathematical equations and subject to the inexorable press of the scientific method.

But what if modern academic thought doesn't go far enough? How else are we to understand the immense body of evidence accrued through the admittedly subjective experiences of millions of people down through the ages who claim to have somehow experienced a reality outside our perception realm? Could all these folks be misguided? Or could unseen realities, existing beyond the capabilities of our measuring devices, be doorways to a much larger experience that could change the way we humans view our lives and subsequent future? Could the acknowledgement of such unseen realms actually alter our human condition on Earth in the twenty-first century?

Some investigate the new frontier using methods such as dowsing, meditation, hypnotism, or other metaphysical techniques. Some experience religious conversion and speak of heavenly messengers and miracles. Others simply keep quiet, not wishing to be thought crazy. Still others claim to have been abducted by aliens.

Whatever these people felt about their supernatural experiences, however they described them, many were changed forever. Almost all who have had such experiences claim they were more "real" than day-to-day reality. These people were changed forever as a result. Their world was turned upside down.

They found themselves on a quest for the supernatural. They now believed in magic.

A Map for the Quest

In this book we're going to engage in such a quest. In "Part I: The Object of the Quest," we'll prepare ourselves by learning how the ancients first perceived and came into contact with forces that existed way beyond their daily experience. Deep in the great painted caves, humans depicted such entities as animal envoys and earth spirits. This happened only after a profound shift in human consciousness, which was perhaps brought about by a period of evolutionary change known as "punctuated equilibria." In the cosmos above, they visualized metaphysical manifestations and developed theories about religious concepts such as theism to try to come to terms with the reality of otherworldly beings. Our day has seen the influx of visitors from afar expressed in the phenomena of mythological motifs found in comic book form and TV shows such as *Ancient Aliens,* which also popularized the idea of abduction and the "Wounded Man" concept found cross-culturally. Whatever the means, however supernatural entities are described, we will attempt to prepare ourselves by reading about the experiences of the ancients who have gone before us. They were the pioneers. They led the way and mapped the territory.

But we're not going to stop with their experiences. We're going to seek to understand not only *what* they saw, but *how* they went about seeing it.

In "Part II: The Method of the Quest," we'll investigate the means by which the supernatural was accessed. Many of these methods, such as astrology, are still in use today. When Dr. Timothy Leary invited folks to "tune in, turn on and drop out" back in the 1960s, he introduced a whole generation to chemical keys indigenous peoples had been using for millennia to open the portals of the supernatural world. Dowsing is still a very popular method to bridge the gap between realities. Dreams are familiar to everyone. Hypnotism, past life regressions, intuition, déjà vu, intentionality, meditation, and Eastern spirituality all have their followers. Miracles, often relegated to the safe, secure past by many moderns, still claim headlines when they occur. Books about out-of-body and near-death experiences fill many bookshelves. Psychics and sensitives still ply their traditional practice, as do followers of shamanism and spiritualism.

One of the most surprising discoveries of the twentieth century was the complete overturning of traditional, Newtonian science, at least as it pertained to the ultimate reality that undergirds our universe. Explorations in theoretical physics and the world of quantum reality have mystified people all over the world. Thanks to advanced mathematics, nothing will ever be quite the same again. Ancient supernatural experience and modern science seem to have blurred together in quite surprising ways.

"In Part III: The End of the Quest and Beyond," we'll try to sum up the results of our survey and look ahead to what might be coming next.

The path ahead is now open. The way of the supernatural. The way of magic. The quest begins.

> Even the most die-hard skeptics among us believe in magic. Humans can't help it: though we try to be logical, irrational beliefs—many of which we aren't even conscious of—are hardwired in our psyches. But rather than hold us back, the unavoidable habits of mind that make us think luck and supernatural

forces are real, that objects and symbols have power, and that humans have souls and destinies are part of what has made our species so evolutionarily successful. Believing in magic is good for us.

—Matthew Hutson, in *The Seven Laws of Magical Thinking*,
Hudson Street Press, 2012.

PART I: THE OBJECT OF THE QUEST

Matter and Spirit. As above, so below. Science teaches us to believe that the material world is the primary and only reality. But … this is absolutely not the case. What we call the material world, our "consensual reality," is only part of the pattern—probably not even the primary part. Viewed through the lens of ayahuasca (for instance), another "world" becomes visible, another reality, perhaps many of them. And because these worlds interpenetrate our own, *effects* in this world may turn out to have *causes* in the other worlds. Perhaps the material world is indeed the creation of spirits, but if so then presumably they made it because they need it (for their own experience/evolution/development). The material world, if cut off from the spirit world, becomes meaningless and empty. So the material world needs the spirit world too.

—Adapted from Graham Hancock, *Supernatural*

INTRODUCTION

A DISCOVERY IN THE DESERT

Begin at the beginning and go on till you come to the end: then stop.

—Lewis Carroll, in *Alice's Adventures in Wonderland*

In 2004, while researching the book *Armageddon Now: The End of the World A–Z*, my wife, Barbara, and I were living in a camper in southern Arizona, working out of the border town of Nogales. We spent many happy but rough hours scrambling over and around canyons and rock outcrops searching for clues that might help explain the sudden disappearance of the ancient Puebloans, commonly referred to as *Anasazi*. Rock art is everywhere in that part of the country. What intrigued us the most, besides the many versions of the *Kokopelli* motif, were the countless spirals pecked into rock faces. What did they represent? What was the meaning behind the designs that obviously meant a great deal to ancient artists?

Some people believe that spirals depict ancient starbursts. They search the cosmological record for stars that exploded thousands of years ago and might have been visible in these parts.

Carl Jung, the famous disciple of Sigmund Freud, taught that the spiral is an archetype—a symbol representing cosmic forces.

Since the spiral is so common in nature, found in everything from tornados, the pattern distribution of seeds in plants such as sunflowers and ferns, the shape of a nautilus shell, and even the double helix of our DNA, many think spiral depictions simply echo what early humans found in the world around them.

Others prefer a mystical interpretation with spiritual overtones. These folks claim to see a pathway leading into and out of the center of our being or a vortex passageway between worlds.

Whatever they mean, spirals are found carved into the rocks of enigmatic places such as Ireland's Newgrange, a megalithic archeological wonder that dates back at least 5,200 years. Clearly, spirals meant something very special to people who were physiologically and mentally similar to us even though they lived a long time ago. The fact that spirals are found in every culture around the world means that people everywhere had a similar intellectual or spiritual need to preserve this figure in stone. It obviously meant something very important.

THE GREAT DISCONNECT

So if those folks were in every way similar to us in terms of mental, intellectual, neurological, and physical capabilities, we have to ask why we don't have the slightest idea what they were trying to convey. What meant a

A detail of the Newgrange site in Ireland shows spiral patterns. Spirals may have physiological, natural, and spiritual significance in our lives.

lot to them means relatively little to us today. Clearly, there must be a huge disconnect somewhere between them and us. Our ancestors, from sea to shining sea and all around the world, felt the spiral was important. They understood its significance and continued to relate to it for thousands of years. They preserved its image in stone that will last forever. They revered this symbol!

We not only don't know what the importance was, we have completely forgotten almost everything about what the spiral might symbolize. We are reduced to wild speculation.

Why? What's happened to us?

There is obviously one way in which we differ from the ancients. We have a written language with which we can record out thoughts, beliefs, ideas and innermost feelings. If we were to carve a spiral in a rock face today, we could write down why we are doing it. We could tell others what it *means* to us.

This doesn't mean we are smarter than the old ones. It just means that they practiced an oral tradition rather than a written one. To them it was important to look someone in the eye when you expressed yourself. They would no doubt think our current practice of Facebook-once-removed rants in which we vomit forth our thoughts to no one in particular and then check to see how many "likes" we receive is a very immature and childish practice. "If you have something to say," they would probably argue, "say it directly to the person in front of you who is listening! Don't hide in a darkened room behind an anonymous computer."

Viewed in this way, we are forced to wonder who is more fully evolved and complete—them or us?

We say history began with the invention of writing. Everything else is pre-history. But that is *our* definition. It doesn't mean it has any relevance to those who came before us. They're not around to argue the point so we have the luxury of acting condescending and patronizing. After all, they can't hear us anymore.

But remember this. Their cultures flourished a lot longer than we "moderns" have been here. Countless thousands of years passed back then but there are only six or eight thousand years on our side of the arbitrary line in the sand that divides what we call "history" from "pre-history." Just because they're dead and we're not doesn't mean we're "right." Some might even argue that the very technological superiority that makes us feel so smug might actually kill us off before we obtain anywhere near their longevity.

Here's the point. The spiral *meant* something to them and we have forgotten what that "something" is. But given their architecture and their propensity to carve spirals in all kinds of out-of-the-way places, there must have been a method to their madness, and it probably had something to do with religion. There is no other force on earth that affects people so. It may not have been any religion we would recognize, but it affected them deeply.

And what is the common denominator of all religious thoughts? It's the belief that something exists "out there," "in here," or "up there"—something Other. The ancient shaman dressed in his animal skins and the Baptist clergyman wearing his black pulpit robe have one thing in common. They both believe there is a realm somewhere that we can contact through prayer and to which we "go" when we die. It is peopled by beings without corporeal bodies who have communicated with us in the past and still, from time to time, are at least felt in our reality. *We* call them angels. We don't know what *they* called them.

The spiral could very well be the oldest symbol of the pathway between worlds. In that sense, it would have been important to them. We may have replaced it with a cross, a menorah, a candle, or a visionary tunnel but the symbolism is the same. The realm that exists "out there," "in here," or "up there" is accessible. We may reach it by journeying, visualizing, meditating, praying or even "climbing Jacob's ladder," but, at least in our minds or souls, we can travel there. Others have done it. They have mapped the way. Those maps are found everywhere on earth. They are called religions. They may depict different routes but they all lead to the same source. That source is where we came from. It's also where we are headed. It is The Object of the Quest.

In Part I we're going to peruse some of those ancient maps. Perhaps some of them, which many may think are outdated, might still show the way.

ANIMAL ENVOYS FROM CAVE AND COSMOS

The animal envoys of the Unseen Power no longer serve, as in primeval times, to teach and guide mankind. Bears, lions, elephants, ibexes and gazelles are in cages in our zoos. Man is no longer the newcomer in a world of unexplored plains and forests, and our immediate neighbors are not the wild beasts but other human beings, contending for goods and space on a planet that is whirling without end around the fireball of a star. Neither in body nor in mind do we inhabit the world of those hunting races of the Paleolithic millennia, to whose lives and life ways we nevertheless owe the very forms of our bodies and structures of our minds. Memories of their animal envoys still must sleep, somehow, within us; for they wake a little and stir when we venture into wilderness. They wake in terror to thunder. And again they wake, with a sense of recognition, when we enter any one of those great painted caves. Whatever the inward darkness may have been to which the shamans of those caves descended in their trances, the same must lie within ourselves, nightly visited in sleep.

—Joseph Campbell in *The Way of the Animal Powers*.

To enter a great cave is to enter another world. Nowadays most of us cross such thresholds in guided groups, walking on manufactured paths while traversing shored-up passageways lit by strings of electric lights. In ancient times the journey was quite different. The underworld cathedrals of Paleolithic times were dark, dangerous, dank, and depressing. There were no enlarged, government-inspected, certified passageways. You had to crawl through small openings carrying torches or some other light source, fully aware that if it went out, leaving you in darkness so profound you couldn't even see your hand in front of your face, you would probably die there. The sharp, ragged rocks scraped your back and knees, and unfathomable drop-offs opened up suddenly before you at every turn. You risked your life and sanity every time. Who would do such a thing?

As it turns out, artists did. Again and again. For thousands of years.

I caught a glimpse of what it must have been like to leave the world of the familiar and enter a portal to the unknown a few years ago when I was invited to speak at a gathering in Cornwall in the United Kingdom. The day before I was scheduled to give a talk about the roots of world religions my hosts took me to visit the ancient village of Carn Euny.

The energy there was wonderful. Surrounded by the remains of an old, old village that dated back to megalithic times I immediately felt the presence of children at play. It was a peaceful feeling, a happy place. People had lived here. They had loved, dreamed, worked, and probably thought their way of life would last forever. I could easily believe that children had been born on this spot of ground, grown to adulthood, and died in peace, never having traveled very far from the site of these rolling hills.

The ancient village of Carn Euny in Cornwall, England, dates back to the Iron Age. In the center of the ruins is a "fogou," a stone-walled underground passage.

But beneath their feet lay a completely different world.

What follows is pure speculation. There's no archeological proof that the theory I'm about to put forth is, in fact, the truth about what happened here. But this is what it felt like to me. Similar stone-age communities, existing into historic times and thus available for observation, tend to agree with my conclusions.

At an inconspicuous place in the village there is a small, enclosed opening in the ground that leads to an underground chamber. It had recently been excavated and a new entrance built so we could actually walk almost upright into a subterranean, human-constructed cave. But back when this village was used you had to go to quite a bit of trouble to reach it, crawling on your hands and knees down into the darkness. I imagine that if the entrance was covered and protected by a strong warning whenever a new generation of kids discovered it, the youngsters might never have known it was there.

But there would inevitably come a day when youngsters were old enough to be initiated into adulthood. Suddenly the mystery was right before them, and I imagine they were frightened out of their wits. Here was a whole realm, which they never knew existed, right beneath their feet. It must have been a spiritual awakening, discovering new worlds, adult worlds, magical worlds where children were now expected to behave in a new way and take on new responsibilities.

What went on down here? What did they learn? What mysteries were revealed?

We'll never know, of course. But it makes me wonder. What might happen if our kids today were suddenly made aware of a world that existed right beneath their feet—a world that they had never before imagined—an adult world that demanded adult behaviors and responsibilities—a world of spiritual power? Nowadays we just give them a driver's license and send them forth. It's not much of a transition. Is it any wonder the passage to adulthood is fraught with such difficulties today? There are no more real rituals that link adulthood with spiritual growth and responsibility. Church confirmation just doesn't cut it. Even Bar Mitzvahs fall short these days. This was the real thing. This was a ritual that said, in no uncertain terms, "Today you become an adult. Act like it!"

Sitting beneath the peaceful village of Carn Euny, all I could think about was that there really *is* a secret world beneath our feet. Even our scientists have discovered its existence, right there on the other side of the Higgs field. It's the world of reality that exists outside our senses, above and below our range of sight, smell, hearing, touch, and taste. We know this world exists. We can prove it using the scientific method. We can deduce its existence by reading thousands upon thousands of years' worth of mythology about elves and fairies, leprechauns, magic, and earth energies. The problem is that today's

Author Jim Willis sits inside the stone chamber at Carn Euny.

elders, most of them anyway, seem to have forgotten where the entrance is. They have forgotten that the world below the surface even exists. Their entire life is lived up above, in the sunshine. They haven't experienced the world below and beyond, so they can't perceive it.

But once you get down on your hands and knees and make the effort to crawl through the tunnel, as Alice traveled down into the rabbit hole, you will, like the children of Carn Euny, never be the same again. You will discover a world where much is the same, only more so. You will discover the world of spirit, the world of alternate realities, the Multiverse, the place of alternative perceptions. It's right there underneath your feet. But you'll never experience it unless you start searching. "All who seek will find. To all who knock, the door will be opened," we read in Matthew 7:7.

Alas, it's far easier just to claim such ideas to be superstitious nonsense. Then you can get home in time for dinner so you can rest up for tomorrow's scheduled complacency. Don't worry. You'll never know what you have missed, right there beneath your feet.

THE CAVES

We come now to the subject of the great painted caves that intrigue so many people today. What did the ancients find when they crawled back and down into these subterranean Meccas of magic?

In two words—animal envoys. They were greeted by mystical messengers. When you enter the famous European caves of El Castillo, Lascaux, Chauvet, Pech Merle, Altamira, or more than three hundred others, all containing magnificent rock art, you are greeted by a whole menagerie of hauntingly beautiful representations of animal envoys. Bison, mammoths, bear, deer, and sea creatures abound, painted in such a way that the very rock formations of walls and ceilings accentuate their features. The famous Hall of the Bulls in Lascaux is a gallery that will easily accommodate up to fifty people.

This immediately raises a comment and two questions. First, the comment: the ancients were artists. These paintings stand right up there next to Michelangelo's work. They are not as polished or composed, of course. After all, they're from a different tradition and use different material for pigment. But the raw effect is the same.

The first question: what were they thinking?

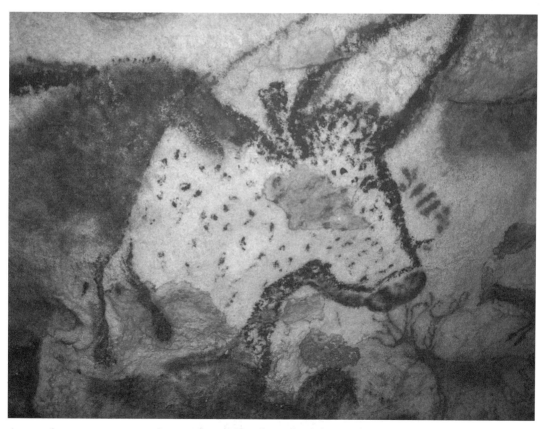

Among the many creatures and scenes depicted on the walls of the Lascaux caves in France is this bull. Such pictures may have been made ritually to increase hunting success or to record spirit journeys.

Explanations abound.

1. Henri Breuil (1877–1961) believed the paintings were meant to serve as magical aids to increase the success of the hunt or to initiate young boys into the society of men. This was a predominate theory for years, popularized in the 1970s by the late Joseph Campbell (1904–1987).

2. David Lewis-Williams (1934–) decided they were the work of Paleolithic shamans who, beginning as long as 40,000 years ago, figured out how to induce a trance state, either naturally or through the use of psychedelic plants or mushrooms, in which they would "journey" to what they perceived as parallel spiritual dimensions. Upon their return they painted what they saw during their "trips." He believed, however, that the paintings were simple representations of hallucinogenic illusions. Being a trained scientist, he dismissed parallel dimensions out of hand. Others question his hypothesis. They wonder if the realms to which the shamans journeyed actually exist. In any case, this is when the great awakening of symbolic/religious thought began. In those caves we became specifically human.

3. R. Dale Guthrie (1936–) wondered whether the paintings were graffiti by adolescent boys who fantasized about becoming great hunters. The presence of so-called "Venus" figures—richly endowed, voluptuous female figures—fueled his speculations. Recently, however, while analyzing hand prints and stencils in both French and Spanish caves, some of the work is now thought to be done by female artists. This discovery helped push Guthrie's work into the background. Not many today believe the caves to be an ancient version of *Playboy* magazine.

Now, the second question: How did they do it?

It's not just the technical questions about materials that concern us here. It's much more basic. Why did they crawl as far as a mile into such dangerous, cramped places? What was their light source? What was their motivation? Why animals? One would think the place to placate the spirits of the hunt would be the forests and plains—the natural abode of the animal kingdom. Bulls and bison never roamed the galleries of Lascaux.

THE COSMOS

Animal envoys didn't make their presence known only in the caves, however. In Psalm 19:1, when an unknown musician declared that "the heavens declare the glory of God," he was speaking a truth reflected in almost every religion on earth.

In my book, *Ancient Gods*, I pointed out that:

Given clear skies and an unimpeded horizon, you see a full moon once every 29 or 30 nights. When it rises it does so against a pattern of stars. Every month or so, that pattern appears to change by a little less than 30 degrees to the east because, due to earth wobble, the moon appears to have moved along the horizon. So over the course of a "lunar" year, the pattern of stars behind the full moon will have changed twelve times. (Remember, this is an approximation.)

In other words, over the course of a lunar year, the full moon will have risen in front of twelve patterns of stars, each of which makes up one compartment, or "house," about 30 degrees wide. To assist astronomers in identifying each house, the ancient Babylonians superimposed an image of a different animal over the stars that formed that particular compartment. One was a lion (Leo), one was a fish (Pisces), one a dragon (Draco), one a bull (Taurus), etc. This system was taken over by the Greeks. The Greek word for animal, or "living being," is spelled, in English, *zoon* (from which we get our word "zoo"). The twelve animals together formed, in Greek, a *zodia*. It means "animal circle." In English we spell it *Zodiac*.... It wasn't long before these animal figures were given god-like qualities, seemingly affecting life on the planet.

AS ABOVE, SO BELOW

In short, our ancient ancestors saw gods or god-like figures in both cave and cosmos. As above, so below. In their mind, the gods both created and direct-ed the activities of humankind, and the images of those gods were depicted both in the sky above their heads and the earth below their feet.

There is even evidence that certain humans had somehow developed the ability to travel between the upper and lower worlds of the animal spirits and the middle realm of human perception on earth. Some of these shamanic figures were known as shape-shifters. They were thought to be able to take on the properties of certain animals and actually change their physical form into those creatures.

Is this the answer to riddle of the *Therianthropes* (from the Greek *therion*, meaning "beast," and *anthropos*, meaning "human"), the half-animal, half-human fig-

Satyrs, fauns, and the god Pan are all half goat, half man creatures from mythology. They may have originated from shamanic tradition and the belief that spiritual people could transform into animals.

ures that appear in rock art all over the world? Is this the explanation that lies behind the various horns and antlers found on helmets and headdresses from Africa and the American west all the way to the Vikings of northern Europe? Is this why the devil of Christianity and Pan of the Greeks are often pictured with horns?

Other shamans and visionaries, while not changing their physical form, encountered animal envoys while the seeker was in a trance state brought about by physical ordeal, sickness, or intentional spiritual journey.

When an animal appeared to a young Native American engaged in a spiritual quest, that animal became a totem. If it was a hawk or eagle, for instance, the young man was expected to obtain a feather from his totem animal and carry it with him in his medicine bag for the rest of his life. The animal would be his protector and spiritual guide forever.

A MODERN EXAMPLE

I don't want to imply that this behavior is necessarily old fashioned or out of date. Vision quests involving animal envoys can happen even today to those who are open and ready. Sometimes they even happen to those who don't expect them. I've shared this personal example before, but what follows happened beginning in the year 2000. Here is how I presented it in my book *The Dragon Awakes*, in which I stated the facts as they happened. You can draw your own conclusions.

> The first act of this metaphysical play I call life began in a cabin in the woods of central Massachusetts. I wrote about it first in *Journey Home*, back at the turn of the century in the year 2000. But by the time I wrote *Faith, Trust, & Belief* seven years later, more events had happened and I had a broader context in which to better understand the symbols. Here's the later version. Little did I realize at the time that this would be the single event that divided my life into two sections—before and after:
>
> For thousands of years, and even to this day in some cultures and areas, our ancestors believed they could receive messages and guidance from forces and powers that inhabited and governed the natural world. This belief system was, and maybe still is, the most predominant faith system in the history of the human race. We drew pictures on cave walls in Spain, dragged megaton boulders across the landscape of England, buried our dead along with tools they would need in the next life, raised huge pyramids in the deserts of Egypt, and built medicine wheels on the tops of mountains in America's Northwest, all to contact or appease the gods. We humans spread pollen, traced the stars, and studied ani-

mal entrails. We observed the paths of planets and suns, went on vision quests, feasted, fasted, and contemplated sunsets. We talked to the trees, listened for voices from the ocean's foam, and consulted hermits and oracles, all of whom inhabited the wilderness so as to be close to natural spirits.

Then came the Age of Enlightenment when, at least in academic European circles, we left our primitive superstitions behind and became fully mature, rational, scientific adults who no longer believed that the great and wonderful natural world, awesome as it was, really possessed anything that could be construed as consciousness, let alone the ability to converse with us. We still wondered how fish could find their way home after years in the oceans, how birds and butterflies could keep such a precise schedule, and how a million or two minor miracles of coincidence and process could exist within the world of plants and animals. But we assumed it would be only a matter of time before we figured it all out.

I understand that kind of thinking. That describes me completely. I'm rational and of scientific bent, despite being an incurable romantic. For thirty years I have been a middle-of-the-road, mainstream Protestant clergyman. I live most of my waking hours in the left side of my brain, meaning I am normally self-contained to a fault. Often, for me, religion is a matter of "knowing about" rather than "experiencing."

But for almost five decades I have also been a professional musician. I started playing in dance bands in 1960. I love to watch people dance, but I can't dance myself. It's not that I don't have rhythm and can't learn simple steps. It's just that every time I try to walk onto a dance floor a palpable, almost physical force says, "Stop!" It has bothered me for years. Once I even talked to a psychologist friend about it, thinking that if I could learn to dance I could open up secret doors in my psyche that I didn't even know were there.

His advice? "Loosen up!"

Didn't work.

As the twentieth century drew to a close I spent time one summer at a cabin I had built in central Massachusetts. The idea was to commune with nature and get in touch with some issues that were on my mind. Five feet in front of the porch of the cabin was a rock, about four feet long, lying on its side. The best way to describe it is to recall the old "Weebles wobble but they don't fall down" craze. Remember Weebles? This rock looked just like that, right down to the flat face—only it had fallen down. Obviously forces other than those found in nature had been employed to work the top smooth, and I had often wondered why it appeared to be almost face-like.

This was the setting where I spent four afternoons meditating on whatever came to mind, trying to go deeper into myself than I normally do. By the second day I was conscious of sounds I first thought were caused by cars on the highway, about a mile away. It was not until the fourth afternoon that I realized I was hearing the sounds in my right ear, which is completely deaf.

After a moment it came to me that what I was hearing was not highway noise, but drums. Suddenly I was aware that I had snapped my eyes wide open and was experiencing a fully formed sentence ringing in my head. Even though my heart was racing, I didn't hear a voice and I saw no apparition. I hadn't been thinking about dancing at all, but the sentence that seemed to appear, almost floating before my eyes, was, "It's not that you *can't* dance. It's that you *won't* dance!"

As soon as I saw, heard, or somehow experienced that message I felt, rather than figured out, that the reason I could not dance was because at one time dance was so sacred, either to me or the people who danced, perhaps even on this spot of ground, that I could not sully it by making it mere entertainment.

I am one of the most rational people you will ever meet. I'm not sure if I believe in reincarnation or not and I only believe in spirits on the occasional second Tuesday. But in that instant I looked down at the rock I had been contemplating for the last four days and knew, just knew, that it was meant to be standing upright.

Fearing that any minute I would have a perfectly acceptable psychological explanation for what was happening to me, I immediately got a shovel and began excavating around the rock. It took about an hour to dig down to bedrock, only about a foot deep on this ledge, clearing a six-foot circle surrounding the stone. I knew long before I finished what I was going to find.

Hidden beneath the soil at the base of the rock was a tripod of stones, obviously placed by human hands, formed to exactly fit the bottom of the rock. And in a semicircle, spread fan-shaped to the east, were seven hammer stones that could only have been made by pre-European New Englanders.

Next day, when I used a hydraulic jack and ropes to stand the stone on its pedestal, the smoothed face of the stone swung just a fraction around toward the northeast, facing exactly the place where the sun peeked over a faraway ridge on the morning of the spring equinox.

In doing research about the indigenous people of my area I later discovered a possible explanation for the rock. It stands on a natural divide. All the water from the stream to its east eventually flows into a huge reservoir to the south. The water draining from the swamp to the west flows out to the Connecticut River and the Atlantic Ocean at Long Island Sound. This would have made the area a natural place of power to the people who lived here. But the rock itself stood on a small plateau, a natural stage. On all four sides a tribe could have gathered to watch a religious ritual "in the round," so to speak. And right on top of the stage stood a boulder I once nicknamed "Dru" (you can read more about Dru in my book *Journey Home: The Inner Life of a Long-Distance Bicycle Rider*).

One explanation for this particular stone being knocked over might be found in unsubstantiated stories about religious disagreements between Indians and Europeans in early New England. When Indians watched Puritans burying their dead they thought they must be worshipping a common deity. The Puritans used four-foot rocks as grave headstones. Some Indian tribes had similar rituals, dancing around the rock as they prayed for the departed. But Puritans were taught that while their own rocks were sacred, Indian rocks were heathen idols, so they knocked them down whenever they came across them.

I had compiled a list with the names of every person who had owned that property since 1798 when the town was first settled. It is easy to believe the very first pioneer who farmed this land, which was awarded to his ancestral family as payment for participation in King Philip's War, came across this spot in his sheep pasture and, recognizing it for the pagan idol it was, knocked it down, to the glory of God.

There it lay until I, his future town minister, put it back up, also to the glory of God.

The story doesn't end there. I was so impressed by the whole affair that I told some folks about it. One thing led to another and we wound up having a dedication service there on the night of the winter solstice. Not knowing what to do, we drank some mead and burned some incense, hoping the spirit of the place would accept our good intentions.

And that was that until March. On a day of early thaw I walked out to the place for the first time since December. The snow had melted back from around the base of the rock, just as it had around many other rocks in the area. But at the foot of this special rock lay the feathers—not the carcass, just the feathers—of a ruffed grouse.

My first thought was that a hawk had killed a grouse on this spot. Nine days out of ten I still believe that. But I called my daughter that day to tell her the story. She knows a lot about all things Indian and I mentioned the grouse. She called me back a few minutes later and I could hear the excitement in her voice.

"Dad, I looked up the meaning of having the ruffed grouse as your totem animal." She then read to me, "When the Creator sends you the grouse as your spirit guide, it is a message to attune yourself to the dance of life. Its keynote is sacred dancing and drumming, both powerful ways in their own right to invoke energies … rhythmic movement is a part of life … all human activity is a kind of dance and ritual." (Ted Andrews, in *Animal Speak*)

What do I make of all this? I don't have the faintest idea. My rational self accepts the coincidence of a grouse being killed by a hawk at this particular time and place. But why a grouse, with its ancient meaning relating to my own dance phobia? And why this particular time? And why this rock, out of all the many others? And why does it tie in to my discovering the secret of the rock after my time of meditation, exactly when I was attempting to let the woods sort out my confused mindset? And why just feathers with no carcass? I don't really know, but I once told this story to an Ojibwa teaching elder after an all-day seminar. We had spent the day sitting in a circle, learning about his tribe's creation myths. Much to my dismay, he appeared rather bored. As I told the story and commented on his seeming lack of interest, he said, "Okay, the grouse was on the west side of the rock. What next?"

"I didn't tell you it was on the west side of the rock. How did you know that?"

"Because that's where we would have expected it to be. That's the direction the soul takes its leave when it departs. Honestly, why do you Christian preachers always expect your God to answer prayer, but act surprised when ours does?"

I was dumbfounded. "Do you mean to tell me I've been searching for an experience with God all my life and now I discover He's an Indian?"

"No," he grinned back with a cherubic expression. "*She's* an Indian!"

I don't carry a medicine bag, but I had a grouse feather laminated in plastic and I carry it in my wallet. And some more feathers are mounted with words from *Medicine Cards: The Discovery of Power Through the Ways of Animals* in a picture frame in my office—just in case.

Grouse … of the Sacred Spiral,

Leading us on,

To reach the everlasting heights,

Where we can live as one.

–Jim Willis, in *The Dragon Awakes:*
Rediscovering Earth Energy in the Age of Science

THE QUANDARY

When you read about stuff like this from the comfort of your own easy chair, it is easy to make assumptions. Such stories can easily be filed under New-Age, woo-woo nonsense. I know. I did it for years. But when you actually find yourself fully engaged in such a metaphysical experience, you begin to wonder. Part of you, the safe, conservative part, explains it as hyperactive imagination in full display. It's fun, but nothing more. Best keep it to yourself.

But there is another part of you that refuses to let it go so easily. You begin to ask yourself, "What if such things are real? What if parallel realms exist and you are somehow transported to them, in vision or dream? Are all the shamans, medicine people, visionaries and magicians of the past simply delusional? Or did they indeed experience something real and try to explain it?

If you're really honest with yourself you might even ask, "Am I going mad? I'm a person of the twenty-first century! I'm educated and rational! Why animals? I don't live in a cave and I can hardly find the Big Dipper because of all the light pollution in the night sky. Why am I experiencing such ancient visual symbols?"

A MODERN THEORY OF AN ANCIENT EXPERIENCE

Here's a theory. We experience visions of other perception realms because those realms actually exist.

"But why animal envoys?" we ask. "Why not something more mechanical, in line with a modern, technological age?"

Well, some people do experience other realms in that way. This, as a matter of fact, might be the answer to understanding the current wave of alien abductions that we'll talk about later.

But a more thorough explanation might run something like this:

1. In vision, dream, sickness, meditation, or through hallucinogenic material of some kind, defenses built and maintained by our five senses are somehow relaxed and overcome. A crack appears in the window of space-time. We perceive something that is normally outside our mental perception reality.

2. How do we explain it? We almost have to use words. Most of us don't know anything different. A gifted few might be able to use art. They might be able to draw or paint what they saw. That has happened. But the result is the same. We attempt to recreate an otherworldly scene in this familiar dimension so that others will understand what we experienced.

3. Here's where it gets difficult. The only way to recreate such an experience is to run it through the neurological pathways of our physical brains. Thus, we can't really say, "This is what I saw." After all, what we saw was outside the parameters of anything anyone normally experiences in this perception realm, because language was invented for use only on this side of the fence. So the best we can say is, "What I saw was like this...." In other words, we conjure up an image of a similar experience. We resort to metaphor.

4. In order to make an otherworldly vision make sense, our brains have to run through the individual rolodex of experiences we all carry around in our heads, find something similar that we will recognize, and then project it onto the screen of our consciousness. To put it simply, our brains manufacture metaphors. "What you saw was something like this...."

5. What usually appears on that screen? The closest our experience can come up with is—you guessed it—pictures of animals. Do actual animals exist on the other side of our reality? Probably not. But that's the closest image the human brain can come up with, so that's what we see.

Now we've arrived at an old, old idea that goes all the way back to Plato. He taught that an actual animal, a horse, for instance, is not a reality. It's an expression of a reality. A "horse" is an expression of "horseness," according to Plato. What he called his *Idea* is that "horseness" is not this or that horse. It is the general concept of all horses—the universal horse. What we call horses are simply expressions of an eternal idea which is unchangeable and imperishable. According to this view, what we call a solid horse is actually just a passing phase, a material expression of a metaphysical concept called "horseness." "Horseness" is the eternal reality. "Horse" is simply a temporary embodiment of that reality. By extension, everything we see around us, including our own selves, is a material expression of a metaphysical idea. It takes shape as it passes through the Higgs Field and clumps together to form the realm we perceive through our senses—the realm we call "reality."

In the painted caves, this idea is found in vivid relief. The animals pictured there are not as important as what they represent. They are not animals as much as representations of animal envoys. They are pictures of supernatural beings.

In a meditative state, and also in other cases when our senses are relaxed or altered, we can perceive things outside of what we consider normal reality.

When you think about it—why not? Animals have different senses than ours. They see, hear, taste, think, and smell a different reality than we do. In many ways, they inhabit a different sensory world than we do. Sometimes their abilities seem almost magical. Why shouldn't animal envoys be a perfectly acceptable image for what we call supernatural beings?

And if this is the case, why wouldn't our ancient ancestors draw pictures of animal envoys on the walls of caves and project their images in the constellations of stars in the heavens above them?

ANOTHER MODERN EXAMPLE

We must emphasize again that animal envoys can be found even in mundane examples in the twenty-first century. Let me recount another example from my book, *The Dragon Awakes*:

"I call your attention," said Sherlock Holmes, "to the curious incident of the dog in the night-time."

"The dog did nothing in the night-time," said Watson.

"That," replied Holmes, "was the curious incident!"

Rocky alerted his owner to the strange behavior of the beagle pack.

This morning that "curious incident" was most certainly not the case. The dogs were raising a royal ruckus. Not our dog, mind you. No, Rocky was just a bit bewildered at the action of the beagle pack who live up the road from us. But he still insisted on calling my attention to the fact that something was happening down in the valley below our house.

We live a quiet life. Days go by when nothing much happens. A simple "woof" usually suffices to bring us to full alert.

"Woof!" said Rocky. And that began the whole thing.

As I walked down the path to where the action seemed to be centered, I saw a rather strange sight. Jack, a beagle mix, was on the bank of our small stream, looking very guilty but refusing to move. Bebe, a tiny Chihuahua-plus-who-knows-what, was down in the ditch, soaking wet, filthy with mud, and acting both defiant and frightened at the same time. Bebe, you must understand, thinks she's a beagle and is much bigger on the inside than she is on the outside. Neither would come to me, although I've given Jack more dog bones than I can remember, and both were acting out of character. Rocky, our constant companion, elected to stay close to me, even behind me, utterly at a loss while confronting a situation foreign to his experience. He is, after all, a shelter dog still negotiating the process of adjusting to country life.

My first reaction was that Bebe was hurt and Jack was protecting his running mate, so I retreated to our house to call the dog's owner and report on the situation. Barb, meanwhile, headed down the hill wearing her English Wellingtons, prepared to brave both mud and water if duty so required. She was the one who discovered the dead deer. In jumping the creek, just a trickle of water in a deep ditch during this period of prolonged drought, a beautiful doe had somehow miscalculated and broken her neck. She had obviously given birth to at least one baby this year, but by now her young fawn would almost certainly be able to get by on its own. For that, at least, we were grateful. Still, seeing that beautiful doe, dead and filthy with creek water, caused us both a lot of anguish, even though I have stood by the carcasses of many deer, some killed by my own hand.

In order to understand the significance of all this you must understand what it means to live on a small parcel of land that is surrounded by miles and miles of woods. We can walk all day and not see anyone. Surrounded as we are by deer, I'm sure they die all the time out there. We often see road kills, and we come across bones and antlers on a fairly regular basis. What made this death so painful to us is that it happened on a piece of ground we consider to be a most sacred site. It's our church.

Many mornings throughout the year we sit on a small hill and wait for the sun to rise over this little piece of ground that nestles in the bend of the small stream below us. We have been strangely attracted to this place ever since we moved in. It may even have been the reason we came here in the first place. Recently two friends, who at that time were much more spiritually sensitive than me to earth energies, identified it, without my saying anything to them at all about our attraction to it, as an energy vortex, a special place of earth magic.

I didn't know much about ley lines and energy fields back then. At the time I was much too left-brained and scientifically minded to pay much attention to what many of my colleagues in ministry called New Age beliefs. Like many theologians, I was Augustinian to the core.

But here we planted our first tree, thus giving the name Little Tree Manor to our country refuge. (And this, mind you, in the midst of miles and miles of trees in all directions! Why here?) Here was where we greeted the dawn most mornings. And here was where we had recently decided to build our version of a Lakota medicine wheel, a mixture of Celtic tradition and Native American spirituality: Stonehenge meets the Black Hills—that sort of thing. It wasn't going to be a big monument. It was just going to be a place of peace wherein we could meditate in what our church's contemporary music team used to call "the still point of the circle."

And now a deer lay dead in the stream, our altar polluted, our sanctuary defiled. Of all the miles and miles of woods surrounding us, why here? Why now?

Barb and I have, quite naturally for her but with greater difficulty for me, come to expect signs and wonders in nature. Indeed, one of the great truths of my spiritual journey has been a deeper understanding of the Eastern and indigenous religious concept of the unity behind all things. Hinduism describes it with the concept of brahman/atman. Brahman is the unknowable unity behind all things, the truth that language cannot capture. Atman is the individual expression of that truth in the human soul. Truth expresses itself through any media available to it. For us, one of those avenues has been the natural world, and one of the most significant messages we have received over the years has come from deer. I've hunted them all my life and have come to believe that they are almost magical creatures. They are all around us, but we never see them. They leave their tracks on our paths every morning and eat the corn I put out for them. But up until now we never got a good look at them. All we were awarded from time to time was a brief glimpse. They have come to represent, for us at least, the magical spirituality that surrounds us all. We seldom see it in full view, and almost never on purpose. From time to time an insight, a brief glimpse of something greater than ourselves, appears, but then is gone. Evidence of it surrounds us. We know it's there. But we seldom get a good look. Instead we "see through a glass, darkly," as the Apostle Paul said.

A strange thing happened, however, a few weeks before the death of this deer that now lay at our feet. As a matter of fact, it began right after we decided to build the medicine wheel. Deer started to come out and feed right at the foot of our driveway—right during the middle of the day. We could regularly look out our window—and there they would be. Plain as day. Big as life. This went on every day for ten days. We began to get a little spooked, to tell you the truth. It seemed they had a message for us.

Ted Andrews writes, in one of his books on "animal speak," that he believes deer represent the lure to new adventures. "Move gently into new areas," he says. "Follow the lure to new studies. Practical pursuits bring surprising rewards." We decided it was a good sign, an indication that we were on the right track. You can't find a more "practical pursuit" than moving heavy rocks and standing stones around the countryside in 90+ degree weather. So we decided to go ahead with our plans and began to study medicine wheel design. We soon got the right idea in our heads and committed to the project.

But now, on the eve of our actual building, a dead deer lay right on the site we had planned to use to build our sacred space. As my neighbor and I dragged the carcass up the hill for removal and burial, I couldn't help but wonder if there was a message behind it all. (Even though I am still a card-carrying clergyman I'm beginning to think like a traditional Indian more and more.) A deer, with all its magical, mystical meaning for us concerning new adventures and new studies, lay before us, seemingly a sacrificial lamb led to slaughter.

Those of you who have read my books (*Snapshots and Visions* and *Journey Home*, for instance) know about my first external encounter with the Reality on the Other Side. It, too, came through nature. It, too, involved sacrifice. A grouse died, and its feathers anointed another standing stone I had erected. Since then one of his feathers has been with me constantly, laminated in plastic and serving as a constant reminder that life is mysterious (the story is recounted in full earlier in this chapter).

All this made me wonder. Is sacrifice built in to every relationship, especially our relationship with Spirit? Catholics refer to the Sacrifice of the Mass. Protestants regularly hear the words, "This is my body, sacrificed for you." Barb and I had even shared our own communion service down here on this spot of ground, right where the deer died. Our two friends who sensed this spot to begin with had each performed different ceremonies, from different traditions, to consecrate this ground. So Barb and I felt compelled one evening to go down and share some bread and wine. (Rocky even joined in, marking the first time I had ever served communion to a dog!) After eating the bread and drinking the wine, we poured some out upon the ground, thus sharing communion with Mother Earth. (Another first for me, I'm ashamed to admit.)

Three ceremonies from three different traditions. One was designed to open a spiritual portal—a place in which the healing powers of Earth could come forth. One was designed to bless and sanctify a holy place—to recognize and acknowledge the energies that empower us all. And the communion service represented a sacrificial event whereby the Divine shares our humanity and experiences our pain through us. Three—the number of the Holy. Interesting. Unplanned, but interesting.

The ancient Hebrew writers told a story about First Man and First Woman's banishment from a mythical Golden Age of unity—of Oneness and Paradise. After the expulsion from Eden an angel was given a flaming sword and posted as a guard at the gate. The implication seemed to be that there is no return to Wholeness without suffering a death of some kind.

Abraham is said to have offered to sacrifice his own son. God provided an animal instead, in a ritual called substitutionary atonement. It's a weird story, until you read carefully what Abraham is reported to have said prior to the rather gruesome event. Here's a paraphrase: "We're going up the mountain to give God a sacrifice. Wait here until we return." You can read it for yourself in Genesis 22:5. Did you catch the second we? He never intended to come down alone. Somehow he knew that God would provide the sacrifice. But consider the situation. Abraham was said to have built an altar out of stone—a Hebrew medicine wheel, if you will. Later, the son of the man said to have been spared on that mountain reportedly fell asleep at a place called Bethel, with a stone for a pillow. He experienced a dream in which angels ascended and descended at the place he rested (Genesis 28). He called it "the gate of heaven." Ever since then, Christians have sung about "climbing Jacob's ladder." Could the story be referring to Jacob resting for the night, leaning up against a standing stone and receiving a vision? If so, it sounds more Native American campfire than Christian Sunday school.

Every religion has within it an element of sacrifice, a basic truth that I have come to abhor. I have no intention of ever sacrificing an animal anytime, anywhere, and for any reason. I don't even believe in a God who demands such things. But I do believe that life is full of sacrifices. In this sense, life is full of death—the death of a dream, a way of living, a hope or lifestyle. But death also leads to resurrection. Indeed, new life cannot take place without the death of the old.

Is this body in which we are living going to be sacrificed some day? "If I deliver my body to be sacrificed," says the apostle, "but have not love, I gain nothing" (I Corinthians 13:3). Are these bodies simply a sacrificial victim placed on the altar of time's experiences? Is it true, in the words of the *Star Trek* movie *Generations*, that "time is the fire in which we burn?" Have I been too quick to throw out the deeper meaning of sacrifice, which was, after all, one of the earliest religious rituals we know about?

Even in Christianity we receive the old, old message only if we have ears to hear. Mary, first mother of a new spirituality, represents the material world, the earthly plane. After a visitation from an angel (the angel is not pictured as an animal; that would be too much to ask of Christianity. But Gabriel is usually pictured with wings as he "flew" through the heavens. Close enough!) she was quickened by the spiritual world, the great and eternal I AM of the invisible realm. The motion of time was, at that moment, filled with the stillness of eternity. That which was conceived in her, the great product of body and spirit, grew up to call us brothers and sisters and was sacrificed for his belief. But first he said, "Follow me. You've got a cross to bear, too!"

Nowadays I'm forced to consider a pattern in my own spiritual growth. Years ago a grouse, nature's drummer, gave me a message beside a standing stone, the first I ever raised. I understood that message to mean that I had to attune myself to the dance of life. My religion had become too intellectual. I had separated myself from the Spirit of Mother Earth, from which we all arise.

Face this fact. If animals can make you think thoughts such as these, are they not "messengers from God"? That is why in shamanic tradition, animals—both in spirit and in flesh, in dreams and in actual encounters—are seen as "threshold guardians." They stand at the point of contact between the world of material reality and the spirit. American Indian tradition often required a vision quest of young men on the threshold of manhood. After fasting and praying for as many as four days, the initiates would often encounter an animal guardian that would be their guide for life.

The "Way of the Animal Spirits" is a common mythological motif. Even today, if we pay attention, animals have much to teach us.

ANIMAL ENVOYS

To put it simply, then, one way to understand the pictures and mythology behind *animal envoys* is that animals represent the deep mystery found in our psyches and minds. In our day we tend to capture these realities and lock them safely away where they won't cause too much trouble as we observe them from afar. Our animals, and the psychological realities they represent, are not wild and free. We cage them in zoos. We collar them so they can be restrained safely on a tight leash. By extension, we keep what they represent safely buried in our subconscious. Once in a while, some author comes along and urges freedom—urges us to let the wild beast loose. Read, for instance, *Women Who Run*

Animals represent the deep mystery found in our psyches and minds, and hence they have entered the realm of the mythological and spiritual in our lives.

with the Wolves: Myths and Stories of the Wild Woman Archetype by Clarissa Pinkola Estes. But in polite society we tend to downplay this kind of activity as quickly as possible. It might upset the safe, secure status quo.

Shapeshifting Superheroes

It is considered likely that the earliest depictions of shapeshifting capabilities comes from the Cave of the Trois-Frères, located in southern France. Though the purposes behind the images discovered there are constantly up for debate, and are unlikely to be definitively decrypted in the near future, many scholars believe that some of these drawings indicate a pre-historic belief in the ritual of transformation. The cave's depiction of "The Sorcerer," for example, gives the impression of both animal and human parts, his awkward position explained by placing him in the physical moment of alteration. If modern scholars are right about this, then beliefs in shapeshifting and transmogrification can be traced all the way back to 13,000 B.C.

—Ryan Stone, "Evolving Forms:
An Intriguing Look at Shapeshifting,"
Ancient Origins: Reconstructing the Story of Humanity's Past

Ask almost any modern child and he or she will tell you that Hogwarts' Professor Minerva McGonagall can turn herself into a cat, Remus Lupin becomes a werewolf when he glimpses the full moon, and Harry Potter's godfather often transforms himself into a dog. By the same token, scientist Bruce Banner becomes the Incredible Hulk when someone ticks him off and, if you're lucky, the frog sitting on that lily pad by the side of the pond might become a handsome prince if you get close enough to kiss it. The kids might not know that Zeus sometimes used to become a bull, a swan, or even an ant, but they will almost certainly be aware that some of the X-Men have the ability to become wolves or eagles.

These are only a few examples of an age-old belief in shapeshifting. The difference is that in the old days it was not considered fantasy. That holds true in some circles even today. Some of the oldest epic poems in literature, including the *Epic of Gilgamesh* and the *Iliad*, recount stories of shapeshifting, and many examples of therianthropes, half-human and half animal, are found in rock art around the world.

Even today, shamans and other out-of-body travelers report meeting astral beings who appear to be half-animal and half-human some of whom maintain the ability to change from one to the other. A few gifted shamans have reported morphing into animal envoys themselves while on a shamanic journey, and some are rumored to be able to step back and forth between shapes even while still in their material bodies.

An ancient fourth-century Coptic text written by a man who called himself St. Cyril of Jerusalem attributes the ability to Jesus. According to his account, when Judas accepted his infamous thirty pieces of silver in return for betraying Jesus to the authorities, they said to him:

> How shall we arrest him [that is, Jesus] for he does not have a single shape but his appearance changes. Sometimes he is ruddy, sometimes he is white, sometimes he is red, sometimes wheat colored, sometimes he is pallid like ascetics, sometimes he is a youth, sometimes an old man.

They arranged a sign. Judas would kiss Jesus on the cheek so they would be able to arrest the right man no matter what shape he had assumed that evening.

Where did all these ideas come from? They are certainly entertaining— Bruce Wayne turning into a Batman, mild-mannered Clark Kent donning

An illustration based upon the painting at the Trois-Frères Cave depicts a half-human, half-animal shaman.

cape and form-fitting jumpsuit to become a Superman, Diana Prince turning around three times to become the red, white, and blue-clad (or maybe not-so-clad comes closer to it) Wonder Woman—these are the stuff of legend and pop culture. But where did the idea first originate?

Evidence seems to trace the practice back to the picture of the *Sorcerer of Trois-Frères Cave* at least 15,000 years ago, but it may go back even further than that. Do the legends recall our evolution from animal to human? Are they fantasies that reflect our desire to soar like the eagle or pad wolf-like through the primeval forest night? Perhaps they are merely wishful thinking.

Or is there an even more fantastic solution to the question?

Shapeshifting and Psychology

Do such creatures actually exist, if not in our material world then perhaps in an adjacent parallel dimension? Do beings beyond our ability to describe exist there, forcing our brains to form fantastic mental images in order to make some sense of what we are encountering when a veil is lifted for a time in dream or vision?

This is, of course, a pretty radical idea, but there is some good evidence, albeit from non-traditional sources, that claims our familiar surroundings are an elaborate illusion, reinforced by the collective unconsciousness of the entire human race. We see an animal, a tree, or a bus because that's what we expect to see when energy forms what appears to be the familiar manifestation. But what happens when energy takes on an unfamiliar manifestation? Our brains are forced to make some kind of sense of it. So we say, "That is a half-leopard, half-man," when we probably should say, "That appears to be a half-leopard, half-man." The image sticks, and since our ancient ancestors had brains similar to ours, this process began a long time ago. Back then it became part of religion and folklore. Today it takes the form of popular entertainment. But it is the very same mental process at work.

However we choose to describe it, the fact remains that shapeshifting is a basic and stable component in shamanic journeying and a rather common testimony from those who experience everything from out of body experiences to alien abduction. Thousands of people for thousands of years have claimed to be eyewitnesses to the process, usually in what is normally called the astral plane but sometimes even here in our material world.

Perhaps a clue to approaching the subject is to be found in modern cartoon-like comic books and TV shows. We often fantasize and even ridicule that which is strange or frightening. It is a way of diminishing it and making it less scary.

Is that what is going on with shapeshifting? As long as we keep it securely bound to popular entertainment, we don't have to treat it seriously. It's just a fantasy show.

But what if such things really happen, either in this world or another? After all, our ancestors of 15,000 years ago never saw a TV show. What were they depicting on those cave walls? The folks who invented mythology never read a Marvel comic book. Where did they get such fantastic ideas? Fairytales predate the Incredible Hulk by thousands of years. What was their genesis?

It makes you wonder, doesn't it?

CAVE

The *cave* represents the deep recesses of the human heart and soul—the inner darkness that usually reveals itself only through hypnosis or intense psychotherapy. It shelters the soul. Few of us ever plunge into its depths, but when we do, we are changed forever. Sometimes we emerge converted to a new religion. Once in a great while we return with a visionary piece of art, music, or literature. Perhaps we encounter a new way of looking at the world and are able to express it in a way that influences others.

Joseph Campbell called it *The Hero's Journey*. Merlin returned from the Crystal Cave and mentored the young King Arthur. Luke Skywalker went alone into the cave and there confronted his enemy/father who was really himself. 40,000 years ago ancient artists crawled miles under the earth, entered their Paleolithic cathedrals, experienced whatever it was they sought, and attempted to draw their visions on the walls of El Castillo, Lascaux, Chauvet, Pech Merle, and Altamira.

COSMOS

The *cosmos*, on the other hand, represents the soaring soul set free. The sky's the limit. How far we can fly depends on how far we can see. "First star to the right and straight on 'til morning," said Peter Pan, the eternal optimist. The goal was nothing less than eternal youth and endless summer.

Our guides on the journey surround us. They are the animal envoys, full of mystery, who surround us still. They see things we don't see. They smell things we cannot smell. They sense things beyond our senses. They are oblivious of the passing days.

"Consider the birds of the air," said the great master Jesus in Matthew 6:26. "They neither sow nor reap nor gather into barns." (He might as well have added, "They don't worry about their bills, nor their certain death someday, nor their job stress nor their status in the community.") "Yet God takes care of them. Are you not of equal value?"

When ancient humans undertook, for the first time, a quest for the supernatural, when they looked for ancient gods, they turned first to the animal envoys who surrounded them, fed them, taught them, and mystified them. Here they found spiritual knowledge which would illuminate the human journey for millennia. These were the first "gods," the first teachers.

But perhaps, just perhaps, the earthly animals were only useful visual metaphors for teachers who actually exist, closer than we can imagine, to those who will open their minds and hearts today. Across the small but unfathomable gap of dimensional time and space, they call to us still.

EARTH SPIRITS

If my humanity I'd loose
Which seduction would I choose?
The angel's voice eternal in the stars,
Or the faery folk, immortal mid the flowers?
The angels sing of boundless light and joy
And spirits flight to high rebirth,
The faery folk are in the land
And love the sacred earth.

—R. J. Stewart, in *The Living World of Faery*

THIS HAUNTED WORLD

Judging by anecdotal evidence gathered from millions of people, past and present, we live in a haunted world. Ghosts, otherworldly encounters with spiritual entities from earth and stars, stories of Bigfoot and Yeti, fairytales we read to our children, popular movies and TV programs, extra-sensory perception accounts, and UFO encounters all add to the mystery. If you pass ten normal-looking people on the street, according to current statistics seven or eight of them will confess privately that they believe the supernatural exists.

Quoting a poll from 2013, Daniel Hayes notes that popular belief in God is down while belief in spirits is up. That hasn't happened in recent times. At least 74 percent of Americans now say they believe in God. This was down from polls conducted in 2005, 2007, and 2009. But belief in ghosts, UFOs, and reincarnation is quite a bit higher. (I write these words during an American election year, and it's interesting to note that 69 percent of Democrats believe in the supernatural, compared to only 49 percent of Republicans. I find this fascinating, but I don't know why.)

Virtually every world religion features a supernatural component. The only possible exception is Buddhism, and even that varies from sect to sect. Spiritual exercises such as meditation and Yoga don't require a belief in the supernatural, but virtually everyone who practices such disciplines confesses to some kind of belief in something "other," "out there," or "in here."

If you travel in landscapes traditionally considered sacred, perhaps even haunted, such as those of Europe, Asia, the Americas, Australia, and practically everywhere in between, you will invariably encounter a people who still live close to the land and who will, usually with great reluctance and only after you have gained their trust by sharing a pint or two, tell you about local spirits. When this happens, and you hear the testimonies of folks who tell of such experiences, you have entered the world of *Faery*.

FAERY AND FAIRY

Please understand, now. This is very important. Notice the spelling I've employed. I'm talking about *Faery*, not *fairy*.

Earlier I talked about the importance, and inadequacy, of words. Words are metaphors, invented to produce images in the mind of the listener or reader. When we speak an individual word, that word conjures up a shared image in the mind of the listener. There has to be a common connection or there is no communication. If you don't speak Basque, for instance, the sound of the word *zuhaitz* means nothing to you. But if you speak English and I use the word "tree," you know exactly what I mean. *Zuhaitz* and *tree* mean the same thing. But you have to possess an experience of Basque culture in order to know that. Without a shared experience the words have no relationship at all.

Likewise, people who have had no experience with the world of *Faery* will probably not understand it. Instead they will be thinking "fairy." There is a huge difference.

Fairies are all about entertainment. They are Tinkerbell, Fairy Godmothers, the Good Fairy who places coins under the pillows of toothless children, and the Sugar Plum fairies of Nutcracker fame. They have nothing whatsoever to do with the world of *Faery* we are about to discuss so if any of these images come to mind as you read what follows, do your best to banish them. Like most of us, you've probably read too many books and seen too many movies.

Faery Folk

The world of Faery is a tradition far older than the movies. It goes back to the dim, dark, misty memories of the very earliest humans. It has haunted the dreams, legends, and myths of humanity ever since we were first able to think in metaphorical terms. Maybe even before that. It cares not a whit that modern science has declared it doesn't exist. Modern science deals with material realities. Faery deals with energies—with non-material realities that lie, usually, beyond our senses. As such, the world of Faery has no size and, especially important, cuteness. Even the work of J. R. R. Tolkein, as entertaining as *The Lord of the Rings* is and much closer to approaching the original tradition of Faery than Walt Disney, fails to capture the ancient essence.

Modern-day people, when they hear the word "Faery," think of dainty creatures with gossamer wings. Faery, though, is not just a people but also an entire world filled with Earth energy.

Definition

What is Faery, then? In short, the world of Faery is the realm of elemental Earth energy. We might even call it Earth "Spirit," if by that we mean individualized, local energy, unencumbered with corporeal existence, that demonstrates all the evidence of intelligence.

Here's how R. J. Stewart puts it:

Faeries are one step, one change of awareness, beyond humanity. They are also those which, out of the wide range of spiritual beings described in tradition, magic, religion and folklore, are most close to humanity. Once we make this change of awareness, our entire perception of other living creatures changes also…. The commercialized images of little beings in gossamer dresses mainly deriving from 19th century sentiment, are not part of the living Faery tradition…. The theme of diminishing and trivializing is a reflection of something within the consciousness of Western culture, for it demonstrates our flight from, our rejection of, the subtle holism of living beings.

—R. J. Stewart, in *The Living World of Faery*

Of all the concepts presented in this book, this might be the hardest for modern folks to grasp. You may have to really work at it. We moderns have been truly inundated with cultural baggage concerning fairies. It consists of the worst kind of prejudicial treatment and works by trivializing and dismissing the whole field by employing it only as a playground for children or silly quacks. It is very important we try very hard to shed this baggage. Our relationship with the earth may very well depend on our doing so. If you live in a town with lights, stores, paved streets, and apartment buildings, you may find it almost impossible to do so.

Such was not the case when our earliest ancestors walked the earth for millions of years before modern humans stalked on to the stage. The ancients were in touch with their environment in a way we simply cannot be today. They felt the subtle presence of what Francis Hitching once called *Earth Magic*. They sensed not only a unity but an actual communication with it. They perceived an intelligence behind it. Is it any wonder they pictured it as human and gave it names such as *Gaia*—"Mother Earth"? Isn't it only natural that they pictured it in human form and thought about it in human terms? How could they have done otherwise? Even the sophisticated Michelangelo, when asked to paint a picture of deity, made God look like an old, bearded man in the sky, reaching down to Adam with a touch of magic. There is simply no other way to do it. Once we sense intelligence in a form outside our experience, we picture it as Human 2.0. There is no other way to think about it.

That's Faery in a nutshell. It's one step beyond our experience—far enough away so as to remain aloof, but close enough for us to personally experience from time to time when our perceptual guard is lowered.

But make no mistake about. Faery is real. It may be easily dismissed as a simple, naturally occurring force that we don't yet fully understand. It may be measured and explained away as a sort of residual energy left over from "somewhere" or "something." It may even be described as parallel quantum reality. But that doesn't mean it isn't intelligent, mindful, and accessible under the right conditions.

Comes the Dragon

When I wrote *The Dragon Awakes*, I used the dragon as a symbol for Earth Magic. I described it in this way:

Were the first people so in touch with earth magic that the places in which they chose to invest their spiritual energy either formed or followed a grid of tangible, vibrant earth energy that they could feel but that those of us less spiritually attuned have lost touch with? Evidence at the great stone buildings around the world seems to indicate the presence of something very real and compelling.

This is the question that brings us into the present and introduces anew the whole topic of earth energy. We have synthesized, using in most cases accepted historical data, the following thesis:

• Our ancestors experienced something in their environment that was so powerful it caused them, even at very early stages of human development, to build monuments, road-ways, temples, and rock structures to mark or honor its existence.

- Because of the locations of these structures, sometimes quite remote and difficult to reach, the force they recognized seems to be connected to an energy flowing from the earth itself—an energy that we no longer understand or even consciously experience except in rare cases.

- Because of the nature of the monu-ments they constructed, we can assume that they interpreted this energy in a spiritual manner. The stone structures seem to link Earth and Cosmos. The result was early religion.

- This spirituality either arose or was carried all over the world, from Turkey across the Fertile Crescent to Europe, the British Isles, and into the Americas.

Earth Magic is a very potent force in the world, and so author Jim Willis chose a dragon to symbolize its power in his book *The Dragon Awakes*.

THE WORLD OF FAERY

How is it that plants respond to human contact in a meaningful, mea-surable way? How do birds, fish, and butterflies know when to migrate and exactly where to go when they do? How do sunflowers decide to follow the arc of the sun as it moves through the skies?

They are all part of the world of Faery. But it goes much deeper than that. Our ancestors believed they could actually call upon individual "beings" who inhabit this world. Do such beings exist? And if so, what kind of an envi-ronment do they enjoy?

Perhaps the answer to the second question might go something like this: It is just like ours, but more so. Perhaps it even overlaps a bit. In *The Tao of Physics*, theoretical physicist Fritjof Capra wrote these words:

I "saw" cascades of energy coming down from outer space, in which particles were created and destroyed in rhythmic pulses; I "saw" the atoms of the elements and those of my body participat-ing in this cosmic dance of energy; I "felt" its rhythm and I "heard" its sound, and at that moment I knew that this was the dance of Shiva, the Lord of Dancers, worshipped by the Hindus.

—Fritjof Capra, in *The Tao of Physics*

That might be the closest words can come to describing the realm of Faery. But what about the inhabitants, if such there be?

A Personal Testimony

It's now time to get personal. There's simply no other way. I said earlier that words only work if there is a shared experience between speaker and listener. For most of my life I never had an experience of Faery—of Earth spirits or of Magic—of beings from another realm, unless it was an oblique one that I didn't pay attention to sufficiently.

Then, one day, I did. In a moment of time, I changed from a disbeliever, even a *disdainful* disbeliever, to a card-carrying member of the ancient society of Faery.

I can't expect words *about* an experience to change anyone's mind. But maybe the words can help someone have a similar experience that might open their mind to possibilities. Here it is. Take it with a grain of salt if you will. But this is what happened as recorded in my journal (and published in my *The Dragon Awakes*:

July 2013: Mid-Afternoon

As has been my custom of late, I retired to my meditation spot, turned on my favorite hemi-sync music, which is music designed to help synchronize the brain's left and right hemispheres, and prepared to relax, go with the flow, and see what might happen.

At first, nothing. But I have come to expect that. I spend so much time these days in intense thought and speculation that it sometimes takes as long as half an hour or so to calm down enough to even begin to scratch the surface of possibilities. Sad to say, sometimes, no matter how hard I try, I get nowhere—probably because I'm trying too hard. (I often wish there was a phone number for dial-a-muse or some such thing.) So whenever something good does happen it invariably catches me by surprise, and that's how I recognize it. It is oftentimes very subtle—a sense of motion or a mental picture that seems somehow more "real" than "reality." I sometimes feel a sense of being out of balance, of leaning one way or another. Often I have the experience of being outside myself—of standing about five feet off to the left and looking at myself from that distance. At such times I've learned that the only way to continue is to relax and go with it. Any kind of excitement or "Wow—here it comes!" will invariably bring the experience to an end.

Still, there is always a little of that. The secret is to stay calm and focused and to let the experience develop on its own. To describe such times, Bob Munroe used the phrase, "Body asleep—Mind awake." That pretty much covers it. I am very alert and conscious, but my body is completely still. Some might call this a waking, or lucid, dream. Others, creative imagination. To many, this is the beginning of an out-of-body experience, or OBE. Probably others would call it wacko. Whatever your opinion, just stick with me.

At such times I am often conscious of a change in my appearance and a sense of light vibration all over, especially in what I call the "doughnut," a sort of circle in my head—somewhat like a halo, but inside. It's difficult to describe it. Sometimes I see a physical body, but it seems non-material. Often it seems luminous, sometimes appearing simply as a beam of light. Many times I have had, however you may explain it, contact with a spirit totem animal. Hawk, deer, crow, or eagle are quite common. Once, during a very powerful meditation, a large, self-sufficient and very dedicated black panther led me to a gate that occurs quite frequently during my meditations. I first saw this gate a year ago, and it has recurred over and over again. Imagine my surprise when, while watching a TV movie, I saw the gate of my dreams. It looked exactly like the gate with which I had become so familiar, and it stood at the entrance to the cemetery at the Wounded Knee Memorial in South Dakota. Barb and I once visited there, and it was a very depressing experience. I have approached this dream gate many times but have rarely been able to venture through. Sometimes it is closed to me. At other times, for whatever reason, I just seem to stop and look through. The feeling has always been that it is the entrance to another reality. The landscape just drops off on the other side, and I view it as if from a high cliff, with the world below me. It always appears bright and shining with green grass and blue, blue skies, a few wispy white clouds and streams of cool water. I love the view.

> I sometimes feel a sense of being out of balance, of leaning one way or another. Often I have the experience of being outside myself....

On this particular afternoon I was hoping to meet up with a totem spirit animal. That is always a pleasant experience and leaves me feeling very relaxed and content when I open my eyes and return "home." That's exactly what happened. But not at all in the way I expected.

After about a half hour of listening to music I feel very relaxed. Even if nothing "happens" during a time of meditation I find it very restful.

Just before I decide it's time to open my eyes, however, I sense a shift occurring. I am taken completely by surprise. Something very powerful seems to be surrounding and overwhelming me and I am almost frightened by the feeling of powerlessness it engenders. But curiosity triumphs over fright. That's a good thing, because I have never had a bad experience while meditating and

An 1891 photograph shortly after the Battle of Wounded Knee shows American soldiers burying Indians in a mass grave.

I really don't feel there is ever any need to fear. Perhaps "anticipation" is a better word. There is the feeling that you are about to jump off a diving board into the deep end of the pool. There is a feeling of justification in the sense that, afterward, waking doubts are almost always present—"Am I just making this up?" But when you are in the moment there is no doubt at all that this is the real thing, and it's bigger than anything life has to offer.

Suddenly I am aware that before me are many, many totem spirit creatures—way too many to count. It's as if they are all dancing or whirling around together, caught in an immense vortex. The colors are the colors of nature—greens and browns, blacks and tans—but all swirling around until they mix together like paint in a bucket and merge into one huge, powerful, green, gold, and silver fire-breathing dragon. That's right, a dragon! I've thought about dragons a lot lately while preparing this book, but this is the first time I've ever seen one in a vision like this.

I suppose I should be frightened, but I'm not, even when in the next moment I am riding the dragon just as Harry Potter might have. Up, up we go, until the earth below is only a soft, green vision. I am conscious, all of a sudden, that the familiar gate of my vision is now far below. I see it as if flying over it in an airplane. The dragon even banks to the left to give me a better view. There is no stopping to peek across this time! We simply fly right over it until it seems to be only a speck in the distance.

What lies before us is an immense field of gray, silver, gold and white. It is perfectly flat but, at the same time, seems to have waves upon waves rippling across its surface. It seems soft and comforting, but infinite in size. It just goes on and on forever. The dragon flies down closer until we are almost skimming across its surface.

In thought, I ask the dragon to drop me off here—to simply roll over and let me tumble down to the surface, but the dragon answers, "No, that is something you must do yourself!"

And I do! I just jump off, not knowing what to expect.

Suddenly I am aware that before me are many, many totem spirit creatures—way too many to count. It's as if they are all dancing or whirling around together, caught in an immense vortex.

What happens is beyond my ability to describe, but I'll try. It seems somehow that all my fears and anxieties, all my guilt, doubts and embarrassments, all my misguided hopes and aspirations, are somehow absorbed into the field of gray and white. They disappear—and I'm left bouncing on the surface like it's a great big trampoline. I'm like a kid again. I have never before in my life experienced such unmitigated joy. Bouncing up and down, doing jumps and spins, inscribing great arcs and flips. Never have I had such fun!

I'm at play in the fields of Akasha—and having a ball!

Next thing I know, I'm back home in my chair with a silly grin on my face.

What just happened? Was it a dream—a flight of imagination? Was it an actual OBE—did I really "go" someplace? Did the whole experience arise through some kind of mental activity?

At that moment I'm reminded of Dumbledore's answer to Harry Potter when Harry asks him if an experience he is having is real or just in his head:

"Of course it is happening inside your head, Harry, but why on earth should that mean that it is not real?"

Back to the Present

I am fully aware that many will read these words and consider them nothing more than a hallucination at best or a possible symptom of psychosis

Saint Paul and other figures of the Bible experienced what could only be described as otherworldly trips.

at worst. But if we are going to talk about Earth spirits and the world of Faery perhaps the best way to approach the subject is to simply point out that these kinds of visionary experiences have been happening to humans since we first climbed down from the trees and wandered out unto the Savannah. Or, at the very least, when we ventured into the great painted caves 40,000 years ago and came out with a severe case of religion that has never abated.

Here's the point. These experiences formed people thousands of years ago. They continue to affect people today, even college-educated, practical minded, left-brain analytical writers such as myself.

Sure, it might be that some human brains such as mine are wired in a way that produces hallucinations. I can't *prove* that I experienced something otherworldly. The means or mechanisms to prove such things don't exist. I believe it because it *felt* real. I believe that if a similar experience were to come your way you would believe it, too. But even then, we would simply be two believers, living in a world pretty much committed to unbelief of such things. That's just the way it is.

What's more, it's always been like that. When the first shamans crawled out of the first cave and tried to explain what they had experienced, I can almost guarantee that most of the tribe looked at each other and said the Paleolithic equivalent of, "Yeah! Right!"

But let me give another example. Now that you've read about my experience, let me tell you about a similar one by a man who lived two thousand years ago. And this one comes straight out of that revered Bible you have somewhere up on a shelf in your home. You can look it up!

> I knew a man in Christ fourteen years ago—whether in the body I do not know, or out of the body I do not know, God knows—such a man was caught up to the third heaven. And I know how such a man—whether in the body or apart from the body I do not know, God knows—was caught up into Paradise and heard inexpressible words, which a man is not permitted to speak.

II Corinthians 12:2–4

Coming right out of the experience of someone revered as Saint Paul, we have to admit that such otherworldly trips are pretty universal. It's interesting to note that even he, that long ago, was reluctant to admit that the man he was talking about was himself. "I knew a guy...."

Belief in Faery is apparently something that even that long ago was not to be taken lightly. Not many liked to admit to it, no matter how important they were.

Is there anything more to these stories? Are they just hallucinations?

A Wealth of Tradition

The myths, legends, and traditions of Faery that come out of the dim, misty past say, "No! Such worlds exist. Such beings exist. We are not alone!"

But we do experience it differently today than people did even a few hundred years ago.

For one thing, our approach is different. In the old days, people tended to try to avoid Faery as much as possible. Perhaps because it was so real to them, they were afraid. Traditions arose, for instance, that Faeries would sneak into your house at night and either steal your child or leave one of theirs—a changeling. When the "Banshee," a "woman of the mounds" in Irish lore, was heard keening in the hills it meant someone had died or soon would. Sensible folk stayed indoors on such occasions. When ancient Celts ventured into the lair of the Faery they tried to be out and home by nightfall. Why tempt fate?

But today people actively try to contact Faery. Through deliberate intention they pay good money to attend workshops where they learn techniques that will put them in touch with the Faery world. Our ancestors of a few centuries ago would probably be appalled.

Another difference between them and us is that most folks used to think that Faery was a localized phenomenon. We hear, for instance, about a particular house that is "haunted." The ghost never seems to leave. The place next door experiences

Even in modern times, there are places such as houses or glades and springs deep in the woods that people feel are haunted or mystical in some way.

nothing unusual. A particular mountain, grove of trees, or forest spring is said to be home to spirits. As long as you stay clear, you'll be fine. Trolls live under specific bridges. Others were certified troll-free.

Although this belief hangs on today, it is not nearly as prevalent. It is not uncommon for instance, to attempt to try to contact spirits far removed from their primary locality. If a downtown hotel has a convenient facility, that's where people go to conduct their seminars. It's more convenient than a Faery grove in the woods somewhere. If your deceased Uncle Fred wants to talk to you, he is just as apt to do it in your medium's studio as the place he used to hang out.

Even so, the "haunted house" belief is a strong one. Anyone who has ever spent time in the woods knows that certain spots feel different from others. Energy vortexes such as those in Sedona, California, attract thousands of tourists every year. Famous places such as the Bermuda triangle and similar triangles in Massachusetts and Lake Michigan are equally sought out. People make pilgrimages to Stonehenge and Avebury because they expect to feel a different energy there. Ireland is "haunted" in a particular way. Australia is haunted in a different way. On and on it goes. When it comes to the experience of Faery, it's location, location, location.

UNDERSTANDING FAERY IN THE TWENTY-FIRST CENTURY

So what are we to do with all this tradition? How do we view it through twenty-first century eyes? Is it real?

Well, let's be honest. A great deal of it is probably nonsense. Some of it is probably hysterical reactions to common phenomena blown up through years and years of retelling the stories so many times that they grow with practice. A certain percentage is no doubt New Age silliness.

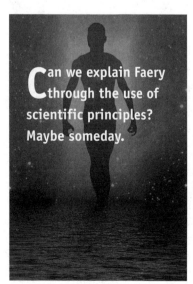

Can we explain Faery through the use of scientific principles? Maybe someday.

But after all is said and done there remains enough well-documented, studied, proven, and verified evidence to say that the world of Faery is real. Fully justifying that statement would take a whole book and many that do just that are listed at the end of this book in the bibliography.

Yes, there is evidence galore that something traditionally labeled Faery exists, and we who have polluted our planet, trampled all over nature, and puffed ourselves up with unjustified pride at our own accomplishments would do well to remember it.

Can we explain Faery through the use of scientific principles? Maybe someday. The field of quantum reality, as we shall see shortly, may be in the process of doing just that.

Can we explain Faery away by saying it consists of personified, anthropomorphized explanations of non-human energies? Sure. But such an explanation doesn't explain away the reality.

Will modern, physics-driven explanations of parallel worlds suffice? Of course! But now we're dealing with semantics. Whatever we choose to label the world of Faery, it's still real. Why not stick to the tried and true tradition but view it through modern eyes?

Fear of Faery

So why do some, maybe even most, moderns tend to trivialize, delegitimize, and demean a tradition that has been around as long as we've been here to experience it? Why are they so reluctant to admit that the universe might be a bigger place than they want it to be? Why do they still fill the darkness of night with light and sound?

In a word—fear.

To admit that the possibility of Faery might exist is to relinquish our place in the cosmos. It is to confess that we are not alone. It is to admit that we might not be in charge of our own lives after all. It is to let loose our fears and face the fact that we aren't the hottest commodity around. It is to acknowledge that we might not be at the top of the proverbial food chain. It is to return in spirit to the frightened child who hears a bump in the night and cowers under the sheets. It is to release the primal fear that the universe is a frightening place.

Do you spend your days worrying that a comet might hit our planet and destroy life as we know it or that our sun will someday go nova and burn everything in the neighborhood clear out to Pluto?

Of course not! But it's going to happen someday. It's a proven fact. The only way around the fear is to ignore it.

We treat the world of Earth spirits, the world of subtle "magic," the world of hidden energies, the world of Faery, in the same way. We ignore it. We almost have to. But in dreams, in unexplained experiences, in forgotten memories suddenly brought to the surface, in sudden glimpses on moonlit nights, it continues to haunt our lives. Something is out there. We sense it. We know it. And despite our blustery confessions and braggadocio, secretly we believe it.

Call them *Earth Spirits*. The world of *Faery*. It's as good as any other phrase we can come up with. It's life. It's power. It's energy.

But don't fear them. You're a part of it. They're not out to get you.

And when you finally open your eyes to them their message will be, "Welcome home, child of Earth! We've been waiting for you."

EVOLUTION AND PUNCTUATED EQUILIBRIA

For some people, God is a convenient explanation for questions that have yet to be answered.

Q: What happened before the Big Bang revved up the universe?
A: *God only knows*.

Q: How did life arise from lifelessness?
A: *God created it*.

Q: What causes seemingly miraculous events to occur?
A: *God is working from the shadows*.

In short, wherever a gap appears in human knowledge, our tendency is to fill that gap with God. It's a convenient explanation.

This is the idea behind the principle known as the "God of the Gaps." It avers that God is the unexplainable force beyond what we can ever know. It's a safe principle and a convenient one. Whenever we are faced with a seemingly unsolvable riddle, we can attribute its solution to God.

There, is, of course, a problem with this theory.

It used to be thought, for instance, that lightning was the result of Zeus hurling his mighty thunderbolts.

Now we know better.

People once believed that the sun rose because Apollo hitched his chariot up to his divine horses every morning and set out on a cosmic journey across the heavens.

Modern telescopes tell a different story.

People once explained natural phenomena as the actions of the gods. For example, the Greek god Zeus threw lightning bolts.

On and on it went. As the gaps grew smaller and smaller, it seemed as though God had less and less to do. Believing in the "God of the Gaps" theory eventually became a bit of an embarrassment as proponents were forced to retreat and retrench after each new discovery. As this process developed, and as God was shoved backward toward irrelevancy, at least when it came to playing a significant role in creating and sustaining the universe, a principle called *phyletic gradualism* developed. This was the idea that evolution occurred uniformly by means of gradual but steady transformations, step by step and piece by piece.

We developed our upright posture, for instance, by gradually spending more and more time on our hind legs. Since this seemed to be a superior method of transportation, nature gradually, over the course of thousands of generations, selected for this trait. Those who stood upright were better able to function. They lived longer and better lives and passed the trait on to their offspring, who, in turn, functioned more efficiently and passed on the trait to their children. On and on it went. It was a matter of *survival of the fittest*. Those better equipped to live survived and passed on the more productive traits they had developed. The others died out and became extinct. We are the end result. It sounds logical and makes perfect sense. God wasn't needed to explain how humans who walk upright differ from apes who don't. Nature itself offers a perfectly reasonable explanation.

EVOLUTIONARY QUESTIONS

But this so-called "reasonable" explanation came with some problems that refused to remain swept under the rug.

Take the evolution of the eye, for instance. For everything pertaining to sight to work correctly, a lot of different things need to evolve independently at the very same time. Even Charles Darwin had trouble with this concept:

> … if numerous gradations from a simple and imperfect eye to one complex and perfect can be shown to exist, each grade being use-

ful to its possessor, as is certainly the case; if further, the eye ever varies and the variations be inherited, as is likewise certainly the case and if such variations should be useful to any animal under changing conditions of life, then the difficulty of believing that a perfect and complex eye could be formed by natural selection, though insuperable by our imagination, should not be considered as subversive of the theory.

That's a lot of "ifs."

Nevertheless, there are those who believe the eye may have evolved independently at least fifty times.

Others aren't so sure.

Two of these people, Niles Eldredge and Stephen Jay Gould, published a ground-breaking paper in 1972 in which they attempted to prove that gradual evolution, such as that described by Charles Darwin, simply didn't fit the fossil record. They believed instead that evolution proceeded by fits, starts, and jumps of mutation in a process they called *punctuated equilibria*. By no means did they attribute these jumps to divinity. They believed that by luck and happenstance, the right processes came together and produced, by accident, something useful—such as an eye that worked, however primitive it might be. After that, the eye could start to improve naturally and develop increased function as it went along.

Punctuated equilibria, now most often called *punctuated equilibrium*, soon became the preferred theory and is almost universally acknowledged as the bedrock of evolutionary theory today.

But there are some jumps that seem too big for even hardcore evolutionists to accept.

Alfred Russel Wallace, for instance, pondered three watershed moments in human development that he simply couldn't explain away:

- *How did life develop from non-life?* How could it possibly happen that a dead cell could, in the next moment of time, become a live one complete with DNA that could replicate itself in its offspring?

Evolutionary biologist and paleontologist Stephen Jay Gould (1941–202) believed, along with colleague Niles Eldredge (1943–), that evolution was not a gradual process so much as one that proceeds in fits and starts.

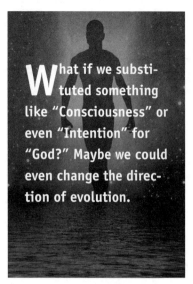

What if we substituted something like "Consciousness" or even "Intention" for "God?" Maybe we could even change the direction of evolution.

- *How did consciousness develop?* Which was the first animal to suddenly become conscious of itself as a unique individual? Who was the first human ancestor to wake up and realize he or she was different from his or her parents, or even be aware of the fact they it was a "he" or a "she"? Or, for that matter, a "who" rather than a "what"?

- *Who was the first "modern" man?* What made such a person different from all those who had come before? How were they different? Why were they different? Apes don't appear to contemplate the stars, or eternity, or existentialism, or their next meal. When did we start to do so?

These are tough, philosophical questions. But we don't even need philosophy to wonder about such things. Biology offers questions as well.

Why, for instance, did our ancient ancestors start to lose their fur and become, in the words of Desmond Morris, a "naked ape?" What evolutionary advantage could we possibly have gained? This is precisely the time when we began to think about wearing fur coats to survive the cold winter. Why would nature have selected for nakedness if, in order to survive, we needed to cover up? It just doesn't make any evolutionary sense.

A New Name for an Old Idea

With all these questions percolating around the halls of academia, an old idea began to rise to the surface. The old "God of the Gaps" idea was outmoded, but perhaps it could be of use after all with some spruced-up verbiage. What if we substituted something like "Consciousness" or even "invention" for "God"? Maybe we could even change the direction of evolution. Maybe we aren't evolving "from" something, but "towards" something. Maybe there is an end product out there somewhere—a perfect human—that is drawing us inexorably towards itself. Plato once speculated that "a horse" is in the process of becoming something he called "horseness." Pierre Teilhard de Chardin (1881–1955), a French Jesuit priest who was for a while censored by the Catholic Church and vilified by most philosophers, agreed, calling our final destination the *Omega Point*, which he believed to be the maximum level of complexity and consciousness—in short, God—to which the universe was evolving. Father Teilhard has since been praised by Pope Benedict XVI (1927–), but during his lifetime he endured some pretty heavy criticism. Like most visionaries, it was only after his death that people other than religious philosophers began to understand his ideas and take them seriously.

Back to the Supernatural

But with the idea of the Omega Point, the supernatural reenters the story of human evolution. If the word "God" gives you trouble, substitute "consciousness" or "destiny." Perhaps you might even grant nature a bit of consciousness and use the word "intention"—as in "Nature *intends* a fully evolved species." How about aliens from out of town manipulating our genes from time to time? What about future programmers double-clicking on the matrix that surrounds us even though we cannot comprehend its existence? Or consider the possibility that such jumps are pre-coded into our DNA, ready to boost us upward and forward when the time is right.

However you phrase it, there now seems to be room within the structure of evolution to permit a discussion of a supernatural force—that is, a force outside of the material world—that seems to be somehow, consciously or not, directing our development and shaping our very essence.

The ancients recognized it and called it "God." Religions formed around the idea. Philosophers intuited it and gave it substance. Now, with the idea of punctuated equilibrium, perhaps even paleontologists can embrace the concept.

Is there a "God of the Gaps," an outside force shaping our evolutionary destiny? Obviously, we have a long way to go in terms of understanding such a force. It would—by definition—have to be considered *super*natural: above nature. But at least the idea is being talked about and roundly scoffed at by traditionalists. That's always the first step toward acceptance.

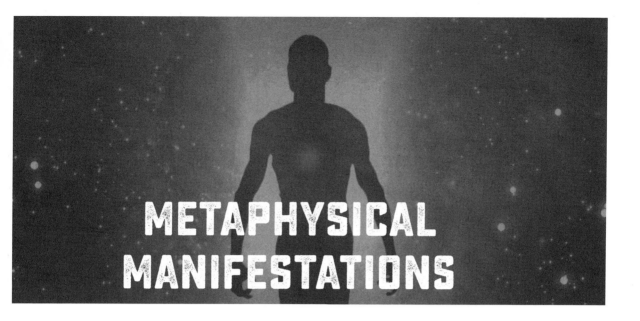

METAPHYSICAL MANIFESTATIONS

THE ESSENCE OF REALITY

Parallel universes. String theory. Quantum entanglement. Alternative consciousness. Worm holes. "M" theory. Warp drive. "God" particles.... These are words that have come to be part of twenty-first-century vocabulary, even if most folks don't really understand the mathematics and theory behind them. Whatever the phrases mean in a technical sense, they have come to represent a central truth: the universe is a strange place, and it doesn't behave only in the way our senses seem to perceive.

Sir Arthur Eddington (1882–1944), the great astrophysicist, was right when he said, "The universe is not only stranger than we imagine, it is stranger than we *can* imagine."

Note the following:

First, a headline and opening paragraph from an article published on June 8, 2015, in *Second Nexus* stated:

A new study published in *Nature Physics* appears to show that time in fact may move backward, things may exist in multiple states, and whether a tree fell in the woods not only may depend on whether anyone ultimately saw it, but also on whether something somehow knew it would be seen.

"It proves that measurement is everything. At the quantum level, reality does not exist if you are not looking at it," said Associate Professor Andrew Truscott from the ANU Research School of Physics and Engineering.

Second, an article cites the research of Professor Howard Wiseman (1968–) and his collaborators. Wiseman is a physicist at Griffith University, Australia. The article begins with a headline and basic premise:

A new theory explains many of the bizarre observations made in quantum physics … other universes are real, exist in vast numbers and exert influence on each other.

—Bryan Nelson, *Mother Nature Network*, November 6, 2014: http://www.mnn.com/green-tech/research-innovations/stories/ parallel-worlds-exist-and-interact-with-our-world-say)

We'll consider this theory more fully in the next chapter, but for now, we simply have to face the fact. Whether or not we understand it, whether or not we believe it, whether or not we accept it, our understanding of the world has changed. It's changed a lot. Ready or not, things will never be the same.

Reflections

Consider a few thoughts I once had while humming an old, old melody that got caught in a loop in my mind one day:

Row, row, row your boat, gently down the stream
Merrily, merrily, merrily, merrily
Life is but a dream

Theoretical physicist Howard Wiseman favors the theory that there are many universes interacting with each other.

For a moment it seemed to be one of the most profound songs ever written. Even its form is important. It's designed to be sung first by one person alone. A measure later, a second person joins in, but not in harmony. The second voice repeats what the first started, from the beginning. Each is singing the same melody, but the two melodies form a harmony. Then a third person joins, and it continues. If you listen to each voice you will hear a complete song that stands by itself, independent of any other singer. But if you listen to them all together you hear a complex composition. Then, when the first singer finishes, that person is reincarnated, so to speak, and starts over again. After a while, you don't know who started to sing, who came in second, or even how many times each has sung the whole song. It just continues on and on—a seemingly endless loop.

And what is the message of the song? What are the singers reminding themselves?

To row their boat, possibly the material body that carries their spirit, *gently* down the stream of life. They are reminding themselves to be gentle with the craft that carries both their mind and soul. Be merry; take joy in the journey because life is, after all, just a dream.

We each sing our short little song. Each song is independent and stands alone. But together, as we each start at the beginning, singing what someone else has sung before, we build a great, harmonious chorus, with complex counterpoint and expression. When we finish our song, we return to the beginning, reincarnated, and sing it again.

How many repetitions? I guess we just keep singing until we feel we are finished. Then we drop out and let others carry the score. It really doesn't matter. There's no hurry, because it's all happening inside us anyway. We create, and are creating, the whole universe. That's who we are—creators. And what of the individual lives we lead here, on this earth and maybe others as well? Don't worry. They're just a dream. Learn from them, but be gentle with yourself while you do it. And be merry!

These thoughts sum up for me the idea, now being explored by physicists, that life is an illusion. The ancient Hindu *rishis* first said it more than five thousand years ago. Even the venerable words of the Bible hint at this message:

Eye has not seen, ear has not heard, neither has entered into the mind of [anyone] what God has prepared for God's people....

—I Corinthians 2:9

Now I see through a [window] dimly, but [someday] I shall see face to face....

—I Corinthians 13:12

Faith is the confidence that what we hope for will actually happen; It gives us assurance about things we cannot see....

—Hebrews 11:1

And now these old writers are beginning to have their theories vindicated by ideas stemming from the complex, mathematical, and endlessly fascinating, emerging field of quantum physics. Out of the laboratories of science comes the new gospel. *Nothing is as it appears to be!* Metaphysics, disparaged in our time as the esoteric work of quacks and silly, superstitious simpletons, is now being revived in the laboratories of modern physicists. We've come a long way, baby!

A Mental Construct

How do we visualize reality if what we see and ultimately experience is an illusion? It would probably be of help to think of a way to conceive of all of this, but that's not an easy task. We need a mental construct of some kind, but how can we trust that it's anywhere near accurate if we can't even trust the fact that the chair we're sitting on is solid?

Perhaps what follows might help. Being a "seeing-is-believing" kind of guy myself, I've tried, over the years, to arrive at a visual representation that merges theology, philosophy, and science. This might not prove to be the ultimate answer. It might even be simplistic. But it might serve as a place to start. Please remember, though, it's only meant to serve as a metaphor. Don't get too literal with it.

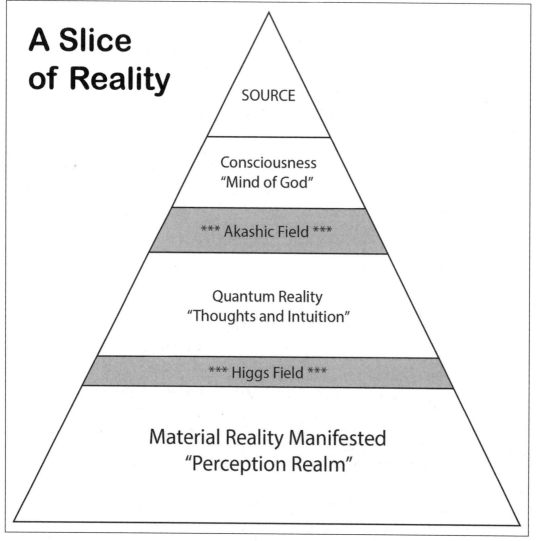

A Slice of Reality

SOURCE

Consciousness "Mind of God"

*** Akashic Field ***

Quantum Reality "Thoughts and Intuition"

*** Higgs Field ***

Material Reality Manifested "Perception Realm"

The above graphic illustrates how our perceived world emanates down from a higher Source.

First, look at the illustration called A *Slice of Reality* on the previous page. Picture it as a piece of a greater pie—concentric circles, moving out from a central point called the *Source*. The *Source* is in the middle, the quiet point around which everything that exists revolves. In our illustration we place it at the bottom, the point of the piece of pie.

What is the *Source*? Well, we don't know. Traditionally we call it *God*, but that's a word that has so much baggage attached to it these days that some might not be comfortable with it. You might prefer something like *Great Mystery* or *Ultimate Unknown*. The Indians of New England called it *Kitchi Manitou*. Others used the term *Great Spirit*. Call it what you will, but for purposes of this illustration we'll use the term *Source*.

Now picture yourself as a wave of some kind of energy within that Source. You have no shape or form. You take up no space but contain infinite possibility. You travel at no speed and exist in perfect rest but have infinite potential.

Along with you in the *Source* there are an infinite number of other waves but that fact isn't really apparent because all waves are One Wave. You certainly can't say there exists anything approaching individuality because all is One. But you cannot grow and personally develop through such one-ness. The only way to do so is to develop uniqueness. And the only way to do that is through individual experience.

And so it begins. A single wave breaks out, beginning its journey toward uniqueness, toward individuality, towards singular experience. When every wave in the *Source* undergoes such transformation, each on its own journey, total potentiality becomes possible. All it requires is space and time for every single, possible experience to become realized. When all such waves finally unite back home, the *Source* will then have become—and personally experienced—everything. Every potentiality will have been realized. The *Source* will have become infinite, realized possibility.

There are, of course, problems inherent to this process. *Realized* possibilities are not always *nice* possibilities. To put it simply, potentiality has a downside. Good and bad, yin and yang—pairs of opposites now enter the picture.

Whatever the Source is, religions all over the world and down through time point to the fact that love is at the center of existence. We might even say that the *Source* is love. The Bible and many holy books agree—"God is love" (I John 4:8).

But when you begin a journey out from the Source, out from Love, out from Unity and toward individuality, you begin the process of establishing your "Self," which, by definition, is separate from Unity.

This is where things get interesting.

AN ANCIENT METAPHOR

Perhaps the best way to visualize our separation from Source is to study anew an ancient but familiar metaphor found in the third chapter of the book of Genesis in the Bible. It's the well-known story of the banishment from Eden.

Is it possible that whoever wrote this story had experienced a mystical vision of the very thing we've been talking about in the last few paragraphs? He or she wouldn't have expressed that vision in the scientific terms we just used. Instead, the writer would have utilized thought-expressions drawn from their own culture.

The beginning of the Genesis story finds our first parents living in a state of blissful unity. They are one with each other, one with nature, and one with God, with whom they "walk in the cool of the evening." They eat whatever nature provides and enjoy each other's company.

This is the way the early writer would have pictured life within the source. One-ness. Unity. Perfect contentment. Peace. Love.

But this unity is about to be broken. In order to experience individuality—the "self"—we need to leave Eden, the place of perfect unity. Thus it was that Eve ate the apple from "The Tree of the Knowledge of Good and Evil." She offered some apples to Adam and they "became as gods, knowing good and evil." No longer would they experience perfect bliss for all eternity. They now knew what it was to be two "selfs" standing side by side, rather than united in perfect harmony.

In a humorous side paragraph, the couple even have their first argument.

"It's not my fault!" says Adam. "Eve made me do it!"

"It's not my fault!" says Eve. "The snake made me do it!"

The snake looked around but there was no one left to blame.

We all know the outcome of the story. All the "selfs" involved would now experience pain. Eve was to give birth in pain. Adam was to work to earn his living "by the sweat of his brow." The snake was to crawl through the dust on his belly. Even God was "grieved."

The story of Adam and Eve being banished from the Garden of Eden is one about the pain of becoming separated from the Source.

There were still to be found moments of bliss, of course. Adam "knew" his wife and Eve gave birth to twins. This seems to tell us that the early author recognized that marital bliss was found in the expression of a return to unity—"the two shall be as one." In unity, in family, in community, in one-ness, we can still find a vestigial memory of the unity of the Source.

But the primary result of dis-unity, of leaving Eden, of leaving the Source, is pain. "All life is suffering," said the Buddha. And he was right. Because life consists of having to mix with a whole bunch of other "selfs." And sometimes that creates conflict.

Is this where the concept of the Devil came from? Is the sense of self we all experience the cause of our discontent? Is "self-ishness" the root of all evil—the Devil himself? In other words, is the experience of "self-ishness" the devil that we created when we ventured out of the Source, seeking the very experience that now leads to so much heartache in the world? Are we, ourselves, the source of our own dissatisfaction? Can real love, real "self-*less*-ness," be experienced only when we enter into harmony with one another?

Even more interesting, is such "self-*less*-ness" the ultimate goal of the whole evolutionary process? Are we moving toward what now seems impossible—the experience of individuality within unity?

If this is true, then all the world's heartache, which ultimately stems from some expression of selfishness, may be only a necessary stage the human race is now experiencing.

Think of it this way. We cannot become emotionally mature as adults without experiencing the pain of separation from first our mother and then our family. There is no other way to grow.

Thus, if we can learn lessons from our current stage of adolescent "self-ishness," we may finally grow into a fully evolved species who can experience *individuality* within *unity*.

Think of it! Not only will we experience bliss, we will retain our individuality while doing it. The many shall become one. We will have grown up.

A Wedding Ceremony

At many Christian church weddings it is customary to place a single, unlit candle on the altar during the service, flanked by two lit candles. The two candles symbolize the bride and groom. At the end of the service the new couple steps forward and lights the center candle—a potent symbol illustrating the words, "The two shall become one."

In the past it was often traditional that the two would then blow out their own candles, signifying the creation of a single entity from two individual people. More and more, however, the current custom is to leave all three candles burning. This changes the symbolism. The meaning now is that they have created something new—their marriage—while retaining their individuality.

This custom is much closer to the imagery we are discussing here.

If this is what the original author had in mind when he or she wrote the opening chapters of the Bible, it causes us to read the story with a brand new mindset, doesn't it? It puts our lives into perspective. The whole process of evolution becomes a mechanism through which we move from *innocent* unity, through an agonizing experience of separation and heartache, to the point where we return to *mature* unity accompanied by individual experience and development.

With this in mind, let's get back to our journey outward from the Source.

The Greek philosopher Plato pointed out the differences between the physicality of a thing and the eternal reality of its qualities—the difference between "horseness" and the actual, physical horse.

Picture again that wave of potential that is you. Your journey begins. You move out from the *Source*. Where do you find yourself? What environment do you now inhabit?

I like to use the word *consciousness*. It is what both Albert Einstein (1879–1955) and Stephen Hawking (1942–) once called "The Mind of God."

Although you still have no mass, either physical or metaphysical, you are now what I might describe as being a little "thicker" or "heavier." You haven't yet visualized where you are going or what you will look like, but you are aware that eventually you will.

The "Mind of God" is an interesting place. There is still complete unity, but there is also an awareness that something we can only call uniqueness and individuality exist. What's it like to be different from every other wave? What does it feel like to be alone, for instance? How will you react to an experience no other wave has ever known?

There's only one way to find out. You have to travel onward.

Your journey now takes you through your first defining field. It's a place wherein you begin to take on shape. Not mass. Not yet. But you grow a little heavier as you begin to transform yourself into something truly unique and separate.

Taking a cue from the ancient Hindus, I call this place of transformation the *Akashic Field*. Everything that we know and experience around us, every rock, tree and flower, every person, every animal, every bird and every fish, was first conceived in *Akasha*.

Earlier we talked about how Plato differentiated "horse" from "horseness." "Horseness" is the eternal reality. The "horse" quietly grazing on clover in the pasture by the side of the road is just its physical manifestation.

Well, a "horse" doesn't exist in the *Akashic Field*. But this is where "horseness" is born. Here we find the field in which uniqueness is first given birth—not in fact but in principle. There are no "horses" here. But there is an idea about what a horse might be as differentiated from a dog or cat.

Once again, you have slowed down a little. You have gathered metaphysical mass. You now understand the concept of individuality expressed both in final form and in idea. You understand that unique individuality leads to unique experience. You pass through the *Akashic Field* and become something different. You now have some direction. What's next?

QUANTUM REALITY

When you emerge from the *Akashic Field* you find yourself in a totally different realm. You have now entered *Quantum Reality*. This world was discovered by our scientists only about a hundred years ago. We are just now beginning to explore it.

Sir James Hopwood Jeans (1877–1946), who died the year I was born, was a brilliant English physicist, astronomer, and mathematician. One of my favorites among his great quotes was his observation that "humanity is at the very beginning of its existence—a new born babe, with all the unexplored potentialities of babyhood; and until the last few moments its interest has been centered absolutely and exclusively on its cradle and feeding bottle." But by far his most famous quote, appearing in almost every physics textbook and quoted in hundreds of lectures throughout the world of quantum physics, was this: "The universe begins to look more like a great thought than a great machine."

For this reason I call the world of *Quantum Reality* the place of "Thoughts and Intentions."

You're not human yet. You still have a way to go. But here in this world you can now form what might be called a thought as to what "human" is and form an intention that you're going to be one.

Quantum Reality is a place of potential. Humans don't really live here. Not yet, anyway. But what Plato called "humanness" now exists. The potential

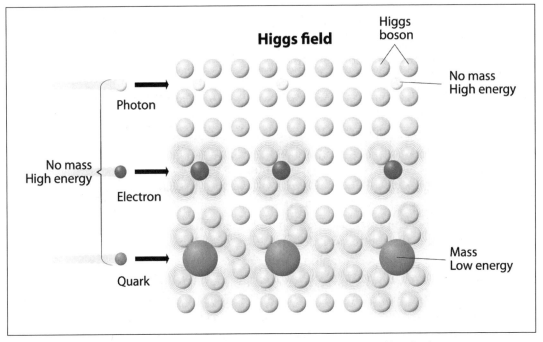

The Higgs mechanism creates a Higgs field that fills space and breaks down symmetry in fundamental particles called bosons, giving them mass. Without the Higgs mechanism, there would be no mass to our universe, only energy.

for any one human is here. That potential will soon be realized when it takes one more step. In order for "humanness" to become "a human" it must first "collapse" into the environment humans experience. To do that it must pass through the newly discovered *Higgs Field*.

Ask physicists whether or not they're excited that the *Higgs Field* is now proved by experimental method and they will say, "Yes! Empathically yes!"

But ask them to describe that field, now that they know it's there, and they will begin to get a little edgy. Some might even giggle.

It's a reality. That's for sure. But no one quite knows how to describe it. Earlier, in the Introduction to this book, we took a brief stab at it. Maybe we should now let a scientist try. Here is the simplest definition I could find, from Andrew Zimmerman Jones:

> The Higgs field is the theoretical field of energy that permeates the universe, according to the theory put forth in 1964 by Scottish theoretical physicist Peter Higgs. Higgs suggested the field as a possible explanation for how the fundamental particles of the universe came to have mass, because in the 1960s the Standard Model of quantum physics actually couldn't explain the reason for

mass itself. He proposed that this field existed throughout all of space and that particles gained their mass by interacting with it.

Does that help? There are many other definitions out there, but they all involve some pretty complex mathematics. Suffice it to say that when energy passes through the Higgs Field it emerges on the other side with, for the first time in its journey from the *Source*, mass. In other words, it becomes material. It is now within our *Perception Realm*. We've come home.

MATERIAL REALITY MANIFESTED

We've now entered the world of our five senses. We're in the material realm of the scientist, who can now breathe a lot easier because he has something to measure, study, dissect, and put under a microscope. This is the world I call our *Perception Realm*. It's the world we see around us.

But even this world has its hidden realms. When I say "Perception Realm" I'm referring to the cosmos in all its many manifestations. Here lies the *Multiverse* in its infinite capacity for creativity. Here dwell all possible manifestations of every single possibility. Here lie an infinite number of "you's," each living their own life in woeful ignorance of their doppelgangers in parallel universes. This particular universe seems to be supported by mysterious *Dark Matter* that pushes it out towards infinity. Here we find the mysteries inherent in the mathematics of modern physics. This is the home of *String Theory*, *Membrane Theory*, and all the other fantastic ideas circulating around the great universities of the world, eventually percolating out to television's *Discovery Channel*. Here we find everything that intrigues and mystifies us.

But all this is only the outer core of an even greater mystery. It all began back at the *Source*, with a vague notion of individual expression encased within perfect one-ness. Out here on the edge, every one of those expressions is manifested. Infinite being. Eternal experiment.

As we row our boat down the stream of what we call life, is it any wonder we can sing that "life is but a dream?"

So what, ultimately, is there, and what is it like? Honestly, we don't know and we're not sure.

But we're getting closer. Until we do, let's not get rid of the term *Supernatural*. It is still pretty useful.

PARALLEL UNIVERSES

Nothing drives a theoretical physicist batty faster than having to listen to pseudo-scientific psycho-babble about the existence of parallel universes. But the existence of such "super-natural" mysteries seems to be the only thing that makes much of the math undergirding the physics of the universe work out.

What's a poor theoretical physicist to do? Complex math demands something that sounds wacky when put in practical terms that a layman can understand. It's a tough spot to be in. But almost every modern theory about how the universe came to be seems to have loose ends that can be tied up only by projecting hypothetical universes that, according to the theories themselves, cannot even be comprehended, much less measured and observed in compliance with the scientific method. It forces a physicist to rely on unproven and unprovable speculative "belief." That's not a comfortable place for a scientist to be.

To make matters worse, there is not "a" theory of parallel universes. There are many.

For that reason, we now offer an armchair tour guide into different realities. Without leaving the comfort of your own body, this guide will take you on a few mental trips to some of the most popular theories regarding realms which, if they really exist, can only be described as "supernatural"—that is, outside of what we consider "natural."

But wait—there's more! Here's an added bonus. If beings exist in these parallel universes (and, according to the theories, they do!) and if these beings have learned to communicate with some of us, just as some of us swear we can communicate with them—then we may have found the source of what some people call "supernatural gods."

Are you ready to take a trip or two? Here it goes. Consider this an excursion into bifurcating timelines, cosmic bubbles, and entangled realities. We'll begin with the ones closest to home and work out from there.

Gottfried Leibniz (1646–1716) once suggested that we live in "the best of all possible worlds." Voltaire (1694–1778) had a field day with this suggestion in *Candide* but since his day the phrase has been given a much more respectable title. It is now called the *Anthropic Principle*.

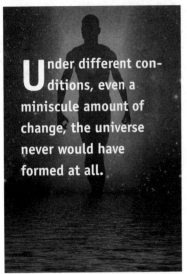

Under different conditions, even a miniscule amount of change, the universe never would have formed at all.

What that means is this: the universe seems to be fine-tuned to produce life. If any of the major forces that sustain us were even a little out of wack, life would not only cease to exist, it never would have formed in the first place. Think, for instance, of what might happen if gravity became a little stronger. We'd all be flattened into nothing. If it became a little weaker, we'd all float off into space. Under different conditions, even a miniscule amount of change, the universe never would have formed at all.

Yet it did. Why?

For many, the answer is simple. God planned it that way. God created a "Goldilocks" universe, neither too hot nor too cold, too this or too that—so that humans would have a comfortable place to live.

Scientists, understandably, are not happy with that theory. So they postulated a variation on it that is much easier to swallow if you're not given to religious, "God-of-the-gaps" explanations. Here it is:

The universe supports the evolution of humankind because if it didn't humankind would never have evolved.

There it is. It's simple and easy to understand. Things could have happened differently. If they had, we wouldn't be here. But because we are here, that, in itself, is the proof that things happened the way they did.

In other words, our universe is uniquely structured so as to produce life as we know it. You might even say the universe was uniquely structured "for" humans—thus, the *Anthropic Principle*, from *Anthropos*, meaning "man" or, more properly, "human being."

The problem with the theory is that the nagging question, "structured by whom?" usually crops up. But the fact that the universe *is* structured doesn't mean it is *purposely* structured. It might have happened by accident.

However it happened, the fact remains that we're here because everything worked out just right. It is, indeed, "the best of all possible worlds." Had it not been, we wouldn't be here to ask the question and form the theory.

Alternative Realities

Here comes a science-fiction staple. A man invents a time machine and travels back into history. There he changes something. When he returns to his own time, everything is different. He has altered the time-space continuum. That, by the way, is a no-no. If you ever go back in time, don't touch anything! The slightest change can magnify out to unthought-of proportions. What if you reach out to hug your grandfather and, by mistake, push him into the path of a speeding truck? You'd never have been born.

Get the picture?

This is not as far-fetched as it seems. The latest projections of Einstein's space/time theories seem to indicate that it might be possible to travel back in time, though probably not forward. What might that mean? If a future time traveler comes back to pay our ancestors a visit, he might change the reality we are currently enjoying.

But what if that has already happened? What if someone already launched a new timeline, an alternative reality, and we're living in it? Is the unique story we are forging subject to change because of some future bungler? We won't know until we know if time travel is possible. But that won't happen if the discovery of time travel is someday postponed by a malcontented time traveler who comes back either to delay the discovery or somehow "make things right," according to his or her ideas, Arnold Schwarzenegger (*The Terminator*) and Michael J. Fox (*Back to the Future*) to the contrary.

Does this make you just a little bit dizzy? Then try this: it is theoretically possible, given the open-ended aspect of eternity, that this has already happened an infinite number of times and will continue to happen until all possible alternative realities are lived out in time. In short, every possible universe that *could* ever be, *will* be, given enough time. And who are the time travelers who have shaped the current history we know and love? We call them "supernatural gods." If they wanted to create a new universe, all they had to do was go back to "in the beginning" and start over.

There's a thought that will keep you up nights!

That leads us to the next theory. Now things heat up a bit. This one is courtesy of Richard Feynman (1918–1988).

One theory about the nature of reality is that we could be living in one of many possible worlds.

Theoretical physicist Richard Feynman speculated that the many possible paths reality could take eventually cancelled themselves out, leaving us with the reality in which we actually live.

Conduct a thought experiment in your mind. Picture a particle that decides to travel from point A to point B. There are, of course, an infinite number of paths the particle could follow. Each of these paths can be given a mathematical probability of being the one the particle will choose based on things like ease of travel, shortest distance between two points, and so on. (If picturing particles throws you off, think instead of a hiker—the particle—who wants to walk through a forest and has an infinite number of paths he or she can go to accomplish the task. Do they choose the shortest one, the most convenient one, the one with the best view, or whatever else comes to mind?)

Now remember this: particles are also waves! Waves spread out as they move. The individual "particle path" now becomes what is called a "probability amplitude." As the waves spread out they take up more space and bump into one another, either canceling each other out or amplifying each other. If you carry this idea to its logical conclusion, at the end you will be left with one, and only one, possibility. That's the possibility we're living in. It's the "Sum Over All Paths" possibility.

(If you switched from particles to hikers two paragraphs ago, think of it this way. Our hypothetical hiker, with every possible path open for selection, decides to take the shortest and easiest path, but only after trying them all, and getting very tired in the process!)

According to this theory, we live in a universe that exists only after all other possible universes were given their time on stage. Our path is what we call reality. We can never experience any of the others. They are outside our realm of possibility. In other words, they are not "natural," but "super-natural." We can deduce that they exist as very real possibilities, but we can never know for sure their nature or their aspects.

This is where Feynman leaves it. The sci-fi writers can take it from here.

Quantum theory is a wild and wacky place, to be sure. But of all the mind-boggling interpretations, none is crazier than a theory put forth by Hugh Everett (1930–1982). The trouble is, he might have been right.

Here's his theory in a nutshell, according to Nick Herbert in *Quantum Reality*:

Of all the claims of the New Physics none is more outrageous than the contention that myriads of universes are created upon the occasion of each measurement act. For any situation in which several different outcomes are possible (flipping a coin, for instance) some physicists believe that all outcomes actually occur. In order to accommodate different outcomes without contradiction, entire new universes spring into being, identical in every detail except for the single outcome that gave them birth. In the case of a flipped coin, one universe contains a coin that came up heads; another, a coin showing tails. Paul Davies champions this claim, known as the many-worlds interpretation.... Science fiction writers commonly invent parallel universes for the sake of a story. Now quantum theory gives us good reason to take such stories seriously.

The "Many-Worlds Theory" was developed by Hugh Everett in 1957. Niels Bohr (1885–1962) hated the idea of many worlds existing simultaneously. He didn't even want to believe in one quantum reality, let alone an infinite number. None of the scientists of Everett's day would give him the time of day. Eventually, Everett became disgusted at the close-mindedness of his colleagues and left physics altogether. Even though he had worked for the Pentagon and wrote the letter that probably became the impetus for the doctrine of "mutually assured destruction" that may have saved the world from nuclear holocaust during the Cold War, he couldn't get a job, dying relatively young of a heart attack.

In his book *Our Mathematical Universe*, MIT professor Max Tegmark (1957–) says Everett's work is as important as Einstein's theory of relativity. If so, Everett was certainly a man ahead of his time. His ideas are now considered both important and influential.

Although it sounds like a crazy idea, it is important because it solves the measurement problem. How can a conscious being actually have the power to change a universe simply by choosing one method of measurement over another?

The answer is that they can't. The wave doesn't "collapse" into a *single* piece of cosmic "stuff." It collapses into *every possible* piece of cosmic "stuff." All possible outcomes occur. You don't realize it because you're stuck in one universe and experience only one outcome. But if it's any consolation, the other versions of "you" exist in parallel dimensions. In one universe you're standing there wondering why you made the choice you made, while in a parallel universe your counterpart is standing there wondering why they made the choice they made. Both are unaware of the other, of course, and continue on as if nothing special has happened.

Think of it this way: When a particle (a quantum) is measured (or observed) it can become manifested in many different ways. Each manifestation, as we have seen, is dependent on an observer or a measurement device. If we are the observer, we see one such random manifestation.

But what about the others? What happened to them?

Everett's novel explanation is that they all occurred, but outside out sensory experience. In other words, there are other "yous," each existing in your own space, and each observing a different result. All possible "real" states are manifested, but each in its own universe.

Suppose that when measured an electron has a 50 percent chance of rotating clockwise and a 50 percent chance of rotating counter-clockwise. Which will occur when you check it out?

Only one. At least, you can handle only one. So you get a clockwise rotation, write it down in your book, and go home for the day.

What about the other possibility?

Everett says there is another "you" who got a counter-clockwise spin, wrote it down in his book, and went home for the day.

Like lovers across a crowded room or ships that pass in the night, you both remain unaware of the other's existence. You live in parallel universes, separated, perhaps, by less than the width of an electron, but you are completely oblivious to your other, quantum self. Your two outcomes, caused by two measurements, both transpire, but in different universes. And you never know it. (Unless you experience something akin to déjà vu. But we cover that in another chapter.)

How many such universes exist? Some have calculated the number to be somewhere near 10^{100}. But who's counting?

There is something else we need to look at when it comes to the Many Worlds Theory and it's very important. As we have already seen when we looked at "The Best of All Possible Worlds," our universe is finely tuned to create and support life. There are many, many things that have to be just so. Too much gravity, too strong or too weak a nuclear field, too much of this, too little of that, and life could never have arisen.

What a strange sensation if you could see all your alternative selves! But just because you can't doesn't mean they don't all exist, all making slightly different choices in their lives....

So why did it? How did it happen that the Goldilocks universe (not too hard—not too soft) we call home turned out just right for us?

Religionists say it's because God made it that way. Others attribute it to dumb luck. Still others say it's the way it is because if it wasn't we wouldn't be here to wonder about such things.

The plain truth is that if you leave it to mathematics, the chances are pretty low. Almost non-existent. According to statistics and probability studies, our existence is pretty near impossible. But according to Everett, every possible thing that *can* happen, *does* happen. That makes our existence a certainty.

When the Big Bang happened, for whatever reason, individual "bubble" universes began to split off right away. They were right next to each other but followed totally separate evolutionary paths. Most of them, according to probability studies, couldn't develop life as we know it. But ours did. For that, we can be thankful. Then again, in those that didn't, there are no people around to offer thanks anyway.

What does this have to do with supernatural gods?

Everything!

Suppose you are a supernatural deity who wants to experience everything there is? What better way to do just that than to create a cosmos where everything that *can* happen, *does* happen?

It's not as if space is a problem. You have infinity to work with. One universe, or even a few billion, is not going to clutter up the place. Go ahead! Spread out! Experience away! You've got all day. Time and space are connected, after all. It takes an infinite amount of both to accomplish your goals, but infinity is what you've got. So knock yourself out! There's no hurry. Create a sentient being in your image who can go live the life, or lives, and report back after his or her mission is accomplished. Just think about the possibilities! Every action can produce every possible outcome, so infinite experiential wisdom is conceivable. And with parallel universes all moving along at the same time, you don't even have to wait. It all happens right now, at the same time!

Admit it. Have you ever wondered whether you like this dish or that dish best, so you cooked them both and performed a taste test? Of course you have. Now just multiply your taste test times infinity, add an infinite amount of curiosity, give yourself an infinite amount of space and time, and sprinkle the whole thing with a dash of omnipotence.

You get the idea. The Many Worlds theory becomes a playground for divinity in action. Some people find this whole idea comforting. Just think of the stories you'll be able to share with your quantum doppelgangers when you, and they, finish with life and return to the Source!

Now—is there any evidence that Everett or his followers even thought about these things?

Absolutely not. Everett was a devout atheist to his dying day. He would no doubt be appalled by this kind of reasoning. Most of his followers are far away from anyone who could be considered religiously motivated in the traditional sense.

But ideas, once released, tend to move through the spiritual ether like wave forms, collapsing into all sorts of spiritual realities never intended by the founders.

And who knows? Maybe that's a good thing.

The universe is infinitely large. The elements that compose it are finite. What this means is that if you mix the finite components together, there will be a limited number of ways to combine them, but infinite space in which to do it. So sooner or later some "mixes" are going to start to look similar to others. What this means is that if you travel "out" far enough, you're bound to come across areas that look very much alike.

If you like this idea, and take it to its logical conclusion, somewhere out there a bunch of chemicals and cosmic stuff came together in a way that is very similar, if not identical, to the way the chemicals and cosmic stuff that make up your body formed you. In other words, there is a nearly identical "you" way out there somewhere who thinks he or she is unique and "you" are simply a mathematicians' dream. According to Paul Halpern (1961–), maybe they are even "reading this article on a parchment scroll illuminated by a glowworm."

Hey, we said it was *nearly* identical out there—not perfect!

Current thinking in cosmology involving the birth of the universe revolves around an idea called "inflation." It was developed in the 1980s but described in mathematical detail in 2002 by physicists Alan Guth (1947–), Andrei Linde (1948–), and Paul Steinhardt (1952–), who all won the Dirac Prize "for development of the concept of inflation in cosmology."

The basic idea is that at the very beginning of the universe, right after the Big Bang, the universe expanded exponentially at a rate much faster than the speed of light. The period of expansion is called the "Inflationary Epoch." If you don't remember it, it's because it happened way before anything else of consequence, including you, formed. Also, you might have missed it because the whole epic lasted less than second. To be precise, it began at 10^{-33} seconds and lasted all the way until 10^{-36} seconds. You may not have noticed it at the time if you were busy doing something else. The universe is still expanding even as you read this. But not nearly that fast.

Now we get weird.

According to the Big Bang theory, "in the beginning" an infinitesimal point that became the universe, a point/field of unimaginable energy that still

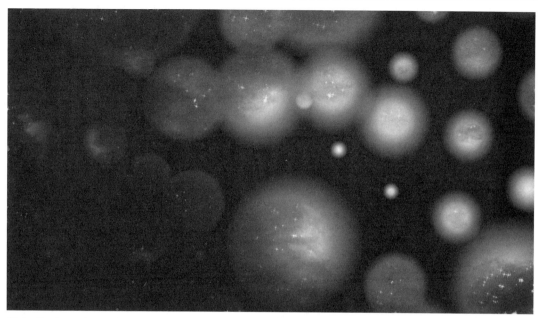

If the Big Bang began from a singularity to form our universe, who's to say this event did not happen many times, engendering many universes?

existed only as potential, was somehow triggered by something that caused space and time to grow, virtually instantaneously, into material that built the universe we view today. Here's the key, though. If the explosive expansion took place in one part of space, it must have also happened in other parts. In other words, bubbles formed. Each one became a potential universe. Ours is just one of many.

Think of sitting in a bathtub and watching soap bubbles form on the surface of the water. Some are big and some are small. They merge. They become bigger. Some of them pop right away. Others take longer.

Each one is a metaphor for our universe. We live in one that stayed together, obviously. No one living in any one bubble can possibly be aware of anyone living in another one.

Whoa! Back up a minute! Think about what we just said:

No one living in any one bubble can possibly be aware of anyone living in another one.

We can't be aware through normal means, of course. We can't reach across the gap and touch another bubble. That's scientifically impossible.

But is there another way to do it?

Go back to the bathtub metaphor. What if the bubbles form in a sea of something that we call Consciousness? The bubbles aren't forming on their own. They're forming on the surface of the water. "Water," in this metaphor, is Consciousness. If human beings can discover ways to separate their individual consciousness from the barriers caused by their five senses—the barriers that separate us from a greater reality—they might be able to peer across the vast divide that is now impossibly far away from us and experience realities existing in other "bubbles." We can't physically travel such extreme distances, even at the speed of light. But what if we can learn to travel at the speed of thought? If Consciousness is the water that supports everything—all the "bubbles" floating on the surface of Consciousness—then Consciousness itself is the unifying reality. Call it God. Call it Akasha. Call it Unity. Call it anything you want. But this theory begins to plunge us into a "supernatural" idea that is both scientific and religious. It has to do with the concept of an underlying unity upon which an infinite number of universes float, expand, experience their time on the surface, and then pop away into oblivion. This is very much a Hindu religious concept. It goes back thousands of years.

Once again, religion and science meet up. Like it or not, when you ask the same questions you eventually arrive at the same destination.

STRING THEORY AND MULTIPLE DIMENSIONS

The last kind of universe we're going to look at concerns higher dimensions. This one takes us out to the extremes.

String theory is the best attempt so far to unify what we call the "natural" forces that govern our universe. The basic idea is that at the root of everything lie vibrating, one-dimensional objects called *strings*. Strings interact with each other in very specific ways. On the surface, a string looks and acts much like a particle in that it has mass and charge. But that's where the similarities end. When the string vibrates, it produces the gravitational force. In that sense, string theory is a quantum theory of gravity. That makes it a candidate for the illusive "Theory of Everything," or the "Grand Unified Theory" (GUT), a single theory that unites what we know about the four principle forces that hold everything together—gravity, electromagnetism, and the strong and weak nuclear forces. Up to now, gravity was the one that gave scientists fits. For various technical reasons it doesn't play well with the others. But string theory made allowances for it and managed to tie them all together. It was so much fun to work with that it soon matured even farther into a theory called superstring theory.

(If your eyes are starting to glass over about now, stick with it just a little longer. We're almost at the end.)

For reasons known only to very gifted nerds, superstring theory only works if you posit eleven different dimensions. It's almost impossible for people like you and me to picture these in our heads. We do well with up and down, side to side, and time. But after that we get easily lost.

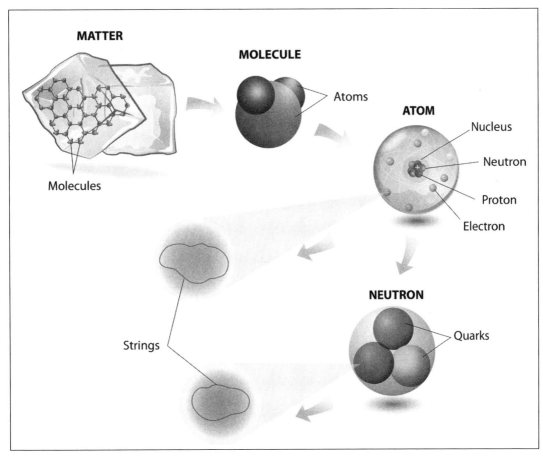

String theory posits that, once you dig down past molecules, atoms, and subatomic particles, eventually you find that all matter is made up of infinitesimally small strings that exist in eleven dimensions.

Theoretical physicists, however, aren't as limited. They exist in a mental world that honors powers far beyond those of mortal men. So what happened was that some very gifted people began to think about string theory so much that the whole idea morphed into what is now called M-Theory. ("M" stands for Membrane [sometimes shortened as "'Brane"], although some scientists substitute "mystery" or even "magic.")

Once again, if such membranes, dimensions, or parallel universes exist, the only way to travel to them is through the mysteries of math or the soaring imagination of our minds. To those of us trapped on this side of the Multiverse/Membrane fence, such things appear quite supernatural. But really, it's only a matter of frequency. Do other universes occupy the same space as us, but simply vibrate at a faster frequency? Perhaps time will someday allow us to answer that question.

(Meanwhile, read the entry in this book about NDEs and OBEs. Seen in this regard, such things are fascinating!)

Our armchair guide to parallel universes and dimensions is now complete. Is any of it true? Who knows? But the fact that serious scientists consider such things is illuminating. If any of it proves viable, the human race could be in for a trip that will take us to unimaginable places.

Think of it this way. If you had told people who were living in the Middle Ages that they were living in the "middle" of something that was about to change drastically, they wouldn't have known what you were talking about. They had no idea a Renaissance was coming that would turn their world upside down and completely change the way they viewed their future and defined themselves.

Who is to say we are any different? We probably can't even imagine that we may be on the cusp of a brand new way of thinking about what we now call *supernatural*. If it breaks through and becomes known reality, everything will change. The human race will evolve overnight into something quite different than anything we have ever known.

So be it. Bring it on!

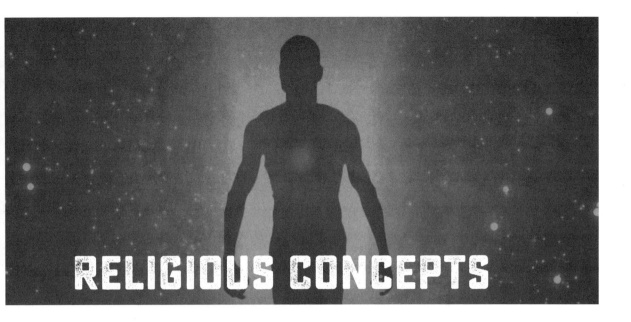

RELIGIOUS CONCEPTS

THREE PILLARS OF RELIGIOUS THEORY

"Religion" is one of those words we all use and seem to understand but then are misunderstood when we use it in a sentence. To some, religion speaks of unbelief versus belief. If you believe in God, you are religious. To others, religion is a code word for prejudice and, in some cases, bigotry. To many, religion means rules and regulations. To others, it has come to mean comfort and security in a confused and confusing world. To some people, who believe in a power higher than themselves, "religion" is a confining word. They usually prefer the word "spirituality." According to their definition, a "religion" forms around an initial spiritual concept and then proceeds to build doctrinal walls, incrusted with centuries of accumulated dogma. Many swear that the surest way to start an argument is to talk about politics or religion. Often, they're correct.

Within the pages of this book, we cannot hope to address the broad spectrum of religious concepts. For that, I recommend my book *The Religion Book: Places, Prophets, Saints, and Seers* as a place to start. But we need to discuss religion in order to travel further on our quest for supernatural gods. So we're going to need to attempt at least a broad definition. It may not be one you agree with. But that's okay. At least we will know what the word means when it is used between the covers of this book.

For purposes of clarity, "religion" as it is used here refers to a broad spectrum of belief systems organized around a basic approach to understanding the supernatural. There are three such systems:

- Nature Religions
- Revealed Religions
- Conceptual Religions

Let's take them one at a time.

Nature Religions

This is, as the name implies, a broad group of religions that take their cue from the natural world. Such religions include animism, shamanism, Wicca, and Druidism; tribal practices in the Americas, Africa, Polynesia, and elsewhere are strongly connected to the natural world. They have ancient roots and reflect our first ancestor's awareness of what they must have considered to be the "magic" that surrounded them.

Animals demonstrated behaviors that humans couldn't duplicate. Fierce storms defied human strength and ingenuity. Mysterious sicknesses, seemingly miraculous cures, and serendipity on steroids all contributed to the idea that the environment was a supernatural place, inhabited by unseen spirits that animated everything. Hence, the world's oldest religion—*Animism*. This was the belief that everything in nature was "animated" by spirit. Spirits inhabited trees and grasslands. They lived within glaciers. They drove the seas and could be sensed brooding in the mountains. Ultimately, spirits were to be found in woodland springs and oak groves, in dark caves and distant stars. They were felt in the rain and sun, experienced in dreams, and sought in visions.

It was only natural that such spirits were personified and soon referred to as "gods." They were *super*-natural gods—"above" nature. As such, it was

A Malaysian shaman performs a ritual to appease Akinabalu, the guardian of Mount Kinabalu. Shamanistic beliefs have strong ties to the natural world.

only prudent to want to keep them on your side—to appease them with gifts of recognition, thanksgiving, and gracious attitudes. Accordingly, rules developed that defined how you should interact with the gods who interacted with you. It became habitual to offer certain gods certain gifts on certain days. A professional clergy was formed whose only purpose was to become experts in such things. They devoted their time to figuring out how to act in the presence of gods. They carved out a niche that enabled them to serve as intermediaries. A layman or laywoman couldn't very well be expected to talk to a god and have the god talk back to them. So clergy came to represent the god in such conversations.

When we consider this process, it becomes obvious that virtually every religion begins with a shamanic component.

The original founders displayed shamanic abilities. The disciples who followed them then turned stories about the founders into dogma and doctrine.

Even Hinduism, which is not a "founder" religion in the sense that there was no one figure such as Moses, Jesus, or Muhammad who began it, demonstrates shamanic influences. The first Hindu rishis describe communicating with supernatural beings when they drank the mysterious, plant-derived brew they called *Soma*. Consider these verses from the *Rigveda*, the oldest of the Hindu scriptures:

> Like currents of wind, the drinks have lifted me up. Have I not drunk soma?
>
> One of my wings is in heaven, the other trails below. Have I not drunk soma?
>
> I am huge! Flying to the clouds. Have I not drunk soma?
>
> —*Rigveda*, Book 10. English translation by Ralph T. H. Griffith

No one knows what soma was, but the best guesses seem to indicate it was produced from mushrooms with psychedelic potential. Drinking this brew seems to have produced visions similar to the shamanic tradition of preparing and ingesting ayahuasca.

Revealed Religions

Nature religions and the shamanic experience are thus at the root of every single religion that now exists. Most people today don't think about their own religion in this way, but consider some examples taken from three familiar world religions still in existence. They are called "revealed" religions because they all believe that God "revealed" the core truth of their religion and either dictated or, in various ways caused to be written, that central truth. The result is scripture—a holy book. But think about how these religions came to be:

Judaism

Judaism began when a naturalist couple, living in a plentifully abundant environment, came across a talking snake who offered them the gift of knowledge that would make them equal to God. Before this they were close to God—walking and talking with him in the cool of the evening. But after they succumbed to the snake's temptation, they were separated from nature and separated from God. It even seemed to put a strain on their marriage. Life was tough from then on. They had to work to produce their food and they raised two kids, one of whom proved to become an unmanageable juvenile delinquent. (This story, by the way, is found not only in Judaism but in many other religions as well.)

When "men began to multiply on the earth," Judaism took another turn in a way that would seem right at home on a modern episode of television's *Ancient Aliens* series. As a matter of fact, it is often employed there. Here it is, right out of the pages of the Bible:

> When men began to increase in number on the earth, the sons of God saw that the daughters of men were beautiful, and they married any of them they chose....The Nephilim [*some translations use the word "Giants"*] were on the earth in those days—and also afterward—when the sons of God went to the daughters of men and had children by them. They were the heroes of old, men of renown.
>
> —Genesis 6:1–7

As the story of Judaism unfolds throughout the pages of the Bible, angels appear to people who are often unaware that they are in the presence of supernatural beings. Abraham, for instance, was visited by two of them who were on their way to destroy Sodom and Gomorrah. Moses underwent a classic shamanic experience when he confronted a voice in the desert speaking to him from a bush that burned but was not consumed. The voice told him that before he could approach, he must take off his sandals because he was walking on holy ground. (Exodus 3:1–5). The young prophet Samuel was called to his ministry because he heard disembodied voices in his room (I Samuel 3). Apparently no one else could hear them. Ezekiel confronted a strangely technological craft that propelled him into his life's work (Ezekiel 1). He was later transported up to "heaven" in a "fiery chariot" (II Kings 2:11).

On and on it goes. Were these stories not found in what has become a revered holy book they would be considered very similar to stories right out of shamanism, Wicca, or ancient Druidism.

"Your sons and daughters will prophesy," said the Jewish prophet Joel in chapter 3 of his famous prophecy from the pages of the Hebrew Bible. "Your old men will dream dreams and your young men will see visions."

To which any respectable shaman would say, "Amen!"

Christianity

It's always important to keep a level head when it comes to religious matters. Many Christians have heard the story of the founding of their religion so often, and have formed such a barricade of doctrine and respectful dogma around it, that it sounds as if we are speaking heresy when we remind them that the incarnation, celebrated every Christmas in song and pageant, tells a typical story that is found in almost all Nature religions around the world. It is a saga called the "virgin birth"—an account of a human female who is impregnated by a god. The story is found in the New Testament of the Bible in two short sections in the Gospels of Matthew and Luke, both of which were written many decades after the event they recall was said to have happened.

In this version, a young girl is visited by an otherworldly visitor who says his name is Gabriel. She is going to become "quickened" by a supernatural being. Her betrothed, a man named Joseph, immediately decides to call off the marriage, but he, too, is visited by a supernatural being who assures him to go ahead with the wedding.

Later, when *Yeshua*, the boy born of that union, is grown, he finds it necessary to retreat into natural surroundings, specifically mountain tops, to pray alone. On one such journey, while accompanied by three followers, two figures from the distant past, Moses and Elijah, both of whom had undertaken shamanic experiences, step out of the ether to counsel him. Yeshua later makes headlines by healing the sick, casting out demons, and performing miracles. This follows the job description of a typical shaman even today.

When Yeshua was crucified, a strange detail recorded in Scripture begins to make sense. There is a common motif in shamanic visions, depicted

Revealed religions are those in which the truth is revealed to people by God or His messengers. This is the basis for Christianity, for example. An angel reveals to Mary she will give birth to a savior (as depicted in numerous works of art, such as this one by Dutch painter Adriaen van de Velde), who then reveals God's Word to the masses.

in the great painted caves, called "The Wounded Man," or, more commonly, "The Pierced Man." We're going to study it in more detail in a few chapters. Rock art especially portrays this event in which a shaman, while undergoing a shamanic journey, feels himself "pierced" by spears or arrows. This is the same experience described in many alien abduction stories. The abductees recall being "pierced," during what are usually described as medical procédures. The shamanic experience is generally described as a "death and resurrection" metaphor. During a vision, the practitioner is "killed," often dismembered, and then restored so as to become a healer—a full-fledged tribal shaman. In the same way, Jesus was "pierced" while hanging on the cross (John 19).

Why? Wasn't crucifixion enough? Why the added necessity of being pierced by a spear? The explanation given in Scripture seems somewhat artificial. But it makes perfect sense if the author of John's Gospel was drawing from shamanic tradition to explain who Jesus was—a great shaman.

Early Christians, among them a group called the *Gnostics*, seemed to understand this viewpoint. They taught a mystical version of Christianity that never caught on. They were declared to be heretical, persecuted, and eventually destroyed so thoroughly that were it not for the accidental discovery of some of their writings found at Nag Hammadi in Egypt in 1945, we never would have known about them.

The idea of "piercing" is not limited to Jesus, either. Saint Teresa of Avila underwent the classic shamanic experience of being exquisitely "pierced" by an angel who held "a long, golden spear at the point of which a small flame seemed to flicker." Both Saint Ursula and Saint Justina wrote about being "pierced by arrows."

Saint Paul wrote about experiencing a vision of a supernatural being he called "the risen Christ." The impact was so great he was knocked off his horse and was assumed to be dead (Acts 9). Later he described the experience in a manner fully consistent with what today would be labeled a near-death experience (II Corinthians 4). It changed his life.

We also have to wonder about Middle Ages descriptions of the many appearances of Mary, the Mother of Jesus. At Lourdes, Fatima, and many other such holy places, she is described as "a lady dressed in white." This corresponds to many similar descriptions of "the white ladies" who step out of the Faery Realm time and time again in European mythology.

Finally, we would be remiss if we didn't mention another Christian myth that is celebrated at the same time as the birth of Jesus. We refer, of course, to Saint Nicholas—Santa Claus himself. Anyone who gets around as fast and far as he does at the time of the winter solstice and who is associated with magical journeying and chimneys, which, with their ascending smoke and tunnel-like qualities, are common "take-off" places for shamanic journeying, is certainly a "right jolly old elf" indeed! He displays other godlike qualities as well. After all, he "knows if you've been bad or good." So how did he get tied in so closely with Jesus?

Perhaps Santa and Jesus share a much more common shamanic tradition than is usually acknowledged.

Earlier we quoted the Hebrew prophet Joel. He spoke of "sons and daughters" prophesying, dreaming, and seeing visions. Isn't it strange that while preaching the first recorded Christian sermon, the Apostle Peter quotes this very same verse? As fire came down from heaven with the sound of a mighty wind, as people began to speak in strange tongues and see ecstatic visions, Peter felt inspired to describe what was happening:

The mythological Santa Claus might be considered to be godlike—as well as elflike in terms of coming from the Faery Realm—in nature.

> This is what was spoken by the prophet Joel, "In the last days, God says, I will pour out my Spirit on all people; your sons and daughters will prophesy, your young men will see visions, your old men will dream dreams. Even on my servants, both men and women, I will pour out my spirit in those days, and they will prophesy.…"
>
> —Acts 2

And again the shamanic choir says, "Amen!"

Islam

Islam began when a young, devout caravan master in the Middle East went on retreat to a cave in the desert, following the typical quest pattern of a young holy man of any indigenous tribe. In the cave he received a visit from Gabriel, the same otherworldly being we met in Judaism, when he appeared to Daniel, and in Christianity, when he appeared to Mary. He now completes his trilogy of visits when he dictates the Quran to Muhammad.

Later, Muhammad is given a white horse to ride as his famous *Night Vision* carries him up and through the seven-fold realm of heaven. Ever since then, the famous Black Stone, or Kaaba Stone, is the destination of pilgrims to the Grand Mosque in Mecca every year. Thus, they relate to a "Visitor from Afar." It may be an inanimate object, but it still exerts a spiritual pull. The rest is history and continues to unfold to this day.

Conceptual Religions

In virtually every religion in the world today we find the same central truths and accounts of similar events. When they are recalled orally and passed down by word of mouth, they are said to be legends of nature religions. When they are written down in a holy book, they are called revealed religions.

Surprisingly, however, such incidents are also found in what we have labeled "conceptual religions." These are religions formed around concepts that don't include a god at all. In that sense, they are more psychology than theology. Perhaps the three best known are Buddhism, Confucianism, and Daoism.

Buddhism

Divinity did not reveal itself in supernatural form to Prince Siddhartha Gautama. At least, not at first. You don't have to believe in God to be a Buddhist. But there is a supernatural component to be found in the brilliant, deeply psychological construct out of which Buddhism was born. Here's the story:

When Prince Siddhartha Gautama was born, a local priest visited the family compound and prophesied that the youngster would grow up to be either an emperor or a Buddha, an Enlightened One.

Quite naturally, the child's worldly father preferred the former to the latter, so he sequestered young Siddhartha within the walls of the palace, hoping to discourage any untoward spiritual development by supplying everything the young man desired in the way of material delights.

But young men are curious, so one day Siddhartha had his chariot driver take him out into the real world. The journey changed his life.

Soon after departing the palace grounds, the young prince encountered an old man. He had seen elders before, but this was an aged man who had not benefitted from the cosmetics money can obtain. Siddhartha began to suspect that life exacts a toll, and he wondered about the path his own life would take. Fear began to cloud his still-inexperienced mind.

If that weren't enough, he soon encountered a man who was afflicted by a hideous disease. With a shock, he thus discovered that life contains an element of suffering.

Then he caught his first glimpse of a corpse, and the reality of death was seared into his consciousness.

Siddhartha later reflected on the lessons he had learned from his excursion thus far:

I also am subject to death and decay and am not free from the power of old age, sickness and death. Is it right that I should feel horror, repulsion and disgust when I see another in such plight? And when I reflected thus … all the joy of life which there is in life died within me.

—Robert S. Ellwood and Barbara A. McGraw,
Many People, Many Faiths

His heretofore-held illusions had evaporated. He now knew he needed to place his trust in something besides wealth and family position. Pleasure could not prevent age, illness, or death, and so could not be the pathway to happiness.

While contemplating this, still unaware that he was about to completely change course in life, he was perplexed to come upon a holy man who seemed quite content. Something within Siddhartha suddenly shifted. He took a leap of faith. His mind at once understood what his heart had already come to appreciate.

From that moment on, the dancing girls back home didn't do it for him anymore. He decided he had to study the meaning of life by becoming a holy man. His father, in trying to keep him from seeking a spiritual path, had instead catapulted the young man toward a destiny that would change the world. Siddhartha determined to go off on a journey of exploration even though he didn't know where that journey would lead. If you had asked him what he was searching for and how he even knew there was something worth finding, he probably could not have answered. But he knew he had to look for it.

There was still the matter of convincing his father who, as expected, refused to let the boy leave. In lieu of what would later occur, it is instructive to observe the young man's method for obtaining what he wanted. Siddhartha simply waited, saying he would not move until he had his father's consent. Dinnertime came and went. Siddhartha stood patiently in place. It got dark outside, time for the household to go to bed. His father, sure that by morning the boy would return to his senses, said goodnight

A 1914 illustration of Prince Siddhartha Gautama leaving home to go on a journey that would transform him into the Buddha.

and retired to his sleeping chamber. But morning's light found the boy still standing in the living room, ready to have his way or die.

Needless to say, the young prince eventually got his way. Saying good-bye to his family, Siddhartha and his faithful charioteer left the family compound, never to return. He began to search for a reality he could trust.

For six years he wandered and studied. He talked with *brahmins*, Hindu holy men. He learned yoga disciplines and meditation. He practiced extreme asceticism, eventually trimming his diet down to one grain of rice a day and then deciding that since he could exist on one grain, why not try slicing it in half to make it last twice as long? Eventually he became so thin and emaciated that it was later said a person could grasp Siddhartha's backbone from the front.

Even after all this, enlightenment eluded him. He joined a group of traveling holy men, none of whom were making any more progress along the spiritual path than he was. They had nothing new to teach him.

Terribly discouraged, he resorted to the technique that he had successfully used with his father. Seating himself beneath a type of fig tree known as a Bo tree (sometimes called a *Bodhi* tree, or "Tree of Knowledge"), he vowed he would meditate right there, not moving until he either reached enlightenment or died.

There in the wilderness of his own confusion he met *Mara*, the devil, who tempted Siddhartha with the traditional three temptations. This is where the supernatural first appears in the story of the Buddha.

- First, the temptation of the flesh. Three beautiful women walked by, begging him to follow. (Legend does not explain why three beautiful women were interested in an emaciated man whose backbone could be grasped from the front!)

- Second, the temptation of the spirit. Ferocious demons attempted to frighten him enough to make him flee from his place beneath the Bo tree. Smiling, Siddhartha simply touched the ground upon which he sat, saying, in effect, "I have a right to be here and here I will stay!"

- Traditionally, the third temptation is always the sneaky, subtle temptation of pride. Whispering in Siddhartha's ear, Mara congratulated him on his spiritual growth, telling him that his insights and dedication were too profound for normal people to understand and that it would be profitless to attempt to teach them to others. But Siddhartha resisted and conquered. At last, Mara left him alone.

With this spiritual victory over temptation, he passed through all stages of awareness. In a vision he saw all his previous incarnations and understood their connectedness, how they had brought him to this point in time and place. Now he sensed *karma* at work—the guiding force that propels life forward. More important, in a sudden intuitive leap, he grasped how to break out of *Samsara,* the wheel of life, death, and rebirth. He had finally found that for which he had been searching, even though he hadn't known what he was looking for. He achieved the goal of his quest. He became the Buddha, the Enlightened One.

(At this point, although the legends are silent, he probably went someplace to eat dinner, for he is never pictured as being thin and frail again.)

He called his insight the *Dharma,* the Middle Way that leads between the poles of all opposites to *Nirvana,* the place beyond, which embraces all dualities.

"Duality" means pair of opposites. For every up there is a down; for every left, a right. Cold cannot exist except in comparison to heat, joy without the contrast of sorrow. One half of every pair of opposites is uncomfortable. The natural human tendency is to identify with that which is good, comfortable, or otherwise desirable. The Buddha saw this was impossible. Unless both poles of opposites are embraced, one cannot be content, because both poles are real and make up the fabric of life. To remain insulat-

A central concept of Buddhism is following the Middle Way—the avoidance of extremes in one's life; that is, all things in moderation.

ed from one pole or the other is to live in denial. Eventually, even if someone dwells in a palace, he or she must journey outside the walls to experience the reality that is comprised of life in all its totality. Denying or even ignoring death and sickness doesn't make them less real. All it creates is anxiety, because the human psyche knows they are inevitable.

What the Buddha came to understand is a profound psychological truth that has become a part of every culture on Earth. It is so common that we forget that Siddhartha was the first to put it into words, to frame it in a way that easily transcends culture and language.

He condensed his insight into what are called the Four Noble Truths.

1. All life is suffering
2. Suffering is caused by desire
3. There can be an end to desire
4. The way to achieve that end is to follow [what he called] the eight-fold path

As you can see, this religion is contemplative and psychological rather than supernatural. But there remains the supernatural component in that *Mara*, the devil, showed up to tempt Buddha away from his teaching. The theme called "The Threefold Temptation" appears in many religions, including Judaism with its story of the serpent offering three temptations to Eve, and in Christianity with its story of Jesus in the wilderness being tempted by the devil.

There are other *Conceptual Religions*, of course. Two of the most well-known today are:

Confucianism and Daoism

In the fifth century B.C.E., China began to face a long period of war and political turmoil. People at all levels of society were caught up in a struggle that was both secular and spiritual. In those days, Chinese spirituality revolved around the balance of *Yin* and *Yang*. These two forces represented the opposite poles through which the Buddha embraced the Middle Way. Yin was feminine, while Yang was masculine. Yin was romantic, intuitive, feeling oriented, and right-brained. Yang was rational, thoughtful, intellectual, and left-brained. Together they represented the contrasting but all-encompassing principles of the *Dao*. Found in both male and female and throughout the natural world, Yin and Yang had to be in balance if people were to function completely and harmoniously. But the cultural power struggles had destroyed the people's balance. They began to wonder what had gone wrong, what they had done to destroy the harmony of daily existence.

The revered Confucius taught that we need not overthrow existing society in order to make it better.

In some ways, the times were similar to the destructive, largely intergenerational conflicts many Americans experienced during the 1960s. Power and politics, religion and psychology, gender and racial equality, war and peace—all were examined anew. Traditional values were turned upside down. Almost every guiding principle that society at large once believed to be true was thrown open for debate. It was a time of long-haired "hippies" and flower children who competed for space on the evening news with dark-suited, crew-cut businessmen and politicians. In confusion, some young people who protested against war donned uniforms and formed paramilitary cells. It was Woodstock versus the New York Philharmonic—communes versus Wall Street—protest marches versus "My country: Love it or leave it!"

In fifth-century B.C.E. China, just as in 1960s America, liberal and conservative traditions developed.

The conservative faction was represented by the teachings of a scholar named K'ung Ch'iu, who became known to the world as Confucius. His advice was not to overthrow existing society, but rather to do it better. He taught that people had to learn how to be better farmers, better politicians, better friends, better parents, and better children. He believed that people must strive to become what, in fact, they already were, even if they had forgotten what that was. The cultural infrastructure was already intact. People just had to make it work as it had been intended to work.

Confucius personified the Yang side of Chinese philosophy. His object was not to destroy what was already in place, but to reform existing social institutions, thereby reforming the people who lived within those institutions.

Lao-tzu ("the old man") was a contemporary of Confucius. Today he is recognized as the founder of what has come to be known as Daoism, or the "Way."

Lao-tzu was *Yin* to Confucius' *Yang*. He was the liberal to Confucius' conservative, the hippie to Confucius' establishment. Lao-Tzu was romantic, intuitive, feeling-oriented, and right-brained. He thought that cultural traditions and social infrastructures were not answers to the problem. Instead, they were the problem itself. If he were to survey today's western culture, he would probably insist that big business, religious institutions, and political systems are not corrupted by society. They are the very cause of the corruption. If you fire the board of directors, he would say, vote out the majority party and defrock all the clergy; those who fill their positions will fall victim to the same corruption. According to Lao-Tzu, power, inherently imbedded in the systems themselves, was the root source of systemic corruption.

A story, which may or not be true, has been passed down that Confucius once met Lao-tzu, who was somewhat older and thus, according to Chinese custom, worthy of the respect given to an elder. After the interview, Confucius said:

> Of birds, I know they have wings to fly with, of fish, that they have fins to swim with, of wild beasts, that they have feet to run with. For feet, there are traps, for fins, nets, for wings, arrows. But who knows how dragons surmount wind and cloud into heaven? This day I have seen Lao-tzu, and he is a dragon.

> —Robert S. Ellwood and Barbara A. McGraw
> in *Many People, Many Faiths*

If the two men had been interviewed by CNN following their meeting, and if they had been asked about spiritual growth in fifth-century B.C.E. China, Confucius might have said, "Reform society!" Lao-tzu would have replied,

"Burn, baby, burn!" In essence, what for Confucius was the sum total of the ideal society—order and material gain, structure and formal learning—was, for Lao-tzu, the epitome of death and decay.

What eventually happened teaches us a lesson. Most Chinese, raised in the tradition of balance, prudently adopted both approaches to their spiritual ideology. Confucianism spoke to their social and family needs. Siddhartha's Buddhism answered questions about life and death. Lao-tzu's Daoism freed their inner nature. It was said that Chinese leaders were *Buddhist* by religion, *Confucian* at work, and *Daoist* in retirement. Their response was to allow inward spirituality to affect the social network and infrastructure already in place.

These two religions, working together, do not manifest a supernatural component. But they provide a framework in which the supernatural forces of Yin and Yang can be balanced and blended in our lives.

Putting It Together

How does all this work together to further our quest to discover how the supernatural first became important to our ancient ancestors?

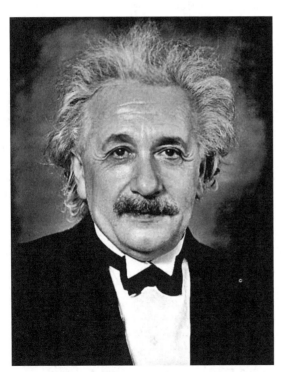

Genius mathematician Albert Einstein considered the unknown entirety of the universe to be the mind of God.

Think about this for a minute: when did humans first start to think in these terms, and why did they begin to do so in the first place?

It might be said that early humans didn't invent religion. Religion formed us into the human species we are today. In short, with the discovery of religion, we became human. We made the leap from the animal kingdom to humanity. Nature religions eventually evolved into revealed religions. Revealed religions began to cohabitate with conceptual religions, eventually adopting many of their more intellectual components. Sometimes, as a matter of fact, they became so academic in their practice that revolutionary groups such as the Christian charismatic movement or the Islamic Sufi sect were formed in order to shake things up a bit by lending a more passionate, free-wheeling, right-brained component to the mix.

In our day, conceptual religions seem to be in the process of merging into science-based religions. Both Albert Einstein and

Stephen Hawking referred to the great unknown as "the mind of God." We use sophisticated technology to measure and chart the brain waves of meditating Buddhist monks. We are beginning to see yoga and biofeedback used as medical tools. We look for the science behind biblical miracles. At laboratories such as the Institute of Noetic Sciences in California, scientists subject metaphysical phenomenon to scientific scrutiny. These are all indications of a religion/science merger.

EVOLUTIONARY SPIRITUALISM

Go back to the beginning of the process. One of the big questions of anthropology concerns a huge jump in symbolic, artistic, and religious thought that occurred about 40,000 years ago. For at least 160,000 years before that time, maybe more, the archeological evidence indicates that, for the most part, homo sapiens were developing like any other animal species. We were using some hit-or-miss tools, just like chimps and some ape species do today. There is no clear-cut evidence of advanced thinking, even though the brain size of our ancestors and their basic anatomy was identical to what we know today.

Then, about 35,000 to 40,000 years ago—for no reason that is made apparent in the archeological record—we suddenly evolved symbolic thought, art, and music. We know this because this is exactly the time when the first art appears on cave walls, musical instruments were developed, and rock art reveals religious imagery.

Why? What evolutionary advantage would it have provided?

It gets even more complicated. Many of the rock art pictures from this time contain the very same imagery that modern people have described during flights of hallucination. The hallucinations couldn't have been inspired by the art, because in most cases the art wasn't discovered until after a long history of such hallucinations had already been written down.

There are a number of ways to look at it.

1. Somehow nature programmed such images into our brain. Hallucinogenic images are hard-wired into our minds so that visions experienced in vision and dream 40,000 years ago are the same we experience today. The problem with this theory is that there doesn't seem to be any evolutionary advantage to the process. What possible purpose could it serve? Why would nature develop such a thing?

2. Somehow the ancients discovered mushrooms or other such hallucinogenic plants that mimic, or were the predecessors of, chemical hallucinogens that are in use today. Ancient shamans ate the mushrooms, experienced the visions, and then crawled back into the caves to paint what they had seen.

3. The only other possible explanation is the weirdest to some people but seems to explain all the facts: 40,000 years ago the ancients, by some means, learned to perceive a parallel realm that was actually there. We can't usually perceive such a realm while experiencing normal consciousness. But under certain conditions we can slip the bonds of what we call "reality" and perceive things that are always present but not normally available to us. In other words, when the ancient ones (under specific conditions such as approaching death, the ingesting of hallucinogenic drugs, deep meditation, long, monotonous drumming kept to a specific cadence, sickness, or other consciousness-altering ordeals) saw visions and heard voices, they were experiencing something that was really there. Upon return to "normalcy," they tried to describe their "trip" in art, words, or music.

This is an old, old method of experiencing the supernatural.

When indigenous peoples around the world sought to enlist the realm of the spirit, they often resorted to such methods. Aborigines danced. Brazilian shamans ingested ayahuasca. Some North American plains tribes utilized voluntary ordeals such as the sun dance or vision quests involving fasting for four days at a time. Fasting is also an activity that is celebrated in the Bible. Moses fasted for forty days in the desert. Elijah journeyed through the desert without eating for forty days. Jesus fasted for forty days in the wilderness. The Christian season of Lent has, in our day, become a pale comparison, but echoes the custom.

What these customs depict is a classic visionary quest that is as old as humanity itself. Its purpose was to contact the supernatural realm. People near death often talk about seeing a tunnel and meeting loved ones or spirit beings. They're called near-death experiences (NDEs). Others, either on purpose or by accident, report out-of-body experiences (OBEs) and meeting spirit guides.

Is all this attributable to simple hallucination? Or are these people actually seeing something that is really there but normally outside our experience because we are caught in a perception box built by our five senses? In order to experience these realities do we need to learn to, quite literally, think "outside the box"?

The Great Leap

It is estimated that about two percent of the population alive at any given time has the ability to spontaneously see through the perceptual barrier. They are usually the ones who, like Albert Einstein, Thomas Edison, and so many original thinkers, have contributed to sudden, intuitive leaps of under-standing. The rest of us have to work at it. In Part II of this book we will study some of the tried-and-true methods.

But whatever happened, however it happened, the truth according to anthropology and archeology is this: 40,000 years ago the human race changed drastically. It was by far the biggest single evolutionary leap we ever took. We "got religion" and became fully human. We've never been the same.

Now come the questions. Did our ancestors "discover" supernatural realities? Or did the realities discover us? Did ancient humans invent the "gods?" Or did the "gods" learn how to break through to us? Did intelligent beings from a parallel reality see some potential in us? Could it be possible that these beings even manipulated our DNA so as to begin the process of making us over "in their image?" Or did DNA manipulation begin four billion years or so and automatically "kick in" when we evolved to a certain level? If so, might this happen again in the future? Are there more hidden messages lying dor-mant in so-called "junk DNA," ready to awaken when the time is right? Are we a work in progress? And did that process begin some 40,000 years ago? Or even four billion years ago when life sprang into existence out of non-life?

We'll examine these question in greater detail in the pages to come. Meanwhile, we've just taken a big step forward on our quest. But we've a long way to go!

THEISM AND THE AGRICULTURAL REVOLUTION

The generally accepted version of how civilization came to be is that we humans took a giant stride up from our primitive, hunter-gatherer ancestral culture during a period known as the Neolithic Revolution. This theory, put forth in the 1920s by V. Gordon Childe (1892–1957), a flamboyant Australian British thinker with a gift for synthesis, went something like this:

About six thousand years ago, in an area called Sumer, some clever humans, probably women, since they were the ones who presumably gathered plants and seeds while the men hunted, discovered that due to warming weather patterns in the wake of the last ice age they could now plant wild grains, take care of them for a while, water them when the weather refused to cooperate, pull a few weeds, and then, after a reasonable wait, harvest them. The advantage was that this provided a predictable, reliable food source. The disadvantage was that they had to stick around while the crop matured. Before this time, for thousands upon thousands of years, humans had survived by following wild game and gathering what food crops they found while living in whatever shelter nature happened to provide. These were the "cave men" we learned about in grade school.

Domesticating crops, however, changed everything. It sparked what has since been called the Agricultural Revolution and marked the beginning of civilization. A stable, local food supply led to the birth of settled towns, which soon exploded into cities. Populations flourished. People began to adapt special occupations. A cobbler, for instance, could practice his trade and get paid for it in consumer goods. He didn't need to go out and hunt anymore. Eventually money was invented to represent commodities such as food, thus making transactions easier to handle. Writing was developed to keep track of who got what and how much was paid. Economy was born. One city might grow barley while another grew wheat. Trade flourished. A merchant class grew to oversee caravans. You can see where this leads.

And, so the theory goes, there was yet another byproduct. Trade between regions led to an immense social upheaval in the field of religion. Prior to agriculture, gods took the form of animals. After, gods were needed to oversee grain production by sending rain in due season. A priestly class arose. Because they lived in one settled place and now had the manpower to build, temples were constructed.

Here the story takes a dark turn. Inevitably one town's fields began to encroach on another's. Resources had to be protected. "This is *our* field, not yours!" To enforce that claim, armies developed. But armies need strong male gods. The Goddess can't intimidate as well as the God. Mother Earth is gentle. Yahweh, Baal, and Zeus are not.

The Bible tells the story in myth and poetry that stems from this very region of the world. Cain, the agriculturist, kills Abel, the pastoralist. He immediately goes out and builds a city. Genesis 4 lists some of the specialized occupations that developed: builders, agriculturalists, musicians, industrialists, soldiers, priests, lawyers. No wonder the final verse of the chapter says, "At that time, men began to call on the name of the Lord."

Shortly after, a man named Abraham left Ur of the Chaldees, taking with him his own family army, and traveled across the Fertile Crescent to Israel. (The biblical writers used the name Canaan.) He went forth armed with an idea: "My God is better than your God!" (Later Hebrew composers would say it much more poetically in their psalms: "Our God is a great God, above all other Gods.") From this journey evolved the concept of monotheism. Abraham emigrated because God told him to. Judaism, Christianity, and Islam followed.

From these simple beginnings in the Fertile Crescent sprang specialized tools, pottery, writing, cities, trains and buses, wars, stress, high blood pressure, obesity, Facebook, Twitter, and all the other benefits of modern civilization.

This is the accepted story. It has been poked and prodded, shaped a little differently and molded into academic shape, but it remains basically the same since Childe first called it the Neolithic Revolution, the Agricultural Revolution that took place in the New Stone (*Neo-Lithic*) Age, a radical change, fraught with revolutionary consequences for the whole species. He declared it to be "the greatest event in human history after the mastery of fire!"

A NEW PARADIGM

That's the way things stood until 1995, when a researcher named Klaus Schmidt (1953–2014), then with the German Archaeological Institute, began to dig at a place in Turkey called, by the locals, Potbelly Hill, or Göbekli Tepe. What Schmidt found there caused him to report, "In 10 or 15 years, Göbekli Tepe will be more famous than Stonehenge. And for good reason!"

Göbekli Tepe is a temple built of immense stone pillars arranged in sets of rings. The tallest are 18 feet high and weigh 16 tons. Carved into their surfaces are bas-relief totemic animals of prey—a whole menagerie. The hillside in which all this was built is littered with flint tools from Neolithic times—knives, projectile points, choppers, scrapers, and files. The T-shaped pillars themselves are immense, and they appear to form a very complex structure.

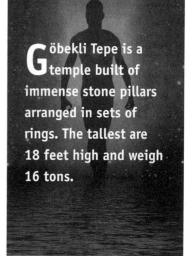

Göbekli Tepe is a temple built of immense stone pillars arranged in sets of rings. The tallest are 18 feet high and weigh 16 tons.

But what makes the discovery so fantastic is this: Göbekli Tepe was built 11,600 years ago! That's seven thousand years older than the Great Pyramid of Giza and thousands of years before even the beginnings of Stonehenge. And, so far at least, there is no evidence whatsoever of existing agriculture in the surrounding area. The temple seems to have been built, impossibly, by hunter-gatherers with no communal support structure except for hunting teams that would fan out, kill what game they could, and bring it back to the workers. The bones of their evening meals consist mostly of auks and gazelles.

How did a hunter-gatherer culture supply the manpower to carve and move sixteen-ton rocks? It must have taken thousands of laborers. What motivated them? Religious temples supposedly didn't come into play until generations after the Agricultural Revolution, but here was a huge religious temple found springing up from the landscape thousands of years before religion was thought to have been organized enough to even attempt such a thing! As far as we knew when Göbekli Tepe was discovered, it was by far the largest building project ever attempted by humankind up to that point in history and there seem to be no precursors—no trial and error, no history of evolving concepts, no evidence of any "practice sites" as is evidenced, for instance, by the pyramid-building tradition in Egypt or the standing-stone tradition culminating at Stonehenge. And it didn't precede those traditions by a few hundred years. It was built almost seven thousand years earlier! If anything, the tradition seems to devolve rather than evolve. The most sophisticated building happened first, at the bottom of the dig. It appears that later generations built on top of it. But their work exhibits less and less skill with each succeeding layer. It seems as though Göbekli Tepe illustrates the unraveling of a tradition rather than the building of one. And at the end, it was completely and deliberately buried like a time capsule, preserving it intact so that it could be dug up and studied in 1995.

THE BIRTH OF RELIGION

What was the motivating force that gave birth to this amazing temple? In a word—religion. In an article written for *National Geographic* magazine (June 2011), Charles C. Mann calls this temple site "the birth of religion." The presence of so many carved shamanic totem animals, the lack of any contemporary nearby towns or support villages, and the almost certain conclusion that this temple marked a religious site seems to cry out that these people were in touch with something so big, so meaningful, so stupendously important in their lives that they had to build a monument to it. The result is Göbekli Tepe.

We can never know what specific beliefs inspire and motivate someone. Most often, we don't even know what our own personal belief system consists of, and it's apt to change many times over the course of a single lifetime. We

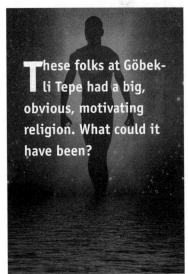

These folks at Göbekli Tepe had a big, obvious, motivating religion. What could it have been?

may have a basic ideology. We may use a catch-all identifier like "Christian." We may narrow that down to "Methodist." But even two "Methodist/Christians" probably disagree about much of what their faith proposes. What stands out however, and what we *can* measure, is depth of commitment. To paraphrase the Gospel of Matthew 7:20, "By their deeds, ye shall know them." In other words, if someone does something big and obvious in the name of faith, they probably have a big, obvious faith. Their faith has either inspired them or caused them to fear their God in a big, obvious way.

These folks at Göbekli Tepe had a big, obvious, motivating religion. What could it have been? At this stage in human development it apparently had something to do with animism. This is the belief that spirit animates everything in nature—that animals, trees, rocks, landscape, and humans meet in Mother Earth's protective embrace. But it is just as obvious that astrology figured in somehow. In other words, the very structure of Göbekli Tepe "marries" the earth to the sky. There are too many star, sun, and moon sight lines to ignore.

Göbekli Tepe isn't an easy place to get to. The builders were motivated by what they saw and felt on the landscape, not by where they found it convenient to work. There is no nearby water source. There were no towns, villages, or fields because these hadn't been developed yet.

No, they built where they did because they felt called to a particular spot of ground in order to manifest a very powerful religion that ties an earthly landscape securely to a heavenly perspective.

Archaeologists are beginning to suspect that Childe's theory about the Agricultural Revolution leading to, among other things, religion, may have to be revised. Now it appears that there is good evidence to support the fact that religion came first, and agriculture, leading to what we call "civilization," arose to support those who lived around these sacred places. Such places exist all over the planet. They may not be as spectacular as Göbekli Tepe, but they draw thousands of seekers each year. And it is intriguing to know that as spectacular as Göbekli Tepe is, only a small portion has been uncovered so far. What else lies beneath the sands and stones of this wonderful place? What secrets still await discovery? Will they reveal the truth behind the lurking connection between belief in supernatural gods and the discovery of agricultural? Only time will tell.

VISITORS FROM AFAR

It is a great mystery that people from many different cultures in many different epochs all report encountering supernaturals who are unwilling to be confined to supernatural realms and who—even while they initiate our shamans and bestow the "second sight" and healing powers upon them—seem to want to take something of our materiality and incorporate it into their own non-physical lineage. As the first manifestations of these ancient supernatural forces in the technological age, UFO abductions and encounters with aliens have been subjected to an unrelenting campaign of ridicule and abuse by scientists who are strongly wedded to the materialistic paradigm. It has been said, however, that "the greatest trick the Devil ever played on us was to convince the world he doesn't exist." Living in societies elevated by technology to almost godlike heights, we have convinced ourselves, against the advice of our ancestors, that there are no supernatural intelligences—that spirits do not exist, that fairies are crazed delusions and that aliens are just figments.

We may be wrong.

—Graham Hancock, *Supernatural*

In 1959 the great Swiss psychologist Carl Jung (1875–1961) published a book about flying saucers. In this landmark study, he didn't talk about aliens. Instead, he studied the fact that more and more people were lifting their eyes to the heavens and reporting objects that he associated with what he called the collective unconscious. He believed flying saucers to be archetypes of "gods," the product of a collective change taking place in the human psyche.

Jung thought that the collective human mind undergoes changes from time to time. People begin to view the world differently. These changes take place roughly every 2,160 years, coinciding with the astrological signs of the zodiac. The Christian era that began 2,000 years ago is identified with the constellation Pisces, the sign of the fish. According to Jung, it was no accident that early Christians chose a fish symbol for their new faith, just as it was no accident that the Christian story identifies the first followers of the Christ as fishermen, and that Jesus invited them to follow him in order to become "fishers of men."

But that was then. This is now. As the groundbreaking, so-called "hippie" musical *Hair* pointed out in 1967, "this is the dawning of the Age of Aquarius!" As any astrologer worth his or her salt knows, Aquarians, under the sign of the water bearer, often go about accomplishing their goals in ways that are quite unorthodox. They are prone to philosophical thought, and although they can become victims to sloth and laziness, they are also artistic, poetic, and generous to a fault. Does this sound like any "hippies" you knew back in the sixties and seventies?

The great mythologist Joseph Campbell (1904–1987) pointed out that in many of the ancient myths of the hero's journey, the hero would pass through water into an enchanted land, where his or her adventure would begin to unfold. Water was the dividing line, whether it was represented by Alice going through the looking glass or Arthur confronting the Lady of the Lake. Once you passed through the water, you were entering enchanted realms. Your worldview was about to be drastically changed. This is one of the many mythical motifs co-opted by the Christian Church in its practice of baptism. Candidates for baptism "pass through" the water and emerge on the other side, supposedly changed people.

The Lady of the Lake gifts King Arthur with the sword Excalibur in this illustration by Henry Justice Ford in Andrew Lang's *Tales of Romance* (1919).

According to Jung, during the Age of Aquarius, the age that we are now beginning, people would start to move up out of the "water" that was the home of Pisces, the fish. The "water bearer" would begin the work of lifting people up to new heights.

So it was that after the explosion of the first atomic bomb taught everyone about the futility of the path technology has been following—after two thousand years of wars and rumors of wars and after the Christian age began to deteriorate into denominational bickering and institutional persecution—humankind began the journey into a new realm. Looking up from the mud and sludge that we had suddenly noticed was pulling us down into the earth, we raised our sights to the skies. And what did we discover? Flying saucers! Chariots of "gods" from a different realm. Hope from the skies!

SALVATION FROM ON HIGH

This was also the time in history when the fundamentalist, which soon evolved into the evangelical, wing of the Christian church adopted the idea of the rapture—the "snatching up" and out of the world experience of all true followers of Christ. Although many believers today assume this doctrine goes back to the very beginning of church history, the term "rapture" was introduced in the United States in the early 1800s. John Nelson Darby (1800–1882), a nineteenth-century Irish evangelist, discovered through his study of the Bible that passages in the New Testament seemed to indicate that Jesus would return at the end of an age that he called a "dispensation." Further study revealed that human history consisted of seven of these dispensations, the sixth of which he called the "Church Age." This, he said, is the age in which we currently live. It began with the birthday of the church at Pentecost, soon after the resurrected Jesus' return to heaven. It will end just before the seventh dispensation, which is called the thousand-year reign of Christ or the millennium. Because Jesus would return before the millennium, this doctrine was called "Premillennialism." The return itself will take place in two stages. The first event is called the Rapture (from the Latin word *raptura*.) Jesus will "snatch up," or rapture, his believing church before physically returning to Earth, either immediately, three years later, or seven years later, depending on the interpretations of the different Christian sects.

The rapture theory continued to grow in popularity among evangelicals largely due to a preacher named William Eugene Blackstone (1841–1935). His book *Jesus Is Coming*, first published in 1878, sold more than one million copies before 1940. All in all, the phenomenon illustrated Jung's "hope from the skies" theory, and it continues to this day.

The *War of the Worlds* (both the book by H. G. Wells [1866–1946] and the radio broadcast read by Orson Welles [1915–1985]), *Star Trek*, and *Star Wars* didn't become blockbusters by accident. This was the world prophesied by Jules Verne (1828–1905) and Wells. Arthur C. Clarke (1917–2008) was its publicist, and Carl Sagan (1934–1996) and Erich Von Daniken (1935–), although from two different cultural and academic "denominations," were its theologians.

And the age is just beginning. It's difficult to turn on the Discovery Channel, or even the History Channel, without seeing shows about alien encounters from on high. The famous actor and narrator Morgan Freeman (1937–) regularly takes us *Through the Wormhole*. Quantum physics has revealed a world much stranger than fiction.

Even the Bible seems to point to evidence that until the age of UFOs, seems to have been hiding in plain sight. Take this passage from Ezekiel, for instance, which was quoted in full at the beginning of this book:

> I saw a windstorm coming out of the north—an immense cloud with flashing lightning and surrounded by a brilliant light. The center of the fire looked like glowing metal, and in the fire was what looked like four living creatures. In appearance their form

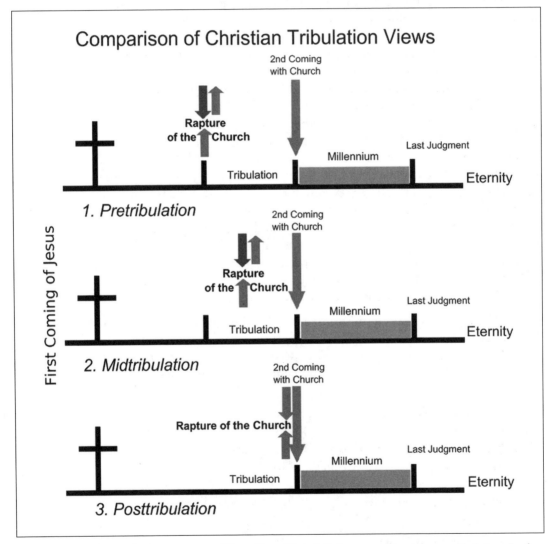

There are three versions of Premillennialism beliefs: pre-, mid-, and post-tribulation. In the first, the Rapture occurs before a seven-year period of tribulation (extreme suffering for humans); in mid-tribulation, it happens during that period; and in post-tribulation, it happens afterwards.

was like that of a man.... I saw a wheel on the ground beside each creature ... they sparkled like chrysolite ... their rims were high and awesome ... spread above their heads was what looked like an expanse, sparkling like ice and awesome. Above the expanse over their heads was what looked like a throne of sapphire, and high above on a throne was a figure like that of a man ... and I heard a voice speaking.

If that weren't a passage from the revered scriptures of three religions, but was instead a fragment of an unrelated ancient text from the same time period, it would certainly raise some interesting questions!

The fact is that many structures on the earth—perhaps the most notable example being the famous Nasca (or Nazca) lines of Peru, which are perfectly straight lines that traverse deserts, mountains, and gullies for as many as sixty miles and appear to be in the shapes of animals and geometric figures—are only really visible from the air. As a matter of fact, until the invention of air travel few people seemed to know they were even there. The same is true of the straight roads that run from Mexico to the border of Colorado. They were not visible until satellite images from space revealed their whereabouts.

This begs an obvious question. Why did prehistoric humans go to this much trouble if the only way to view their work was from the air? Why did they climb to inhospitable places, labor long and hard in scorching deserts, and undergo such tremendous hardship, only to have their work go unnoticed for millennia? Perhaps they did it for reasons that had to do with something we can't even begin to understand—summoning, honoring, or even signaling something, or someone, who lived and moved "on high" but occasionally visited us here on earth.

Help from Above—or Within?

Shamans journey to other realms. Christians look to the skies for the return of a supernatural being. Both ancients and moderns look to the heavens for the presence of beings from above.

What do they all have in common? They all seem to share identical stories. They claim to have experienced supernatural beings who seem to have unlimited knowledge or at least superior technology. These beings came, sometimes in secret and sometimes flamboyantly, did whatever it was they needed to do, and then left. Sometimes they poked and prodded. Sometimes they pierced and dismembered. Sometimes they offered helpful advice. Sometimes they formed a new religion. Sometimes they kept to themselves or zoomed off into space. Sometimes they looked like us. Sometimes they didn't.

But when you read enough of these stories, and there are so many of them that even if you try you'll never get through them all, you begin to

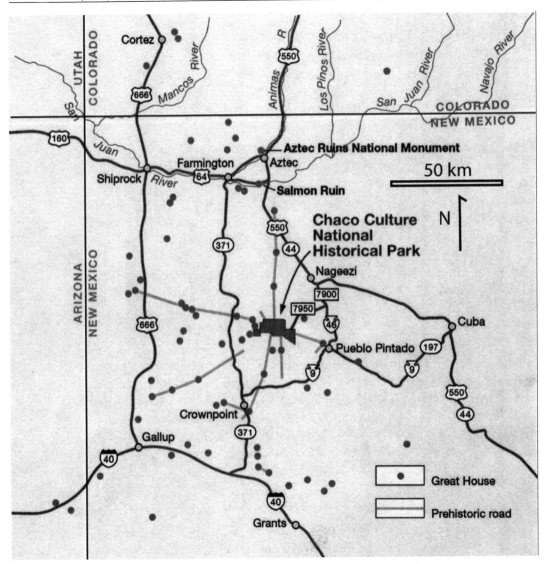

The network of roads constructed by the Chaco culture (light-gray lines in picture above) in the Southwest part of North America about a thousand years ago are amazingly straight, despite even geologic features that were in the way. This fact was only made evident when photos could be taken from the air by modern-day people.

notice a common thread. It's easy to forget whether you're reading the testimony of alien abductees from last year or an anthropologist's report on a shamanic encounter from a hundred years ago. Pictures of alien "grays" look very similar to rock art painted 35,000 years ago. Testimonies about near-death experiences, tunnels of light, meeting lost loved ones, and returning from a transformed environment span all cultures.

Could it be possible that all these phenomena are related? Might people from many different time periods and civilizations have experienced the same thing? Are we dealing with cultural representations of an encounter with so-called "supernatural" beings that actually exist in alternate dimensions? Have these witnesses, for a moment, broken through the box created by their five senses and glimpsed a reality most of us normally never experience?

Before you shake your heads and dismiss the whole idea, first consider the evidence. Until recently it has been primarily circumstantial—stories, writings, mythologies, and belief systems of the participants. But in the last ten years we have seen evidence of so-called "parallel" dimensions, including alternate copies of "you," arising out of the equations of theoretical physicists, many of whom ridicule almost everything we have been talking about so far in this chapter. It's important to remember that theories imply real things, not just mathematical constructs. If the math indicates that multiple universes and alternate identities exist, that means that those universes and versions of

These paintings found on the Wandjina rocks of Western Australia date back about four thousand years. The faces bear a resemblance to the alien "grays" that have been more recently reported and are, indeed, linked to aboriginal tales of the "Sky People."

"you," if ever proven, are just as real as you are. You may not believe in them. But they probably don't believe in you either.

To follow the path that leads from nonbeliever through skeptic and questioner to believer takes a good deal of courage. It's never easy to face up to the unknown. Early pioneers were subjected to ridicule. In many cases, they still are. But let's follow the path and see where it leads. You don't have to tell anyone you're doing it.

Let's state our thesis plainly, without equivocation, so we all know exactly what we're talking about and where we're headed.

Most of us live our lives within the confines of a comfortable illusion. We think we're the only beings that exist and our cosmos is all there is.

This is a false assumption. It is understandable because we have evolved a set of five senses that help us relate to our surroundings. But those senses are inadequate when it comes to experiencing what amounts to "real" reality.

Our brains, constantly processing information, are not sufficient. In effect, they have evolved to serve as "step-down" transformers. They are filters that keep out much of the information that constantly assails our senses. Their function is to make it possible to deal with the here and now so we don't feel overwhelmed by information overload.

But it is becoming clear that a small number of people through time have, either by accident or on purpose, glimpsed a reality beyond the normal range of our senses. They have seen, dimly, to be sure, that parallel dimensions exist and are populated by other intelligent beings who live in worlds that follow a completely different set of physical laws. The mathematics of theoretical physicists has only begun to predict that these realities exist.

Some of these supernatural beings have, from time to time, figured out how to step into our world. They are Visitors from Afar.

In different eras these visitors have been described in different ways. Sometimes they are seen as interdimensional spirit helpers. Sometimes they are interpreted as being space aliens. During some eras they have been called angels. Mythology has labeled them everything from faeries to leprechauns. Psychologists see them as collective archetypes. Most often they are considered figments of our imaginations.

What we're saying now is that they are real. Misunderstood? Yes. But real. When science and mythology begin to overlap, we simply must at least consider the facts, as foreign as those facts feel to our world-based senses.

We have been, and are being, visited.

If this theory proves to be true, we stand at the threshold of the greatest discovery in the history of the human race. The headline in the newspapers can state the thesis in a simple, declarative sentence: "WE ARE NOT ALONE!"

Are We Visitors from Afar?

This leads to another fascinating thought. What if Visitors from Afar turn out to be our creators? As a matter of fact, what if we *are* those visitors from afar?

Think about it. Every single living cell, from pond scum to ferocious tiger, from tree leaf to elephant, from one-celled amoeba to those of complex human beings, exists because DNA programmed them in a special way. We are the result of DNA evolutionary development. It's that simple.

But no one knows how DNA came to evolve in the first place. And that's an inconvenient problem.

In his book *Supernatural*, Graham Hancock (1950–) recalls a conversation he had with Jeremy Narby (1959–), a Swiss anthropologist who thought deeply about this subject and eventually wrote the book *The Cosmic Serpent: DNA and the Origins of Knowledge*. When Hancock visited with Narby, he asked whether or not it might be possible that there is a message encoded in our DNA that, under the right conditions, we might be able to decipher.

Narby replied, "Or a bunch of messages. I think that we haven't even found all that goes with it."

"Who put the messages there?" Hancock asked.

"I don't have the faintest," Narby replied. "But I think it was some entity; or several entities, that were rather clever!"

Narby's ideas in *The Cosmic Serpent* are mind-blowing:

> DNA and the cell-based life it codes for are an extremely sophisticated technology that far surpasses our present understanding and that initially developed elsewhere than on earth— which it radically transformed on its arrival some four billion years ago.

Could it be possible? Did life begin somewhere else and arrive here on earth, either purposefully or by accident, four billion years ago? That would certainly explain how it began to do its work with no antici-

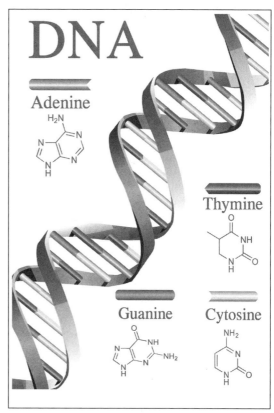

To some experts, the idea that the complex structure of the DNA molecule somehow generated itself on Earth is unlikely. Could DNA have been engineered by an alien race and then brought here?

Francis Crick, the co-discoverer (with James Watson) of DNA.

patory buildup. So far at least, there is nothing in the fossil record that even approaches the evolutionary development of DNA.

Some experts have theorized that it would be statistically more likely for a tornado to blow through a junkyard and accidentally put together an automobile than for all the "moving parts" of the DNA double helix to come together by accident at the same time. This is an extension of the old "monkeys accidentally typing the works of Shakespeare" argument.

So let's go one step further out on a limb. What if DNA-carrying bacteria were deliberately sent here? What if an ancient civilization faced extinction due to, for instance, its star going nova or another cosmic catastrophe? Such a scenario is usually confined to the sci-fi genre, such as a famous *Star Trek: The Next Generation* episode ("The Inner Light") wherein Captain Jean-Luc Picard finds himself living an earlier, parallel life on a planet that is about to be destroyed. The inhabitants send out a "message in a bottle" to whomever might come across it so that they won't be forgotten.

A surprising number of scientists are willing to consider such a thing. They reason that our so-called "junk DNA," the 97 percent of DNA that we can't figure out, really contains coded messages that tell us who we are and why we are here. In other words, *we* are the aliens.

In my earlier book, *Ancient Gods,* I wrote about the discovery of DNA:

In July of 2004, Francis Crick, co-discoverer of the double helix structure of DNA molecules, died at the age of 88. Soon after his passing a little-known fact about his accomplishment surfaced. It was revealed that when Crick was working at the Cavendish Laboratory in Cambridge, England, during the 1950s, he frequently used LSD as a "thinking tool." The drug was legal back then, but few knew about it. Timothy Leary hadn't yet been exposed to the general public.

It was on one of Crick's LSD-fueled "trips" that, in his words, he "perceived the double helix shape" of DNA and began to unravel its structure.

In other words, one of the greatest discoveries in the history of biology happened because someone "expanded his mind."

Earlier we said that one theory advanced about humankind's "Great Leap Forward" in the great painted caves of Europe some 35,000 years ago, the first expression of symbolic, or religious, thought, was that shamans ate hallucinogenic mushrooms and experienced mind-altering spiritual visions.

It certainly appears as though mind-altering experiences have entered into the human evolutionary experience more often than we would care to admit. No one wants to talk about it, but there it is.

—Jim Willis, *Ancient Gods:*
Lost Histories, Hidden Truths and the Conspiracy of Silence

In our quest for the Supernatural, we have now arrived at that place where we are beginning to search out the source of the mystical knowledge that, from time to time, a few gifted, shamanic-type mystics have been privileged to glimpse. Could it be possible that for most of this time we have been searching in the wrong place? Does the answer lie not "out there" but "in here"? Is the secret to life going to ultimately be found within the very DNA structure that created life as we know it in the first place?

Think of the implications! The biotechnology that made us who we are may have arrived here from somewhere in the cosmos. Either by accident or design, it seeded itself on earth and went about the process of evolving thousands upon thousands, then millions upon millions, of life forms that have called this earth home. Eventually, there arose a species that had the potential to take the "Great Leap Forward" into intelligent, feeling, caring individuals. Some 40,000 years ago, perhaps by the same mind-altering process Francis Crick used to discover DNA's existence, our species stepped forth out into the sunshine. In only a second of cosmic time, we moved out of the great caves into what we now call civilization. It was a great leap toward fulfilling our ultimate destiny and becoming who we can be.

Cosmic children though we may be, it remains to be seen whether or not our species will live long enough to mature. But if we make it through our rocky adolescence, what other messages await us in the so-called "junk" DNA that makes up 97 percent of the bioengineered miracle that is a human being? What other "Great Leaps" might lie before us?

If any of this proves to be true, we can only say, quoting the Bard himself:

What a piece of work is a man! How noble in reason, how infinite in faculty! In form and moving how express and admirable! In action how like an Angel! In apprehension how like a god!

—William Shakespeare, *Hamlet*, Act 2, scene 2

Perhaps the ancient psalmist had it right after all:

You are gods; you are all children of the Most High.

—Book of Psalms 82:6

To mangle the famous quote attributed to Pogo in the old comic strip: "We have met the supernatural and they are us!" The magic *without* begins *within*. The Visitors from Afar have revealed themselves. And they have been with us all along.

The universe is, indeed, a magical place.

STORIES OF HEALING AND TRANSFORMATION

He was pierced through for our transgressions, he was crushed for our iniquities; the punishment that brought us peace was on him, and by his wounds we are healed.

—Isaiah 53:5

ENIGMATIC ROCK ART FROM ANCIENT TIMES

Deep within the Grotte du Pech-Merle in the French Pyrenees, hidden from the time of the Solutrian culture of 25000 B.C.E. until its discovery in 1949, lies an enigmatic cave painting called *The Wounded Man*. It depicts a seemingly shamanic-like figure who is pierced by a number of spears. No one knows the meaning behind the painting. Certainly we will never know exactly what was in the original artist's mind or exactly what he meant to depict. Traditional guesses usually revolve around the idea of a man who was wounded in a fight with a neighboring tribe or a depiction of a ritual killing of a hypothetical tribal wrong-doer, but there is absolutely no evidence to suggest that either of these are correct. They are simply guide-book conjectures that have echoed down through the years.

The motif of "the wounded man" who is pierced by a spear, however, reverberates from ancient mythology right down to the present day.

We find it prominently described, for instance, in the death of Jesus of Nazareth in the Gospel according to St. John:

When they came to Jesus and found that he was already dead … one of the soldiers pierced Jesus' side with a spear, bringing a sudden flow of blood and water. The man who saw it has given testimony, and his testimony is true. He knows that he tells the truth, and he testifies so that you also may believe. These things happened so that the scripture would be fulfilled: "Not one of his bones will be broken," and, as another scripture says, "They will look on the one they have pierced."

—John 19:33–37

This is the passage that forms the basis of the story about the mythical Spear of Destiny that was used to pierce the side of Jesus. Although the story has been embellished down through the centuries, the basic theme was that this spear, or Holy Lance, was originally made by Tubal-Cain, who appears in Genesis 4:22 and is described as the first man to "forge all kinds of tools out of bronze and iron." The spear was passed on down through the ages until it eventually fell into the hands of a Roman soldier who pierced the side of Jesus after he was crucified.

The only biblical passage that contains this information is found in the last of the four gospels, written some sixty years after Jesus died. One can only

The spear that a Roman soldier stabbed into the side of the crucified Jesus is now known as the Spear of Destiny, Holy Lance, or Lance of Longinus (after Saint Longinus), a religious artifact that some say has mystical powers.

wonder whether the author post-scripted this story because he was influenced by non-Christian mythological accounts of similar incidents and wanted to add to the growing body of mythology that was even then being bandied about to pad the résumé of Jesus. The theological explanation about "not one of his bones being broken" seems a little contrived, to say the least. This certainly seems to be a later add-on to the crucifixion account.

The spear supposedly continued its journey through history, being passed from generation to generation. Richard Wagner (1813–1883) immortalized it in his operatic *Ring Cycle*. The story grew that Hitler somehow acquired it. By his time, it was rumored that the owner of the sacred lance would rule the world. At least three different churches, including the Vatican archives, are said to be hiding it away. It became a centerpiece in the plot of the 2004 made-for-TV movie *The Librarian: The Quest for the Spear*, starring Noah Wyle (1971–), Sonya Walger (1974–), and Bob Newhart (1929–).

Brad Meltzer (1970–) searched for it in his *Decoded* TV series, describing it with the usual TV-inspired hyperbole:

> What if I told you that for two thousand years, many of the world's most powerful men have pursued an ancient artifact they believed would bring them unparalleled power? It's the lance that allegedly pierced Jesus' side while he was nailed to the cross. Known as the Spear of Destiny, it passed through the hands of leaders like Napoleon and Adolf Hitler, and today there are a number of shadowy institutions around the world that are still chasing the Spear. Yet the question remains: does the Spear really exist, or has it been lost forever?

FROM SHAMANIC INITIATION TO ALIEN ABDUCTIONS

However the "wounded man" motif is depicted in art and literature, there is a common theme that weaves its way throughout its history. Many early shamanic stories tell of an astral initiation ceremony wherein a young man is "wounded," usually dismembered, and then "reassembled," so to speak. The motive is really not much different than that employed by the armed forces during basic training. The idea is to break young recruits down, destroying the person they once were, and then rebuilding them in the image of a soldier who will respond to commands, do what needs to be done, and generally become a productive member of the service.

Drill sergeants don't actually pierce young men with spears, of course. Their weapons are usually verbal rather than material. But the purpose is the same and the result just as powerful. In a vision, the young shaman is taken apart and reassembled as a useful member of the shamanic tradition, able to heal and care for the tribe. In this sense, he becomes a "wounded man" who,

In the Native American Sun Dance spiritual ceremony, some young people have their chests pierced with hooks from which they are then suspended in the air.

upon recovery, sets out on a new path through life—the path of healing and service. Is this what appears on the cave walls of the Grotte du Pech-Merle?

Perhaps the picture depicts a common motif central to the theme of the *Star Wars* movies. Anakin Skywalker is "wounded," his essential life burned away, and he emerges as the mystical Darth Vader, made in the image of a machine-like servant at the beck and call of an evil emperor. Luke Skywalker, his son, loses his good right hand in his quest for redemption. He must be "broken" before he can truly serve the Force and restore righteousness to the galaxy. When you think about it, there's not much difference between a spear and a light saber.

We are almost forced to wonder if an ancient shaman from the Solutrian culture experienced this visionary "initiation" 25,000 years ago, crawled back into the sacred cave of his ancestors, and recorded the event for all time on the walls of the great cathedral-like holy place that served the shamanic community for generations.

But "piercing" isn't limited to shamanic traditionalists. In contemporary society, the same thing might be happening, transformed by modern culture into quite a different experience.

Now many people today are familiar with the ancient shamanic experience of initiation by piercing. But thanks to TV and many magazine articles, they are familiar with alien abductions. Is that why so many abduction stories contain the element of being "pierced" or "probed" by aliens who seem to want to know what makes humans tick? Is that why abductees are sent back into society, having undergone some kind of medical-sounding procedure? In other words, can some alien abduction accounts be explained as an experience common to the human race for thousands of years but described differently in culturally relevant ways? An ancient shamanic "piercing" might describe the same experience as an alien "probing." Shamanic stories about figures from Jesus to Darth Vader might simply be the result of their disciples recognizing the need for a dismemberment or a severe "wounding" before a hero can take his or her rightful place as a spiritual leader.

A Personal Testimony

I would be remiss if I didn't reveal a relevant story at this point. It's very personal and I almost hesitate to bring it up. But I feel the need to illustrate how what we sometimes talk about in theory has actual physical relevance. I want to share an entry from a journal I sometimes keep. This particular incident happened in 2014. I confess that I don't fully understand it. All I know is that back then I knew little about the "wounded man" motif or shamanic initiation. As a matter of fact, this was the experience that began my research into the subject. I simply recount it, unembellished and unedited, as it appears in my journal:

October 14, 2014

I've had some out-of-body experiences (OBEs) in the last two weeks, but, for some reason, haven't wanted to write about them. Perhaps doubt. Perhaps sloth. Perhaps a nagging fear that my imagination might sometimes run amuck. But there's no imagining what happened today. There is physical proof. In short—I received a healing.

Two of my recent OBEs involved meeting a feminine energy being I have labeled Brigit. In the first I thought she was a lost soul. She was standing by a bay of water and looking out to sea. I thought she must be waiting for a lost husband to return from a voyage and I tried to help her move on. But I couldn't get through. The second one revealed the truth. She wasn't lost at all. She is a patron saint of Ireland, "baptized" by the Christian Church to adopt her from her original incarnation as a pagan goddess of women, among many other things. I figured that my recent desire to go to Ireland might have inspired this thought, so I was a bit skeptical and didn't follow it up much. But then I saw her again. I began to think that the desire to go to Ireland might have somehow opened a door to her, inviting her to enter my life. Little did I know how important that open door would become.

For the last week I've been on my feet a lot and a recent badly sprained, perhaps broken, ankle has been giving me nagging problems. For the last three days I've been wearing a brace and using a cane. To say the least, I've been very discouraged.

Today it rained. It's slippery outside. For the third straight day I've been confined inside. To make matters worse, I've been gaining weight again and riding a bike seems out of the question. At my age, that's the only thing that helps keep my weight down. On top of that, I've had small epileptic seizures for the past two days, and this morning I had a big one.

Around noon I had a strong yen to go down to our gazebo, so I took a book and walked out towards the woods. Because I was trying to get away without getting Rocky, our dog and constant companion, all excited I snuck out the back door and, in my hurry, forgot my ankle brace. I didn't want to go back inside so I decided that even though it was really slippery I'd just be careful. When I got there I sat down and read a little, then tried to meditate. Within seconds I felt something happening. A moment later I was out of body and standing

The Medicine Wheel constructed by the author and his wife in South Carolina.

by the small monument of stones we've built overlooking our Medicine Wheel.

I look down at the Medicine Wheel and see Brigit standing there at the center, welcoming me with open arms. When I went down to greet her I asked if she was an incarnation or manifestation of Gaia. She said she was Gaia's daughter, a manifestation emanating from the Earth Mother. The circle was filled with women engaged in a ritual of some kind. They stood in a ring around the Medicine Wheel, watching me. I suppose I should have been a bit bashful. I was completely naked and obviously a man. But I wasn't uncomfortable at all. Instead, I told Brigit that my ankle was hurt. She immediately knelt down and began to stroke my ankle with both hands. I remember thinking that the problem wasn't in my astral ankle, it was in my real ankle up in the Gazebo. But I didn't say anything because I was aware of a healing touch, a kind of vibration, in my ankle. So I just let it happen.

(I seem to remember here being told that I had to submit if we were to go further. "Submit" is a bad word. It has negative connotations. But this feeling wasn't negative at all. There was no hierarchy or ranking involved. It was just a need to let go and permit what was to come. And I did—consciously.)

At any rate, my attention was immediately drawn away from the ankle because I was, in the presence of all the female witnesses, given a crash course in sexuality. Not just sex, although that was involved, but sexuality. I really can't go into all the ins and outs, so to speak, but it became obvious that human sex is merely a crude grasping for something that is spiritually very profound—a search for timeless individuality within unity. I was made instantly aware of why I, and everyone else, has certain things that "turn them on," so to speak. Questions I've had about my early childhood, way before I was sexually active or even capable of it, were answered in explicit detail. Now it all became clear that there was a greater purpose being acted out.

When the lesson was over (there's more, but let's leave it at that!), a strange thing happened. I was placed prone on the ground and somehow kind of "pressed in" to Gaia herself. It wasn't sex; it was a more profound and complete merging with the earth, soil, moss, and drippy, moist things. I was, in short, partially dismembered and buried. But it was very pleasant. I really enjoyed the experience.

When I stood up again, there was Sobuko, my out-of-body friend and spirit guide, walking down the hill and joining us at the Medicine Wheel. He stood in the center with Brigit as they faced each other and joined hands—male and female. One by one the women in the circle would walk to them and stand in the center of their held hands and arms. Sobuko and Brigit would lift their arms and then—whoosh!—the women would shoot up into the air and out of sight. When my time came I could hardly wait. Both Sobuko and Brigit were smiling. It seemed to be a wonderful game. They lowered their arms on both sides of me and then lifted them again. Suddenly I seemed to be transformed into a beam of rainbow-hued light. I shot up into the air and out of the universe, looking down on planets and stars. It was a similar experience to what I've had before, of looking at the universe from above and outside, but I wanted more. I wanted a cleansing. So I flew instantly to the sun in order to burn away all impurities. It was wonderful. I flew right into the sun and enjoyed every second of it.

Immediately, however, I was back in my body in the gazebo. I felt that I had just awoken from a powerful dream, half here and half there. I decided to go back to the house and tell Barb about it.

It was only when I was halfway back that I realized I was walking normally, without any pain at all. Even on the slippery ground I began to dance and was sure-footed, without a twinge. I took a short nap and slept like a baby for half an hour, then drove to town and went to the grocery store. No cane and no pain. When I got back to the house and told Barb about the story, I even danced around the living room. Unheard of two hours ago. My ankle was completely healed.

I don't understand what happened, but you don't "imagine" or "dream up" a healing of this sort. This is physically real. All I can do is accept it and say thank you. Which I did. And do!

There it is, for better or for worse. I don't understand it, I wasn't expecting it, and I certainly don't blame anyone who refuses to accept it as anything other than a figment of my fertile imagination. For much of my life that's what I would have believed, too. I only know this. I haven't had any problems with my ankle from that date to the present time.

Life is indeed mysterious.

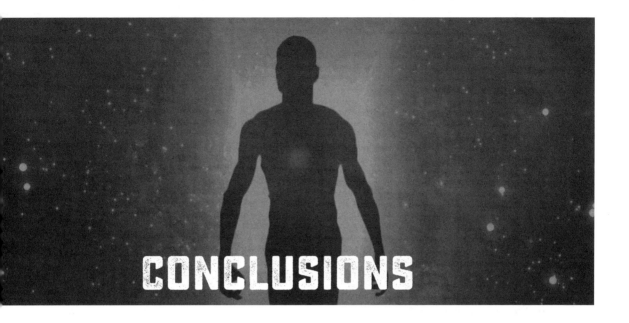

CONCLUSIONS

Once again the question arises—who are these ancient teachers, who some call "gods," and some call "aliens" or "spirits," who come to us in altered states of consciousness with strange messages that have shaped the course of human history?

—Graham Hancock, *Supernatural*

Our quest for supernatural gods has now been defined. We've discovered that our earliest ancestors probably came out of the great painted caves with a new sense of the mystical and magical. Deep in those caves, they had portrayed their spirit guides in the form of animal envoys. They had identified some of those same envoys in the constellations of the cosmos above. Here in the middle world between heaven and earth, they recognized earth spirits that animated every aspect of their environment. They began to sense what we now call metaphysical manifestations that evolved into religious concepts that many of us still hold today. They experienced the first stage in an ever-changing experience of meeting visitors from afar. Over the years, their ways of describing these visitors may have varied, but, stripped of their cultural trappings, the experiences demonstrate amazing similarities.

Finally, we speculated on the idea that these "visitors" may be within each and every one of us, the evidence of which might even be coded into our very DNA. We don't sense their presence in normal, waking consciousness. But if we can let down the barriers through various spiritual, chemical, or physical practices, they make themselves known.

We are proceeding under assumptions based on the calculations and complex mathematics of theoretical physicists, which seem to confirm the

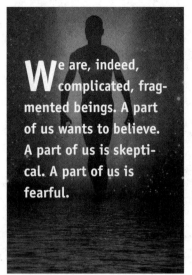

We are, indeed, complicated, fragmented beings. A part of us wants to believe. A part of us is skeptical. A part of us is fearful.

anecdotal evidence of millions of people down through the centuries from virtually every civilization that has ever existed.

Namely—we are not alone. The reality we experience in our day to day lives is not the only reality. Hidden outside the boundaries of our five senses, other realities exist and are very probably inhabited by beings so different from ourselves that many people today take refuge in sarcasm and patronizing attitudes whenever the subject of their existence is brought up in polite conversation.

All this, while we still retain at least a quasi-belief in angels and aliens from outer space and devour the latest scientific research on time travel and alternate dimensions.

We are, indeed, complicated, fragmented beings. A part of us wants to believe. A part of us is skeptical. A part of us is fearful. A part of us would hop aboard the first flying saucer that showed up in our backyard. We sense the power of something beyond ourselves but, in the light of day, doubt that it really exists. We yearn to live by faith but, when the chips are down, pull back in skepticism. We want to believe in supernatural gods, but hold back.

What's a poor seeker to do?

THE OBJECT OF THE QUEST

In olden times, the quest for the Holy Grail began in earnest when an image of the sacred relic first appeared in the air before the knights assembled at Arthur's famous Round Table. Before they could seek it, they had to glimpse it. They had to believe it was real. They had to know what it was they were looking for.

In Part I: The Object of the Quest, we have glimpsed our Grail—supernatural gods. We have seen that new discoveries in cutting-edge science are now putting flesh on the old bones of mythology and the experiential testimonies of people from all times and all ages. Ancient rock art illustrates modern religious motifs. Shamanic journeys lend experience to current alien encounters. The question hovers constantly before us: are we alone?

Behind the Illusion: Reason, Time, and Essence

Before we continue, though, there may be those who might have found themselves turned off by all these theories and the search for material evidence of a non-material reality. So let's offer a symbolic metaphor—a different perspective. Perhaps it's easier for artistic types, for instance, to think about musical metaphors. Can we find, in an appreciation for music and its accompanying symbols, a different way of meditating on the search for how the universe works and whether or not there is a supernatural reality beyond the reach of our senses?

Imagine for a minute, a single musical note:

It's nice, in its way. It has an interesting substance and shape. It seems to imply a certain function. It has movement and form. But, assuming you know nothing about music, its essence and very purpose, remains a mystery. You have no idea what it *means*. Because you are viewing it out of its context, it is, for all practical purposes, worthless. You cannot determine its sound, its pitch, or how it fits in to any piece of music. Indeed, unless you know something about music, you can't even figure out what it is. If an archeologist dug up this image a million years from now, and music notation had been completely forgotten, he or she would have no idea what the image is about. A circle and a stick. What does it mean? Who could possibly understand that this symbol represented vibration, pitch, speed, and duration? Who would think to link this image with a word or a particular timbre voiced on a particular instrument?

To figure all this out you need to go on a quest—a search for meaning found in symbols. What would you find?

Well, you might discover an image that had substance. What if it appeared like this?

Now you are beginning to zero in on what the image means. You still need to learn a lot more, but the symbol is linked to similar symbols, and they are placed on some kind of graph, giving them a bit more meaning. At the very least, you might sense some kind of message behind the picture. It makes you want to look further into the mystery.

Without drawing out the parable too much more, let's add a clef sign:

Now we're getting somewhere. Assuming our future archeologist gains some background in ancient music, this simple addition adds an important element—pitch! The treble clef sign and the five-lined staff tell us the vibration that this particular symbol represents. Specifically, and here we're going to have to give our future archeologist a lot of information, this symbol represents a musical note that is vibrating exactly 440 beats per second. The musical staff and the treble clef sign lock this note in space. They indicate exactly how high or how low the pitch it represents will sound, no matter what instrument or voice is producing it. A soprano's vocal chords, an organ's pipes, or a violin's string must vibrate at 440 beats per second in order to reproduce the note its composer is calling for.

But we still have a long way to go. We have indicated this note's place in space. But music also deals in time. If all notes of a composition were played at the same time, Beethoven's entire *Fifth Symphony* could be played in about three seconds—and it just wouldn't sound the same. That's why music needs some further symbols.

How about this?

Now we're getting somewhere. The time signature tells us how long each note is to be sounded, thereby anchoring the symbols in both space and time. We know the exact pitch of the note and the length of time it is to be sounded.

We are still lacking many aids. If this were all that were needed, the audience could go home after the oboe sounded the note at the beginning of the concert so that the other musicians could tune to it. No—of course we need something more. We need someone to write the music, someone to perform it, and someone to listen to it.

Without all this, the music simply wouldn't have any sense, any essence, or any meaning.

Let's review: In order for music symbols to produce that which they symbolize, they must be anchored in space and in time. They require a composer who has some sense of conveying, through those symbols, a meaningful composition that, when interpreted by many musicians playing, perhaps, many different instruments, will produce an understandable piece of art.

But think this through a little. What about the audience who is hearing the music? Anyone trained in musical symbols can pick up a score, flip through the pages, and see the outcome. Perhaps they might even, if sufficiently trained, be able to imagine the results. But in order to hear the music, in order to experience the art, they have to sit down over a course of time and hear it unfold. Beethoven's *Fifth Symphony* takes a full orchestra, a mature conductor, some talented soloists, a gifted orchestra, and a trained chorus about forty-five minutes to produce. You can glance through the score in a minute or two, but you won't hear the art unless you wait it out and listen to it develop.

If you jump to the end, it is a magnificent sound. But if you haven't *heard* the composition—you haven't heard the art.

So it is with the human story and our experience of supernatural gods. And that is the purpose of time. You can dip into it at any point, as we have just done, and see great magnificence or extreme foolishness. But until the human symphony reaches its ultimate conclusion you simply cannot hear the entire composition. Our essence can be revealed only through time.

Books have been written about individual themes. They are repeated, it would seem, every generation or two. Scholars have debated about the intent of the composer. But does an individual note, no matter how many times it is repeated, have the ability to deduce its real function? How can an individual note, let alone a phrase, see how it fits in to the whole composition? The variations have not played out. We don't even know if the last movement has yet begun.

Life may be a cabaret, my friend, but it is also a symphony. And you won't get your money's worth unless you stay for the final note. Only then will the applause begin. Only then will the supernatural gods reveal themselves.

BACK TO THE QUEST

This musical illustration is an attempt to put the quest for supernatural gods into a different perspective. We can find evidence in the written texts of hundreds of religions written over thousands of years. We can talk and talk about the supernatural and find evidence for it, even as we can talk about written notes on a page of manuscript. But to experience what those notes mean, we need to listen for the music.

In the very same way, to experience the supernatural, we need to go beyond written evidence.

Our thesis is now clear. To paraphrase what we wrote earlier: It is becoming clear that a small number of people through time have, either by accident or on purpose, glimpsed a reality beyond the normal range of our senses. They have seen, dimly, to be sure, that parallel dimensions exist and are populated by other intelligent beings who live in worlds that follow a completely different set of physical laws. The mathematics of theoretical physicists has only begun to predict that these realities exist.

Some of these supernatural beings have, from time to time, figured out how to step into our world.

In different eras, these visitors have been described in different ways. What we're saying now is that they are real. Misunderstood? Yes. But real. When science and mythology begin to overlap, we simply must at least consider the facts, as foreign as those facts feel to our world-based senses.

If this theory proves to be true, we stand at the threshold of the greatest discovery in the history of the human race. The headline in the newspapers can state the thesis in a simple, declaratory sentence: "WE ARE NOT ALONE!"

Now that we have a solid idea about what we're looking for, we can begin to explore the many historical methods of personal exploration available to us. That is the goal for what comes next. It's time to plan The Method of the Quest.

PART II:
THE METHOD
OF THE QUEST

Those of us on a spiritual path, and more specifically on a Vision Quest, believe that we are put on this earth for a special reason, but that reason is not always clear to us. We want to know what we need to accomplish in life for our highest benefit, and, in turn, the benefit of the world. The quest can reveal our life's purpose, but it is an arduous journey into the core of our being that we should only embark upon with sincerity.

http://native-americans-online.com/

INTRODUCTION

The only true wisdom lives far from mankind, out in the great lone-
liness, and can be reached only through suffering. Privation and
suffering alone open the mind to all that is hidden from others.

—Quote from Inuit shaman Igjugarjuk, as translated by
Joseph Campbell in an interview with Bill Moyers

The quest for supernatural gods is not a new endeavor. When our ancestors
first became acquainted with ancient gods, they began a process that led
inexorably to the present day. Along the way, they felt hidden energies
beneath their feet and wondered what the source might be. They compiled
much of what, regrettably, is now lost mystical knowledge, though they left us
tantalizing clues to its nature in the form of art, rock structures, customs, religious texts, and mythology.

In Part II we now turn to a survey of their endeavors, some of which are
still in practice today. From organized, somewhat structured activities such as
astrology, dowsing, meditation, shamanism, and spiritualism to more open and
free-form experiences such as dreams, hypnotism and past-life regressions,
intuition, and claims of miracles, there comes a growing body of evidence to
aid in the search. Psychics and sensitives still peer into the unknown. Some
seek "Chemical Keys," believing that their use of drugs and plant derivatives
might expand their minds in order to find openings to other worlds of reality
that exist outside our normal perception. People who experience such realities
in out-of-body experiences called OBEs and NDEs often return with fantastic
tales of adventure. Even those who work in the rather new field of theoretical
physics report strange new worlds implied in their mathematical equations.

We'll look into all of these "roads less traveled," to borrow a phrase from Robert Frost, but before we do it's important to lay some groundwork. We need to look at some basic assumptions.

FAITH STATEMENTS

Let's put this as simply as we can. When people report similar, cross-cultural experiences with supernatural entities, does that mean those entities really exist? Or are they just images hard-wired into our brains? Are they real, intelligent beings or anthropomorphic figments of our imagination? Are there other realities "out there" or do people who possess a healthy imagination merely conjure them up?

The more we study supernatural phenomena, the more amazed we become that this question has gone unstudied by classic academia for as long as it has. Perhaps the reason lies in the fact that a person's approach to supernatural reality is almost always guided by the conclusion that person has already reached, knowingly or not. He or she is either a "believer" or an "unbeliever." In other words, first comes the "Faith Statement": "I believe in the supernatural" or "I don't believe in the supernatural." Everything follows from there. Usually, facts are gathered and cited to prove the initial statement rather than to examine the question. Once a person's mind is made up, that's usually it. There is little possibility of changing it.

Once a person becomes a believer (or an unbeliever), and asserts that position in their life, it is extremely difficult to shake that faith.

This is a common human foible. We like to think we are creatures of intellect who arrive at our beliefs rationally and logically. But that is almost never the case.

In the field of religion, for instance, people have died for their beliefs, even if those beliefs are subsequently proved wrong. In politics, people regularly view "their" candidate as right and the other candidate wrong, even if secretly they harbor doubts. The field of science is cluttered with the bodies of those who have refused to give up their confidence in a particular fact, whether or not that fact has withstood the test of time. It's simply what we do: "My mind is made up. Don't confuse me with facts!"

Belief in the supernatural is no different. Most people who read this book have already decided, based on an unexamined belief already formed by their experience, education, and upbringing, whether or not supernatural entities exist. By the time they read this far, they are either thrilled to discover something that justifies their belief, or they grit their teeth while wondering if they should continue to waste their time on what they believe is unmitigated drivel.

As a public speaker, I've seen it too many times to count. You stand up before an audience who has already decided your message is silly, and you simply cannot pierce through the fog of derision that arises from the gathered assembly, no matter how polite they are. Or you stand before another audience, defending what you fear they might reject, and are met with boredom. "You're preaching to the choir," they say. "You don't need to defend your conclusions. We already believe." Even worse, you deliver your talk knowing you could say virtually anything as long as the people have accepted your basic premise, and they will never question you even if you don't have your facts straight.

A PLEA FOR SANITY

Consider this a plea, then, for us to proceed together with an open mind. Let's consider the evidence.

"There isn't any evidence!" roar the unbelievers, thereby turning their backs on not only the testimonies of millions of people over thousands of years who claim to have experienced the supernatural, but also ignoring the equations and observations of modern science even while being woefully ignorant of most of its contents.

"Of course there is evidence!" shout the believers. "Don't waste our time. Just get to it!"

And so the polarization of humanity gains ground in this field, as it has in so many others.

To the best of our ability, then, let's begin at the beginning and see where the evidence leads.

Am I guilty of harboring a Faith Statement? Have I come to a conclusion in my own mind before I lay out the facts as I see them?

Of course! I'm only human. I really couldn't write a book unless I had a point of view.

My only excuse is that I am a human who has stood on both sides of the fence. I used to be a rational skeptic. My Faith Statement was, "I'll believe it when I see it!" But then I experienced a radical transformation. My Faith Statement became, "I've seen it so I believe it!" It happens. At least what follows comes with a promise. I will be as objective as I can be.

To those who are skeptical, but willing to put their skepticism aside for a moment, I offer the prayer of my favorite Christian disciple. His name was

In the Bible, the disciple Thomas refuses to believe in Christ's resurrection until Jesus allows him to actually probe the wound in His side with a finger. Only then did Thomas believe.

Thomas, and he is most often referred to as "Doubting Thomas." Being of a rational bent, he simply could not believe in life after death. But when confronted by his first supernatural being, in this case the risen Christ, he prayed the prayer that I believe is the most profound expression of openness found in the entire Bible: "I believe," he said. "Help thou mine unbelief!"

Truly an open-minded and honest seeker after truth!

THE HUMAN BRAIN: GENERATOR OR RECEIVER?

Let's begin our quest, then, with an examination of how we go about the process of thinking in the first place.

Understanding begins in the mind. That's just the way we operate. But what is the "mind?" Is it synonymous with our brain? In other words, does Mind = Brain?

Surprisingly, although there are loads of opinions offered, often with strident force, on the subject, the truth is that no one knows. Worse yet, we are often coerced into a particular understanding without even knowing it happened.

To understand how this might work, consider an example drawn from the legal profession. Pretend, for a moment, that you are selected to serve on a jury trial. You will soon discover that the judge sets the definitions and limits of the debate. No so-called "peripheral" issues will be allowed during the trial, whether or not they might later seem very important to your decision. Within the rules of the courtroom, none of those things matter. The issue has been defined, and the jury can only base its conclusion on evidence allowed and presented.

The verdict, of course, is now guaranteed. According to the limits of the law, as set by those who define the evidence allowed, you can only make up your mind based on what you hear within the courtroom.

But is the issue really that simple? Has truth really prevailed? What if other issues were allowed to be discussed and evaluated? Another point of view might certainly have sprung to mind if other opinions had been allowed in court. But including them might have muddied the waters and questioned precedents of law. Past "simple" verdicts might become very, very complicated and have to be reevaluated.

To forgo this messy outcome, and to preserve the status quo, the judge sets limits on the evidence considered. He or she "defines" the terms of the trial, thus ensuring the outcome. Accepted precedent and tradition have won.

In much the same way, probably unintentionally, the "judges" of traditional academia, those who have written the texts, published the papers, and taught in the schools, have set limits on any discussion concerning human perceptions and the nature of consciousness itself. Many even declare that the very words "perception" and "consciousness" are vague, indefinable, and inadmissible to scientific scrutiny. After all, if some people use the words one way and others another, how can we study them? It becomes similar to comparing apples to oranges. We certainly can't put perception, let alone consciousness, under a microscope or define them in mathematical terms. So perhaps it's best to simply ignore the subject, at least in scientific circles. Leave it to the philosophers, religionists, and New Age fringe groups!

But recently, something strange has happened. Those who study the human brain have begun to suspect that mind and brain might be separate things. "Mind" consists of thoughts, emotions, memories, feelings, and intuitions. You can't put those under a microscope. "Brain" means neurons, protoplasm, and cells. Those you can study.

For a while, "mind equals brain" held sway. "Mind things" were simply a product of neurons firing away with electromagnetic energy. This can be measured and quantified. So "mind" remained within the confines of measurable brain research. In many universities, this system still prevails.

But as the twentieth century began to wind down, a few young scientists, new to the game and perhaps more open to curiosity and rebellion, began to say that "mind" might equal "consciousness" and that the brain might be a *receptor*, rather than a *transmitter*, of consciousness.

Picture a radio, for instance. It receives electrical signals and transfers them into meaningful sound waves, thus producing music. You can study a radio, connect it to dials and gauges, see where it lights up and how it converts energy into music. But you can't say, "That's where music comes from," even though it appears from all your blinking lights and graphs that you've tracked down the source of Beethoven's *Fifth Symphony*.

As soon as this metaphor began to be seriously considered, philosophy, religion, metaphysics, and science began to overlap. Representatives of the various disciplines began to ask difficult questions. "Can we really understand the brain without at least considering the source of perception, consciousness,

Imagine your consciousness stems from a source outside your body, just as a radio program doesn't come from the radio itself but, rather, from an outside broadcaster.

and mind? Can we arrive at a complete understanding of one without considering its connection to the others?"

As long as traditional scientists, like our metaphorical judge, were allowed to set the courtroom limits on definitions and strands of allowable evidence, the verdict was obvious. Mind equals brain! End of discussion. When you are brain-dead, you cease to exist.

But this verdict came into public question on a nationwide stage when a woman named Terri Schiavo suffered brain damage in February of 1990. The legislative, executive, and judicial branches of both the state of Florida and the U.S. government became involved in the case eight years later, when Michael Schiavo, her husband, sought permission to remove his wife's feeding tube, thus ending what was called a "vegetative" or "brain-dead" state. In effect, he said, "Her brain has died. She is gone. Let her body catch up."

Two days later, Terri's parents intervened. The feeding tube was reinserted. That simple act sparked a national debate that grew to involve governors, churches, doctors, lawyers, religionists, philosophers, and scientists. "Talking heads" from both sides dominated the news programs. The conversation eventually grew to include those who held institutionally vested opinions about life after death. If we die when our brain ceases to function, do we live on after the body stops breathing? What, after all, is death? Is there a universal God, a universal Mind, or a universal Consciousness from which we arise and to which we return at physical death?

It was, and remains, an important debate. But to engage in that debate it appears we may have to involve cross-discipline dialogue. If one side or the other has the right to define terms and conditions, the jury will never be able to reach a considered opinion. The "judge"—and by this I mean our personal sensibility, mind, brain, ego or consciousness—simply has to allow evidence from all corners into the courtroom of our own thought process before we can, individually, reach our own verdict. Any action short of this will affect the outcome of the trial.

How does this play out in actual terms? How do we each consider evidence from many sources when we internally debate the nature of existence and the existence of mind and consciousness in their relationship to possible supernatural energy forces?

To begin with, we have to remember that most of us have been trained since birth to depend upon the five senses of sight, hearing, touch, taste, and smell. Through these senses we have developed something called "logic." Everything that comes consciously into our thoughts usually enters through one of these senses. We then "decide" whether or not it is true. Carried to its "logical" conclusion, buttressed by repeatable experiments and tests of observable, measurable phenomena, this is the basis for what we now call the scientific method.

But consider this. What if those senses, as important as they are, could deceive us? What if in limiting our evidence to their testimony, we have, in effect, predetermined the outcome of the debate? What if there are other ways to perceive the world around us? What if the mystics are on to something? Or the religionists? Or the spiritualists? Or even those who study quantum reality?

To illustrate, try this thought experiment: imagine that you live in a world of sight, but you can't hear anything. In a very short time you would come to believe, and believe deeply, that sound doesn't exist. Your scientists would prove, over and over again, through a thousand different experiments, that sight is the only thing there is. And according to their parameters, they would be right. So you would teach this reality in your schools, and your vocabulary would evolve around metaphors of sight. You wouldn't say, "It sounds fishy to me!" You would say, using sign language, of course, "It looks suspicious." You would probably ridicule anyone who suggested even the possibility of sound, because no one in your world could prove its reality. Why waste time even fooling around with the concept of sound? For all practical purposes, unless you could place sound under a microscope and study it, you wouldn't believe it. You would ban its possibility from your laboratories and refuse to speculate on its existence at your scientific gatherings.

Then one day an archaeologist unearths some evidence that seems to indicate that a long-dead ancestor, who lived perhaps thousands of years ago, once believed that sound existed. Maybe he or she even claimed to have heard something. You would, most assuredly, chalk it up to primitive ignorance. If a "New Age" cult of sound sprang up, you would scoff and discount the whole thing as mere superstition. You would not allow it to be taught in your classrooms and you would heap scorn upon the idea, hoping that it would go away.

But then you would never come to fully understand your universe, would you? Sound would remain undiscovered because you refused to even consider its existence.

This is exactly what has happened within today's materialistic, technologically based, left-brained, scientific-method-anchored culture when it comes to what we label "reality."

What if we lived in a world where nobody had a sense of hearing and everything was visual? Then someone came along and announced there was something called "sound" and that they received a message this way. Would we believe them?

To put it another way, how would you describe the color blue to a person who is colorblind? You could explain the frequency of light waves or quote the "red-orange-yellow-green-blue-indigo-violet" rainbow spectrum we all learned in school. To someone who just can't see the color blue, however, you could try different words from now until the end of time and they just wouldn't get it unless they were open enough to meet you halfway, use their imagination, and really try to believe you were seeing something that they could not. Only then could you have an interesting conversation and an exciting time of discovery together. In effect, the person, in trust, would be saying, "I understand that you are experiencing something I am not. I want to at least have an idea about what you see when you look at the sky. Talk to me!"

But what if the person would simply not believe that you were capable of experiencing the color blue in a way that he or she could not? What if they said, in a patronizing way, "I don't see the color blue and you can't seem to find words precise enough for me to understand what you're talking about, so obviously the color blue does not exist!"

The conversation would be over.

MEANING IN THE METHOD

Let's try to sum all this up. What does it mean?

To put it in a nutshell, we are considering the fact that what we call the "mind" is different from the lump of tissue that houses all the chemical soup and electrical neuron pathways that we call the "brain." There seems to be some good evidence that the "brain" is a biological receiver and step-down transformer, the function of which is to receive, just like a radio or TV, information that is surging around us all the time but exists at a frequency outside the normal range of our five senses. After this information is "stepped-down" so that it resonates at a frequency we can perceive, our "minds" go to work putting a "form" to these energies—a form with which we can identify. It has to be familiar or we might not even see it.

How many times have you looked right at an object but not seen it because it somehow appeared different than what you were expecting? You glance at a distant forest, for instance, and don't see the deer standing in plain sight because you didn't expect to see a deer there. Once you see it, you wonder how you could have missed it. It is now obvious.

What happened was simple. You brain "saw" the deer, but your mind didn't convert it to reality. As far as you could tell, there was no deer, even though it was standing in plain sight. It was real, but to your brain, it didn't exist.

If a friend was standing right next to you, and saw the deer when you didn't, you might even get into an argument.

"There was a deer right there!"

"There was no such thing. You're crazy!"

"But I saw it!"

"No you didn't, because if you had seen it I would have seen it too!"

Do you see where this is going?

How many times have you looked right at an object but not seen it because it somehow appeared different than what you were expecting?

In the very same way, many people may have glimpsed other realities for their whole lives. As children, they might have had "imaginary" friends. As adults, they may have been impressed with the content of a dream and even derived meaning from it. Perhaps they had fleeting glimpses of unidentified flying objects in the sky.

But they are conditioned to treat such things as figments of their imagination. Our society frowns upon seeing visions and hearing voices. So they chalk it all up to imagination and forget about it. Such things don't exist.

But what if they do?

In Part II we're going to survey various methods employed by folks down through the centuries who claim to have caught a glimpse of the supernatural. We're going to consider the facts and, to the best of our ability, given our "modern" education, take them seriously. We're going to assume these people aren't charlatans and quacks. We'll honestly study what they have come to believe and why. Remember that some of these methods have been in place for thousands of years—much longer than any world religion now practiced. Remember also that some very smart people have studied these methods and pronounced them sound. When no less an authority than Albert Einstein, for instance, says he believes dowsers are for real, that means something. When indigenous shamans bring about healing, that healing is just as effective as any produced by modern medicine. When theoretical physicists point to the fantastic parallel dimensions that arise out of their equations, those dimensions very probably exist.

We do not make the claim that science misleads us as far as understanding what we call "reality." We simply ask whether what we call "reality" has bigger bounds than what science is capable of studying with instruments designed specifically for *this* reality. Maybe, if we're going to venture out of bounds, we need to do so with methods science will not acknowledge. Perhaps those methods are a lot older than we think. Maybe our ancestors, living a lot closer to those realities than we do given our antiseptic lifestyle, were more equipped than we are to experience what we have forgotten. Hidden energies and lost mystical knowledge await, beckoning us forward. Our quest continues.

ASTROLOGY

The fault … is not in our stars,
But in ourselves.…

—William Shakespeare, *Julius Caesar*, Act 1, Scene 2

Astrology, reduced to a basic definition, is a search for meaning, purpose, and direction on earth. To find that meaning, purpose, and direction, astrologists look to the heavens above. They believe that what happens up there influences what happens down here. It's as simple, and as complicated, as that.

Ancient megaliths such as Stonehenge were designed and built by astrologers. Way before that, however, ancient seekers who lived up to 40,000 years ago attempted to record times and seasons by carving on rocks, cave walls, and bones. Such carvings and structures are often explained as being necessary so early farmers would know when to plant their crops. But such claims simply don't stand up to even superficial scrutiny. To begin with, many astrological markings and structures predate agriculture by, in some cases, thousands of years. As a matter of fact, studies at such places as Göbekli Tepe in Turkey seem to indicate that agriculture may have been invented to support workers who were already hard at work building such astrological structures. If that is the case, astrology came before agriculture. Secondly, if you want to know when to plant your crops, there are easier ways to deduce the correct seasons than to lug mega-ton boulders all over the landscape. Frost doesn't pay any more attention to rocks than it does to the *Farmer's Almanac*.

Astrological texts, such as those discovered in Babylon, Sumeria, Mesopotamia, Greece, and China may indicate a date later than agriculture, but undoubtedly the texts were written long, long after the practice itself had become a full-fledged religion.

We have no way of knowing whether early astrologers believed the heavens *caused* events on earth, or merely *foretold* them, but there is no doubt that the basic principal of *As Above, So Below* has held sway in human consciousness for thousands of years.

No one knows what the ancients believed, or how they pursued their craft, but most modern astrologers believe that the positions of the planets at the moment of our birth were indicative of energies that reflect our character and spiritual focus throughout our lives. To appreciate that belief, we need a basic primer in astrological horoscopes.

Is astrology a valid system of divination today? Does it work? Is there any truth behind the theory? If so, how could the position of stars and planets in the cosmos have any influence on what happens in our personal life down here on earth?

Those questions are at the heart of the current, violent disagreements out there concerning the whole field. There are those who swear *by* astrology. There are even more who swear *at* it. When reporters discovered that First Lady Nancy Reagan had invited an astrologer to help President Reagan make decisions while he served in the White House, the press had a field day!

Although a few words written in a book will not convert anyone either *to* astrology or *away* from it, we can at least attempt to try to understand a little about the whys and wherefores of the subject.

There are prominent and famous people who believe in astrology. The late First Lady Nancy Reagan did, even inviting an astrologer to the White House.

We'll begin with the idea of energy. What is it?

Energy comes in two forms: *potential energy* (stored energy) and *kinetic energy* (moving energy). As the name implies, potential energy doesn't really accomplish anything. It merely has the potential to accomplish something. So what interests us in this discussion is moving energy—energy that is going somewhere and doing something. Another word for that is vibration. When vibration slows down to the speed of light, we can measure it. It's within our perception of reality. Einstein swore that nothing can travel faster than the speed of light. That's why space travel of any distance is so problematic. The universe is so darned big that it would take a person four years just to get to the nearest star, assuming he could travel at the speed of light, which he or she can't, because all sorts of weird things happen in *time* when you get to that speed. Time and space are, after all, connected.

Remember, though, that just because Einstein said it, it doesn't mean it's true. There might be all kinds of wonderful things happening in the fast lane out beyond the speed of light. We just don't know what they are because we can't perceive them with any instruments we now have at our disposal. Maybe someday we'll fold space and fly at warp speed. But that day is still in the future, Captain Kirk to the contrary.

So we're left with energies that vibrate at the speed of light or slower.

Or are we?

ENTANGLEMENT: SPOOKY ACTION AT A DISTANCE

Theoretical physicists have discovered a strange phenomenon called "nonlocality" that would defy belief were it not for the fact that it has been tested time and time again and has never proved to be false. Carefully constructed laboratory experiments have shown that when two connected particles are separated and sent on their merry way, one in one direction and one in another, they remain forever "entangled." That means that when you do something to one of them over *here*, the one over *there* reacts instantaneously, even though they may be on opposite sides of the galaxy. (Albert Einstein called this "spooky action at a distance." At first he refused to believe it possible because he was so committed to the fact that no information could pass between them that traveled faster than the speed of light, let alone instantaneously.)

Now comes the fun part. Remember that space and time are connected. That's why scientists refer to them as space/time. So particles remain entangled, or connected, not only throughout space, but throughout time as well.

In order to understand this, we have to put it very simply. That means we are about to lose our scientist-readers. But if we start quoting all sorts of mathematical equations, we're going to lose our non-scientist-readers. On the assumption that more non-scientist-readers than scientist-readers have come this far, let's skip the equations and get to the bottom line.

There is good evidence that our perception of the "river" of time or "time's arrow" is an illusion. That's right, time may not even exist. (For more information on this topic: my wife, Barbara, and I wrote a book a few years ago called *Armageddon Now: The End of the World A–Z*. In it, we spent some time analyzing the theories of the English physicist Julien Barber. He's a fascinating man and the intervening years have only strengthened his stature among scientists. In short, Barber believes that what we call "time" is a series of what he calls "nows." A "now" is simply where everything is in the universe at a given point.)

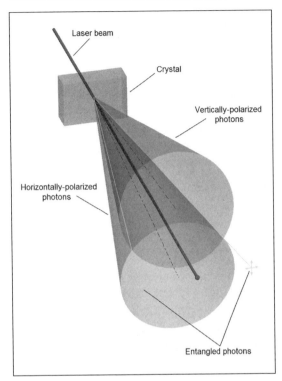

Laser beam

Crystal

Vertically-polarized
photons

Horizontally-polarized
photons

Entangled photons

This diagram shows how entangled photons have been created in the laboratory by directing a laser through polarizing crystals.

When we step outside our little perception box and view the cosmos through a bigger lens, we are faced with the fact that energies present *here* and *now* might also be perceived as being present *then* and *now*. The energies present in the vibrating, energetic particles that caused you to be first conceived and then born, the miracle of life that formed you in the first place, might very well be entangled with, or connected to, the energies present everywhere in the cosmos when you first experienced life.

Your biological body began at a specific time and place in the cosmos. That is undeniable fact. At that instant, everything in the universe occupied a particular, unique place in both space and time. Is it such a large leap to imagine that those energies, inherent in those particular vibrating particles, might have an entangled effect on you throughout the rest of your life, no matter how far or how fast they might have traveled since then?

This kind of thinking violates every notion that is considered intuitively true in classic, Newtonian mechanics, but makes perfect sense on the quantum level, as wacky as it may sound. (But don't be discouraged. As we will see in a later chapter, quantum mechanics sounds wacky even to the folks who study it.)

What all this means is that, theoretically, by studying the location, shape, and tendencies of what was going on in the stars when you came bawling on to the scene, it might be perfectly logical to assume that we are somehow able to see those tendencies played out in your life, decades later.

The thought that quantum reality, existing at the micro level of existence, might have anything to do with biology, existing at the macro level of existence, was considered outlandish just a few years ago. Anyone claiming such a thing would have been laughed out of the symposium. But fewer people are laughing now.

What this means is that if you can accept even the possibility of such a connection, you have to accept the fact that ancient astrologers discovered all this thousands of years before modern physicists. They didn't have all the math figured out, of course. They just saw that it worked. And that's all it took. You don't have to understand the parabolic tables to know you'll trace an arc off a cliff if you jump. You just have to observe that if you get too close to the edge you'll fall off and then observe the pattern of your trip down. That's simple logic.

Ideally, given enough time and a big enough computer, it is perfectly possible to trace the trajectory of every particle in your body, for that matter every particle in the universe, both forward and backward in time—where it is and where it was. If we could do that, we would have perfect omniscience about where everything has ever been and where everything is going to be, thus observing everything that has ever happened and everything that will ever happen. We would, in every practical sense, be "gods."

Given the rapid increase in computer power over just the last forty years, who is to say that won't happen someday? And then take the next step. Who is to say it hasn't already happened, and we are simply living out some future astrologer's predictive computer program? Reputable scientists have given this problem serious thought and have come to the conclusion that such a scenario is not only possible, but probable. Whether you accept it or not is, of course, part of your Faith Statement. But even acknowledging that such a thing is possible opens a lot of doors. It makes astrology a pretty tame subject and not nearly so esoteric or outlandish as we might have first believed.

If any of this is true, we are faced with the prospect, as we will be time and time again as we continue on together in this book, that the ancients intuited long ago what we are just beginning to understand: the world is a strange place that operates under rules that we are just beginning to figure out. Who knows what tomorrow may bring? Maybe astrology can tell us.

CHEMICAL KEYS

It may at first seem absurd that anything like a genuine religious experience could be induced by activities as simple and apparently as materialistic as eating, drinking or smoking certain species of plants. But we should feel less surprised when we remember that the plants in question contain chemicals intimately related to brain hormones and neurotransmitters such as dopamine and serotonin. Although the neurological details are difficult to grasp, the fact is that these chemicals, and others like them, are intrinsic to all the functions of our brains, while our brains in turn are involved with everything we experience—even if we choose to define some of those experiences as real and some as non-real. Whether we like it or not ... it is beyond serious dispute that these chemicals *already* play a fundamental role in spontaneous religious experiences.

—Graham Hancock, *Supernatural*

In American society there now exists a "war" on drugs. And make no mistake. It is a war. If you are caught behind enemy lines carrying mind-altering drugs, you will be captured and marched off to prison.

But what are mind-altering drugs? Ah, there's the problem. The three most common are caffeine, tobacco, and alcohol. The vast majority of Americans and Europeans regularly consume at least one of these substances. What makes it worse is that when you listen to music, stare at a painting, observe a sunset, or perform yoga exercises, your brain produces chemicals that, if synthesized and encapsulated in sufficient quantities, would constitute grounds for your arrest and conviction resulting in a prison sentence.

Peyote plants have long been used in the American Southwest as a source for a hallucinogenic drug taken to create a spiritual experience.

Indians of the southwest eat peyote as a religious rite. Christians drink wine in memory of Jesus and his disciples at the Last Supper. Some actually believe the wine is literally transformed into blood. South American shamans drink ayahuasca as a prelude to journeying to other perception realms. There is evidence that the religious practices of ancient Greeks, Hindus, Egyptians, and Mayans all included healthy doses of mind-altering substances.

Let's get even more specific. When a severely depressed person is treated by a medical professional, he or she is often prescribed a mind-altering substance. Prozac and its cousins regulate serotonin, a naturally occurring chemical produced by the brain that affects mood. It is structurally similar to DMT, or Dimethyltryptamine, which is manufactured in your pineal gland. Every animal and most plants produce DMT internally. It is also a major candidate in the quest to understand why human beings first made the great leap into symbolic, or religious, thinking when they entered the great painted caves of Europe.

Physicists have their "God particle." Biologists have their "God chemical." But it's important to remember that DMT doesn't "manufacture" feelings. It enables your brain to soothe out your body so you can appreciate and experience feelings associated with a reality that already exists but that you don't fully appreciate at the time. Nothing changes except your mind. You simply see reality in a different light.

Isn't that exactly what happens when a person undergoes a religious experience? He or she doesn't "manufacture" God. God is simply revealed. Two thousand years ago an unknown blind man is said to have reported, "I once was blind but now I see" (John 9:25). John Newton (1725–1807) immortalized his statement in a song called *Amazing Grace*. The truth is this. Drugs don't necessarily cause a reality to spring into existence, but by altering the way we look at life they sometimes allow us to see it in a different light.

Drugs have been around longer than religions and have been a part of our lives since we stepped out of the primal soup four billion years ago. Is it any wonder that they play an integral role in our spiritual development? Whether manufactured individually in the body, naturally in our environment, or unnaturally in the test tube, we are all composed of, surrounded by, and exist within a chemical ocean that determines who we are, how we feel, and whether we live or die. Testosterone, estrogen, adrenalin, and serotonin—they all shape us as people.

When it comes to discussing brain chemistry or mind-altering drugs, I am certainly no expert. I can speak about the stimulating effects of caffeine in the morning and the attitude adjustments inherent in a glass of bourbon in the evening, but that's about it. I've never smoked anything at all, whether grown in Virginia or Mexico, and I missed the entire 1960s drug scene because I spent most of my time in a practice room at a music school. So my knowledge of this subject comes secondhand.

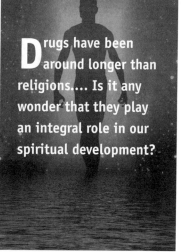

Drugs have been around longer than religions.... Is it any wonder that they play an integral role in our spiritual development?

Dr. Rick Strassman, M.D., however, has studied the subject exhaustively and scientifically. The results of his study can be found in his best-selling books, *DMT: The Spirit Molecule*, *DMT and the Soul of Prophecy*, and *Inner Paths to Outer Space*.

Strassman knew that DMT was produced naturally in our bodies and is found in nature, especially in those parts of the thousands-of-years-old shamanic ayahuasca cultures of South America. After giving volunteers carefully controlled doses of DMT in a laboratory setting, under the watchful eye of the government, he carefully monitored their sessions with up-to-date equipment. His were the first controlled experiments involving psychedelics in twenty years. What he discovered was amazing.

In an interview conducted for the Reset.Me website in April 2015, this clinically trained scientist was moved to say:

> I think that the universe, including humans, exist out of God's beneficence, and once having created us, He would like us to know and love Him, to the extent that those concepts/words capture the essence of that "desired" relationship. In my new theory of theoneurology, I propose that the brain is so designed that we are able to communicate with God, and perhaps endogenous DMT is involved in mediating the phenomenological contents—visions, voices, emotions, etc.—that accompany the interactive religious experience with God.

This is not the kind of language one would expect from a distinguished scientist. But it is exactly the kind of language one hears when interviewing people who have undergone similar experiences, whether artificially induced or naturally experienced. The common denominator seems to be, "It felt more real than reality!" Or, "Everything in my life now seems like a pale dream in comparison!"

Virtually everyone who has experienced chemically induced alternate perception realms agrees that:

- First, those realms are inhabited by intelligent beings who seem to be aware of us. They may be described as saints, angels, Jesus, the deity, aliens, mythological figures, therianthropes, animal envoys, or spirit guides, but they are real, ready, and waiting for us to make contact.

- Second, "over there" is real. Life on this side is a bit of a drag after such an experience.

Strassman describes why he got into this kind of research:

My original impetus to do the DMT work was noticing how similar the effects of psychedelic drugs were to descriptions of the effects of certain Eastern religious meditations and near-death experiences. It seemed that there must be some common biological denominator. That is, perhaps psychedelic drugs and meditation techniques activated the same part of the brain, to the extent that the two syndromes resembled each other. I only became aware of the correspondences between the DMT experience and the alien abduction literature after finishing my study.

My theory of theoneurology suggests that God designed the brain in order for us to be able to communicate with Him and His intermediaries/angels. I think it is more complicated than simply an antenna; rather, perhaps a better analogy would be a television set which is able to display information received from an outside source using a number of different modalities. In the case of the brain, that would involve all of the components of subjective experience, including perception, cognition, emotion, and so on.

Research such as this raises some pertinent questions. First and foremost, what does it all mean? Is our conception of God simply a chemically induced illusion? Is there anything real about such hallucinations? Is the entire culture of scriptural and mythological religion simply a product of people's drug-induced imagination?

THE "GOD HELMET"

Perhaps an experiment that runs along similar lines might shed some light on these questions.

Stanley Koren, while working in Laurentian University's neuroscience department, built a device according to specifications provided by Dr. Michael A. Persinger (1945–), who was the head of the department. It was called the Koren Helmet, and its function was to measure certain areas of the brain that were being stimulated by a mild electrical current.

When the press found out that many of the volunteers reported visions of supernatural beings, it was inevitably nicknamed the "God Helmet." They soon asked the question, "Is the supernatural only a product of electrical stimulation or chemically induced hallucinations?"

Todd Murphy reported on the *Inner Worlds* website:

> The experiences of those who have come face to face with God might be just an example of a very rare brain activity. If they actually met the true God, then why did they do so in this controlled experimental setting, but not at other times?

> The implications for theology are obvious. Perhaps God exists, but has been waiting until humanity developed enough to find him in the brain before he would appear under any circumstances he could control. Perhaps God exists only in our brains. Perhaps he exists, and chose to bless the 1% of Dr. Persinger's research subjects with visions of him, because those people were beloved to him. Perhaps he exists, but he appears to those with the right neural history in moments when the right pattern of brain activity is present, and not according to what he sees in their hearts.

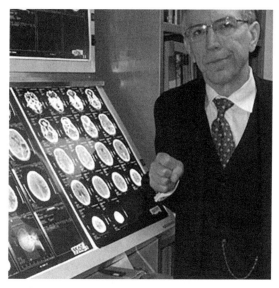

Michael Persinger is a cognitive neuroscience researcher who has studied and published on telepathic and remote-viewing communication.

Not every subject saw God. Many simply became aware of other beings present in the room with them.

So what's going on here? Three theories come immediately to mind:

1. The God Helmet produces an electrical effect in the brain that causes hallucinations involving the presence of imaginary figures that might include an image of a deity.

2. The God Helmet stimulates those areas of the brain that form our connection to other worlds. The volunteers didn't really see those worlds, but the part of their brain that might connect them to those worlds reproduced the experience.

3. Other worlds exist all around us, but we don't see them because our brains have evolved to filter out their existence in favor of presenting only the information we need to survive and thrive in our everyday lives. The God Helmet resets those filters, allowing the test subjects to glimpse another perception realm.

In other words, the God Helmet does electrically what drugs such as DMT do chemically.

What do we do with all this information? What does it mean?

The simple answer is, no one knows.

Those who don't believe that supernatural worlds, let alone supernatural intelligent beings, exist are quick to claim that such visions are simply hallucinations that seem real, but are not. If we can produce them electrically or chemically, that in itself is proof that supernatural realms are figments of our brain-induced imaginations. We might call such people "supernatural atheists."

Those who are on the fence, straddling both sides of the whole supernatural argument, want to believe such things are possible, but doubt that we're going to meet God in a laboratory setting. Therefore, they argue, what such experiments prove is that part of our brain jumps to the fore when we experience the supernatural, and laboratory experiments with electrical currents or chemicals simply stimulate those specific areas of the brain. We can call such people *supernatural agnostics*.

Others, however, hold closer to a theory that says we relate to everything, supernatural or not, through thought processes that take shape in our brains before being translated into words and images. Normally we don't experience the supernatural. It's not something we need during our morning commute, for instance. But under the right conditions, which might be induced by everything from religious practices, such as prayer and meditation, to chemical or electrical current experiments, the brain "filters" that usually serve us well can be opened to allow glimpses of glory. We might label such people *supernatural believers*.

These distinctions were placed on vivid display in America during the 1960s. Widespread use of psychedelic drugs caused millions of people to suddenly experience mind-altering worlds beyond anything they had ever considered. It was frightening to those on the "outside" of the scene to hear Timothy Leary (1920–1996), associated with no less an all-American institution than Harvard University, advise young people to "turn on, tune in and drop out." He may have been an accredited psychologist, have conducted LSD experiments under controlled, laboratory conditions, and been

American psychologist Timothy Leary did experiments with LSD in the 1960s at Harvard. He advocated the drug's use as therapeutic, even spiritual.

on to something important, but the established mainstream American family, sitting at home watching on their televisions, were shaken to the core. It wasn't long before the "War on Drugs" was an official policy of the government. The effort eventually led to the famous "Just Say NO!" slogan.

People who had seen things beyond their wildest imaginations and experienced realities they had never dreamed of, who had met what appeared to be welcoming, life-affirming, intelligent beings who existed in indescribable perception realms, were quick to respond.

"Just say NO!" to experiencing reality for the first time? "Just say NO!" to a life-changing experience? "Just say NO!" to the adventure of being a pioneer in humankind's evolution to another level of consciousness? Why, in heaven's name, should they say "NO!" to that?

Daniel Pinchbeck (1966–), quoted in Dean Radin's book *Supernormal,* summed up the situation succinctly:

> In the sophisticated contemporary world, it seems absurd to propose that the dismissed and disgraced psychedelic compounds might be real doorways to neighboring dimensions, and within those other realms there are beings we can contact who are waiting to welcome us with disconcerting glee. It is even more absurd to suggest that some of those beings resemble our folkloric archetypes, because they are the source for those archetypes in the first place.

—Daniel Pinchbeck, *Breaking Open the Head*

After quoting Pinchbeck, Radin went on to say:

> But the fact remains that practically anyone who explored those realms has returned stunned after learning that the shamans, and the yogis, were probably right: Everyday reality is just one provincial way of perceiving the world. There are others that are equally valid, and it's in some of those worlds where the supernatural resides.

—Dean Radin, in *Supernatural*

Things to Remember

In summary, before you decide where you stand on all this, think about a few things:

- First—virtually everyone who has a supernatural experience, whether chemically induced or not, insists that they have undergone a life-changing experience. Their lives are, quite literally, changed. They are never quite the same.

- Second—people who have undergone these experiences return with amazingly similar descriptions. They may live in an Amazon rain forest or a European city, they may be contemporaneous with us today or have lived in biblical times or even earlier, they may be educated or primitive, religious or non-religious, devout or heretic, but they all report the same visions over and over again. It seems much more probable to believe that they all perceived a similar world and then reported it, biased only by their own culture and language, than it is to believe that somehow evolution found it expedient to build visions of other realms into our collective psyches. What would be the evolutionary point of that?

- Third—virtually everyone who experiences the supernatural insists that what they saw "over there" was much more *real* than that which they normally experience "over here." They adamantly swear that it didn't feel like a dream or an illusion. It was "real," and they go to their graves insisting on it.

It's hard to let testimonies like these go, simply because they may differ from our own version of reality. And there are so many of them. Their numbers grow daily. Is it time to start taking them seriously?

DOWSING

The Lord said to Moses, "Take your rod in your hand and I will go before you to the rock at Horeb. Strike the rock and water will come out of it for the people to drink."

—Exodus 17:5–6

The British Society of Dowsers, formed in 1933, is the leading organization for dowsers in the United Kingdom. Its stated purpose is "to encourage the study and enhance the knowledge of dowsing in all its forms amongst members and the public." According to its publications, dowsing is:

> A technique for bringing information from the intuitive or subconscious senses to the attention of the rational mind, it has potential value in almost every area of human endeavor, research and activity, and dowsing practitioners find it a valuable tool in both their work and their everyday lives.

A similar group exists in the United States called the American Society of Dowsers, Inc. Its mission statement is as follows:

> The American Society of Dowsers, Inc. is a scientific and educational non-profit organization whose mission is "to support, encourage and promote dowsing and dowsers in a manner consistent with the highest standards of personal integrity and behavior; to provide dowsing education and training to dowsers and non-dowsers alike to bring them to a level of proficiency they are comfortable with; to promote and foster communication and fellowship among all persons in any way interested in dowsing.

Until relatively recently, dowsing was primarily used for finding water. Although many well-driving companies won't admit it, and they certainly don't publicize it, they often employ dowsers to check out a site before going to the trouble and expense of bringing in heavy equipment and setting up drilling rigs. It's not uncommon at all to see an old-timer with a forked willow or hazel stick slowly walking back and forth over a potential site while trucks idle quietly a few hundred yards away. What happens next, if one is unprepared for it, can sometimes appear quite shocking.

Suddenly, for no apparent reason, the stick, or "wand" as it is called, will quite forcefully be drawn toward the earth, dipping down toward the ground, seemingly out of control. As a matter of fact, dowsers have to be careful, so sudden and violent is the movement. The dowser will try a few more angles, sometimes mumbling to himself in deep concentration. He or she may walk away a few steps, turn and come back slowly to the original point, sometimes changing dowsing equipment to a pendulum or an "L"-shaped rod held in each hand. Different tools produce different effects. The pendulum will swing around in a circle, often very fast and almost perpendicular to the ground. The L-rods will suddenly either cross or separate, with no discernible movement of the dowser's hands.

A man searches for water using dowsing wands. Using this technique to find water is what comes to mind to most people when you mention dowsing.

After a while, the dowser will mark a spot on the ground, often placing a stone or stick at a particular place that looks no different from any other spot of ground on the landscape, and announce that there is a good vein of water to be found right there at, for instance, 250 feet below the surface.

The trucks move in, begin to drill and, lo and behold, strike water within a few feet of the predicted depth!

How is this possible?

The truth is, no one really knows. Not even the dowser. But it has happened so often, so predictably, so consistently, and through so many years of history that people who have witnessed the phenomenon simply accept it. It saves too much money, time, and effort to question the process. Simply put, you don't have to understand it. It just works. You don't have to buy sensitive equipment. There are no moving parts to speak of, and it doesn't take a lot of time and effort. All you need is a sensitive, experienced dowser and a little faith. And even the faith comes by experience. Do it often enough, and you stop thinking of it as faith. You don't *believe* any more. You *know*.

This is by no means a knock on intelligence. No less an authority than Albert Einstein admitted to "believing" in dowsing while not understanding how it worked. In a letter to Herman E. Peisach of Connecticut, dated February 15, 1946, Mr. Einstein admitted that although the art of dowsing was often "regarded on the same mystical level as astrology," he explained it as a "way of using the human nervous system to detect factors that are unknown to us at this time."

Dowsing is not a new phenomenon. Its usefulness and practicality have been recognized not just for generations but for thousands of years. Even very early examples of writing talk about it. And its usefulness is not limited to finding water. Early geologists employed dowsers to locate tin mines on the coast of Wales. Dowsers have been hired to search for gold and other precious minerals, as well as oil, in California. Although modern police departments usually don't want the practice publicized, they often have dowsers on hand to search for lost people. A dowser will sit in a back room of a police department, miles away from the scene, and hold a pendulum on a short string over a topographical map showing the area where the person was last seen. The pendulum will begin to change the direction and intensity of its swing when it passes over a particular mountain range or stream course. Often enough, the person will be found in that area. Healers, too, sometimes use dowsing with a pendulum to find out exactly what is going on inside the human body—a practice that is entirely noninvasive and requires no preparation on the part of the patient.

Is it magic? Are dowsers sensitive to electromagnetic forces? Is it metaphysical or is parapsychology at work? Is it a cultish phenomenon, as some conservative Christian denominations claim? Or is it simply luck and New Age mumbo jumbo?

If you are of a modern, left-brained, scientific bent and have never experienced dowsing at work, you are probably inclined toward the mumbo-jumbo explanation, comparing it disdainfully with such outmoded superstitions as "women's intuition," "clairvoyance," or "beginner's luck." If you follow a religion that looks down upon it, you might call it the work of the devil. But if you ever witness a good, credible, personable dowser practicing their craft, although you probably won't fully accept the evidence before your eyes, you will undoubtedly never forget the experience and will be inclined to keep, at the very least, an open mind toward the subject. And if you take the next step and actually hold a dowsing implement in your hand under the expert tutelage of an experienced adept, and if you are sensitive enough to get your first response, it could very well change your life.

Let me share a personal experience.

A SKEPTIC'S SOLILOQUY

For many years I had been skeptical of folks who dowsed for water with rods or willow sticks. I had watched a few dowsers at their work, seen the rods or stick move or plunge downward, and tried to figure out how they were doing it. I had been told that some well-drilling companies won't even drive to a property without hiring a dowser to tell them if there's water present and where to drill. But I thought it was all poppycock.

Nonetheless, one day I decided to try it myself. Why? I don't have the faintest idea. One moment I was a skeptic. The next, I wanted to try it.

After doing some Internet research (we don't do anything these days without Internet research, do we?), I decided the simplest way to get started was to get some brass rods, bend them into what are called "L-rods," and see if it worked.

I didn't dare tell my wife, Barb, what I was doing, so I just quietly made a surreptitious trip to the local hardware store. They didn't have any brass rods. So I got some solid copper wire in the heaviest gauge I could get, cut it into two 18-inch pieces, bent them into a shape roughly like the letter "L," and went forth to find water.

And I struck out, totally. I had been told by numerous websites that the rods would either cross or open up if I walked slowly over an underground water source. Didn't happen. Even when I walked over the spot where I knew the water line ran from the well to the house, I got nothing. Zip! Thoroughly discouraged, I did what any modern researcher would do. I went back online for more study.

I came across some sites that, at the time, seemed quite wacko. They said you could dowse for the presence of spirits. That was even stranger than dowsing for water. I at least believed in water. I also found a site that talked about dowsing for earth energy. Now, that was more up my alley! While skeptical about certain human practices like dowsing, I have always been a confirmed nature mystic. So armed with my L-rods, confident that Barb was taking a nap and wouldn't see my foolishness, I started off across sections of our woods' paths and the small yard we have cleared from the forest around our home.

There, right in front of our house, I received the shock of my life. While concentrating as best I knew how, I took the step that has probably changed me forever. One step—nothing. Another step—the rods suddenly crossed, all by themselves, and this in the hands of someone who up until that moment had been highly skeptical. I stepped back and tried it again. Same thing. I straightened them out in my hands and walked a little farther. A few steps later, they moved again. It was almost as if I was crossing a stream from one shore to the other. When measured, the apparent river of energy turned out to be about 85 inches wide. When I came from one direction and reached the "shore" of the energy, the rods crossed. When I crossed over and came back from the other side, they crossed again.

One step—nothing. Another step—the rods suddenly crossed, all by themselves, and this in the hands of someone who up until that moment had been highly skeptical.

I asked whatever "Powers That Be" if this was an underground stream—kind of a prayer "to Whom it may concern." Maybe I had found water. But no, when I stepped onto the area with water on my mind, nothing happened. The only way I could get the rods to move by themselves was to concentrate on earth energy.

Quietly and only to myself, I asked "someone" or "something" or "whatever" which direction the energy was flowing. Both rods slowly turned to the southeast. When I asked what direction the energy was coming from, they slowly turned to the northwest.

I walked about fifty or sixty feet "upstream" and tried again. Same thing. Eighty five inches across. I drew an imaginary line through our house, lined up a tall tree for bearings, went around to the backyard and tried again. There, too. I continued downhill, taking bearings on trees so as to keep a straight line, and kept measuring. Every place, 85 inches. Same results. I had discovered a perfectly straight line of energy that ran through our property from northwest to southeast. I had, in fact, discovered a ley line, or what is now more and more being called an Energy Lay. (Since that time I have traced the line on a topographical map and dowsed it out miles in both directions. Sometimes it takes a little walking to find it, even with a large-scale map. But when I do—85 inches every time! I have also extended the line cross-country, on a road map, and was amazed to discover the number of Native American sacred sites it bisected.)

Thoroughly spooked and out of breath, I waited until Barb joined me to repeat the exercise. I kept saying to her, "Watch my hands. Make sure I'm not moving them!" I even tried to get the rods to stand still. But every time, without exception, even trying it with my eyes closed so I wouldn't know when I came to the edge of a line, when I crossed the flow of that powerful earth energy, the rods crossed of their own accord. I couldn't make them *not* do it. It was as if they were hitting a wall and collapsing in on themselves.

Once the ice was broken—the skeptic converted, so to speak—the sky became the limit. I could ask for the presence of water and the rods would cross whenever I stood over an underground source. I could even deduce the direction of flow and determine, by a series of bracketing questions, how deep the water was. I stood over our well, for instance, and figured out how many feet down it was. When I checked the figures left by the driller, I found I had come within five feet. Over and over again, with expanding confidence, I discovered that there was almost no limit to what I could discover about the "magical" outdoors that I had lived in all my life. (I also discovered the presence of what others might call "spirits." That was a complete surprise to this retired preacher!) I delighted in asking a question to which there was no way to discover the answer until I could verify it after the fact. I have rarely been disappointed.

All my life, I had heard people who had the reputation of having a "green thumb" swear that plants grew better when they talked to them. I had even seen some verifiable scientific experiments done in this field. Imagine my surprise when I discovered that trees had "auras," circles of energy around them. As an experiment, I dowsed the aura energy surrounding a small cedar

tree that we were particularly fond of and decorated with lights each year at Christmas time. I discovered an energy aura about six feet out surrounding the tree. Then, when we were sure no one was looking, we actually talked to and, yes, hugged the little thing. We let it know it was loved. When I then dowsed it again, the energy aura had expanded to three times the original distance—eighteen feet! Over the course of many, many months we repeated the experiment, with different trees and plants, always getting the same result. Then we moved on to people. Once, with my heart in my mouth, I dowsed the aura of a close friend and neighbor, not telling her what I was doing. I dowsed an aura that went out about four or five feet in a circle around her. Then

When in the meditative state, a person's aura will actually increase in size around them.

I asked her to close her eyes and meditate deeply for a few minutes. While she was deep in meditation I dowsed her aura again. It had expanded to almost twenty feet! From that moment on, I have never doubted the results of hospital experiments that determined that intercessory prayer "works." Something seems to change and affect our personal energy when we pray, meditate, or otherwise intentionally focus on positive thoughts and emotions.

The question is, of course, how does it work?

Although no one can answer that question finally and unequivocally, there seems to be a gathering consensus among dowsers that is at once highly sophisticated yet very simple to understand. Ancient folklore, brain research, and quantum physics seem to have come together to offer an elegant hypothesis that goes something like this:

A THEORY OF DOWSING

Dowsing seems to be a way to transfer intuition into waking consciousness.

What is intuition? Simply put, it's the process by which right-brain-hemisphere experiences are translated into left-brain-hemisphere consciousness. How did you "know" that your friend was going to call? How did you "know" something special was going to happen? How did you "know" to turn right in order to get to your destination?

The answer is simple. Somehow you perceived something below the level of conscious thought and transferred that perception into action carried out by the cognizant, decision-making part of your brain. You acted on instinct. The right hemisphere felt something and then sent a message to your left hemisphere to act intentionally, even though it might not have known why.

Athletes do it all the time. It's called "visualization." Jazz musicians, too, "know" what notes someone else is going to play, sometimes even before that person knows himself. They don't think about the chord changes or the rhythmic riffs they are using. They just play. When they're in a groove, they don't even know what's going to come out until they hear it. It's not that they don't understand the framework of the music. It's just that the harmonic structure, the key signature, the time signature, the phrasing, is so instinctual, so much a part of their subconscious being, that they are not aware of it. And until music gets to be that instinctual, it sounds stilted.

Many believe this is exactly how dowsing works. There is nothing magic in the dowsing rods themselves. They are not moved by mystical forces from paranormal realms. They are the instrument by which the music of the spheres is translated into visible signals. The body, a receptor for consciousness itself, experiences something below, and maybe even above, the level of conscious thought. By concentrating on the rods in their hands, dowsers see those feelings converted into a visible sign. The rods tell them what it was that they were experiencing that didn't register within the left hemisphere of their brains. The dowsers read the energy through which they move even though they are not fully conscious of it. Are small muscles, beyond the conscious awareness of the dowser, actually moving the rods? Possibly. But that's not the point. The body is acting apart from the conscious awareness of the dowser. That's the important thing to know.

This is the basic idea underlying what has been called the "ideomotor response," a theory that proposes unconscious and involuntary muscle movements go into effect when a person—in this case, a dowser—expects something to happen at a given time and given place. If a novice dowser, for instance, is told that there is a water line below the surface of the ground and his or her rods will cross when they pass over it, the rods will invariably cross at that point. Because the novice isn't conscious of moving any muscles at all, the effect can seem to be a bit mystical.

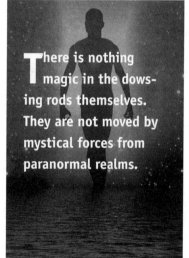

There is nothing magic in the dowsing rods themselves. They are not moved by mystical forces from paranormal realms.

This explanation brings comfort to those who have already decided dowsing is a simple parlor trick. But there is a serious flaw in its basic premise. A real dowser who is trying to locate a good spot for a well doesn't have the slightest idea where water can be located. Why here and not over there? How can he or she have even a vague notion of how deep the vein will be? And yet time after time dowsers will pinpoint the exact location and depth for an effective well to be dug.

I had a similar experience a few years ago when a work crew pulled up to widen the road we live on. They had been told there was an old water line somewhere on the road and didn't want to break it with their equipment. Without giving it a thought, the driver of one of the trucks rummaged around in the back of his truck and came up with a pair of dowsing rods. He soon located the line, which was well out of range from where anyone thought it would be. With the utmost confidence they proceeded to widen the road with no mishaps.

Dowsing rods are a gauge, a visible way to register an impression of energy all around you, even though it is not consciously perceived and thus "translated" by your left brain's language skills. In the words of the British Society of Dowsers, they are tools "for bringing information from the intuitive or subconscious senses to the attention of the rational mind."

Think of it in this way. Those of you old enough to remember when television consisted of a small, black-and-white box with "rabbit ear" antennas

Dowsers may be channeling energy through their bodies and through the wands they hold.

on the top probably also remember a time when you discovered that if you stood in a certain spot with the antenna in your hand, the picture improved. What was happening?

Well, your body was serving as an antenna. It was picking up the broadcast waves and transferring them to the TV set. Until you saw this demonstrated on the screen you had no idea that the very air you breathed was awash with television signals—that they were, in effect, going right through you all the time.

Then the TV became, in effect, your dowsing rod. It proved, beyond the shadow of a doubt, that unseen forces filled your environment. You could see them right there on the television screen. In the left hemisphere of your brain you weren't consciously aware of any such broadcast waves. But your body "knew" they were there, and proved it the first chance they got. It showed them on TV.

In the case of TV and radio band signals, technology has simply produced an electronic dowsing rod.

DOWSING THROUGH THE YEARS

The present-day world is filled with examples of this phenomenon. Sometimes we ignore them because, for the most part, modern culture tends to denigrate activities usually associated with, for example, shamanism or aboriginal religion. But this is exactly the kind of experience much of the drug culture of the 1960s and 1970s was seeking. "Magic mushrooms" and synthetic psychedelics both were used for the same purpose. They were an attempt to bring about an altered state of reality, to bypass the traditional way of processing the world, to view life from an intuitive, rather than a rational, perspective.

It seems as though humans have been experimenting with dowsing earth energies, water, or even paranormal or metaphysical energies for a long time.

In 1949, for instance, a group of French explorers, while exploring in the Atlas Mountains of North Africa, found a system of caverns now called the Tassili caves. Many of the cave walls were decorated with prehistoric murals. One of them seems to depict a dowser who holds a forked branch in his hand, possibly searching for water. He is surrounded by a group of, presumably, tribesmen. The paintings were carbon dated and yielded an age of at least 8,000 years.

No one can tell, of course, exactly what prehistoric artists meant to portray, but etchings from Egyptian temple walls that are 4,000 years old seem to show similar scenes. And although there are many uses for pendulums, the Museum of Egyptian Antiquities in Cairo has displays featuring ceramic pendulums from thousands-of-years-old tombs. Are they dowsing implements or merely plumb-bobs? No one knows.

In historic, but still very ancient, times, records from Greece refer to dowsing, and the art was practiced on the Isle of Crete as early as 400 B.C.E. Some dowsers even believe the oracle of Delphi used a pendulum to help answer questions posed by pilgrims.

Bible scholars don't have any idea what the mysterious *Urim and Thummin* were that appear so often in Old Testament texts such as Exodus, Ezra, and I Samuel, but they seem to be some kind of dice that, when thrown, were believed to indicate the will of *YHVH*, Jehovah God. And the prophet Ezekiel reports that King Nebuchadnezzar of Babylon first consulted dowsers, or "diviners," as they were also called, before deciding whether or not it was wise to attack Jerusalem.

In Germany, during the 1400s, miners used dowsing rods to search for valuable minerals. They referred to the forked sticks they used as *Deuter*, a German word meaning "to show," "to indicate," "to point out," "to auger," or "to strike."

Closer to home, it's interesting to note that the first "official" use of the word "dowsing rod" is attributed to John Locke (1632–1704), a writer whose ideas inspired the framers of the U.S. Constitution. In 1650, Locke wrote an essay in which he said that through dowsing one could discover not only water but precious minerals as well. He coined the term by employing English words from the old language of Cornwall. The Cornish *dewsys* meant "goddess"; *rhod* was the word for "tree branch." Hence the term "dowsing rod," and thus it remains to this day.

Even more interesting is the fact that the 1912 edition of *Mining Magazine*, published in London, England, mentioned dowsing when it produced the first translation of a Latin work into English. It was called *On Metals* and had been written 356 years earlier. The translator was a professional American mining engineer who went on to become the thirty-first president of the United States—Herbert Hoover. Author Chris Bird, who wrote *The Divining Hand*, has noted, "God knows, had President Hoover been an expert dowser himself, he might have predicted, and therefore prevented, the great stock market crash of 1929!"

In 1959, Verne Cameron of California issued a challenge to the U.S. Navy. He offered to pinpoint the position of every U.S. submarine, using only a map and pendulum. The navy accepted the challenge. Mr. Cameron was successful, and he threw in a bonus. He located the Russian fleet as well! Speaking of the armed forces, it is reported that some U.S. Army soldiers in Vietnam were trained to dowse for land mines.

Speaking of the armed forces, it is reported that some U.S. Army soldiers in Vietnam were trained to dowse for land mines.

Why aren't these activities widely reported? Well, dowsing, like music and effective public speaking, is as much art as it is science. Even very experienced dowsers sometimes get it wrong. You probably wouldn't want to follow a dowser into a minefield any more than the dowser would want you to. Furthermore, we have to remember that no one fully understands how dowsing works. It can be an inexact process, even at best. But it has proven to be so reliable over the course of its long, long history that it certainly is worth studying.

EARTH MAGIC

Perhaps the most important outcome of the dowser's craft is an enhanced appreciation of what the ancients might have called "earth magic." Hamish Miller (1927–2010), until his death, was England's most well-known, and certainly most beloved, dowser. The founder of the Parallel Community, an online group of like-minded souls, and the author of many books and articles, Miller was drawn to dowsing after a near-death experience in 1982. In his 1989 book, *The Sun and the Serpent*, written with Paul Broadhurst, he expresses his appreciation of the art with these words:

> The question of meaning arises ... in connection with modern discoveries of aligned sacred sites ("leys") throughout the world,

of temples orientated astrologically to receive light and energies from certain heavenly bodies, of the mystical science of geomancy and of the cosmological patterns of formulae which sustained ancient civilizations. Revelations abound.... Together they amount to a statement, given directly by nature; a statement that our present way of understanding and treating the earth is wrong, that we inhabit a living planet and must give it the respect due to any living creature. From that follows a quite different perception of our relationship to nature, leading to a rediscovery of the ancient spiritual sciences. We do not know why serpentine energies spiral around the course of the line of St. Michael sites from the far west to the far east of England. Others before us have recognized the phenomenon, and they have made their sanctuaries and pilgrimage routes in relation to the earth energies. The ancients, as Plato reminds us, were simple people. They did not ask reason from nature but accepted things as they were. Plato also emphasizes that everything, all human science, knowledge and wisdom, originates from divine revelation.

If dowsing teaches us to experience the magic of life itself, if the use of rod, wand, or pendulum helps us to visualize or make manifest the earth energies through which we move, it changes our whole concept of our relationship to the earth—to our place in nature itself. The earth becomes a living, breathing, life-supporting organism named, perhaps, *Gaia*, after the Greek primordial ancestor of all life. It is no longer a simple manufacturer of resources. Mother Earth not only gives birth to her children, she sustains them throughout their physical existence and receives them back at the end. Earth and earth's species become one in a cosmic dance of life energy, manifested on this physical plane. Once we have accepted this Gaia Hypothesis, the idea that the Earth is a living breathing being, we have embraced the essence of supernatural.

DREAMS

Life is but a dream…

—From an English-language nursery rhyme

Sigmund Freud (1856–1939) was the first modern psychiatrist to bring the study of dreams to the attention of the general public. He still has a large following. His theory of dreams was that they were a representation of unconscious desires, motivations, and thoughts. He came to believe that we are driven by sexual and aggressive instincts that, due to social pressures, we repress from our conscious awareness. Because these thoughts are not consciously acknowledged, they find their way into our awareness through dreams. (Hence the oversized boxing gloves you used to find in the offices of Freudian psychologists. They were for expressing those aggressive feelings.) In his book *The Interpretation of Dreams*, still the "bible" of many dream analysts, Freud wrote that dreams are "disguised fulfillments of repressed wishes." He went on to say that there are two different contextual categories of interpretation that need to be addressed during dream analysis. *Manifest content* pertains to actual images, thoughts, and content. *Latent content* refers to hidden psychological meanings. (Of course, "a cigar is sometimes just a cigar." Sometimes there is no hidden meaning. It depends on the latent content lurking, or not lurking, in our psyche.)

Dream research didn't stop with Freud. It remains a controversial topic today. Here are just a few examples of modern schools of thought:

- The Activation-Synthesis Model: This theory was proposed by John Allan Hobson (1933–) and Robert McCarley (1937–) in 1977. They believed that circuits in the brain come alive during rapid eye movement (REM) sleep, causing areas of the limbic system that are involved in emotions, sensations, and memories, including the hippocampus, to become active. The brain synthesizes and interprets all this activity in an attempt to find meaning, which results in dreaming. This model, in other words, suggests that dreams are a symbolic interpretation of signals generated by the brain during sleep. The symbols, if interpreted correctly by a trained analyst, can reveal clues to understanding what is going on in our subjective unconscious. Hence the proliferation of various "dream dictionaries"—a car always means "this," a dog always means "that." A variation on this theme is that dreams are the result of our brains trying to make sense out of noises that are happening around us. A car driving by an open window might become a stimulus for a car appearing in our dream. A song on the radio might become part of a story the brain makes up in order to produce nonverbal, symbolic images.

- The Computer Model: When your home computer "sleeps" at night—in other words, when you're not using it—some programs automatically kick in that spend time cleaning up and organizing "clutter." (At least they do if you keep the darned thing turned on. I shut mine off. What does that mean, Sigmund?) They defragment and systematize things so the computer will work more efficiently. This dream model speculates that your brain operates in the same way. When you "shut down" in sleep, your brain goes to work organizing all the thoughts and external stimuli you encountered that day.

- The Quiet Therapist: This popular model proposes that dreams operate as a kind of therapeutic psychotherapy session. The brain tries to make sense out of things while you sleep in the safe environment of your bed, somewhat akin to a therapist's couch. Things that happen to you are analyzed for meaning and projected on the wall of your conscious mind when you wake up and remember. Your emotions help make sense of the symbols.

We might very well discover that one or more of these models is correct. Perhaps the truth lies in combining parts of all of them. But for thousands of years, shamans and mystics have taught that in dreams our normal waking consciousness is let out to play. It separates from its confines within the material body and brain and returns to its mystic union with the One in the creative, ground zero, imaginative, zero-point field of the Source. That is the purpose of sleep, they remind us. Without this daily renewal, life in this material world would simply be too hard to endure.

Modern sleep-deprivation and dream-deprivation studies seem to indicate that this is, indeed, the case. When we are tired and deprived of sleep, our creativity fails first. Then we start to forget things. Finally, we go completely mad and die. In this day and age, we may not fully understand what sleep and dreaming are all about, but we know that the material body ceases to function without them. Death is the result. That seems a pretty good indication that the ancients knew something. Indeed, traditional wayside hosts, the "keepers of the shrine" of the old road hostels in Britain, used to pronounce the final words of the evening to the gathered guests: "May the gods send you a dream."

Shamanism goes even further. Shamans claim that when released from the normal bounds of restraints of the waking, analytical hemisphere in our brains, our true nature, our consciousness, returns to the Source. They believe that with practice we can actually follow along while fully conscious.

American psychiatrist John Allan Hobson is noted for his research on rapid eye movement (REM) sleep. Along with colleague Robert McCarley, they established that dreams occur during the REM state.

DREAMTIME

Nowhere is this more evident than among the aborigines of Australia. They may well be the world's foremost teachers when it comes to understanding the ultimate nature of dreaming.

Although it is very difficult for most Westerners to grasp this concept, the indigenous Australians had no words in their language to express the idea that time is a "river" that flows from the past, through the present, to the future. They simply did not resonate with what Sir Arthur Eddington (1882–1944) called "the arrow of time." To them, time was something quite different.

This idea began to percolate through popular Western consciousness when Paul Hogan's movie *Crocodile Dundee* made a great splash back in 1986. The hero of the movie, Mick "Crocodile" Dundee, raised by tribal aborigines, was asked how old he was. He didn't know. "I once asked a tribal elder when I was born," he said. The answer came back, "In the summertime." To westerners who lived by the clock, this was an intriguing concept.

Australian aborigines trace their religion, indeed their whole culture as a people, back to prehistoric times. Recent DNA research confirms their claim. They are an ancient, ancient people. According to their belief system, at least as much as they share with outsiders, everything that exists is part of a vast, interlocking web, a network that extends back to their original ancestors who lived in what they call the *Dreamtime*.

Dreamtime is not simply a mythological construct. It still exists and is accessed whenever people "dream the fire" or enter into spiritual communion with the ancestors who still inhabit the landscape of the Australian outback. Dreamtime is the invisible plane that supports what most of us perceive as visible reality.

The great mental construct of the West is *pragmatism*. We deal with things in a way that we consider sensible and realistic. We base our actions and beliefs on practical, rather than theoretical, considerations.

Dreamtime is quite different. It manifests itself in ways that are much more mystical. Telepathy, for instance, is generally disparaged in western society. In traditional Australian circles, it is considered normal to the point of being taken for granted.

When Europe "discovered" and subsequently exploited Australian culture, they completely misunderstood the richness and depth of what they found. They considered native Australians primitive beings who needed to be "elevated" out of the quagmire of superstition. It wasn't until late in the twentieth century that a few westerners began to realize, to their horror, what they had done. Australian aborigines recognized right away the dangers inherent in Western culture. They understood that Western concepts of time, especially when it came to rushing it and cramming it full of activities primed by multitasking, would lead inevitably to anxiety-provoked diseases and general malaise.

When pressure built up too much, the Australian went "walkabout." He would simply drop out for a while, head off away from all the nonsense and bustle, and come back when he was good and ready.

To European overlords, this was incomprehensible behavior. To Australians it made perfect sense. How could a person live without being connected to the very essence of Dreamtime? When anxieties built up, when life became too complex and needed some perspective, when a person felt cut off from the ground of their being, it was of utmost importance to regain balance and stability. Dreamtime is real. Life is the illusion.

In the ritual of the dance, accompanied by clap sticks and the music of the didgeridoo, through the ritual of closely observing the land in ways westerners just didn't understand, traditional Australians released the power of Dreamtime into their present reality. By sharing their histories and telling their stories, they passed on to their younger generations the hard-earned wisdom that was present long before westerners showed up, and would be present long after they disappeared into the mists of time.

In our book, *Armageddon Now*, Barb and I summarized Dreamtime in this way:

The aboriginal peoples of Australia live in a culture that is not obsessed with issues of time—as in the West—and that appreciates the reality of Dreamtime.

Aboriginal customs have stood the test of time, coming to the aid of people who have seen their world turned upside down in just a few short years. And Dreamtime is validated when people feel the pressures of modern life and want to establish roots in a fast-changing world. When those pressures build up and threaten to overcome us, when too much information floods our souls, perhaps we all need to "go walkabout" or spend some quiet time "dreaming the fire."

To accept a theory such as the metaphysical reality of Dreamtime, the modern analyst must first acknowledge that our consciousness, our mind, exists independent of our brain. He or she has to at least consider that there is something else bigger than us, a *super*natural reality, that is really running the show. It is the stage upon which we play our small part.

This is something not many specialists are willing to consider. They would have to visualize the brain as a receiver, not an originator, of consciousness. That implies there is an "Out There," an "Other," that is actually the source of consciousness.

"Look how the brain lights up under an MRI," they say. "We can show you exactly where different kinds of thoughts originate in the brain. We can even stimulate those areas and produce those thoughts in our laboratory experiments!"

But modern shamans disagree. "I can do the same thing with my old radio," they retort. "I can show you exactly which tubes light up when I listen to a Hank Williams song. I can even cause those same tubes to play Hank's voice whenever I want. But Hank Williams doesn't live in my radio."

So, does consciousness reside in the circuits and neurons of the brain? Or is the brain an evolved receiver that picks up consciousness from outside—perhaps from what Ervin László (1932–) called the *Akashic Field*? Let's take a brief detour away from Dreamtime and consider:

THE CLOUD

I think I received a good picture of this whole thing from a man who installed the sound system in our new house. I call him Mel the Installer Guy. He's really into these things and was trying to describe to me how far the whole computer/MP3/hand-held/Kindle/Blackberry/gizmo/smartphone culture has evolved since the Internet went public back in the dark ages of, oh, 1970 or so. I had voiced my fear of losing my "stuff" if my computer ever crashed. But he informed me that he could throw his entire computer in the nearby lake and not lose a thing. (I told him I've had the same thought many times!)

"Where's all your information, your pictures, your tunes?" I asked him. "How do you back them up?"

"They're in the Cloud," he said.

"What cloud?" I wanted to know.

That was my introduction to what, apparently, everybody else in the world but me understands. So I looked it up online, thereby using "the Cloud" to tell me what "the Cloud" is. Here's what I discovered, according to Eric Griffith in *PC Magazine*:

> In the simplest terms, cloud computing means storing and accessing data and programs over the Internet instead of your computer's hard drive. The "Cloud" is just a metaphor for the Internet. It goes back to the days of flowcharts and presentations that would represent the gigantic server-farm infrastructure of the Internet as nothing but a puffy, white cumulonimbus cloud, accepting connections and doling out information as it floats.

At the risk of sounding naïve here, it seems to me that when we humans invented the "Cloud," we invented something that sounds suspiciously like what the ancient Hindu mystics first called *Akasha*. According to their writings, all the information (or what we would call "bits" today) is out there in Akasha. It's the source of Consciousness. We access it through our brains, the "hardware" of the analogy. The "software" corresponds to the various religious/philosophical outlooks we espouse. We even call it the same thing—"memory."

The analogy is perfect, except that *our* cloud, the Internet, is an invention of humankind. The *other* cloud is the Great Mystery, or God, or Vishnu. (Fill in your own word here.) In other words, it is not enough that we have created robots and artificial intelligence in our own image. We unconsciously followed the cosmic model and built it into the way our computer network thinks and acts. If we ever *do* manage to create a completely artificial sentient being (like the android Data on *Star Trek: The Next Generation*), we will have mimicked the exact same structure of intelligence as Akasha, the intelligence we are now experiencing here in the material world, even though we don't acknowledge that it exists.

"But that's different!" you exclaim in frustration. "We were the ones who placed the information in *our* cloud in the first place. There is nothing supernatural involved. It's only human knowledge. The information was already there before the cloud was ever invented. We put it up there. That's why we can now download it!"

Exactly! First the information, then the cloud. After the information, then the download. The "stuff" gets placed in the cloud and then the receiver, our computer, picks it up.

The "Cloud" is simply the collection of servers that store programs and data off site, which can then be downloaded for access on your electronic devices. Cloud technology is, in a way, a kind of metaphor for a Creator and our access to it.

"But the Internet cloud is a product of intelligence," you insist. "It had a creator. Us!"

Right again, but with one important difference. Akasha didn't just *have* a creator. Akasha *is* the Creator. And then we came along, made in the image of the Creator, and were able to not only access the information, we were able to do it in full consciousness while being aware of the fact that we were doing it! Consciousness thus accesses consciousness while being fully conscious. It's beautiful. That's Akasha!

"Now, hold on," you shout. (You're now getting extremely frustrated.) "The 'information' that you're talking about isn't really hanging around in a 'cloud.' It exists in millions of computers that are sitting around out there in every country on earth. It's accessed by the electromagnetic, quantum grid that connects every computer on the Internet to every other computer. It's real. It's a verifiable fact!"

Exactly! Each and every human being (the computer of our analogy), everything in all of creation, is, in fact, connected. So you, too, can consciously experience that connection in the form of an electromagnetic, quantum force that the ancients recognized. It all exists in a universal field, an "information" field that Carl Jung labeled the "collective unconscious" and the ancients dubbed the "Akashic Field." It is a power field, the ground of our being—a mystical field that is at the same time supernatural and real. It consists of every bit of information and the experience of every thing that ever existed.

But there is so much information out there that our brains can't possible let it in all at once. It would be like trying to explain advanced calculus to a five-year old. They couldn't possible understand it. You need to dribble out the basics a little at a time or they would get swamped.

Very few people are wired in such a way that they can access information beyond the rest of us, but a few are more highly advanced and pull it off. We call them geniuses.

Einstein accessed Akasha, the cosmic "Cloud." What do you think he was doing when he engaged in "thought experiments?" So did Newton and Socrates and Brahms and Mozart and the builders of ancient monuments and dowsers and Hindu mystics and every other genius who ever lived. The reason people built similar pyramids in Egypt and way over in Central America was that they were accessing the same information field. The reason societies started doing the same things with stone at the same time was because they were all tuned in to the same source. When it appears in Akasha everyone, everywhere, has access to it. The reason human society evolves in bumps and jumps and punctuated equilibrium is because of the wisdom found in the words: "When the time is right, you'll know it!"

What goes around comes around. We, the participants, recipients, and final products of Akasha have invented our own version in our own image. We call it the Cloud. ("May the Force be with you!") And the allegorical individual, the personal expression, the human counterpart in this metaphor, sits right in front of me on my desk as I type these words. My computer and me. Two peas in a cosmic pod. Each of us is a physically manifested expression of a possibility wave that originated in Akasha.

There are many ways to access the Cloud of information and potential we have labeled the Akashic Field, but the most common point of entry to this supernatural realm is dreaming. Every night, when your brain "shuts down" and "re-boots," when you leave normal, waking reality behind for a moment, having relaxed the brain filters that served you so well all day, you enter an environment of spirituality and possibility. Because this environment is foreign to us, different from our waking reality, our brains need to select images that come close to representing what it sees so as to present it to us in a manner we can comprehend. Even then, sometimes the scene gets a little wild. After all, we're dealing with a wholly different level of reality here that often doesn't include any similar previous experience your brain can find rattling around in there. But if we learn to pay attention, we can reap great benefits.

The late Joseph Campbell used to teach that dreams are a great source of the spirit, so maybe there is no greater blessing than the traditional one: "May the gods send you a dream."

HARD-WIRED FOR SPIRITUALITY

Given their intelligence, it seems to me likely that the Neanderthals contemplated, in some way, the mysteries of life. Wouldn't they have wondered not only about unexpected and surprising weather events and sky events but also what happens when our lives comes to an end? If they thought about these questions, did they do so with awe, dread or reverence?

More relevantly for a scientific analysis is this question: Did they come together in groups to evoke gods, spirits or ancestors to help themselves make sense of the world?

—Barbara J. King, *Were Neanderthals Religious?*

THE FIRST FUNERALS

In the autumn of 2016, archeologist Enrique Baquedano (1958–) reported on an archeological dig ongoing at a cave in Spain. The evidence being examined included the grave of a small child encircled by several fire hearths and thirty horns of various animals, including bison, red deer, and a rhinoceros skull. That was the hard evidence. But the report included something else that hard evidence couldn't verify. The researchers believed they had discovered the site of a funeral ritual. What was even more surprising was that this was, without question, a gathering of Neanderthals, human cousins who modern humans would someday encounter and with whom they would even procreate. But at this time they were most certainly a different branch of the human tree.

Neanderthals were long considered to be primitive, hulking, ignorant "cave men" of the *Alley Oop* comic strip variety. That idea has long since been displaced. But still, funerals imply religion and symbolic rites affirming an afterlife. Those things have traditionally been the hallmark of modern humans. So the question is inevitable. Were Neanderthals really religious? And if so, had they discovered religion separately or had they learned such things from contact with modern humans? The evidence in the cave had been dated from about 40,000 years ago, just about the time so-called "modern" humans were discovering such things. So it might be possible that the Neanderthals were merely mimicking behavior they had observed in wondering bands of religious Cro-Magnons. But, given the lack of any such evidence, it seems a stretch. It is far simpler to draw the conclusion that these were religious Neanderthals engaged in the business of doing what modern humans still do today—gathering to mourn the loss of a loved one and speed him or her on the way to another plain of existence.

It's a highly disputed theory, to be sure, but if it is true it might indicate that modern humans, including our distant ancestors, are somehow hard-wired to believe in supernatural gods. Because such a belief is subjective, at best, it is very difficult to find hard evidence proving it. But the question lingers. If even Neanderthals believed in an afterlife, could that in itself be evidence that a Creator or Creating Force hard-wired such a belief into our very DNA?

> If even Neanderthals believed in an after-life, could that in itself be evidence that a Creator or Creating Force hard-wired such a belief into our very DNA?

The Spanish archeological site doesn't stand alone. Lots of other grave burials found all around the world display similar evidence, including pollen left from gifts of flowers and carefully crafted tools. You don't bury a perfectly good tool unless you think your dearly departed will have a use for it. It is possible that all these sites together simply show a tendency for humans, including human-like cousins, to contemplate death and wonder what's on the other side. But the idea that spirituality and religion are built into our very being is certainly a viable theory.

Like all such theories, skeptics tend to argue against it and believers tend to argue for it. As always, the sides seem to predictably rally around predetermined Faith Statements. But it does cause us to wonder.

It caused Barbara J. King (1956–) to wonder as well. She wrote to Professor John Hawks, a specialist in Neanderthal studies, at the University of Wisconsin. This was his reply:

> Religion, as many people recognize it, is built from highly detailed symbolic narratives. If we separate that out, though, and look only at the material manifestations that an archaeologist might find, there is really very little in most religious traditions that is different from what Neanderthals do.

So I don't think it is at all improbable that the Neanderthals had a humanlike religious capacity. But to be honest, I think this is not what many Americans or Europeans would recognize as religion.

—John Hawkes, as reported by
Barbara J. King, *Were Neanderthals Religious?*

As King points out, religion is more a practice than a belief. After all, lots of people attend church and synagogue, to say nothing of celebrating Christmas and Passover, without really believing in God. But it is tempting to think that as much as we moderns try to act intelligently sophisticated and "above" the notion of superstition and religious formality, most people still hesitate when a black cat crosses their path while they carefully walk around, rather than under, ladders on Friday the 13th. Similarly, we are often told that "there are no atheists in foxholes," and we attend funerals where prayers are offered, no matter how much we attest to the psychological, rather than spiritual, need for such rituals.

Is there more? Is there something deeply buried within each of us that cries out in a still, small voice, "You are more than a material body!"

Polls and Modernity

CNSNews.com reports that 74 percent of American adults believe in God. That's down from 82 percent a few years ago. But it's still a pretty significant number.

On the other hand, even skeptical scientists seem to wonder from time to time when it comes to a belief in the supernatural and the significance of religious thought.

Read, for instance, the quote from Robert Jastrow (1925–2008), an eminent American astronomer, physicist, and cosmologist, in his response to discovering the background radiation that appears to prove the theory of an initial Big Bang:

For the scientist who has lived by his faith in the power of reason, the story ends like a bad dream. He has scaled the mountains of ignorance; he is

Socialist philosopher and economist Karl Marx believed that religions were just human constructs designed to help the oppressed deal with am unjust world.

about to conquer the highest peak; as he pulls himself over the final rock, he is greeted by a band of theologians who have been sitting there for centuries.

When I taught courses on world religions, I always began my first lecture with an explanation designed to put religion in its proper place. I spoke about the two prevailing human opinions as to why religion existed.

The first position was that expressed by Karl Marx (1818–1883). He believed religion to be a human invention designed to salve over the human need to solve questions about the great Unknown:

> Man makes religion, religion does not make man.... Religion is the sigh of the oppressed creature, the heart of a heartless world, and the soul of soulless conditions. It is the opium of the people.
>
> Karl Marx, *Deutsch-Französische Jahrbücher*,
> 7 & 10 February 1844

The rest of the course was based on the second explanation. That is the view that postulates an "Other," another side "out there." People who subscribe to this second hypothesis believe that there really is a great Unknown, and that we can communicate with It, and It with us.

In my book *Ancient Gods*, I described our ancestors like this:

> Why should these folks have been any different from us? They might have turned to a Higher Power in thanksgiving or for help through difficult times, just as many do today. They might have sung the equivalent of the Christian hymns, "We Gather Together to Ask the Lord's Blessing," or "Come, Ye Thankful People, Come." They cried when they were hurt. They laughed when they were happy. Their children sometimes made them proud and sometimes let them down. They must have felt the encroachment of the years on their tired bodies. They must have sometimes wondered, "God, why did You allow this to happen?" They probably celebrated weddings and funerals, were sometimes afraid of the dark and welcomed the warming of spring every year.

> Here's the point. Sometimes, if you are quiet for long enough and can sit still in meditation while gazing at the artifacts the old ones left behind, you can make a journey through the centuries and feel at one with the ancients. The illusion of time breaks down. The scales fall away.

> And why not? The blood of our ancestors flows in our veins. We are what they became. They once were what we are today.

We cannot prove, and maybe never will, that we are hard-wired to be spiritual. We have not yet discovered a "religious" gene in our DNA sequence. But given the universality of spirituality found in our history, and still present around the world today, we are forced to admit that such a possibility exists.

That inevitably leads to questions:

- If a "religious" gene exists, how did it get there? What evolutionary advantage did it provide?

- If spirituality is part of our make-up, when did it start? Who was the first "religious" human to pass this trait on to his or her children?

- In spite of the onslaught of academic attacks upon religion today, a large majority of people still believe in supernatural gods. Why?

- If spirituality is, indeed, hard-wired into our psychological make-up, could it be that Something, or Someone, is waiting for us to acknowledge it?

The jury is still out.

HYPNOTISM, PAST-LIFE REGRESSION, AND CHANNELING

In 1952 a best-selling book took America by storm, prompting discussions, arguments, family feuds, and public sermons from prominent Christian evangelists. It was written by Colorado businessman Morey Bernstein (1920–1999), who also happened to be an amateur hypnotist. Paramount Studios purchased the rights to the book and made a successful movie out of it. Titled *The Search for Bridey Murphy*, it told the story of how a woman named "Ruth Simmons" (her actual name was Virginia Tighe) had been placed in a hypnotic trance and suddenly found herself transported back to Ireland in the year 1806. Speaking in an Irish brogue, she began to describe in great detail her life as eight-year-old Bridey Murphy, who lived in Cork. She was the daughter of Duncan Murphy, a barrister, and his wife, Kathleen. When she was seventeen, Bridey married Sean Brian McCarthy and moved to Belfast. She provided vivid details of a fall that caused her death. She also talked about watching her own funeral and described her tombstone. She felt neither pain nor happiness in death, she recalled, but was later reborn in midwestern America as Virginia Tighe in 1923. Tighe had no trace of an Irish accent, even though when she spoke as Bridey Murphy it seemed quite pronounced and authentic.

The story, even in those pre-Internet days, caused a sensation. Half of America, it seemed, was intrigued and began to seriously consider past-life regression hypnotism with eager eyes. Some claimed that a scientific proof of reincarnation had finally been discovered. A whole new area of research blossomed almost overnight. Professional psychologists began studying hypnotism techniques so they could use a patient's previous-life experience to unlock keys that would shed light on present-day problems.

The other half of America was more troubled than curious. Christian churches, operating within the typical theological framework of 1950s fundamentalism that, thanks to the influence of men like Billy Graham, was so prevalent back in those days, used their radio and newfound TV exposure to denounce the whole story as either nonsense or the work of the devil. Many pastors forbade their congregation to read the book, thereby boosting sales even more.

This episode marks the popular genesis of a technique called *hypnotic regression,* during which a subject is first placed in a hypnotic trance and then gradually taken back, first to their childhood and then even further to past lives. The technique is still used quite often today and many people swear by it.

Unfortunately, upon closer inspection the tale of Bridey Murphy began to unravel. The publisher neglected to check the details before going to print. As book sales soared here in America, more scrupulous reporters were dispatched to Ireland to confirm the facts. That was when things started to go awry. The very details that made the book seem so authentic could not be verified.

Bridey had said she was born on December 20, 1798, in Cork. She had died in 1864. Official records recorded neither date. She pronounced the name of her husband as "See-an." But Sean is pronounced closer to "Shawn" in Ireland. If that wasn't enough, Bridey recalled that she used to call her husband Brian, not Sean. That happens to be the middle name of the man to whom Virginia Tighe was married.

She claimed to have worshipped at St. Theresa's Church. The church exists but was not built until 1911. She bought groceries at the shop of a man named Farr. No such grocer ever existed.

Even more troubling, it was discovered that an Irish immigrant lived across the street from the young Virginia Tighe when she lived in Chicago as a child. The immigrant's name was Bridie Murphy Corkell. That fact, when made public, raised some eyebrows.

There were some physical descriptions that checked out. Her recollections of certain geographical locations were very accurate.

But most telling of all, Virginia Tighe didn't believe in reincarnation herself. Neither she nor Morey Bernstein seemed to be the type of people who were trying to pull off a hoax. In innocence, they merely reported what happened, wrote a good book about it, and then watched as things spiraled out of their control, as such things often do once they go public and strike a responsive chord.

Bernstein eventually gave up hypnotism and became a philanthropist until his death in 1999. Tighe tried to shrink from the publicity until she died in 1995. For the most part, she succeeded.

Meanwhile, the book version of *The Search for Bridey Murphy* is still in print and readily available.

HYPNOTIC REGRESSION: FACT OR FICTION?

This whole episode succeeded in producing two polarized schools of thought in regards to the "science" of hypnotic regression as a window opening on to the supernatural. Believers, who still exist in considerable numbers, claim that debunking one case study, no matter how popular it was, doesn't negate the hundreds of other cases on record. Many, many people claim to have experienced past lives and can recall in vivid detail facts that they could not possibly have known about before their hypnotic adventures.

An equally large group of unbelievers have declared themselves as well. They claim the entire experience of hypnotic regression can be explained away in any number of ways. Consider the following arguments:

Cryptomnesia—This is the theory that "forgotten" memories might consist solely of information the patient may have filed away and since forgotten. Such information may have come from books and movies, long-lost conversations, or things overheard but not remembered. The subconscious records all this material and then, under hypnosis, brings it back while casting the patient in the starring role of the drama.

Anachronisms—When a person claims to have served in the court of Ramses III, for instance, questions are immediately raised. The practice of numbering pharaohs didn't begin until the reign of Queen Victoria. It would be similar to a person saying he was born in 32 B.C.E. How could anyone know he was born thirty two years before Christ? Case studies cite people who claim to be Vikings while describing themselves as wearing helmets with horns on them. That's the way, up until recently, Vikings were always portrayed. Modern archeologists, however, seem to have proved that Vikings wore close fitting caps that would not be so cumbersome in battle. Horned helmets were reserved for religious ceremonies.

Personality Transference—Psychologists believe from studies of separated identical twins that much of our per-

There are several possible theories that explain how hypnotism brings back "past lives" to patients' memories, including the influence of the hypnotists themselves.

sonality development can be attributed to individual experiences while growing up. How could a personality trait in the twenty-first century be derived from someone who lived thousands of years ago in a totally different culture?

Flawed Hypnotic Techniques—How much does the therapist inadvertently contribute to the existential narrative of the patient? Can the therapist be guilty of "leading the witness," so to speak? Ian Stevenson puts it like this:

Another possible explanation that could overrule the veracity of past-life recall is the influence of the hypnotist, whose suggestion ability is a sine qua non for the effectiveness of hypnosis. The other necessary factor is the receptivity of the patient to the hypnotist's suggestions. Although the two conditions determine the success of hypnosis when used as psychiatric treatment, when expecting to get information from alleged past lives, the suggestion ability of the hypnotist becomes an important hindrance in obtaining true information, since it can contaminate the patient's story.

—Ian Stevenson, quoted by Meryle Secrestin,
"The Reluctant Messenger," *Omni Magazine*, 1988

Imagination—Is the patient merely imagining an entire historical scenario? This doesn't imply deliberate subterfuge. It merely raises the question of mistaken, even if sincere, memories. It's a well-known fact that trial witnesses often remember situations that didn't happen in the way indicated by their testimonies. It recognizes that our minds can be tricky things.

PREVIOUS LIVES

If all this weren't confusing enough, there is another phenomenon to consider. It's called "channeling." This is the practice of a person becoming a channel through which a supernatural entity external to our world or dimension speaks through the vocal apparatus of an earthly host. Mediums have long channeled the voices of departed loved ones, but the practice, popularized in the famous series of "Seth" books compiled by Jane Roberts, many of the works by and about Edgar Cayce, and the well-known *Course in Miracles*, has become a mainstay of the New Age movement.

There is really no way to prove or disprove the phenomenon, unless a dialogue is established indicating, one way or another, that the entity knows things that could not possibly be known by the host. Such things are notoriously difficult to determine.

Once again, then, it would seem that whether or not past-life regression or channeling methods effect our belief in reincarnation depends on an initial Faith Statement. Those who believe, either through personal experience or faith, believe. Those who don't, don't.

So are there any other ways of studying the matter?

As a matter of fact, there are.

Although the fact has gone pretty much unreported in the popular press, there are numerous cases of children recalling events in alleged past lives that are much too detailed to simply pass off as childhood imagination. When a four-year-old child reports names and places with great accuracy and insists he or she has lived before, it is worth noting. In places such as India, where reincarnation is readily accepted, such cases aren't usually even reported. They are simply regarded as fact. In the West, incidents such as these are usually discouraged. By the time a child enters elementary school, he or she has usually been discouraged from repeating such things in polite company and the comments fade away into misty childhood memories.

The case for such soul migrations is buttressed whenever it becomes necessary to search for a new Dalai Lama. Whenever a Dalai Lama dies, a committee composed of high-ranking Lamas and Tibetan governmental officials begins the task of selecting a new one. After meditation, dreams, prayers, and visions are employed over a period of a few years, the committee follows the spiritual clues they have been given and searches out a child whom they believe is the reincarnated spiritual leader. Several toys and personal items are placed before the child. If he chooses the correct ones, the items that were special to the last Dalai Lama, it is considered a sign that the child recognizes his old self. There are other tests of course, and people who knew the old Dalai Lama are consulted, but if the process continues free of doubt, a new spiritual leader is selected and begins his training.

Tibet's holy Dalai Lama is a supreme example of the idea of souls migrating from life to life. The current Dalai Lama is the thirteenth in the line of Buddhist leaders.

Dr. Ian Stevenson, before his death in 2007, was probably best known for his work in this field. A psychiatrist who worked at the University of Virginia School of Medicine for more than fifty years, he was considered by some to be a genius. Others thought him quite the eccentric. There is no doubt, however, that he produced some groundbreaking work in the field of reincarnation. He believed it could be proved that not only memories but also physical clues such as birthmarks could be transferred through the process of moving on from one life to another. Traveling extensively, especially in places where reincarnation was part of the generally accepted social fabric, he came to believe that what he called "soul transfer" was the best explanation for such things as phobias, unexpected emotions, unusual abilities, and knowledge of past events. His more than three hundred published technical papers and fourteen books on the subject cited case after case and provided the basis for his extensive investigations. *Twenty Cases Suggestive of Reincarnation*, published in 1966, and *European Cases of the Reincarnation Type*, published in 2003, were very popular reference works and are still available. His most important work, however, was probably *Where Reincarnation and Biology Intersect*, published in 1997.

> He believed it could be proved that not only memories but also physical clues such as birthmarks could be transferred through the process of moving on from one life to another.

Although many people sympathetic to Stevenson's ideas called him a misunderstood genius, it was probably inevitable that most scientists simply ignored him. Those who paid attention at all generally thought he had obtained his case studies by asking leading questions of both the children whom he interviewed and their parents who were present at the time. Some say his results were skewed by translators who tended to believe in reincarnation and fed him the answers they thought he wanted to hear. The well-known charge of *confirmation bias*, whereby a scientist edits out any information that doesn't agree with his or her thesis, was leveled at him more than a few times.

Interestingly, a quite novel criticism of his work was raised by some people who one might consider allies. These folks thought that the children he interviewed were not recalling past lives at all. Instead they were, quite literally, possessed by external entities and became channels to them. In short, they claimed that spiritual possession accounted for almost all the cases Stevenson studied. The children became possessed when they were young and vulnerable and subsequently lost their abilities to channel such entities when they grew older and developed a more mature sense of spirituality.

Stevenson himself never thought his case studies proved anything that would satisfy scientific standards. In a 1988 interview in *Omni Magazine*, he said: "All the cases I've investigated so far have shortcomings. Even taken together they do not offer anything like proof."

INTELLECTUAL VS. METAPHYSICAL

Those who are inclined to doubt the whole reincarnation process are legion in the West. They tend to simply discount the beliefs of the teeming millions in the East who do believe. Once again, people usually first form what we earlier called a Faith Statement, then they gather supporting arguments. Those arguments can sometimes seem pretty silly or even petty:

- "Why is it that people who believe they lived a past life are always somebody famous? Why do they always remember serving on the court of Cleopatra? How come they weren't just Joe Sixpack from Tulsa?"

- And then there are the religious arguments, usually delivered with great seriousness, pomp, and circumstance. The Bible says, "It is appointed unto man once to die, and after that to face judgment!" (Hebrews 9:27).

- Another condemnation is one I call the argument from mathematics: "There are seven billion people alive in the world today. They can't all be reincarnated from past lives. There are just too many of them. The numbers don't add up!"

And so it goes. Those who believe, believe. Those who don't, don't. It's as simple as that.

Once again we are faced with a dilemma. There seem to be indications that transmigration of souls—reincarnation—is possible. The laws of science, for instance, declare that energy cannot be destroyed. It can only change form. This implies that who we are could easily become someone else, as long as we are willing to admit the fact that our consciousness exists separate from our bodies or brains.

For thousands of years, old and venerable religions, especially those of the East, have claimed reincarnation is real. One of the most respected men on the planet, the Dalai Lama, is said to be a reincarnated Buddha.

Those who study the time/space continuum wonder if time is even a part of reincarnation at all. They ask if we are currently living many different lives in many different perceived eras, but all at the same time.

There are case studies that illuminate many different possibilities and seem to be very interesting. But so far they all fall short of the testable, repeatable, controlled studies demanded by the scientific method.

Until such evidence is peer reviewed, repeated, and written up, it will probably always fall short. That doesn't mean reincarnation isn't real. It doesn't mean that it is. It continues to be a great dividing line best illustrated by the refrain from *The Ballad of East and West*, by Rudyard Kipling: "East is East and West is West and never the twain shall meet!"

INTUITION, DÉJÀ VU, AND INTENTIONALITY

A controversy is raging today about the power of our minds. Intuitively we know that our conscious thoughts can guide our actions. Yet the chief philosophies of our time proclaim, in the name of science, that we are mechanical systems governed, fundamentally, entirely by impersonal laws that operate at the level of our microscopic constituents.... The question of the nature of the relationship between conscious thoughts and physical actions is called the mind–body problem.... The current welter of conflicting opinion about the mind-brain connection suggests that a paradigm shift is looming. But it will require a major foundational shift. For powerful thinkers have, for three centuries, been attacking this problem from every angle within the bounds defined by the precepts of classical physical theory, and no consensus has emerged.

—Henry P. Stapp, *Attention, Intention, and Will in Quantum Physics*, Lawrence Berkeley National Laboratory, University of California, May 14, 1999

THE MIND–BODY PROBLEM

Are we more than our bodies or can everything from our motivations to our illnesses simply be described as chemically induced phenomena? Is love nothing more than a subjective feeling arising from a flood of endorphins? Where does the body end and the mind begin? Does such a horizon even exist? How do we come to know what we know?

Intuition is a phenomenon in which we seem to suddenly know something without going through the process of acquiring any special knowledge. It comes from the word "intuit," which simply means "to contemplate." Common usage tends to reduce the meaning to a yin/yang simplicity: we either analytically figure something out through "reason" or we skip the whole process and "intuit" the result. In the unenlightened but recent past, we denigrated intuition with the pejorative term "women's intuition." Men, it was said, figured things out. Women jumped right to the end of the process. Men were "left brain," process thinkers. Women were "right brain," intuitive feelers. There was no question as to which method was superior. Before we became politically correct in terms of gender awareness, it led to a lot of very funny sitcoms.

How did we know, that one time, that in order to reach a certain destination we had to steer our car through a sudden right-hand turn? We either figured it out and reached a decision or we intuited it. It either required a thought process or a feeling process. And do you remember that time you not only knew the phone was going to ring, you also knew who was calling?

Intuition, in its most profound form, often produces an almost mystical feeling within us. That's why it is sometimes referred to as a "sixth" sense. How did Bret Maverick, in the 1994 movie starring Mel Gibson, know he was about to draw to an inside straight and win a lucrative hand at poker? He felt it! God was on his side! He just somehow knew! It was supernatural!

Intuition is similar to another phenomenon known as *déjà vu.*

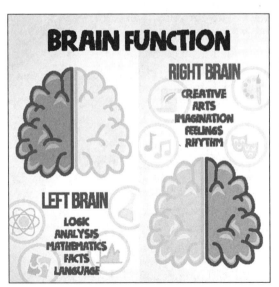

The right side of the brain controls the creative and emotional parts of the personality, while the right side is more logical and analytical.

In the 1999 movie *The Matrix* a committed hacker named Neo (Keanu Reeves) is thrown into a future world dominated by robots. Sometime after their creation by humanity in the twenty-first century, the robots rebelled and began an independent existence that depended upon harvesting human bioelectricity and thermal energy. Humans were grown in pods, unaware of the true nature of their condition because the computers kept their minds under strict control by supplying implants that connected them to a cyber reality called the Matrix. What appeared to be reality was, in fact, an illusion, albeit a mostly pleasant one.

Sometimes, however, the Matrix needed upgrading, and the seam connecting the old reality to the new developed a bit of a hiccup. It appeared as if an event happened, and then happened again as the new reality tape began to roll out. Humans experienced it as *déjà vu*. Those in the know, who existed outside the illusion, saw it for what it was—a glitch in the Matrix.

Déjà vu is derived from the French words "already seen." We see something and feel we have seen it before. We do something and feel we have done it before. We experience something and it feels familiar.

The experience is so widespread that it engendered a song by Richard Rogers and Lorenz Hart called "Where or When":

It seems we stood and talked like this before.
We looked at each other in the same way then,
But I can't remember where or when.
The clothes you're wearing are the clothes you wore.
The smile you are smiling you were smiling then
But I can't remember where or when.
Some things that happened for the first time
Seem to be happening again.
And so it seems that we have met before
And laughed before, and loved before
But who knows where or when?

Some believe the phenomenon to be a memory of a dream. Others, a precognition. Some look for a neurological glitch in which a new event is accidentally sidetracked and appears suddenly in our memory banks instead of our brain's recognition software.

Whatever it is, the feeling is often accompanied by a moment of mystical comprehension. It makes us feel as if something supernatural is occurring. "I've done this before," we say. "Was it in a past life? Did I just glimpse the future?" It feels a bit spooky even to those who are objective and practical when it comes to such matters.

However we logically explain the phenomena, intuition and déjà vu make us feel a bit apprehensive. We sense that somehow we are in touch with the supernatural. We feel the presence of a greater unknown. A higher truth casts its shadow upon us. Whether we believe in it or not makes no difference. For a moment, the hair stands up on the back of our necks. The only proper response is a drawn-out and mystical, "Whoa! Did you see that?"

Is there a mystical proof behind these experiences? Has anyone studied both subjects in the laboratory, written a peer-reviewed paper, and contrived an acceptable theory that anchors intuition and déjà vu solidly within the realm of supernatural mysticism?

Absolutely not!

Prolific inventor Thomas Edison was said to have taken power naps, falling asleep just enough to access the more intuitive side of his brain.

But has anyone fully explained them in a manner acceptable to modern biological reasoning?

No again!

So both experiences inhabit the no-man's land of the gap between what we know and what we feel.

Can we really "know" something if it appears fully formed in our minds, without any way of explaining how we "know" it? Can we sense, in a moment of insight, that we are not "inventing" a truth but "discovering" it instead, as if we had already seen it play out?

It appears we can. The history of science is littered with the uncomfortable knowledge that sometimes intuition and déjà vu are necessary tools of the trade.

Take, for instance, this insight from Cindy Shippy Evans:

Thomas Edison, inventor of the light bulb, had a napping habit which he was often teased about. As the story goes, he kept a rocking chair in his office, which he would use for these infamous naps. In one hand he would hold a rock. Beside the chair, underneath the hand with the rock, was a metal pail. The idea behind the pail was that if he fell far enough asleep for the rock to drop out of his hand, the sound of the rock hitting the pail would wake him back up. Does this make Edison the inventor of the "power nap"? Possibly. I am convinced there is a whole lot more to the story than meets the eye. I believe Edison used his naps to tap into the wisdom of his intuition. He used these "naps" to tap into the mind of God.

Years ago, I discovered there is a place just between awake and asleep where I would occasionally see visions or have an inspired idea. I see this as the place where we can actually tap into the mind of the One—the mind of God. Christians might call it the Holy Spirit. Scientists might call it the Zero-Point Field or the Matrix. It is that which flows in and through all things. Over time, I have tried to tune into this field in order to gain insight and wisdom from that place where truth exists, unfettered by the teachings of this world.

I am convinced Thomas Edison used his "naps" to work out solutions to his inventions' problems. He used the rock so that he didn't fall too deeply asleep! Look back at how much Edison accomplished in his lifetime. In order to do this, he put himself in a meditative state where he could access his intuition—which in my mind is another term for the mind of God. As humans, we all have this ability to connect to this unseen force. We just have to learn to harness it.

—Cindy Shippy Evans, *From Cocoon to Butterfly:*
A Journal of Spiritual Healing and Transformation

INTUITION AND QUANTUM PHYSICS

A possible theory of intuition and *déjà vu* comes, surprisingly, not from the musings of mystics and psychics but from the emerging field of quantum physics. At several points in this book, we have talked about the phenomenon known as entanglement or non-locality. It has been discovered, and proved beyond any reasonable doubt, that particles that have become "entangled" are able, when separated, to "communicate," for lack of a better word, instantaneously over vast distances. When one particle is given an "up" spin, for instance, its partner will immediately exhibit a "down" spin. This flies in the face of classical physics. Einstein proved to everyone's satisfaction that information cannot travel faster than the speed of light. Even at that speed it would take some time for one particle to send a message ("Hey! I'm spinning up. Start spinning down!") to its counterpart. But the message gets sent. And it arrives, for all practical purposes, instantaneously.

This result is accepted at the micro level. Scientists seem to be fine with allowing all sorts of strange things to happen as long as they don't break out into our world of the five senses. Such things may be entertaining when it comes to *Star Trek* episodes. Most good scientists are Trekkies anyway, so when the starship *Enterprise* is able to "open a sub-space frequency" and talk instantly to a planet that is ten light years away, no one complains. Just don't let it happen in the real world. There it would be impossible.

But the evidence indicates that, at least down on the quantum level of the very small, that's exactly what happens.

This has raised some serious questions. If it happens down there, why can't it happen up here? Some interesting experiments have been conducted, notably by the Institute of Noetic Sciences in California, that demonstrate some very meaningful statistical results. Partners in love, identical twins, and other combinations of "entangled" couples seem to be susceptible to ascertaining all sorts of things when separated. Dean Radin's book *Entangled Minds* makes for fascinating reading about this subject.

But more to our point are the theories that arise out of this research. Classical physics pictures the cosmos as a set of objects, separated from each other. If one is to influence another, it must do so by sending information through a *field*.

Gravity, for instance, is one such field. The electromagnetic field is another. Objects existing in such a field operate in a known and mathematically predictable fashion. If you want to talk to me by telephone and I live on the other side of the continent, our voices are turned into electric impulses that travel through wires at the speed of light and are turned back into sound waves on the other end. Even if we use wireless devices such as cell phones and bounce our voices all over the satellite grid, the information still travels at the speed of light. That's very fast. But it's not instantaneous. So how do particles living in the quantum field do it?

Quantum field! That's the key phrase. It appears that space is not empty at all but rather is a field wherein everything is connected to everything else. We live, apparently, in an entangled cosmos. What happens there is felt over here. It's as simple, and as complicated, as that.

Some people appear to have a strong sense of intuition that allows them to sense when something—particularly something momentous—has happened, even when it happens far away.

So why don't we all know everything that's going on everywhere? That's simple, too, according to this theory. If we were aware of everything at the same time, we would overload and burn out in a second or two. There's always a "disturbance in the Force" going on somewhere. Humans, who have evolved within this system, have developed filters. They're called the five senses. Their purpose is to let in what we need in order to survive and function but filter out the rest.

Sometimes, however, stuff gets through the filters. In times of stress, perhaps, or when our guard is down just before we fall asleep, or when we meditate, or pick up dowsing rods, or even just by accident, something slips through. We call it intuition.

A mother, for instance, suddenly feels that her daughter on the other side of the world has had an accident. A man is suddenly struck with the feeling that his uncle George just died. A friend decides to call us on the phone and we pick up the vibes before the first ring. It's the phenomenon of entanglement at work.

Some people are better at it than others. Why? No one knows. They were just born that way. We call them psychics or mystics. Their antennae are attuned a little differently than ours. There's a good chance that the ancients were probably more sensitive than we are. Tribal elders among Australian aborigines are famous for communicating telepathically over long distances. Such sensitivity may have been useful a long time ago, but it could very well have been pushed out of our experience and atrophied due to disuse.

But there are those, and I count myself among them, who wonder if the ability to intuit exists right below the surface and is available to all of us if we attune our senses and expand the receiving radius of our minds.

In an earlier chapter I talked about my experience with dowsing. If dowsing teaches us anything, it teaches us to experience the "magic" of intuition. The dowsing rods become visible signs of forces we feel below the level of thought. It's like standing in the middle of radio waves but not knowing it until you turn on the radio. The radio is tuned in to such frequencies. We are not.

In the same way, information is everywhere around us and coursing right through us, but we don't feel it.

That's where dowsing rods are helpful. They are tools that pick up frequencies below the level of our senses. Do the rods themselves make contact with such energy? Probably not. But they offer visible proof that your body picks up information you don't normally consciously feel except through sudden bursts of intuition.

How do we learn to access that information?

Eventually I discovered that I could ask questions and receive "yes" or "no" answers. It was as if I was having a conversation with another person who could only respond (because of my primitive technology) with those two replies. A "yes" was when the rods crossed in my hands. A "no" was when they didn't move. (It's very similar to computer technology. You have access to all the information stored in the cloud, but that information comes to your laptop through one small circuit that is either open or closed—a zero or a one.)

For the sake of convenience, I began to call this intuited presence Gaia, meaning "Mother Earth." I practiced and practiced, specifically to ensure that I wasn't consciously moving my hands at all. I wanted to make sure I wasn't influencing the rods by even a subtle movement.

After many conversations, "Gaia" even caught on to my sense of humor. When I asked a facetious question, such as, "Are you putting me on?" or "Are you having trouble getting through my thick head?" one rod, the right one, would cross and the other stay still. The old commercial was right. "It's not nice to fool Mother Nature!" It was as if she knew I was kidding around and wanted to join the fun!

Through this kind of dowsing, and after much practice and confidence building, I discovered the existence of another Being (angel, spirit, metaphysical presence, source of intuitive understanding—you decide) whom I began to call "Sobuko," because that was the name that appeared in my head and simply would not go away. There were questions, some of them very personal, that Gaia wouldn't or couldn't answer. At those times I was pretty shocked when suddenly both rods would move emphatically to the right. I began to realize that another presence seemed to control them. After many tries, I discovered that our comfortable twosome was now a threesome. There was another presence at work.

Through many questions, I came to understand that Sobuko was none other than me—the "me" on the other side of the barrier that divides material life from what we call spiritual life. Words fall short, but I came to see "Sobuko" as what I called my "soul." I began to wonder if, when we come into this sphere of the material world, part of us remains behind, perhaps even acting in the role that Christians for two millennia have called our "Guardian Angel."

I have since learned that others have experienced this phenomenon. Some call it the "Higher Self."

All I know for sure is that when I hold dowsing rods in my hands, they seem to come alive with a vibrancy all their own. I have spent hours in "conversation" with these two entities. I have never, ever been stood up or forgotten by them. They are there no matter my mental state or physical condition. I can totally count on them.

Am I saying that two pieces of copper wire that make up my dowsing rods are sentient in themselves? No! Am I saying that independent beings from another dimension take over control of the rods in my hands? I don't think so.

So what's happening? I have come to believe that the rods offer a visible means to actually see what my body intuits. Our bodies are smarter than we are. Do small muscles I am unaware of actually move the rods? Maybe. But if that's the case, it proves that my body is receiving information of which I am consciously unaware. That's what intuition is.

Read again the definition that began this entry:

Intuition is a phenomenon in which we seem to suddenly know something without going through the process of acquiring any special knowledge.

If present theories in the field of quantum reality hold true, it might be that intuition has a basis in hard science after all.

MEDITATION AND EASTERN SPIRITUALITY

I went to the woods because I wished to live deliberately, to front only the essential facts of life, and see if I could not learn what it had to teach, and not, when I came to die, discover that I had not lived. I did not wish to live what was not life, living is so dear; nor did I wish to practice resignation, unless it was quite necessary. I wanted to live deep and suck out all the marrow of life, to live so sturdily and Spartan-like as to put to rout all that was not life, to cut a broad swath and shave close, to drive life into a corner, and reduce it to its lowest terms....

—Henry David Thoreau, *Walden*

Over the last few years I've learned something about meditation. For most of my life I thought I pretty much had the exercise down pat. I was a clergyman who was used to spending time in prayer. If the clergy don't understand such things, who does?

What I've now learned is that I was kidding myself, just as most contemporary Americans and Europeans are probably deceiving themselves today.

Here's the simple truth. The lives we lead in the twenty-first century, filled with techno-gizmos, responsibilities, hard-charging business philosophies and, above all, television sets and light bulbs, isolate us from really deep spiritual meditation. Perhaps they even isolate us from authentic spiritual growth. We just don't realize it because the change happened so gradually.

A farmer out plowing his field used to be able to think uninterrupted thoughts for hours at a time. The same was true for his homebound wife who minded the chores and prepared dinner made from scratch all by herself. By the time that dinner was served, they both had plenty of things to talk about. They had been thinking about them all day long.

When was the last time you thought about something for hours at a time? I'll bet that even the thought of sitting alone in a room with nothing to occupy your mind and hands is a bit frightening. Perhaps it even fills you with dread. No laptop. No smartphone. No tunes. No TV. Not even a magazine. Try it sometime and see how long you last. You'll be surprised how difficult it is.

Yet this was the experience of most of humanity for most of the time we have been on earth—a period of millions of years. Is it any wonder we now suffer from stress-related diseases at an increasing rate and measure our concentration span growing shorter with each passing year?

Sitting quietly for a few minutes, even an hour or so, every morning does us some good. It's certainly better than nothing. But modern human beings are as far removed from real meditation as a lit-up city is removed from the darkness of an ancient stargazer's landscape.

ECKHART TOLLE AND *THE POWER OF NOW*

What does all this have to do with supernatural gods? Just this.

When Eckhart Tolle's book *The Power of Now* was touted on TV by popular talk show hostess Oprah Winfrey, it soon brought meditation and the principle of what Tolle calls *Presence* into the public mainstream. It has since benefited countless stressed-out people and made Tolle a household name in the field of spiritual development.

His principle thesis is that past and present are really an illusion. The idea that anything ever happened in the past or will happen in the future is false. Everything always happens *now*. Even the past and future are really memory streams that we experience now. They are accessed by our ego-centered minds. We, along with every other thing that exists, live in a constant state called *now*. There is no other reality.

Here's where things get really interesting. When we say "I" have a mind that contains memories of the past and dreams of the future, what we are saying is that there are two "I"s: one is the mind that lives in the past and future, and the other is the "I" that has that mind.

Which one is real?

The answer is obvious. The real "I" exists always in the eternal now. The other "I," the one who lives in past memories and future hopes, is our ego. The ego has a short shelf-life of seventy to eighty years or so. When our bodies "die," so does the ego.

Therein lies the problem. Like all living entities, the ego is afraid of the great unknown called death. It tries desperately to hang on to its identity, and, in the vast majority of cases, manages to announce its presence so resolutely that most of us totally identify with our ego rather than our eternal "be-ing."

The ego is the source of the chattering "monkey-brain" that fills our every waking moment. It constantly fills our lives with noise. Sit quietly for a few minutes and listen to it. You will be amazed at how it prattles on and on, switching subjects at the slightest opportunity, filling sleepless nights with fears and worries, and demanding its own brand of tribute. It wants more "stuff" to insure its importance. Then, if we get hold of that "stuff," it wants more. It wants to consume. Even worse, it wants to be "Number 1." It wants to prance around in the end zone of life, triumphantly spiking the football of materialism, showing off its importance and supposed superiority. Most of all it is filled with fear and dread. It knows its career is finite and it is terrified of no longer existing.

The German-born Canadian author Eckhart Tolle created a stir in popular culture with his book *The Power of Now.*

In most cases, hopefully, its whims can be tempered with practical good sense. In a few cases, it can be devastating. Witness the case of famous fallen celebrities whose ego was not satisfied with fame and fortune. Read about powerful politicians whose egos convinced them they were above laws that guided more well-adjusted folks. Think about respected clergy whose egos led them, along with the people they were supposed to guide, into a whole world of hurt.

Like any living organism, the ego wants to be fed. It wants to grow. It wants control and power over others and all things. Above all it wants to win—to triumph over others. That's the whole purpose of sports, isn't it? One person wins and holds up a single finger, pointing toward heaven. "I win! I'm number one! I'm better than you!" We've gone so far as to bring art, music, and even cooking, for heaven's sake, into the arena of competition. Some ego has to win. That means another has to lose. "Winning isn't everything," said the late Green Bay Packers coach Vince Lombardi. "It's the only thing!" And when the ego crosses the line so as to hurt, injure, punish, or cheat in its effort to achieve victory, it becomes demonic in nature.

Whoa! Hold on now! Did we just use the term "demonic?" That takes us into the realm of the supernatural. "Demons" are supernatural beings, aren't

Christian apologist and author C. S. Lewis (this is a statue of him in Belfast, Ireland) was famous for his "Chronicles of Narnia" fantasy series, which has strong Christian connotations.

they? They're right there along with gods and deities. All the religions of the world acknowledge their presence.

Now we come to the central point. We often think of supernatural beings as spooky ghosts, angels, spirits, and goblins with individual identities. Without realizing we are doing so, we thus trivialize the "demonic," reducing it to entities that we know don't really exist. Thus, the truly demonic disguises its identity. C. S. Lewis (1898–1963) once said that Satan's greatest trick was to convince the world he doesn't exist. How true it is.

Three paragraphs ago we talked about "unhealthy egos" using these words:

> Like any living organism, the ego wants to be fed. It wants to grow. It wants control and power over other and all things. Above all it wants to win—to triumph over others.

If you agreed with those words when you just read them in context, then you're treating your ego as an independent entity. That sounds suspiciously similar to what earlier generations called demons. And when we admit that our egos control us in unhealthy ways, then for all practical purposes we're talking about the same thing earlier generations called "demonic possession." Get rid of superstitious beliefs about fallen angels floating around looking for a home, seeking to do mischief. Think of it instead as a metaphor. It's the same thing. Earlier generations may have described it differently than we scientific-minded types, but it's the same phenomenon.

Once we accept that premise, we might as well say it. We live in a demon-possessed world. We create that world ourselves whenever we become possessed by our ego-driven tendencies. We are the source of the evil implied in those early doctrines. To paraphrase the old *Pogo* comic strip, "We have met the enemy and he is us!"

Is there a way out? Is there something we can do to bring things back into line and return our minds to their rightful place—valuable tools that help us negotiate in the ever-present now?

The answer, thankfully, is a resounding *yes!* But it takes intention, thought, and some hard work.

PUTTING THE NOW BACK IN LIFE

When my wife and I retired in 2009, we did so with an agenda. It was much the same as that of Henry David Thoreau, quoted above. We wanted to live deliberately. We went on retreat. Not for a weekend or even a month or two. We wanted to live that way for a period of years to see what would happen. Ignoring the modern academic theory preached by *AARP The Magazine* that retired people need to surround themselves with friends lest they get depressed, we decided to live away from the distraction other human beings might impose on us. Instead, we wanted to find God. We wanted to live in a state of meditation.

A newly retired minister's life can go in at least two different directions. I've talked to many, many colleagues in my position, and the bulk of them, it's safe to say, stay involved with the church in one way or another. Most seem to relish supply preaching and being involved with a local church in a way that assures continuity of the familiar but without much responsibility. This course allows you some respect, the opportunity to serve, and the benefit of being considered a kind of consultant. You get to attend the local ministerial luncheons, and it gives plenty of opportunity to stay in touch with what's happening while earning a small but appreciated income in retirement. It's a nice life and sometimes even leads to the chance for that great retired-ministerial plum job—a part-time position with few responsibilities in which you keep a church together while they search for a new pastor. If the church folks like you, you get to stay for a while as they drag their feet and stall the process as long as possible because no one usually complains about a pastor who doesn't make waves, is pleasant, and won't be around too long.

That was not the direction I took. For me, ministry has always been about spiritual growth. I wanted to experience God. Notice the word "experience." I'm not talking about "knowing about," "studying," or "reading up on." To me, if God is real, then spiritual peek-a-boo just won't cut it. I see no sense in a God who created humans "in His image" and then left them to fend for themselves, without any visible, or even invisible, means of support.

Because of my passion—sometimes I've even been forced to call it an obsession—religion has never been really satisfying for me. God was only exciting when I was learning something new, and I never found one way of thinking or practicing religion that explained and neatly codified all that could be known about God. I've run the gamut. After a full-blown fundamentalist conversion, I served time as an Evangelical, a Charismatic, a main-line conservative, and a flaming liberal. I've studied Zen Buddhism, Hinduism, Daoism, various Indian religions, philosophy, and New Age spiritualities. I've meditated, mediated, illuminated, contemplated, and postulated. I've taught more seminars that I can possibly remember, written nine books, and been a college professor, teaching courses in the fields of comparative religion and cross-cultural studies. I've preached more than six thousand sermons, led Bible studies, and hosted a drive-time radio program called the "Through the Bible Series."

After all this, you would think a person would have the sense to call himself an expert and retire into a life of contentment and pleasure. "Lord, now lettest Thou Thy servant depart in peace."

But it didn't work that way. I never intended to give God a rest. Like Jacob of old, I wrestled with God my whole life, saying, "I will not let you go until you bless me!"

(Writing these words recalls a powerful experience that I need to share because it vividly illustrates how the universe conspires to meet us halfway on our journey toward spiritual growth. A few years ago, I was invited to speak in Cornwall. While in England, I fulfilled a cherished dream to visit a small church in Fenny Compton where my ancestors, clergy associated with the Church of England, used to preach. I had a chance to stand in the pulpit, look out at the same sanctuary that greeted them on Sabbath mornings, and think

about what kind of people they were. I wondered if they ever thought about a possible descendant who turned out to be me. Then, while exploring the stained glass windows familiar to my ancestors, ones they saw each and every Sunday morning, I came across a theme I had never before seen portayed in this medium. It was a picture of Jacob, wrestling with God. Beneath it were the words, "There wrestled a man with him." It was a depiction of the same scripture verse that has influenced so much of my life. And my ancestors saw it each and every week. I admit it. I broke down and cried.)

They say confession is good for the soul, so I have a confession to make. I've never found anyone who I consider to be a saint, in the general sense of the word. Catholics elevate people to sainthood, and the theology of Protestantism considers all Christians to be saints, but that's not how I'm using the word here. What I mean is that

Jim Willis checks out the pulpit at Fenny Compton. although I've met many, many people who claim they have figured it all out—many, many people who say they know "the way"—none of them have ever stood up to close scrutiny. Without exception, they have not experienced God in the way I was looking for. I wasn't seeking some idealized hope based on prayer and coincidence or a reasoned explanation about why we must "live by faith and not by sight." I wanted to experience the Holy. If God could condescend to speak to Abraham, Jacob, and Isaac, I figured God ought to be able to talk to me as well. If the book of Acts is to be believed, God appeared to Paul and knocked him right off his horse!

Don't talk to me, now, about how Paul was special because he was a saint. When he met the one whom he considered to be the resurrected Jesus, Paul was a well-educated Jewish fundamentalist, a murderer, and a persecutor of Christians. I'm no saint, but I've never had anyone thrown in jail because of their religion!

No, I think we've all been fed a line about false humility to insure one of the best-kept ecclesiastical cover-ups of all times, which is, to wit: because our church leaders, for the most part, have seldom experienced the Holy outside of accepted settings, we've been told that no one should. Such a desire, it is implied, reeks of ego and hubris. In other times, such experiences were even called heresy.

But if we are "made in God's image," as the Bible says, then we are one of the hottest commodities in the universe! Why, in heaven's name, wouldn't God want to us to experience the divine any way we can?

I know, I know. "All we, like sheep, have gone astray." There's that whole matter of sin that separates us from God. But Christianity, at least, postulates the ultimate in forgiveness. The sacrifice of the cross has, according to every Christian denomination, "removed our sin from us as far as the east is from the west." So if sin can't separate us from the Holy, then what, in God's name, can? And besides all that, why is it sinful to seek an experience of the presence of God? Even Paul, that old converted scoundrel, stated this firmly in the book of Romans: "I am convinced ['convinced,' he said!] that nothing can separate us from the love of God in Christ."

"Okay," you say, "Paul was talking about the 'love' of God. He didn't mean we could ever really experience the Presence."

And why do you say that? Because if you ever *do* experience God's presence you're going to make two thousand years of church leaders who *haven't* experienced it look pretty foolish.

So we're stuck with the ultimate leveler: "Who do you think you are that somehow *you* should have an experience with God that even Rev. So-and-So has never had? What colossal ego!"

Well, ego or not, I just didn't buy that argument anymore.

All this is to say I retired with that agenda I mentioned a while back. "Okay God, it's You and me. No church structures. No restrictions. No theology. No holds barred. Twenty-four hours a day. You are my only passion. You say you like a challenge? Bring it on!" Like Jacob of old who wrestled with God, I had one prayer on my lips: *"I will not let you go until you bless me!"*

Imagine my surprise when God answered and did just that!

Beginnings

I guess that last sentence needs some explaining. When I retired to the woods, I wasn't exactly sure how to go about my task of experiencing the Holy. I mean, short of the angel Gabriel appearing with trumpet in hand, how can God actually communicate with you? You can get impressions while deep in prayer. You can have coincidences happen. Once, for instance, when I was really strapped for cash I prayed for money and got a check in the mail the next day. Stuff like that happens and for most people, I suppose, that's sufficient. But not for me. It's just too subjective. I wanted something I could see and touch.

The traditional concept of a white-bearded, human-looking God is a personalized vision of the Supreme Being that is unlikely to be anything like the truth.

There's also another problem. By the time I retired, I had long given up on the concept of God that postulates a "Being" somehow separate and distinct from me. I don't picture God as an old man sitting on a cloud, watching with interest what goes on down here on planet Earth, perhaps even wringing "His" hands in worry and fret about the state of the human race. To me, God simply is not that personal. If that's what it takes for some people to try to wrap their minds around a concept of God, far be it from me to argue. But for me it just won't work. The only way I can think about God that makes sense is to think in terms of a cosmic, infinite Consciousness, an eternal Other that is beyond words and even ideas. This is a classic Hindu idea. *Brahma*, "God," is beyond language or even categories of thought. If you try to describe it, you have, by definition, fallen short.

(I once gave a mid-term exam to a college class in comparative religion. In it, I asked for a short, one-paragraph explanation of the Hindu concept of God. One of my students left that question blank and I graded him down accordingly. When I passed back the papers the following week, he was grinning at me like a Cheshire cat. "Professor Willis," he said, "did everyone answer question three?" "Well, they at least tried," I replied. "Then you're telling me that I was the only one in class to get it right!" I had to revise his grade and give him full credit for turning in a blank piece of paper!)

New England Indian tribes had a concept that goes something like this. They called it *Kitchi Manitou*, or "Great Mystery." Other American tribes called it the "Creator." These are phrases that indicate a belief that the mystery of the Other preceded our feeble attempts to invent words that could capture it.

This is not to say that God isn't real or exists in a form somewhat like the Force in *Star Wars*. In our day, as we have already seen, quantum physicists are beginning to toy with the idea that what we call "mind" doesn't exist in our heads at all. It's more like a universal, connected reality. What we call "mind," our brain, is simply the hardware by which we interpret signals from this universal "Mind" that I call Akasha, Consciousness, or even God.

But the ancient writers understood that we are "made" in that Consciousness's image. We are not separate from it. Indeed, we are the very body, the manifested reality of that Consciousness within the material universe, which is also, itself, a manifestation of Consciousness. In other words, we are the first life form on planet Earth, as far as we know, to be able to contemplate its existence or even the possibility of universal Consciousness at all.

Seen in this fashion, our evolution constitutes the shaping of the Divine within the framework of time and space. Doesn't ignoring such a supernatural possibility due to trivial pursuits involving smartphones and TV sets sound a bit selfish and silly?

Seeking Stability

In the first month of the year 2012, I lost my stability. I had been troubled by epileptic seizures for a few years. They had begun, to the best of my recollection, when I lived in Florida, sometime during the years between 2006 and 2009, probably brought on by stress. These were the years I first began to think in terms of vibrational energies separating alternate dimensions.

Epilepsy has been called, since the time of Aristotle, the "spiritual sickness" because people who have epileptic seizures sometimes experience visions and what are usually called hallucinations. Indeed, MRI studies show that what is often called the "shamanic experience" and the OBE experience affect the same portion of the brain that is lit up during epileptic seizures.

There was no question in my mind that my seizures happened more often, and were of greater intensity, when I had been visiting our land in

South Carolina for a while. I could count on them whenever we left to drive back to Florida. After moving up here full time to live on that land, they worsened, culminating in an incident in which I got a speck of wood in my eye while doing some chainsaw work. While Barb drove me to an eye doctor, I had the first episodes of what I assume were grand mal seizures—very severe. As they continued during the next year, a few of them were accompanied by impressions of lights, tunnels, and even, one time, people of light standing off to one side.

I did a lot of Internet research. I was afraid to take meds or even see a doctor. My feeling was, strange and egotistical as it may sound, that there was a good possibility that the seizures were happening for a reason. By then I was flirting with out-of-body experiences, which are usually accompanied by a vibrational phase. I felt that they might be opening up a section of my brain that I, through a lifetime of left-brain, analytical, religious, and systematic theological thought, might have, by habit and misuse, allowed to atrophy.

Now I began to think that this was a shortcoming that needed to be adjusted. Were the seizures my way of opening up the very connections in my brain that I would need in order to be responsive to voices from the other side of what I, up to now, had called "reality?"

In other words, I was afraid that if I chemically closed the door to the "bad guys" of epileptic seizures, I might also be closing the door to the "good guys" of spiritual voices.

That being said, I began to make some allowances. Barb took over most of the driving, and I was very careful. But otherwise I adopted a wait-and-see approach.

> **E**pilepsy has been called, since the time of Aristotle, the "spiritual sickness" because people who have epileptic seizures sometimes experience visions and what are usually called hallucinations.

During the second week of January, I had a vicious epileptic seizure that knocked me right off my feet. The results of the seizure itself quickly passed, but in falling down, I severely hurt my ankle. Although I never had an X-ray done, I think I must have cracked a bone or two. At the very least I sprained, pulled, or tore some ligaments and tendons. As late as August of that year, the ankle was still swollen and tender. My other Achilles heel, the left one, was also quite painful. Walking was very difficult. Running and biking were, of course, impossible. I was forced to spend months at a time, especially during January and February, off my feet, moving only with a cane or walking stick while wearing ankle braces on both feet.

Suffice it to say that circumstances forced me into a quiet, contemplative life. It had certainly been a year of "instability" in that regard. But the instability manifested itself in other ways. For the first time in my life, I began to understand what real meditation was.

There is no such thing as coincidence. Timing is as magical as the event itself.

Back to the Subject

This lengthy personal detour has a purpose. I want to really bring home the fact that many of us don't fully understand what real Eastern spirituality, expressed through the art of meditation, is all about. It is not simply an exercise. It is a discipline. A life-long discipline. A difficult discipline. A profound discipline. A life-transforming discipline.

When we enter into it with our full consciousness and give it the time and energy it requires, we discover that it is not an individual, solitary discipline after all. In meditation we eventually enter into a dialogue, a conversation with the supernatural—that which is greater than ourselves—a higher power. And the supernatural responds in ways that, in my case at least, knocked me off my feet and even took me all the way to England to illustrate its presence, going back generations, in my life and those who eventually produced me.

The Eastern mystics have understood the great mysteries of the universe for thousands of years. It has only been in the last few decades that Westerners such as Americans have begun to listen.

The supernatural is real. It does not reveal itself only in a diaphanous serendipity, although sometimes that happens. (We may call it coincidence, but deep down we know better.)

Here's the point. The Eastern mystics knew about this stuff thousands of years ago and have been practicing the "Presence" ever since. Their methods are now being Americanized, packaged for our convenience and shortened attention spans. They are popularized by famous people such as the Beatles, Richard Gere, and Shirley MacLaine. Yoga and martial arts studios can be found in most strip malls. Tai chi and qigong are a staple of morning television.

But the real masters are still those who have practiced their entire lives. They are the ones who come closest to the supernatural ideal. In many cases, we don't know who they are because it is an important part of their discipline to refrain from public demonstrations that can easily lead to ego-driven displays that impede real development. Usually we learn about them from their students. But they are there. They are in touch with a greater reality that most of us can barely imagine. And they are living proof that there is much more to reality than this materialistic world that occupies our every waking thought.

It takes effort and fortunate circumstances to escape the modern world, but I have discovered it is time and effort well spent. Perhaps if enough people begin to walk the walk instead of simply talking the talk, the world might actually change. Who knows?

MIRACLES

When the Pew Forum on Religion and Public Life asked thirty-five thousand Americans in 2007, "Do you believe in miracles?," a whopping 79 percent responded yes.... This tremendous faith in the miraculous—manifestations of the divine—gives incorrigible skeptics indigestion.

—Dean Radin, *Supernormal*

On December 12, 2012, Robert Wright wrote an article for the *New York Times* recalling a conversation he had with British evolutionary biologist W. D. Hamilton (1936–2000), a researcher and original thinker famous for his views that led to a modern Darwinian theory involving social biology. Hamilton was a darling of the traditional establishment and was venerated by such stalwart defenders of materialism and atheism as the infamous Richard Dawkins (1942–), who paid tribute to him in his book *The Selfish Gene*, written back in 1976. One would not expect Hamilton to wax eloquent philosophically about such things as miracles. He was considered a paragon of traditional scholarship.

That's why Wright was so surprised to hear Hamilton say, "I'm quite open to the view that there is some kind of ultimate good which is of a religious nature—that we just have to look beyond what the evolutionary theory tells us and accept promptings of what ultimate good is, coming from some other source."

Hardly believing what he was hearing, considering the source, Wright quoted Hamilton further. He asked Hamilton to expound on what he had just said. Here is Hamilton's response:

I could enlarge on that in terms of the possible existence of extraterrestrial manipulators who interfere, and so on. There's one theory of the universe that I rather like—I accept it in an almost joking spirit—and that is that Planet Earth in our solar system is a kind of zoo for extraterrestrial beings who dwell out there somewhere. And this is the best, the most interesting experiment they could set up: to set the evolution on Planet Earth going in such a way that it would produce these really interesting characters—humans who go around doing things—and they watch their experiment, interfering hardly at all, so that everything we humans do comes out according to the laws of nature. But every now and then they see something which doesn't look quite right—this zoo is going to kill itself off if they let you do this or that. These extraterrestrials then insert a finger and just change some little thing. And maybe those are the miracles which the religious people like to so emphasize. I put it forward in an almost joking spirit. But I think it's a kind of hypothesis that's very, very hard to dismiss.

Wright begins to speculate:

If you wanted to capture the philosophical significance of what Hamilton was saying, you'd take another tack. Rather than focus on miracles, you'd focus on the idea of "higher purpose"—the idea that there's some point to life on earth that emanates from something that is in some sense beyond it.

He goes on to list four common misperceptions found in what he calls "the scientifically minded community."

The First Myth

To say that there's in some sense a "higher purpose" means there are "spooky forces" at work.

You may consider aliens spooky, but they're not a spooky *force*. And they're not supernatural beings. They're just physical beings like us. Their technology is so advanced that their interventions might seem miraculous to us—as various smartphone apps would seem to my great-great-grandparents—but these interventions would in fact comply with the laws of science.

More to the point: If you ask how Hamilton's aliens had initially imparted "purpose" to life, the answer is that they did so in concrete fashion: by planting simple, self-replicating material on earth a few billion years ago, confident that it would lead to something that would keep them entertained (keeping them entertained being, in this scenario, life's purpose).

The Second Myth

To say that evolution has a purpose is to say that it is driven by something other than natural selection.

The correction of this misconception is in some ways just a corollary of the correction of the first misconception, but it's worth spelling out: evolution can have a purpose even if it is a wholly mechanical, material process—that is, even if its sole engine is natural selection. After all, clocks have purposes—to keep time, a purpose imparted by clockmakers—and they're wholly mechanical. Of course, to suggest that evolution involves the unfolding of some purpose is to suggest that evolution has, in some sense, been *heading somewhere*—namely, toward the realization of its purpose.

The Third Myth

Evolution couldn't have a purpose, because it doesn't have a direction.

The idea that evolution is fundamentally directionless is widespread, in part because one great popularizer of evolution, Stephen Jay Gould (1941–2002), worked hard to leave that impression. Gould was, at best, misleading on this point. He admitted that on balance evolution tends to create beings of greater and greater complexity. A number of evolutionary biologists would go further and say that evolution was likely, given long enough, to create animals as intelligent as us.

In fact, that idea is implicit in Hamilton's saying the aliens could have "set up" evolution in such a way that "it would produce these really interesting characters—humans." This part of Hamilton's scenario requires no intervention on the part of the aliens, because he believed that evolution by natural selection has a kind of direction in the sense that it is likely, given long enough, to produce very intelligent forms of life. (When speaking more precisely, as he did in other parts of the interview, Hamilton would say that the human species per se wasn't in the cards—that it wasn't inevitable that the first intelligent species would look like us.)

A UFO might seem like a supernatural phenomenon, but it is simply technology that is so advanced compared to our own that it appears miraculous and unnatural by comparison.

The Fourth Myth

If evolution has a purpose, the purpose must have been imbued by an intelligent being.

That said, one interesting feature of current discourse is a growing openness among some scientifically minded people to the possibility that our world has a purpose that was imparted by an intelligent being. I'm referring to "simulation" scenarios, which hold that our seemingly tangible world is actually a kind of projection emanating from some sort of mind-blowingly powerful computer; and the history of our universe, including evolution on this planet, is the unfolding of a computer algorithm whose author must be pretty bright.

(The above is paraphrased from the *New York Times* on December 12, 2012, written by Robert Wright.)

Wright's hypothesis is fascinating because it includes both a modern, scientific understanding *and* a place for what we consider to be the miraculous.

What is a miracle, anyway, but that which appears to be a supernatural intervention into our normal affairs? If the Pew Forum on Religion and Public Life is to be believed, 79 percent of Americans believe in miracles. That's a substantial number. Why would that many people believe in miracles if they hadn't experienced such things? It makes us wonder. Is there a possibility that supernatural beings, or supernatural forces, poke through our material atmosphere from time to time and, for reasons beyond our comprehension, perform what we refer to as miracles? If so, why? Why sometimes and not others? Why do some people experience healings, for instance, while others don't? Who gets to be the recipient of a supernatural intervention? Are some people being rewarded and others punished? Do supernatural entities have the ability to "know when you are sleeping and know when you're awake" … to "know when you've been bad or good, so be good for goodness' sake!"?

These questions are not frivolous. They deserve answers. But no answers can be forthcoming unless we first believe miracles actually take place. So we are left with a circular reasoning pattern. There's no sense looking specifically into reasons for miracles unless they are real. But the proof of their reality is to be found in understanding why they occur.

No wonder the subject is fraught with such subjective emotion!

WILLIS HARMAN'S WORLD VIEWS

When Willis Harman (1918–1997) was the president of the Institute of Noetic Sciences, founded by former astronaut Edgar Mitchell (1930–2016) in 1973, he wrote a book called *Global Mind Change: The Promise of the 21st Century*. In it he outlined three different world views held today.

- The first is what he called *Materialistic monism*. This is the view held by most Western scientists today—that everything is made of matter and energy, even the mind. Those who hold this worldview simply do not believe in supernatural forces and, of course, miracles.

- The second is what he called *dualism*. This is the view that recognizes two fundamentally different kinds of substance in the universe—matter and mind. It is a fundamental doctrine of many religious institutions: heaven and earth, God and humanity, above and below, spirit and matter.

- The third view is the one Harman believes is emerging today. He called it *idealism*. In this view, consciousness is primary. It is the Source. Matter and energy proceed from this Source. Humanity, having originated there, is evolving back to it in a mature, intellectual fashion. When Jesus, for instance, said, "I am the alpha and omega,

Former astronaut Edgar Mitchell founded the parapsychological research facility known as the Institute of Noetic Sciences.

the beginning and the end," he was referring to the fact that the supernatural, God, is both our source and our destination."

If Harman is right, if humanity is in the process of beginning to intellectually understand what the mystics have intuited for ages, then it might be that miracles represent the breaking forth into the material world of a greater reality. They might even be considered "tweaks" to the systematic, mechanical workings of forces we now understand to be true, including evolution.

This doesn't answer the basic question of "why," of course. Why do miracles happen to some and not to others? Why are some people healed and others die? Why are some accidents prevented and not others? Why are some people gifted with a miracle while others suffer?

The truth is that we just don't know. But if answers are to be found we first have to admit that miracles might happen. That's a very big step. Perhaps it is time to seriously consider their reality so as to begin the process of figuring them out.

In Dean Radin's book *Supernormal*, he speculates about just such a step:

Perhaps this transformation is precisely what the mystics have been preparing us for so diligently. Maybe the experiences of (the miraculous) are seen as ineffable and mysterious not just because we don't have the language to talk about them yet, but because if we really understood these concepts, it would change everything.

Amen to that!

OUT-OF-BODY EXPERIENCES AND NEAR-DEATH EXPERIENCES

> The most beautiful experience we can have is the mysterious. It is the fundamental emotion which stands at the cradle of true art and true science. Whoever does not know it and can no longer wonder, no longer marvel, is as good as dead, and his eyes are dimmed.
>
> —Albert Einstein

In 1975, Dr. Raymond Moody (1944–) wrote what soon became a perennial best-selling book. It was called *Life After Life* and chronicled what he claimed were the near-death experiences (NDEs) of patient after patient who had, according to his meticulous medical documentation, died and come back to tell about it. Other books had presented similar claims, but this one caught the public's attention like no other. What made Moody's work so compelling, aside from the spectacular stories and his inviting writing style, was his rigorous use of medical procedures and scientific protocols. It challenged the world views of even the most skeptical critics.

Life after Life found a recurring pattern of shared experiences by patients from different countries, death situations, religions, walks of life, and ages:

1. A *buzzing* or *ringing* sound that appeared to originate outside the realty of the patient.

2. *Peace and painlessness.* The patients may have experienced pain while dying, but after they left their bodies the pain vanished. They almost always used words such as "peace" and "loving acceptance" to describe how they felt.

3. *Out-of-body-experience* (OBE). They felt as if they "left" their bodies and usually described seeing themselves, along with accurate descriptions of sometimes frantic activity by medical professionals working to resuscitate them.

4. A *tunnel*. Patients universally described a sort of tunnel of light through which they passed. Alternatively, some described the experience as a rapid upward rising toward a bright light.

5. The appearance of a *being of light*. The being was usually described as God, Jesus, or another religious figure who appeared to comfort them.

6. *Life review*. The being of light conducted an entire life review with the patient. Virtually everything of meaning flashed before their eyes and they somehow understood why they did what they did and how the experience fit in to their overall life journey. This review was never accompanied by judgment or condemnation. Indeed, the word most frequently used to describe the experience was "love." (Note: This is a very common experience. Its universality is evidenced by the phrase, "My life flashed before my eyes," in any joke about a supposed brush with death.)

7. *Reluctance to return*. When patients were told they must return to their bodies, they almost always said they preferred to stay. The experiences were universally positive. People came back changed. They may not have become "religious" in the sense that they immediately joined a religious institution, but they described themselves as spiritual and found themselves to be no longer afraid of death.

This is just one example from Dr. Moody's book *Life After Life*:

I knew I was dying and that there was nothing I could do about it, because no one could hear me.... I was out of my body, there's no doubt about it, because I could see my own body there on the operating room table. My soul was out! All this made me feel very bad at first, but then, this really bright light came. It did seem that it was a little dim at first, but then it was this huge beam. It was just a tremendous amount of light, nothing like a big bright flashlight, it was just too much light. And it gave off heat to me; I felt a warm sensation.

It was a bright yellowish white—more white. It was tremendously bright; I just can't describe it. It seemed that it covered everything, yet it didn't prevent me from seeing everything around me—the operating room, the doctors and nurses, everything. I could see clearly, and it wasn't blinding.

At first, when the light came, I wasn't sure what was happening, but then, it asked, it kind of asked me if I was ready to die. It was like talking to a person, but a person wasn't there. The light's what was talking to me, but in a voice.

Now, I think that the voice that was talking to me actually realized that I wasn't ready to die. You know, it was just kind of testing me more than anything else. Yet, from the moment the light spoke to me, I felt really good—secure and loved. The love which came from it is just unimaginable, indescribable. It was a fun person to be with! And it had a sense of humor, too—definitely!

Although many critics attacked the book as subjective and emotional, the public embraced it with open arms. Indeed, it soon became apparent that those who liked it were "believers" and those who didn't, weren't. In other words, people tended to be grouped on either side of the issue not by

Traveling through a tunnel and seeing a being of light are two common experiences reported by those who have been technically deceased before being brought back.

the facts Moody mustered, but by their ingrained Faith Statement or worldview. Once again, people believed what they wanted to believe despite, or in some cases because of, the research. This seems to be a recurring truth of human nature.

Moody described incident after incident of people seeing details of an operating room from a position of height. They talked about seeing details outside the room that they couldn't possibly have seen from the operating table, in some cases even describing objects such as shoes discarded on the roof of the hospital. They undoubtedly were moved by their experience.

The universality of the experiences shared by witnesses who could not possibly have corroborated their stories was amazing. But many experts still refused to accept the findings. It appears, these many years later, that unless a person actually experiences an NDE or OBE, it is difficult to believe such things occur. But once a person does have such an experience, no amount of argument can convince them it wasn't real.

JOURNEYS OUT OF THE BODY

In 1971, four years before Raymond Moody's book was published, Robert Monroe (1915–1995) wrote *Journeys Out of the Body*. In it, he documented his experiences traveling out of body without the inconvenience of dying first. He was the one who is credited with coining the term "out-of-body experience," or OBE. Up until then, the experience was usually referred to as "astral travel."

Just as was the case with Moody, many critics attacked the book, sometimes viciously, almost always with an attempt at what they probably considered to be humorous scorn.

But many others were not amused. Indeed, even the U.S. military became interested in his work.

Bob Monroe was anything but the kind of man one would expect to be interested in what is often called the paranormal. Up until the 1950s, he was a radio broadcasting executive. While experimenting with various radio frequencies and their effect on sleep patterns, he discovered and patented what he later called Hemi-Sync, an audio method of arranging sound frequencies to synchronize and coordinate the left and right hemispheres of the brain. The results of his discovery were so startling that at first he was reluctant to share it with anyone, lest he damage his mainstream professional reputation.

Eventually, after experimenting first on himself and then a carefully selected few trusted friends, he compiled enough evidence to write *Journeys Out of the Body*. The book became an underground hit but soon was discovered by the mainstream, changing Monroe's life. Two more books were to follow, along with the creation of The Monroe Institute (TMI), the purpose of

Out-of-body experiences allow us to voyage into other realities, the world of the supernatural.

which is to explore and test, within scientific guidelines, the whole area of human consciousness. Located in Charlottesville, Virginia, thousands of people enroll in various workshops held at the campus and satellite locations around the world, to experience the core Gateway Program, developed to be the entrance into the study of consciousness. "You are more than your body," Bob would teach. His emphasis on the state of watchful consciousness, described, in his words, as "Mind awake, body asleep," is attested to by the thousands of people who have undertaken the discipline of a week under the trained tutelage of competent instructors.

The training earned enough respect that in 1978 Monroe was approached by F. Holmes "Skip" Atwater, who was at the time engaged in a secret military program designed to study remote viewing as a possibility of infiltrating enemy spy networks and activity. Skip, after retiring from the army, became a frequent teacher and lecturer on the subject at the Monroe Institute, in films and around the world. His book *Captain of My Ship, Master of My Soul* details his years in the field.

What countless thousands of people have since discovered through personal experience is that it is, indeed, possible to separate from the body and experience other realities—the *super*natural.

From time to time in this book, I have resorted to personal experience because, as we have often seen, only personal experience can convince many of us that there is validity to such things. This is another of those times. Like many who may read this book, I spent most of my life wanting to believe there was an extra dimension to life that I was not personally experiencing. I believed, I suppose, but didn't know. There is a world of difference!

In 2012 I decided to enroll in a week-long seminar taught by William Buhlman and held at the Monroe Institute. Bill's book, *Adventures Beyond the Body*, had held me captivated through at least two readings and I wanted to meet him in person.

In preparation for the seminar I again read his book, along with two by Bob Monroe and one by Skip Atwater. I decided to try some of Bill's methods, even though I very much doubted I would experience any results. Bill had said it would take devoting twenty to thirty minutes a day for at least thirty days to see any results. That seemed like an ambitious goal, but I decided to try.

After three weeks I was getting discouraged. Nothing much had happened, although I seemed to have more dream recall than normal. Following his instructions, I kept a meticulous journal outlining any progress. In my case, so far, it was lack of progress.

Then, in the midst of my skeptical but devoted practice, something happened that would change my life. I present it here, edited only for length but otherwise untouched, from my journal.

August 16, 2012

Was it an OBE or did I imagine it? Here's what happened. I was meditating, guided by Bill Buhlman's CD *Affirmations*.

I was trying to picture myself leaving my body, but my mind, as usual, was jumping around.

First I tried to imagine my astral body leaving my physical body. I tried to bring on the vibrational state Buhlman talks about—all the things I usually tried to do. I affirmed that I was a multidimensional being, capable of moving between dimensions. All the usual stuff. I was getting frustrated. Nothing was happening.

Then, for just a minute, something does happen. I feel myself drawn backwards, away from my body. The feeling of motion is very obvious. I feel vibrations throughout my body and am aware of the taste behind my teeth that I get when I have a severe epilepsy surge.

(If it is, indeed, epilepsy. I'm beginning to think it's not—or at least that epilepsy might be connected to OBEs.)

Suddenly, completely unbidden, I picture myself as a twenty-year-old. I look just the same as I used to look and I feel strong and athletic. I have full awareness of this image and play with it a minute, knowing that I hadn't planned for this and wondering if this is, indeed, an OBE. I think for a moment that if I could talk to this kid, he would make different choices and live a different life.

> **S**uddenly, completely unbidden, I picture myself as a twenty-year-old. I look just the same as I used to look and I feel strong and athletic.

Then I start to fly (not really "fly," but it's the only word that works. "Zoom" might be better) towards the sun. My hands are at my side and I'm moving through space towards a bright light. I'm not at all worried. I want to plunge into the sun because I feel that if I do, it will burn away all my guilt, worries, and fears, leaving only the pure essence of the real me. I look forward to it, but before I get there I awake with a full bladder. (The curse of old age!) I feel very heavy, and have to wait awhile before I can get up out of the chair.

Well, what's the verdict? Was this indeed an OBE? If it was, it was not what I expected. Here are the positives and negatives.

Positive: I never intended to picture myself as a twenty-year-old kid in the prime of life. That was totally unexpected. Also unexpected was the feeling of being drawn backwards away from my body. That has happened once before, but not as pronounced as this. The part about talking to my younger self and changing my life was the farthest thing from my mind.

The part about the sun journey may have been suggested by the previous Buhlman teaching. He mentioned a technique for changing Karma and removing fears and blocks and said that some people experience it as a furnace, or being devoured by a large animal or beast. But the sun seems to have been my idea.

Also, the taste behind my teeth intrigues me. I've experienced it during some *petit mal* seizures, but this was most definitely not a seizure.

Negative: I can honestly say that, except for brief seconds here and there, I was always conscious of being in my chair and was almost always trying to decide if this was real or imaginary. It wouldn't take much to convince me that I imagined the whole thing, but that just doesn't *feel* right. I guess only time and practice will tell. At least I'm encouraged.

August 24, 2012

It's 6:00 in the morning and even as I write these words I am beginning to doubt that what happened did, indeed, happen. But I knew that would be the case. I even laughed at it as I reminded myself that I would think this way when I got back. But as the images begin to fade, and with full knowledge that words will be insufficient, here goes....

At 4:30 in the morning I am wide awake, having slept through the night without having to get up once. I decide to go into the living room, recline in my chair, and turn on Hemi-Sync meditation music. I'm really not expecting anything except a quiet time. Rocky, our faithful dog, comes in and begins his licking routine, which can be pretty distracting. Besides that, I've been so discouraged lately about being close but not quite able to get out of my body, that I've been tempted to quit for a while, rather than develop a habit of failure. I try to envision some of Bill Buhlman's techniques but, as usual, my mind is everywhere and I'm finding it difficult to concentrate. Then I realize a half hour has gone by. I know this because the CD starts over. It's a half-hour long. It skips a little at the beginning and I wonder if it has a scratch on it.

But then my mental image suddenly changes.

I'm lying on a mesh, rope-type hammock, very relaxed. My body has turned into something resembling butterfat and is oozing down through the rope mesh.

I'm lying on a mesh, rope-type hammock, very relaxed. My body has turned into something resembling butterfat and is oozing down through the rope mesh. It's being strained, you might say. As the body melts down through the mesh, what is left in the hammock is a bunch of tiny points of light. They have no form to speak of, but they are clumped together. I guess the only image that comes close is to picture a school of fish, all swimming together—individuals, but collectively whole. I realize that I'm outside the school, watching it, but that somehow the lights are really me—my spiritual essence—my reality. With that thought I decide to unite my mind, on the outside, with the lights. I feel as if that's where it really belongs. Suddenly the lights come alive as one. We zoom off the hammock and begin to move.

Without shock or concern, I realize I'm out of my body. I experience no random thoughts, no distractions. But at the same time, I am somehow amused. I realize that I will soon return to my body and try to convince myself that this is nothing other than self-hypnosis or some such thing. I move over to Barb, asleep in the next room, and try to give her a message, telling her to "remind me, when I get back, that this really happened." I find the whole thing to be slightly amusing, or ironic, in a patronizing way, as if *this* is the reality, but that poor, ignorant guy in the chair will soon think he is the reality. With a sigh, much like a parent feels about the impossibility of correcting a wayward child, I move on.

First stop is our gazebo. I'm there in an instant, and am aware that it is surrounded by a tornado-like energy vortex. I can reach out and touch the sides, much like as in the movie *Surf's Up,* when the surfers ride the tube and touch the water at their side. But as powerful as this is, it's only a kind of refueling stop. The main event is our Medicine Wheel, down in the valley below the Gazebo, and as soon as I think about it, I'm there. Its vortex is shaped a little different than I imagined it. It looks kind of like a chimenea. There is a round, bulbous-shaped area near the ground, and then it swirls into a kind of chimney at the top, much like the spires on Russian churches. There I meet a "being" who is more like a pillar, or tube, of light. He seems bright and, in contrast, I seem dark. [I guess anything would appear dark next to that light.] I now seem to be watching from the outside, although taking part at the same time. Light and dark, the being and I, kind of swirl together, mingling. Soon we will shoot out the top of the vortex together—but we don't. I really want to go. What's out there? What will I see?

But we stay within the confines of the Medicine Wheel vortex. I try, but to no avail. Then I'm back at the house. I'm aware of my body in the chair and try to reenter a few times, but each time I find an excuse to linger. I really don't want to go back and I fight the impulse. One of the things that makes me stay out is the sure and certain knowledge that I will soon find a perfectly good Freudian explanation for this whole experience. All I can do is shake my head and feel sorry for the poor chap in the chair who will be so hard to convince.

Finally, I enter partway into my body in the chair, but I feel as though my body is somehow lopsided. If asked where the center was located, I would have to say about two feet outside on the right. It's as though all the water had sloshed over to my right side. I finally get up out of the chair and go in to tell Barb about this. It takes a while to readjust. Finally I decide to write this up quickly, before it fades.

After all, it's probably just a case of self-hypnosis, right? The whole thing happened in my head.

On the other hand, I'm reminded of that wonderful line Dumbledore says to Harry Potter after Harry's NDE near the end of the final book. Harry wants to know if all this is real or if it is just happening in his head. The old wizard replies, "Of course it's just happening in your head ... but why on earth should that mean that it is not real?"

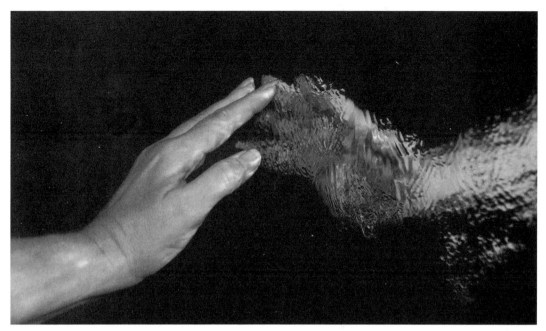

When reaching into other realities, it is extraordinary how the other side can feel more real than the world we call reality.

What are my overall impressions?

- I didn't experience any vibration state that I was aware of.

- Most of the time I was conscious of being in my body, but out of it at the same time. Strange.

- I have never experienced such focus, without distraction, for that long a time. The experience took almost half an hour, because the CD started up the second time and ended. It's at least twenty-five minutes long. I wasn't aware of the passing of time at all.

- I have the impression that I was feeling a need to return, as if vacation was over but I didn't want it to end. Both the feeling of needing to get back and the feeling of wanting to stay were very real.

- I never "saw" my body from outside, but I was aware of it. It was almost as if I was in two places at once. On the other hand, I definitely "saw" my body at the Medicine Wheel with the being of light. Again, I saw it from the outside and yet I felt as though I were there. I suppose if anyone could have come up to me and asked where "I" was, I would have said, "Right here in my chair." But I definitely felt as though I were down at the Medicine Wheel or present in the next room with Barb.

- The overall feeling was one of peace, yet at the same time, determination to explore.

- Somehow it feels like this was a watershed moment in my life. There have been a few of those in the past, but I wasn't able to articulate them, or in some cases even recognize them, until later. With this one, I know.

I have the feeling there will be more to follow.

BACK TO THIS REALITY

I don't make any claims that what I just described was an unusual or somehow special event. I am not, by any means, as experienced as others who work in this field. I have since talked to many people whose first OBE was quite different, and others whose descriptions were much the same, in general, as mine. When I attended a workshop at the Monroe Institute the following month, I heard story after story. Some of them resonated with me. A few of them left me doubtful. Like any group of highly charged New Agers, it was sometimes hard to separate the wheat from the chaff. As a matter of fact, on any given day, I have a hard time believing it really happened myself, even though since then I have had numerous "out-of-body" trips. While they are occurring, they feel profoundly real. I am convinced, usually, that I am not simply practicing an exotic type of self-hypnosis. I am much too honest with myself to allow that to happen and don't have the imagination needed to concoct some of the "right out of left field" stuff that has happened.

Every time I feel a very definite shift in consciousness that alerts me to the fact that something is happening, I become very alert to any possibility that I'm playing head games. Instead, I become quite the skeptic, trying not to be taken in by any psychological tricks I might be inducing in an effort to believe.

Also, whenever I have an OBE, I am very much taken with the fact that there seems a lot more real than here. True reality seems to be outside the body rather than inside. The supernatural seems much more real than the natural.

One more thing, and I say this with a great deal of caution. I very much look forward to making the trip to the other side a one-way journey. I'm not at all suicidal and don't think about ending life before my time comes. But I can't say that I believe death is an enemy to be dreaded. Quite the contrary. It's life that's difficult.

My senses, probably similar to most people's, often seem to form a prison that filters out the true essence of reality. This is so prevalent that the moment after I "return to my senses" my first thought is usually to question the reality of what I just experienced. It seems so far removed from the kind of thinking that fills up my normal life that it seems preposterous to even think about "leaving" the body.

I have tried to debunk the whole OBE thing and "get back to reality." But the honest, seeking researcher within me is forced to admit that something real has occurred. Only my twenty-first century, American-educated mindset is tempted to discard the facts that I know are real in favor of a "normal" approach to the whole matter.

Will this "convert" anyone who has never experienced an OBE?

Probably not. But if it will encourage a few people to try, it will have been worth sticking my neck out, if only in a literary form.

Why is this important?

Simply this.

If enough people begin to believe that we are, in Bob Monroe's words, "more than our bodies," it will change the course of human history. After catching even a glimpse of such a reality, the blathering of world leaders and power-grabbing politicians, to say nothing of the platitudes of many religions leaders, seem somehow silly.

There is much more to life than what we have been told. Perhaps it's time, as a species, to go about the process of growing up.

PSYCHICS AND SENSITIVES

Most people who have included some psycho-spiritual learning in their life will say it has helped them, particularly in actualizing their new-found knowledge. Being a psychic, medium or healer, or implementing spirituality, may not always provide us with a life without difficulties, illnesses or sorrows. Life is likely to present us with challenges, problems to be solved, bereavements to be grieved, and all the myriad experiences an individual may encounter. It may not make the bumps in our road disappear. What it can do is provide us with a stronger vehicle with which to ride more easily over them.

—Julie Soskin, *The Psychic's Handbook*

Julie Soskin is psychic. But because that label has attracted so much baggage over the years, she prefers the title "sensitive." In her book *The Psychic's Handbook: Your Essential Guide to Psycho-Spiritual Energies,* she asks:

What sort of world would it be if we were all balanced human beings? This, of course, is a dream we can only imagine. Nonetheless, it seems to me that we are on the verge of dynamic movement and change and there are tiny sprouts of enlightenment emerging. They are delicate and need a lot of care.

If she is right and we are on the verge of "dynamic movement and change," what might that change look like and how can the average person participate?

Ever since she was a youngster, Julie was aware that she felt things others did not. Like so many other gifted psychics, she at first hid her feelings and intuitions. She was afraid of being "different." She looked upon her gift as being more of a curse than a blessing. It was only after she grew to maturity that she was able to come to grips with the fact that although everyone walks around in a sea of feelings and intuitions, life had somehow given her the ability to discern these energies to a much greater degree than most folks demonstrate. It was as if everyone was inundated by radio waves but she was the only one who had her receiver turned on.

She is the first to admit that this can be confusing:

> Psychic senses can be confusing. Message coming into the consciousness are often misinterpreted, especially the sources of different levels of psychic perceptions. These energies can take time and experience to discern.

But recognizing that they are there is the first step. Learning to discern what they imply is probably a life-time learning process.

It's important to begin any discussion of psychic ability with this caveat: Psychic discernment is supernatural in the sense that it employs intuiting energies that are outside the range of our normal five senses. But supernatural doesn't mean "spooky." It can probably even be considered normal, if not usual. It might very well be that we all have psychic ability to some degree. Some of us are just more developed than others. If that is the case, psychic abilities only seem to be supernatural because we deem them to be.

Think of it this way. Most of us can carry a tune. But few are as gifted as was Mozart. His ability to compose wasn't supernatural as much as it was "super-normal." He had a gift that all of us have to some degree. He just had more of it and developed it to a much greater degree than practically anyone else.

Some people are more attuned to their psychic abilities than others. No one knows why this is yet.

It might turn out that we will someday discover that our ancient ancestors possessed psychic ability to a much more developed degree than we are used to seeing today. The reason for the atrophy of the gift is probably because we stopped using it, for many reasons. We are busier today than we used to be. We follow hectic schedules that keep us from employing long periods of uninterrupted solitude necessary for thought and contemplation. We are more left-brained and analytical than we used to be. And, if the truth were known, our western education systems emphasize math and science much more than intuitive courses of study conducive to art, poetry, and music. Even for those who follow such pursuits, the emphasis nowadays seems to be on "understanding" art more than simply experiencing it.

All this is speculative. We don't know why some people are more attuned to psychic signals than others. We just know that they are. Trying to "figure out" such things is a trap. It can lead us down a primrose path of intellectualizing. Far better to simply accept and appreciate.

THE PATH OF THE PSYCHIC

If you or someone you know is gifted in this regard, what do you do with it? How do you employ your ability?

For some the course of action entails hanging out a shingle and commercializing their gift. A lot of well-meaning, helpful folks have done just that. Sad to say, a lot of fakes and charlatans have done it as well. The Internet is full of such people who give sincere, gifted, psychics a bad name. That is precisely why Julie Soskin prefers the title *sensitive* to *psychic*. False psychics have muddied the waters far too often for far too long.

But having the gift doesn't necessarily mean cashing in on it. If you find yourself developing your abilities, it might mean that you have a different task. Perhaps your path in life is to help yourself and others become better, more well-balanced people.

The philosopher Immanuel Kant (1724–1804), in his *Critique of Practical Reason*, once speculated that "there is an absolute truth if only we could find it." He was probably only half right. If "absolute truth" exists, it most certainly will be found to be the sum total of different experiences of many different people. As a matter of fact, it might be that *only* the experiences of many different people can, when finally realized, add up to what Kant called "absolute truth." What this means is that diversity, not homogeneity, is the goal of evolution. An "absolute truth" must contain the experiences of butterfly and humming bird, elephant and toad, electron and black hole, male and female, and, ultimately, human and spirit.

The goal of the psychic, then, is to be found in diversity—in recognizing the unique ability of all people—in discerning what is beneath the surface, not just the visible universe around us. The psychic learns to see truth even if it means gazing beneath falsehood. We all become very adept at pulling the wool over our own eyes—of seeing the world the way we desire to see it. We can all lie to ourselves very easily, justifying the most outlandish activities. Developing our sixth sense (or is it better described as our *first* sense?) helps us to cut through the fabric of our own, egotistic tendencies. It might be the one most valuable sense we can develop as a human race if we are going to emerge

The Buddha did not consider himself a great prophet but, rather, merely an ordinary man who was awake to the true reality of existence.

from the labyrinthine maze we seem to be constructing for ourselves, given the state of our politics, our environment, our social network, and our dominating technology.

The true psychic can pierce through this curtain of confusion—can see through the illusion to the core reality beneath it all.

Perhaps *sensitive* is a better word after all. Maybe we are becoming *in*-sensitive and need to regain our intuitive sense of who we are and what we are here for.

It was said that a traveler once came across the Buddha, who was meditating beneath a tree beside the road.

"Sir," the traveler said, "I perceive something special about you. Are you a god?"

The Buddha simply smiled and shook his head.

"Are you a prophet?" asked the traveler.

"No," replied the Buddha.

"Then what are you?" said the traveler.

The Buddha said, "I am awake."

If psychics, or sensitives, can open our eyes to see truth behind illusion, if they can pick up the subtle signals that many of us too often bury beneath the hectic activities and subterfuges that make up our modern world, if they can tune in frequencies most of us ignore, then perhaps it is not too late for the human race. Perhaps we can yet make music where too often we have simply created noise. If the ability lies within each of us, then, just like the Buddha, it is time we woke up. The subtle world awaits.

SEX AND THE SPIRIT

Obviously, we can't alter our sexual instincts. What we can do, however, is use spiritual practice to overcome the limitations imposed by nature on our sexuality. In fact, we can transform the inherent mismatch between male and female sexuality into an incredible opportunity for spiritual growth.

—Robert Ping, *Why Sex Should Be Treated as a Spiritual Practice*

Iknow what you're thinking. Where's this one going? I also know you are probably looking a bit askance at the subject. But besides all that, if you're just dipping into a few select chapters in this book, rather than reading it cover to cover, this is probably one of the first chapters you checked out.

No doubt about it—sex sells.

There is undoubtedly a lot of nonsense out there about the spiritual significance of exotic sex. Much of it is simply titillating and superficial, usually designed to sell something, if only the fame of the one writing about it. But there is an ancient and well-studied tradition that comes out of Eastern spirituality that insists sex can be, and should be, a spiritual practice as well as a means of procreation. According to this view, it is a way to access the supernatural. We might do well to at least ask ourselves if there is a valid point hidden in here somewhere.

Consider the following:

- *Sex is powerful.* By indulging in sex with the wrong people at the wrong time, presidents and politicians, priests and pastors, athletes and celebrities, have all risked everything they had for so long struggled to achieve. How could a person strive his or her whole life to achieve a long-held, lofty goal, and then throw it all away for a weekend in Vegas? Who knows? But it happens a lot.

- *Sex is mystical.* The goal of meditation is to achieve one-point focus—to clear one's mind by concentrating on a single, powerful, mystical union with the ultimate, blissful, silence of the unknown. That's what sex does. Hindu *rishis* used to call death "the orgasm that lasts forever." Japanese mystics believed orgasm to be the ultimate spiritual experience and called it "reaching clouds and rain."

- *Sex is religious.* Some religions began because the founder's mother had sex with God. Male supernatural gods are often said to have sought intercourse with human women. Even the Bible underscores this historical oddity:

Now it came about, when men began to multiply on the face of the land, and daughters were born to them, that the sons of God saw that the daughters of men were beautiful; and they took wives for themselves, whomever they chose.

—Genesis 6:1–2

And, let's face it. When someone says "Oh, God!" at the point of sexual climax, is that just a Freudian slip?

- *Sex is magical.* I'm not talking about feelings or emotions here. Magic happens when male sperm connects with female ovum. Life is created. That's magical, no matter how prudish you may be about the process.

- *Sex is unifying.* Males and females experience sex differently. We won't go into a lot of detail here because the subject has been explored thoroughly. But ultimate supernatural reality, whatever else it is, must comprise both sides of the coin. Male and female are the yin and yang of existence, all the way up and down the food chain. It is no mistake that traditional weddings usually close with the biblical injunction, "The two shall be as one."

For all these reasons, traditional Eastern spiritual philosophies have treated sex with a special reverence not often found in Western systems of thought. In Western anthropological studies, for instance, it is common to espouse the belief that sex is powerful because of the need to propagate the species.

In theory, that sounds reasonable. But it flies in the face of experiential practice. In the wild, for instance, it is common for males to not only ignore their young, but to actually compete with them for dominance. And as all humans know, much of the rigmarole surrounding sex involves *not* propagating. That's exactly the opposite of conventional wisdom. Yet the myth continues because it sounds so utterly academic.

Sex and Yoga

In ancient eastern tradition, the energy involved in orgasm travels up the spine and out the top of the head. This is the same path followed by *Kundalini* energy. Kundalini is thought to be the basis of life essence. It energizes the chakras found in the body, uniting them in spiritual force and power. In Sanskrit, life energy is called *prana*. To control *prana* energy is to experience the very essence of life itself.

When viewed through this lens, sex becomes spiritual, not just physical. It may not be possible for westerners to arrive at this stage of understanding, given our training in early childhood development and the constant bombardment of sex-as-advertising and sex-as-entertainment we get from our exposure to daily media. All this incoming propaganda predisposes us to an entirely different attitude about the subject.

But there is no doubt some real value in considering a change of heart toward the topic. Be careful, though. The Internet is full of sites that offer a superficial treatment on this subject. Most are worthless. But if you dig long enough in a diamond mine, you might just find some valuable gems amongst the dirt.

In some religions sex is a spiritual experience, as illustrated in this sculpture found on one of the Khajuraho Temples in Madhya Pradesh, India.

SHAMANISM AND SPIRITUALISM

Shamanism is an ancient and powerful spiritual practice that can help us thrive during challenging and changing times. In our modern-day technological world we have been led to believe that what we see, touch, hear, smell, and taste with our ordinary senses connects us only to the world that is visible around us. Conversely, shamanism teaches us that there are doorways into other realms of reality where spirits reside who can share guidance, insight, and healing not just for ourselves but also for the world in which we live.

—Sandra Ingerman, *Awakening to the Spirit World:*
The Shamanic Path of Direct Revelation

Rational scientists assume there is no such thing as the supernatural. When confronted with unexplained phenomena, even if it seems magical at the time, they believe that there must certainly exist a logical explanation based on laws and rules that are perfectly reasonable even if we don't quite understand how they work.

Shamanism expresses the exact opposite. The conviction here is that supernatural worlds most definitely exist and the reason we don't understand them is because we have to enter into a state of expanded consciousness, a state that goes beyond the perception only of the five senses, in order to perceive them.

Traditional scientists say hallucinations are a product of chemical and neurological stimulation in the brain and claim they can prove it because they can duplicate such hallucinations under controlled conditions.

Shamans believe that so-called hallucinations are glimpses of reality. If science duplicates them under controlled conditions, they do so by stimulating areas of the brain that are hard-wired to conduct such activities anyway. If a live performance of a symphony, for instance, produces a powerful emotion, perhaps even a burst of insight, the experience can be duplicated by a recording. But the recording itself is proof that the real performance took place, not that there was never an original performance.

In short, a rational question or two seems to indicate that shamans have a point. Let's assume that our brains can and do produce hallucinations common to shamanic tradition. When and why did this activity begin in the first place? Evolution works by severely following the principle that the only traits that will be passed down the gene pool are those that offer some kind of advantage. What possible physical advantage could the first hallucination have provided that would benefit the humans who had it and then passed on to their offspring?

Physicists know that parallel dimensions outside our range of sensory input really exist. Shamans claim to have experienced parallel dimensions. Doesn't it seem logical to at least investigate their claims rather than write them off as imaginary, usually on the grounds that shamans are "primitive" and, let's be honest, usually of a race that is not white and college educated?

Graham Hancock puts it like this:

> If we were smart we would listen to what the shamans have to say about the true character and complexity of reality, instead of basking mindlessly in the over-weaning, one-dimensional arrogance of the Western technological mindset.
>
> —Graham Hancock, *Supernatural*

He certainly has a point.

One of the supreme ironies of modern human existence is that in order to see what's on the other side of the newly discovered Higgs Field, the "fence" that separates us from other realms of existence that don't consist of material manifestations of energy, is to employ the talents and skills of a member of a fraternity consisting of perhaps the oldest spiritual practitioners known to humankind—those who are familiar with the art of the shaman. They've been journeying back and forth from this reality to other realities for thousands of years. As a matter of fact, the first shaman might very well have been contemporaneous with the first modern human.

If you have any preconceived ideas about what a shaman is, based on some picture you once saw in an old copy of your parents' *National Geographic*, do your best to disassociate with them. They are, without a doubt, false and an insult to the craft. A modern shaman doesn't have to live in Peru, South

Africa, or Siberia, although many of them do. You might even sit next to one in a bus on your morning commute and talk about the results of the latest football game without ever realizing you are with a unique individual. Being a shaman is almost always a part-time position. You can't go to the metaphysical neighborhoods they visit and stay there. It would probably drive you mad. After a shamanic journey, no matter how vivid and spectacular the trip, you have to come home and do the dishes. That's just the way it is.

DEFINITIONS

First, understand that the word "shaman" itself is a bit of a misnomer. It is a Siberian term that has since been applied to all indigenous practitioners who we once called "medicine men," "priests," or even (shudder!) "witch doctors." It is a catch-all phrase employed by outsiders. As such it is probably not a very good label. But it's out there, so we'll use it.

That being the case, it would probably be best to agree on a good definition of what a shaman is. For that we turn to Michael Harner (1929–), who in the 1980s opened the eyes of the world with his ground-breaking book, *The Way of the Shaman*. He didn't gain his insights by learning about shamanism, as was the custom of that time when it came to doing research in the field. Back then you were expected to remain aloof and unattached when studying foreign cultures. "Observe, don't participate" was the academic mantra. "Remain objective!" "Don't go native!"

Harner was a scientist. But he was open-minded enough to understand that studying shamanism required active participation simply because a typical shaman couldn't possibly teach you anything just by lecturing about it. He quickly discovered that "learning about" wouldn't cut it. The most that method could accomplish would be a physical description of someone experiencing an inward journey—a worthless endeavor. That's why shamans don't usually write anything down about their practices. It is an oral tradition and has been since the beginning.

Harner wrote *The Way of the Shaman* in 1980. Its genius lay in the fact that he was able to synthesize shamanistic tradition

Referring to this man in the Irkutsk region of Russia as a shaman would be strictly correct. The word "shaman" comes from Siberia, but it is now often used for "medicine men" and aboriginal priests in many other cultures.

and package it in a way Americans could grasp. He didn't write his next book, *Cave and Cosmos*, until 2013, and the only reason he wrote the second book at all was that he considered the inevitable approach of death and felt it would be advantageous to share some of the work in *core shamanism* he had accomplished at his Foundation for Shamanic Studies in Mill Valley, California.

According to Michael Harner in *Cave and Cosmos:*

> While the work of shamans encompass virtually the full gamut of known spiritual practices, shamanism is universally characterized by an intentional change in consciousness to engage in two-way interaction with spirits. Its most distinctive feature, which is not universal, is the out-of-body journey to other worlds. It should be noted that in some indigenous societies, there are shamans who do not journey at all, and others who journey only in the Middle World or, if they journey beyond the Middle World, may not go to both the Upper and Lower Worlds. What they all do share is disciplined interaction with spirits in non-ordinary reality to help and heal others.

Let's break that down a bit. A core teaching of shamanism is that there is more than one reality. The reality we live in consists of matter and extends

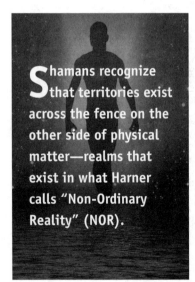

Shamans recognize that territories exist across the fence on the other side of physical matter—realms that exist in what Harner calls "Non-Ordinary Reality" (NOR).

to the end of the universe. You may travel, as has been reported by those who have experienced a typical out-of-body experience, to the farthest reach of the cosmos and hold the universe in the palm of your hand, but you still haven't left the "Middle World." The Middle World is the world of the scientist. It consists of matter that can be measured. Harner calls it "Ordinary Reality" (OR).

Shamans recognize that territories exist across the fence on the other side of physical matter—realms that exist in what Harner calls "Non-Ordinary Reality" (NOR). They also believe those realms are just as present *here* as they are *there*. If shamanism spawned a religion, it was probably the religion known as *animism*—the belief that everything made of matter, rock, tree, and person, is *animated* by spirit. It is alive, as opposed to what one of my shaman friends refers to as the "dead-stick philosophy."

Ordinary Reality, then, is what we experience in what I have elsewhere called our "Perception Realm," a term coined by my wife, Barbara. But there are realms we cannot perceive with the five senses, even though we walk, run, and live amongst and in them. Perhaps Jesus said it best in Luke 17:21: "The realm of God is within (or amongst) you." We have deduced the existence of these realms through the math of quantum physics but cannot experience them physically except in rare cases of splash-over that we often attribute to emotions, *déjà vu*, or metaphysical enigmas. This is the country of Non-Ordinary Reality.

In traditional shamanism, there are worlds on both sides of our perceptions.

- First is the *Lower World*, which is usually associated with animal spirits. This was probably the world experienced by the ancient shamans who went into the great caves of Europe and rendered artistic images in vivid pigments of the animal envoys they met there.

- Second is the *Upper World*, which is usually associated with images of fairies and angels found in mythologies everywhere. In other words, it is associated with flight.

At this point, if your knowledge about shamanism is limited to a few articles picked up from the Internet, you are probably ready to throw up your hands in disgust and turn the page.

DESCRIBING THE INDESCRIBABLE

Suppose you see something completely outside your experience and attempt to explain it to someone. How are you going to do it? They haven't seen it, so all you can do is tell them what it's like.

"I saw this beautiful flower that only grows in India. It is different from anything I've ever seen. It was kind of red and gold, with a gorgeous petal like...."

"Dude, I saw this guy do a totally radical move on his surfboard. He did like a 360 with a kind of backward flip and then tucked into a ball and landed on his feet. Oh man, you had to have been there!

"The music was unbelievable—kind of a cross between Led Zeppelin and Barry Manilow, you know, with some Beethoven orchestrations behind it that sounded like Shostakovich on steroids!"

You get the idea. It's hard to describe something unless your listener has a common point of reference.

Next, suppose you have the good fortune to expand your consciousness to the point of "seeing" a totally different reality. Words were invented to describe experiences in *this* reality. How are they possibly going to work over *there*?

It gets even more complicated. Forget trying to explain it to someone *else*. How are *you* going to process it? You are seeing something that is totally outside the realm that language was invented to explain.

Have you ever tried to describe a dream? Difficult, isn't it? The images are very real to you. But the poor person you're trying to tell about it just sits there with a blank face.

The problem lies in the fact that your right-brain intuitive neurons are experiencing something that can only be processed by your left-brain analytical memories. The left brain has to sort through your entire rolodex of experiences to come up with something that the image looks like.

You probably didn't see a two-headed eagle with the body of a fish, but that's the only image your left brain synaptic memory banks could come up with that looked remotely like the image you did see, which was, by the way, an entity encountered in a perception reality completely devoid of physical matter.

Is it any wonder that shamans may have difficulty expressing that which is, by its very nature, inexpressible?

Therein lies both the problem and the practice. But cheer up! The only "faith" you have to have in the whole process is backed up by what physics and metaphysics have already proved: that parallel universes, or non-ordinary realities, actually exist and that it may be possible to experience them directly.

BEGINNINGS

How did it all start? When did our ancient ancestors first discover the existence of other realms that were outside of this one but still very much "real"?

This is a pot with *ayahuasca* mushrooms in it that are about to be prepared for a ceremony in Ecuador. The psychedelic fungus, when used correctly, can induce a spiritual state in the user.

The speculation, by no means proven, is that "mind-expanding" or "consciousness-raising" journeys, or "trips," to use a term from the 1960s, began the same way they sometimes occur today—by ingesting chemicals found in plant derivatives that open up areas of the brain that we seldom use in day-to-day life.

Our brains have evolved to bring order to the world we live in. That only makes sense. It doesn't mean other realities don't exist. It just means we have forgotten how to access them. Estimates have been advanced that some 2 percent of the human race is born with the correct amount of naturally occurring chemicals in the brain to spontaneously experience other realities and to see with "sacred" eyes. For the rest of us, the windows and doors are still there, hidden in the recesses of our minds, but as we age, we've learned just to close them.

Please don't think that all shamans are druggies, however. Some, indeed, are famous for their use of *ayahuasca* and psychedelic mushrooms. When used correctly they are ingested in a sacred manner after much preparation and are overseen by experienced shamanic practitioners. It is considered to be a sacred, ritualistic journey, not a recreational "trip."

But there are other methods employed in shamanic journeying. Perhaps the most universal is the use of drumming, often accompanied by rhythmic dance. It produces the same kind of effect in modern cultures completely divorced from shamanism, such as is expressed in the well-known Dobie Gray song of some years back: "Give me the beat boys and free my soul / I wanna get lost in your rock and roll and drift away...."

Others practice intense meditation. American Indian tribes were famous for inducing discomfort and even pain through depravation, such as in the *Vision Quest* or, even more extreme, the *Sun Dance*.

All this is not to say, however, that the purpose for shamanic journeying is to experience a kind of personal ecstasy. That happens sometimes, it is true. But the core of shamanism is to obtain information and assistance to help others. Shamans are not priests. Their primary purpose is not to lead ritualistic pageants. Instead, they share more in common with healers. Their purpose is to journey out for help and return with healing.

They are the oldest religious practitioners known to humankind. They are familiar with the landscape of other worlds. They practice to serve. Perhaps the time has now come for scientists, for all of us, to abandon long-held prejudices and turn to the folks who have the experience to explore where test tubes and microscopes cannot go—the subtle world we have finally discovered that lies beyond the Higgs Field.

Old meets New—a marriage made in Heaven!

SPIRITUALISM

Spiritualism is a religion that is not based on a relationship with a particular savior. It recognizes all prophets that have come to humankind throughout the ages, not setting one above the other. Rather, it is based upon the idea that we are all to form our own relationship with God, and to obtain guidance and accept responsibility for our actions based on our interaction with that personal guidance. We are able to have that instant and personal communication directly with God through no intermediary; hence the reason that we do not give anyone a fixed idea of God, only that there is a God. Any attempt to personalize the idea of God only limits the totality of that Intelligence, which is the reason that Spiritualists sometimes refer to that idea of God as "Infinite Intelligence" or "Infinite Spirit."

—*What Is Spiritualism?*, published by the
Cassadaga Spiritualist Camp

Spiritualism might be one of the most misunderstood religions of all time. When you ask most folks, and I have asked many, to describe Spiritualists, the answer often revolves around the idea that "spiritualists worship spirits."

Nothing could be further from the truth.

Spiritualists do seek contact with those who have crossed the border from our world to the next. But spiritualists ranging from the Methodist Sunday school teacher Edgar Cayce (1877–1945) to Arthur Conan Doyle (1859–1930), the creator of the famous fictional detective Sherlock Holmes, would be offended if you accused them of worshipping the spirits they sought to contact. To them, and many like them, God is a reality, even if they define God in different ways from most religious folks. The phrase "the God of your understanding" is frequently used to describe the divine in Spiritualist circles. This is akin to the Alcoholics Anonymous credo defining God as a "higher power, however you conceive of it."

In Spiritualism, it is common to consult someone who has demonstrated an ability to contact spirits. This person is usually called a "medium." Many practitioners believe Jesus Christ was an advanced medium who lived for a while on our earthly plain.

A medium will generally seek to contact spirits during a ritual known as a séance. It is here where Spiritualism has inherited a bad name. Séances are notorious for employing gimmicks and tricks to fool the unwary. Harry Houdini (1874–1926), a gifted magician/entertainer, wanted desperately to believe spirits really existed. Given his considerable experience at fooling audiences, he attended séances whenever he could throughout his life. He never found one he could authenticate. Every one of them employed fakery of some kind. He even promised his wife that he would try to communicate with her if he passed first. To her bitter disappointment, he never did. Séances were held for years on the anniversary of his death, but he never spoke to her. After many years she finally gave up hope and stopped trying.

Although Spiritualism has ancient roots, its beginnings in America can be traced to May 1848 in upstate New York. Margaretta and Kate Fox were sisters aged eleven and eight years old respectively. They claimed they heard a mysterious rapping coming from somewhere in an upstairs bedroom and were able to work out a code understandable to the spirit behind the phenomenon. They were eventually able to communicate with "the other side."

In this circa 1920s photo, the illusionist Harry Houdini shows how an image of Abraham Lincoln could be made to appear as a ghost. Despite such debunking, the magician actually wished to believe in the spiritual realm.

Such news, of course, spread rapidly in a nineteenth-century America caught up in many other religious fads. Eventually "rappings" were heard everywhere. A phenomenon called "table tipping" often accompanied the rapping. Tables would rise up and slowly revolve. Voices of deceased loved ones were heard, giving advice to those left behind. The first patent for a Ouija Board was issued on February 10, 1891. Church attendance dwindled, much to the consternation of preachers across America. Presidents from Abraham Lincoln

(1809–1865) to Ronald Reagan (1911–2004) attended séances. Frauds proliferated. Eventually the tragedy of the Civil War drew attention away from the practice, but Spiritualism continued. Fraud and deceit are common to all religions, claim many Spiritualists, as the fall of so many TV evangelists has proved so vividly.

The claim that life goes on after death is not unique to Spiritualism. It will no doubt continue to influence many people. Labels are contrary things. Spiritualism may suffer from bad press these days, but its claims are no different from those of many other established religions. As is so often the case, who can say for sure what lies on the other side of physical death, the greatest mystery of all?

THE WORLD OF QUANTUM REALITY

> One of the curious features of modern physics is that in spite of its overwhelming practical success in explaining a vast range of phenomena from quark to quasar, it fails to give us a single metaphor for how the universe actually works. The old mechanical metaphor, "The world is a giant clock," condensed in one image the principle of features of Newtonian physics—namely, atomicity, objectivity, and determinism. However, physicists today do not possess a single metaphor that unites in one image the principle features of quantum theory.
>
> —Nick Herbert, *Quantum Reality*

If you think about it, the word "supernatural" is usually understood, at least at a gut level, to mean "spooky." That's how we most often seem to use it. "Supernatural" refers to ghosts and goblins, weird, unexplained phenomena, the "Force" from *Star Wars*, or strange goings-on in the local graveyard.

Nothing could be further from the truth.

If "natural" refers to our normal experience, "super"natural refers to actions that take place "above" or "outside" of our normal experience. That's all.

In the past, "supernatural" was the home of religions and fiction. But in the last hundred years, and especially the last twenty or so, it has become the stuff of science. We can thank the discovery of quantum reality for that. When Albert Einstein referred to the theory of quantum entanglement as "spooky action at a distance," he spoke for the vast majority of scientists of his day and perhaps ours as well. Quantum theory is about "super-natural" activity, to say the least!

The problem is that in almost a century of laboratory tests and experiments, quantum theory, in all its "spooky" splendor, is still batting a thousand. It has never, ever been proven wrong. It is the very best, most tested, and proven theory science has come up with since it discovered gravity.

Is it supernatural?

In one sense, yes. Things just don't behave that way in the natural world.

Is it spooky? Absolutely! Even Einstein thought so.

Is it real?

Oh yes! It has never failed the experiment test.

So we are left with an uncomfortable truth. At the root of all existence lies something that certainly appears to be supernatural. It's as simple, and as complicated, as that. Quantum theory, utilizing the very best and latest scientific methods, has finally begun to reveal the basis of existence that, up until our day, was solely the bailiwick of religion and spirituality. After hundreds of years the two disciplines of science and religion, having struggled through a messy separation, now begin to hook up again. It makes for an interesting and uncomfortable marriage. And what we have seen so far is only the beginning.

Someday, hopefully not too far in the future, after the renewed coupling has had a chance to mature a little, it will probably be noted with great irony that many scientists, in the closing years of the twentieth century, treated religion with the same scorn that religion leveled against science back in the Middle Ages. In those days, the Grand Inquisitor and general bad guy was a man called Tomás de Torquemada (1420–1498). The victims he and his successors persecuted eventually numbered in the thousands and later grew to include everyone from Nicolaus Copernicus (1473–1543) and Isaac Newton (1643–1727) to (in its Protestant version) untold New England witches. The crime of these innocent unfortunates consisted of questioning the facts accepted by the status quo—facts that uncovered the true nature of reality.

Popular New Age author and speeker Deepak Chopra, who is also an alternative medicine advocate, has been one of many targets for attacks by "scientific inquisitors" who doubt the supernatural exists.

Many of today's scientific inquisitors unleash the same brand of scorn on those who question accepted scientific theories about materialism and reductionism and dare to believe there are real supernatural worlds to conquer. The modern inquisition, at least in its public persona, is led by a small coterie of outspoken atheists such as Richard Dawkins (1941–; *The God Delusion*) and Sam Harris (1967–; *The End of Faith*). Thankfully, they don't have the power of the state behind them like the religious inquisitors of the past did. But their vitriol has a familiar ring. Popular writers such as Deepak Chopra (1947–; *The Future of God*) and Fritjof Capra (1939–; *The Tao of Physics*), to say nothing of outsiders ranging from Graham Hancock (1950–; *Magicians of the Gods*) to Shirley MacLaine (*Out on a Limb*), have been forced to endure their literary slings and arrows.

So who is this new kid on the block called quantum theory and why is he so upsetting? What is the nature of the "spooky action" that has opened up a Pandora's Box of surprises and acts suspiciously like what has traditionally been called *supernatural*?

QUANTUM THEORY 101

First, understand this. There is no single quantum theory.

Quantum reality? Sure! Everyone agrees it exists. Its presence has passed every test with flying colors.

But how do we interpret the results of those tests? What exactly is quantum theory?

Let's start with a general definition and go from there.

Back in the closing years of the nineteenth century, physicists figured they had a firm grip on the nature of the reality commonly called the natural world. It consisted of matter (the stuff of the cosmos) and fields (the cosmic ocean in which the stuff floats). That was all there was to it. They pretty much knew the laws that governed both. A young Max Planck (1858–1947) even had a professor once tell him, "Physics is finished, young man. It's a dead-end street! You'd be better off becoming a concert pianist." (Thank goodness young Max, as we shall soon discover, was the kind of student who refused to listen to his elders!)

Classical physics declares that there are four fields. They are called electromagnetic, gravitational, strong nuclear, and weak nuclear. That's it. It's elegant and simple. Anyone can understand the concept.

Why are they important? That's simple, too. There are rules that govern each field that guide the stuff that floats around in them. Drop an apple from a tree, and it falls through the gravitational field while following specific rules that can be mathematically expressed. Learn the rules, and you understand how things work. Shoot a cannonball out into a field, and it follows a predictable parabola that can be mathematically plotted if you plug in variables for speed and trajectory. Increase the speed or trajectory, and it goes farther or higher, but the formula remains the same.

That's traditional physics. It's safe, neat, clean, and predictable. Perfectly normal and natural. This was the world of Albert Einstein. Using acceptable mathematical formulas, he brilliantly predicted all sorts of things that made him the smartest scientist to come down the pike since Isaac Newton. One of his predictions, which would soon come back to haunt him, was that nothing could travel faster than the speed of light. If a particle *there* was going to communicate with a particle *here*, it had to send information across the field and that information took some time to make the trip. That was simple logic.

Meanwhile, Max Planck, in spite of his teacher, decided to major in physics rather than music, a decision that probably changed the world. Without going into a lot of detail, Max came to understand that light and energy were connected in ways no one had yet understood. In short, he discovered that electrons didn't always follow the rules. They didn't act consistent with what had previously been considered "stuff," or, more important, "things."

His thinking went like this: While putting together a formula that would describe the relationship between color and temperature observed in heating metal objects, he found he could make the whole thing work mathematically by making an assumption that energy existed in individual units that he called *quanta*, because mathematical formulas made such measurements quantifiable.

Up to now, electrons were thought to be the smallest parts of atoms. Atoms were visualized as miniature galaxies, a nucleus surrounded by little, orbiting particles such as protons and electrons. They were thought to be the smallest "stuff" in the universe—the building blocks of everything else.

Now all that was thrown into question. In 1924, physicist Louis de Broglie (1892–1987) put forth the outlandish notion that sometimes orbiting electrons acted like waves of energy, and sometimes they acted like particles. If you looked for electrons in order to determine where they were—their position—you would find particles. But if you looked at how fast those same electrons were moving, you'd find waves. So which were they? If atoms, and especially electrons, didn't act like "things," maybe they weren't "things." Could it be that the "stuff" of the cosmos wasn't made of "things" after all? But if not—what? How could something be at least two things at once and neither declares itself until you look?

HEISENBERG, BOHR, AND THE COPENHAGEN SCHOOL

It began with Werner Heisenberg (1901–1976). "Atoms are not things," he famously said. Along with Danish physicist Niels Bohr (1885–1962) of the University of Copenhagen, which gave birth to what is now called the Copenhagen School of Quantum Interpretation, he believed strongly in the world of the five senses—the world of real objects. But he and the Copenhagenists, who probably make up the majority of physicists today, also believe our world of reality floats on principles that we will probably never understand. Bohr and Einstein often argued deep into the night, each frustrating the other to no end. But Bohr could never admit that a deeper reality exists. "There is no quantum world," said Bohr. "There is only an abstract quantum description."

German theoretical physicist Werner Heisenberg is remembered for, among other things, his Uncertainty Principle, which states that you can know the position or momentum of a particle but not both at the same time.

What that means, in layman's terms, is that quantum theory merely describes, to a degree, the workings of the real world we all experience. It is a mathematical representation of reality and helpful to math nerds, but it doesn't really change anything in terms of what we call reality.

If you have trouble with these ideas, you are in good company. Taken to its logical conclusion, the quantum world jumps into existence only when we "measure" something. When we want to find out where an electron is in space—in other words—its position, bam! There it is. It's a particle. We looked for it and we found it. When we want to measure a particle's velocity we look for it and, bam! There it is. It's a wave. A wave doesn't collapse into a particle until we measure it. Until then, it's only potential. Virtual energy doesn't become a thing until we observe it. What is it in the meantime? We don't know. That's why Heisenberg called it the Uncertainty Principle. It's like Forrest Gump's box of chocolates. You never know what you're going to get. To which Einstein scoffed, "God does not play dice with the universe!"

In other words, observers create reality by carrying out the act of observation. Until we look for it, it doesn't exist.

This prompted Cornell physicist N. David Mermin (1935–) to quip, "We now know that the moon is demonstrably not there when nobody looks."

Einstein had problems with this, too. He once said that he had a hard time believing that a mouse could significantly change the universe by simply looking at it.

But serious physicists such as Fred Wolf (1934–) convincingly put forth the argument that you create your own reality. It's not that the egocentric being you think of as yourself actually changes things at the macro level. It's just that the math is very clear that observation, or measurement, does change things at the micro level.

So even though it's one of the most counterintuitive scientific theories ever devised, if we honestly follow the math, that's what happens. Energy does not turn into matter until a conscious observer, human or otherwise, looks for it.

How does this interpretation affect the idea of supernatural gods?

Well, think about it for a minute. What caused the Big Bang to explode into the void, causing the material universe we call home? What caused the preexisting energy to collapse into a cosmos of matter? Obviously, there were no conscious beings around to observe it. So who did the deed? Who was the observer? Who was the measurer?

Obviously something, or someone, not of this material existence. Who, or what, does that point to? It sounds suspiciously like when God said, "Let there be light!" And there was light. Someone observed it—although "measurement" is the term scientists use—and it came to pass.

According to this manner of thinking, all that we know and experience is the result of a supernatural being (God) or deities (the Bible uses the plural form when it says, "Let *us* make man in *our* own image") who dreamed us into existence and made us co-creators. Yes, we are created in God's image, but by studying quantum theory and following it to its logical conclusion, we now create God in our own image as well.

Thus, although the Copenhagenists never intended it, they brought religion solidly into the discussion.

THE STRANGE CONDITION OF SCHRÖDINGER'S CAT

In 1935, Erwin Schrödinger (1887–1961) presented what has become the most famous metaphor to describe the situation physicists found themselves in thanks to Heisenberg. Like all good metaphors, it was simple and easy to understand. The problem was that it was also a *koan* worthy of any Zen Master. In other words, it seemed as though it was an unsolvable puzzle.

Suppose, he said, you put a cat in a box and sealed it up so you couldn't see inside. (Disclaimer—no live cats were used in this explanation.) Along with the cat, you attach a fiendish device containing a vial of radioactive poison. If a single atom of this poison decays, it will trip a hammer that will break the vial and release the poison, killing the cat.

Now comes the question. Is the cat dead or alive? You won't know until you look.

This metaphor illustrates a quantum conundrum called "superposition." It is a word used to describe how matter works at the quantum level—the level

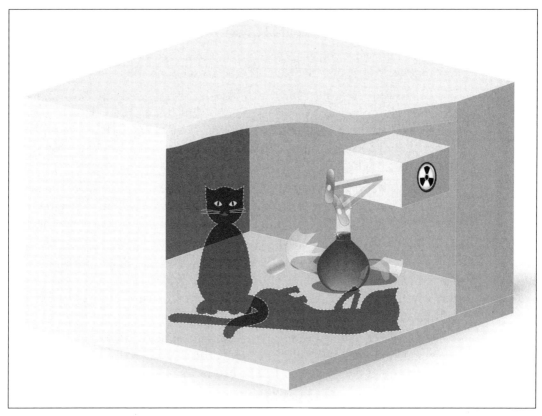

In the mental exercise explained by Erwin Schrödinger, a cat is enclosed inside a box that will release a poison at a random time. Until the box is opened, the cat inside can be thought of as both alive and dead, since its actual state is only realized when it is observed. The cat is, in effect, experiencing a quantum state of existence.

of the very, very small, and how we observe it at our level—the level of the so-called natural world.

The answer out here in the natural world is that the cat is either dead or alive. We don't know which, but it obviously has to be one or the other. We won't know until we open the box and check things out. That seems obvious. It's classical physics. It's the way things happen in the real world. It's what Newton would have concluded, along with Einstein and any other right-thinking intellectual.

But hold on a minute! According to quantum thinking, we're not going to have an answer until we observe the results! An electron, remember, becomes a particle or a wave only when we observe it. Until then, it exists in a quantum state of virtual potentiality that could go either way.

In the same way, Schrödinger said, according to the rules of quantum physics, until we check out our cat's condition, that cat is both dead and alive at the same time. It exists in a state of virtual potentiality that could go either way. It is only when we break open the box that the outcome becomes apparent.

(I know what you cat lovers are thinking. In order to save the cat's life, don't open the box. But that leads to another set of problems, doesn't it?)

This illustrates the paradox called "quantum indeterminacy," or, more popularly, the "observer's paradox." Simply put, the observer determines the outcome. Until you look, strictly speaking, that cat is both dead and alive because either possibility exists. And, from your position, it stays in that virtual state until you look.

(It's a weird experiment that seems to involve semantics more than natural-world facts. But physicists have to think that way when they enter the quantum world. Apparent natural-world conclusions don't exist down there.)

In the same way, Schrödinger concluded, we don't know what an electron is (wave or particle) until we "look inside the box" and measure it. It exists in a "virtual" state, a quantum state of potentiality. It could become either. When we check it out, the virtual electron collapses, or jumps, into our world. This is the genesis of the famous "quantum leap."

Until Schrödinger came up with this metaphor it was a confusing time. (Some might argue that's still the case. By the way, Schrödinger is rumored to have said late in life that he wished he had never met that cat!)

Max Planck was awarded the Nobel Prize in 1918, but a lot more was going on by then. And quickly, too, because by 1925 classical physics fell apart and scientists lost their grip on reality. Where before there had been no theory of quantum reality at all, suddenly there were many. And they're still showing up.

Fritjof Capra and Undivided Wholeness

A second quantum interpretation is found in the work of Walter Heitler (1904–1981) and was popularized by Fritjof Capra in his book *The Tao of Physics*. We'll call this one the *Undivided Wholeness Theory*. In this theory, we cannot continue to think of "us" and an "outside reality." We are not separate. Like the Buddhist monk comes to understand, we are one with everything. We exist in the cosmos and the cosmos exists in us. There is no separation except for that which we perceive with our senses, which are, by the way, deceiving us. In other words, existence as we know it is an illusion. "Life is but a dream." We are trapped in a prison built by an evolutionary development that raised us to function within those very same prison walls.

But there is a deeper reality beneath, or above, the natural world we experience and just as the ancient adepts of many religious traditions have argued for a very long time, we can learn to feel this wholeness, pierce through the illusion, and see Oneness.

In the *Tao of Physics*, Capra wrote these words:

> I "saw" cascades of energy coming down from outer space, in which particles were created and destroyed in rhythmic pulses; I "saw" the atoms of the elements and those of my body participating in this cosmic dance of energy; I "felt" its rhythm and I "heard" its sound, and at the moment I knew that this was the dance of Shiva, the Lord of Dancers, worshipped by the Hindus.

Born in Austria, Fritjof Capra is the founding director of the Center for Ecoliteracy at UC Berkeley and the author of the bestseller *The Tao of Physics*.

Here he finds alliance with a concept that goes back thousands of years—at least as far as the Hindu *rishis*, wise men who first wrote about the god Shiva. They believed that the universe is an illusion. That doesn't mean it doesn't really exist. It simply means that it's not what it appears to be. Everything is in a constant state of change, no matter its outward mask of invincibility.

A tree, for instance, seems to be solid, but it's not. Cut it down and burn it and it becomes energy in the form of heat. Turn it into paper, and it becomes a book. Bury the book in the ground, and it returns to the soil that nourishes a tree. On and on it goes. The various stages of its existence—tree, fire, heat, paper, book, and soil—are merely incarnations over the course of time. A solid tree is reincarnated as heat, paper, book, and soil just as humans go through various incarnations. Even the universe itself is merely a reincarnation of countless previous universes.

Joseph Campbell once described this classic cycle of Hinduism, called *Samsara*, in poetic terms:

> Vishnu sleeps in the cosmic ocean, and the lotus of the universe grows from his navel. On the lotus sits Brahma, the creator. Brahma opens his eyes, and a world comes into being. Brahma closes his eyes, and a world goes out of being. The life of a Brahma is 432,000 years. When he dies, the lotus goes back, and another lotus is formed, and another Brahma. Then think of the galaxies beyond galaxies in infinite space, each a lotus, with a Brahma sitting on it, opening his eyes, closing his eyes....
>
> —Joseph Campbell, speaking to Bill Moyers
> in *The Power of Myth*

This old, old spiritual wisdom and insight now seems to have been given flesh and blood through the discoveries of quantum reality. All that we call "normal" is merely a segment of an eternal unity. It is a snapshot—a still photo that is part of an ever-turning movie reel and we are but small characters in the plot of a supernatural drama, connected on every level but unable, in our present material form, to understand the whole story.

And when we say "connected on every level," we mean exactly that. Every point is connected (physicists use the word "entangled") with every other part. That's what quantum theory tells us. When point "A" way over on one side of the galaxy communicates something to point "B" on the other side of the galaxy, the communication is instantaneous. It doesn't send a message at the speed of light, the fastest speed possible according to the rules of classic physics. The communication is *instantly* delivered. It travels not at the speed of light, but at the speed of thought. And that truth is no longer a claim only of religionists and mystics. It has been verified by scientific experiment time and time again!

No wonder Einstein called it "spooky action at a distance."

Physicist David Bohm (1917–1992) of London's Birbeck College expressed it with appropriate scientific terminology:

> One is led to a new notion of unbroken wholeness which denies the classical analyzability of the world into separately and independently existing parts ... the inseparable quantum interconnectedness of the whole universe is the fundamental reality.

> —David Bohm in *Quantum Reality*, by Nick Herbert

In an earlier chapter ("Metaphysical Manifestations"), we quoted Sir James Hopwood Jeans (1877–1946). Perhaps it would be a good idea to highlight a part of the quote again. Before his death in 1946, Jeans proved strangely prophetic when he said, "The stream of knowledge is heading towards a non-mechanical reality; the universe begins to look more like a great thought than like a great machine."

Picturing the universe as a unified thought, whether it springs from a dream of Vishnu or a divine fiat from Jehovah, is certainly not what physicists expected when they discovered quantum theory. There used to be no room in physics for supernatural gods.

There is now.

ERVIN LÁSZLÓ AND THE AKASHIC FIELD

When quantum theory started out, the founders refused to accept a notion of a deeper reality undergirding existence. Today there are a few daring scientists who refuse to accept anything less. Ervin László (1932–) is one of them.

C. J. Martes is an Akashic Field theorist and founder of Akashic Field Therapy™ (AFT) who describes her Akashic Field experiences in László's book *The Akashic Experience: Science and the Cosmic Memory Field*. In an excerpt from an article she wrote for her website, she had this to say:

> Quantum scientists recently discovered a new area of time and space called the Quantum vacuum. There are newly discovered properties of time and space happening all the time but it seems clear now that this vacuum is a super dense cosmic frictionless medium that carries light and all the universal forces of nature. A well known scientist and philosopher named Ervin László, in his recently published book, *Science and the Akashic Field,* shows that it may not only be a super dense sea of frictionless energy but also a sea of information conveying the historical experience of matter.

Hungarian philosopher of science Ervin László believed that a field made up of information (the Akashic Field) is what made up the universe.

> —C. J. Martes, www.cjmartes.com

She goes on to quote László's theory that a quantum vacuum essentially "generates the holographic field that is the memory of the universe."

So—who is Ervin László and why is he so important?

Theoretical physicist Stephen Hawking claims that the so-called Integral Theory of Everything (I-TOE) is the Holy Grail of the contemporary physicist. Well, László claims he has found it. It lies at the center of his "Akashic Field Theory," released to the world in his 2004 book, *Science and the Akashic Field: An Integral Theory of Everything*.

Born in Budapest, Hungary, László has written more than seventy-five books and published hundreds of scientific papers, among his many other accomplishments. He is certainly a heavyweight in the field of quantum reality. But what I like most about him is that he began his career as a classical pianist and has recorded several of my favorite concertos with the Budapest Symphony. He has since branched out into such fields as philosophy of science, integral theory, and systems theory. When he talks about "developing a holistic perspective on the world," a view he labels "quantum consciousness," he certainly knows what he's talking about. In short, he's my kind of guy—a brilliant synthesist well-versed in many disciplines.

Using math and the tools of the physicist, he claims to have discovered a field of "information," for lack of a better word, that he calls the zero-point field, a place (which is really not a "place" at all) from which all energy comes into existence. It is Ground Zero in terms of being that point from which every single ripple of quantum energy originates. It is the mysterious field that eludes and tantalizes the scientists at CERN's Large Hadron Collider in Switzerland. It is home—the "mind of God"—the place that is both originator and receiver of particles that spring into existence from "nowhere" and go back to "somewhere" just as quickly. It is our home as well—the Alpha and Omega of our existence.

But to better describe this field he turns to that most spiritual of languages, Sanskrit. *Akasha* is a word meaning "space." In his book, he suggests that the Akashic field or the "quantum vacuum," is a field supporting all the fundamental energy and bits of information that manifest themselves as material objects in the Cosmos. (That means you and me, as well as all stars and atoms everywhere.) But he goes farther than this. He believes the Akashic field supports not only this Cosmos, this universe, but all universes, past and present, discovered and undiscovered. (You can use the words "multiverse" or "metaverse" here. I don't think he would mind.)

In other words (as if other words would help), Akasha is the mysterious realm from which everything originates. It is an infinite wave of potential

The Akashic field that Ervin László imagined was a source where all the information to potentially create the reality of all universes is stored.

awaiting incarnation in matter. Every symphony Beethoven wrote, every painting Picasso created, every possible outcome to any choice you ever made, every idea you ever had—all existed *in potential* in Akasha. When you plucked your elected idea out of Akasha, you gave it life through your intention. Akasha is the home of the Muse, but much, much more. It is the Source, the Ground of Being. In short, it is Consciousness itself.

We've been talking in this chapter about the weird world of quantum physics in which an electron does not come into existence until someone looks for it. A possibility wave of potential does not appear until we tease it out by giving it our attention.

Well, that's Akasha in a nutshell. According to László's way of thinking, Forrest Gump was right. At the end of the movie, Forrest speculates on predestination and free will. He wonders which theory is correct. He winds up saying, "I think it's both." And in typical Forrest fashion, he stumbles upon the truth. Everything exists in potential. In that sense, everything is predestined. But it manifests itself only when we choose to collapse it into our existence. That's called free will.

Here's the awesome part. You choose the elected manifestation, thereby bringing it into our universe—our reality. According to Hugh Everett, as we've just seen, another "you" in the infinite Multiverse, or Metaverse, chooses another possible manifestation, until all potential possibilities are manifested somewhere, somehow.

Akasha, or the zero-point field from where all selections is made, is hot right now. You know that's true when no less than a *New York Times* best-selling author such as Clive Cussler (1931–) makes it the critical plot contrivance in his thriller *Zero Hour*.

I could write about Ervin László all day. He's that brilliant. But let's let him present his theory in his own words:

> There is an explanation for the phenomena that puzzles today's front-line investigators; we can understand what processes underlie the nonlocal coherence of the human body, of all life, of the quantum, and of the entire universe. It is the presence of information throughout the cosmos, carried and conveyed by the universal information field we have named the Akashic field. The actions of this subtle but real A-field explains the non-locality of the smallest measureable units of the universe as well as its largest structures. It explains the coherence of living organisms, and their coherence with the milieu in which they live and evolve. It also explains the coherence of the human brain and consciousness associated with it, in regard to the brain and consciousness of other human beings, and even the world at large.

And it explains the astounding fact that the physical parameters of the universe are so finely adjusted that living organisms can exist and evolve on this planet, and possibly on countless other planets in this and other galaxies....

A-field information is the logical explanation of the mysterious way in which quanta are connected across time and space, of the evident but nonetheless astounding fact that we and other organisms have evolved and can live on this planet and, last but not least, of the seemingly miraculous capacity of the universe to bring forth human beings such as you and I, who now ask themselves why this universe is so well tuned that in all essential respects it is both instantly and universally interconnected.

—Ervin László, *Science and the Akashic Field*

Deepak Chopra explains it in layman's terms as well as anyone. In his book *Life after Death*, he talks about consciousness being a kind of three-layer cake. The outside layer is the dimension of physical matter. This is the world of concrete objects we encounter through the five senses—the one scientists observe and measure, quantify, and study.

Inside that is the dimension of subtle objects. This is the world of dreams and visions, imagination and inspiration.

Finally comes the dimension of pure consciousness itself, the field of Akasha. This is that mysterious realm that gives birth to everything there is—the ground of our very being—consciousness aware of itself. The Bible calls it the dimension of *I Am*. When Moses asked the burning bush who was sending him on his mission of freedom, the voice responded, "Tell them *I Am* sent you." Jesus later said, "Before Moses was, *I Am!*"

If you read the last few paragraphs again you will see how easy, perhaps even inevitably, we can move from scientific theory to religious speculation. Seen through the eyes of quantum theory, the proclamations of many wise men of old, some of them founders of venerable religious traditions, take on new meaning.

If you find yourself reacting against the thought of this religion/science mix, it's important to examine your motivations. Are you reacting against the wisdom of the founders and wise men of old or are you reacting against the worldly and often superficial traditions that developed around them years after they were dead?

It's easy to find it hard to utter the word "God," for instance. That word has become so incrusted with baggage that it's hard to know what it means anymore. If visions of TV preachers and door-to-door evangelists pop into your head, it's probably wise to either abandon the name altogether or at least use it wisely and in the right company.

But let's not be too quick to allow the traditionalists to corrupt a perfectly good word. Given the right definition, it can serve to condense a lot of spirituality into a quickly available concept. There's a reason some scientists use "God talk." Both Einstein and Hawking refer to "the mind of God," for instance. It's a good word and carries a lot of meaning when used correctly. You just have to get past the traditional image of a father-figure who doles out blessings to the "faithful" who jump through his hoops.

"Akasha" is another example. It's a spiritual Hindu Sanskrit word that is capable of conveying some deep scientific concepts, perhaps even an explanation of reality. And that is no small thing!

VON NEUMANN AND THE CONSCIOUSNESS-CREATED COSMOS

"In the beginning," humans were at the center of the universe. The cosmos was created for us and didn't get interesting until relatively recently when we showed up.

Then came the age of telescopes and space travel and that idea went right out the window.

Look up into the night sky and you see a reality that is overwhelming but manageable. Follow the moon and the sun through their courses and it's easy to get the idea the universe revolves around us.

But take one look at some Hubble deep space telescope pictures and you'll get humble really quickly. Watch the earth disappear into an infinite smear of light from uncountable galaxies, let alone individual stars, and you'll soon come to the conclusion that if we're really at the center of it all, it's an extravagant waste of space. At such times, the idea of humans being significant in the grand scheme of things is pretty silly.

But thanks to the brilliant Hungarian physicist, mathematician, and computer scientist John von Neumann (1903–1957), who was a prodigy, that's right where we now return.

Von Neumann was a fascinating fellow who became an American citizen in 1937. A jack-of-all trades, he could speak

Hungarian scientist John von Neumann was the author of *The Foundations,* which is considered the bible of quantum physics.

New Testament Greek by the time he was six years old while doing complex math in his head. He was a history buff who also wrote the bible of quantum physics *Die Grundlagen* (*The Foundations*), still revered today. He was a man who loved to eat and drink (his wife used to say he could count everything but calories) and delighted in dirty limericks.

In the midst of all this, he developed a theory that is quite disturbing to a lot of physicists who otherwise love his work. He was a mathematician who insisted on following facts to their logical conclusion.

And that's the problem.

He simply couldn't get away from the fact that quanta collapsed into our reality only when they were being observed by a conscious observer. It isn't a convenient truth. But there it is. There was no escaping it. If he could treat wave function collapse as a simple artifact of quantum mathematics instead of something real that happened in real time and space, things would have been just fine. It would have been something for physicists to chuckle about at conventions.

But he couldn't do that. He was too honest. If quanta made the jump from a virtual "somewhere" to "here" when they were observed, and if humans did the observing, then that put humans right back at the center of the universe. After taking thousands of years to push us off the throne, here we were right back on it again.

It wasn't that von Neumann did this on purpose, or even that he ever really considered the implications of it all. That's the way it worked, however, and religionists, from traditionalists to New Agers, who might not be able to follow the math, certainly jumped at the conclusions.

Consciousness creates reality. There it is. Plain and simple. There's no escaping it. What's a poor physicist to do?

That didn't mean, claimed a lot of believers, that consciousness was centered only in humans. And here's where supernatural gods come into the picture. It wasn't that the universe revolved around humans. It revolved around consciousness. There was intelligence behind it. There was purpose and meaning. We, being creatures of Consciousness, were created. We evolved *for* something. And that made a huge, comforting difference.

Von Neumann's work suggested that most of the universe, most of the time, exists in the same limbo that claimed Schrödinger's cat. Perhaps it exists in the form of the 95 percent of what we can't see but label dark energy. Perhaps it waits over on the other side of the Higgs Field. But it enters our reality when consciousness concentrates on it and begins to observe and measure.

Mind and matter. Matter and mind. Possibilities and probabilities. They are all there, waiting.

Waiting for what?

Waiting to be released into our conception of reality. Jeffrey Kripal (1962–), a professor of comparative religion at Rice University, has written extensively about meaning. He sees the "supernatural" abilities demonstrated by a few gifted shamans, psychics, and mystics as *symbols*. In his word, these symbols indicate:

> … the eruption of meaning into the physical world via the radical collapse of the subject-object structure itself. They are not simply *physical* events. They are also *meaning* events.
>
> —Jeffrey Kripal, *Authors of the Impossible:*
> *The Paranormal and the Sacred*

There are many more quantum theory interpretations out there. Some are pretty weird. Others seem tantalizingly just out of reach. All are revolutionary. We are in the midst of a huge paradigm shift and we don't know how or when the dust is going to settle. It's hard to get our minds out of our five-senses box and take all these ideas seriously. But there are some important things to keep in mind:

- These ideas offer profound religious interpretations and implications.
- They are the results of serious study by a lot of very brilliant thinkers. They are not the work of quacks.
- They talk about real phenomena in the real world.
- They attempt to explain how we came to exist. Maybe even why.
- We are the product of forces that we simply, as yet, do not understand. But they are magical, to say the least.

Where will all this take us? We don't know. But we are on the right track. Stay tuned! The best is certainly yet to come.

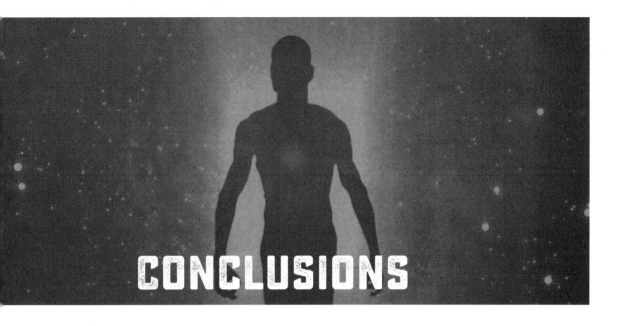

CONCLUSIONS

As science continues to probe the nature of the universe ever more deeply, we've begun to realize that some of our earlier assumptions were based on a naive, "surface" view of reality. We now know that commonsense—our everyday experience while driving down the street, talking to a friend, or buying a melon in the grocery store—is a vastly simplified snapshot of a hyper complex reality.

—Dean Radin, in *Supernormal*

THE EIGHTFOLD PATH

We began the explorations in this book with a simple, three-point premise:

1. What you have been taught about reality is insufficient.

2. You are living within the walls of an illusion.

3. You have the ability, perhaps even the obligation, to break through those walls and glimpse the truth.

Now, after looking at some of the methods people have employed over the centuries to search for supernatural gods, it's time to sum up what we have learned and see if the premise holds up under scrutiny.

First, though, we need to examine the base from which we form what we earlier called our *Faith Statement*. That consists of assumptions, often unexamined, which we hold concerning "facts" we automatically assume to be true.

Most of us are products of a typical modern western education. Dr. Dean Radin, in his position as chief scientist at the Institute of Noetic Sciences, which studies, under strict scientific protocols, what some call "supernatural" experiences, defines the Faith Statement of the scientific method using an eightfold series of beliefs that every one of us absorbed while growing up. According to Radin in his book *Supernormal*:

1. *Realism:* The physical world consists of objects that are completely independent of observation. What this means is that the moon is still there even when you're not looking at it. This belief rules out the possibility that the mind can control matter by bending spoons or that you can make money in the stock market by thinking positive thoughts.

2. *Localism:* Objects are completely separate and unconnected. There is no such thing as "action at a distance." If one object affects another, it's because they either physically interact or some force travels between them.

3. *Causality:* Time is like a river that flows in one direction, from past to future through the present.

4. *Mechanism:* Everything can be understood in terms of cause and effect, similar to the gears of a clock. One gear influences another and on down the line.

5. *Physicalism:* Everything can be fully described in terms of having real properties that exist in space and time. Even meaningful statements are analytically proved or not by using math and logic.

6. *Materialism:* Everything, including mind, is made up of matter. Nothing nonmaterial exists.

7. *Determinism:* All events are fully caused by preceding states.

8. *Reductionism:* Objects can be understood by reducing them to their basic components. An "automobile," for instance, can be best understood as a drive shaft, power plant, steering mechanism, etc.

We might not agree with every one of these statements, but if we consider them carefully and honestly most of us are forced to admit that they form the basis of our particular, day-to-day worldview. They are the primary principles that have formed the basis of our entire learning experience. They serve as the Faith Statement of modern education. They may never have been presented as such, but they are the assumptions upon which a typical education from elementary school through postgraduate studies are based. We don't examine them. We simply accept them.

Here's the problem—the latest scientific research into the mysteries of modern physics, especially in the quantum realm, has proven every one of these assumptions wrong. Since it is terribly difficult to discard cherished beliefs, most of us don't believe in the supernatural because we simply don't want to. It goes against everything we hold true. Throwing facts aside, we take refuge in the phrase, "It just doesn't seem logical to me!"

Albert Einstein, for instance, couldn't accept the idea of nonlocality, a concept we discussed earlier, calling it "spooky action at a distance." He much preferred *localism*. It was only late in life that he was forced to change his mind.

Physicist Anthony Leggett (1938–) writes about reductionism in these terms:

Anthony Leggett, a recipient of the Nobel Prize in Physics for his work on superfluidity and superconductors, has been a leader in the field of quantum mechanics.

> It is difficult to exaggerate the degree to which reductionism is entrenched in the thinking not only of the twentieth-century physical scientist, but also to a large extent of the twentieth-century man in the street.

—Anthony Leggett, *Quantum Measurement: Beyond Paradox*

We could go on and on. Causality has fallen victim to the theory of general relativity. Physicalism is falsified by quantum mechanics. Materialism falls apart when we discover that what lies at the heart of every object is, at root, nothing. Schrödinger debunked determinism and, to a lesser extent, mechanism with his famous cat-in-the-box thought experiment, which proved, logically if not reasonably, that according to quantum theory, Schrödinger's famous cat in a box was alive and dead at the same time. (I know. It doesn't make any sense to most of us. But theorists love this stuff.) As for realism, quantum physics pulls the curtain on that with every new pronouncement.

THE FIRST PREMISE

So what are we left with?

Premise #1: *What our culture has taught us about reality is insufficient.*

The old way of viewing the world no longer stands up to scrutiny, no matter how normal or right it feels to you.

Make no mistake about it. This is hard! Accepting that there may be a supernatural realm, possibly inhabited by inconceivable, intelligent beings that previous generations called gods and deities, is really tough for an educated, Western, modern human being. It goes against every one of our assumptions. It threatens to turn our logical worldview into something that feels suspiciously like medieval superstition. Who wants to turn back the clock to the Middle Ages? Haven't we progressed past those days?

A / B / A¹ Theory

Maybe this will help. I've written about this in almost every book I've ever done because I've found it to be an invaluable tool when it comes to understanding how we look at the world. Those who have read my previous books can probably skip the next few pages. But it might be a good refresher course, so I suggest you stick with me even if you are familiar with the technique. I call it the A / B / A¹ stage method of development.

Stage A

Let's use a belief in Santa Claus as a metaphor for understanding how the method works. In *Stage A*, we, as children, exhibit a blind belief in a man with a red suit and white beard who comes down the chimney on Christmas Eve to bring us presents. We are convinced he knows when we are good and bad and is keeping a record, so we try our darnedest to "be good, for goodness' sake."

We interpret the Christmas myth in a very literal sense. There is a real workshop at the North Pole, a real Rudolph, a real sleigh, and a real Santa. A large conspiracy consisting of television shows, an adult population that participates in the cover-up, peer pressure at school, and our social network convinces us the myth is true. So we believe, even if each passing year finds us asking more questions.

Stage A in this example represents various belief systems ranging from the beginning of humankind up to the Middle Ages, during which humans saw gods and deities behind every bush and taught their children to be afraid and watch their step or "God's gonna gitcha'!" It conveniently placed misunderstanding and ignorance in the lap of a supernatural entity. It lasted for a long time and was only upstaged after a dedicated and sometimes deadly battle waged between religion and science, fought by heroes such as Copernicus and Isaac Newton.

Stage B

Now back to the Santa Claus metaphor.

There comes a time early in our childhood development when Christmas agnosticism rears its ugly head and we enter into a difficult transition peri-

The story of Santa, much like faith in religion, begins in full belief (Stage A), then evolves into disbelief (Stage B), and, finally, becomes a metaphor for something that is real (Stage A^1).

od. Facts cannot be denied. Soon we evolve into Santa Claus atheists. We enter *Stage B*. We are tolerant of the poor, uneducated, simple kids who are not as mature as we are, but we secretly pity them and consider ourselves their intellectual superiors. We don't waste time with many of the rituals and myths. No more milk and cookies on Christmas Eve. After all, it's only Dad who shows up. We don't write the traditional letter to Santa. There are better ways to manipulate the real providers. We may be a little bitter, but we are certainly more savvy, more sophisticated.

We are now Santa Claus atheists who tolerate the system because it serves as a crutch to those we consider to be less mature than ourselves. On the other hand, there is still something in it for us, and we want it to be there when we need it. After all, among other things, it gives us legal holidays. So we outwardly play the game.

That's what we've been doing ever since science gained the upper hand on religion. The supernatural has been reduced to superstition. Gods and deities have been dethroned and replaced. We left the church in droves even though we were comfortable with the idea of having a central place in our town in which to hold weddings and funerals. *Stage A* was fine for a while, just as Santa Claus is probably good for children. Religion's story explained a lot and was a lot of fun. But eventually we had to grow up. It was time for *Stage B*.

But what happens when *Stage B* proves to be a stepping-stone to something bigger?

Stage A¹

With time and providence, something wonderful begins to happen when children grow into adults. They once again find Santa Claus religion. They become believers again.

Not in a literal sense, of course. They know there is no workshop at the North Pole. But the myth becomes a metaphor for something that is very real. They call it the Spirit of Christmas or some such thing. They say wholeheartedly, "Yes, Virginia, there is a Santa Claus!"

And there really is! It turns out that belief in the Christmas myth is much more than a metaphor. It's just that the reality is very, very different from what we were told as children. "Santa Claus" is discovered to be an interlocking network of loving parents and worldwide, fully encompassing, enjoyable, social customs. We come to understand its importance. We feel, probably without being able to explain why, the significance of what Christmas is all about. The season takes on a new meaning. We enter what I call *Stage A¹* faith—a faith that is based not upon the crude myth but upon its importance, which is both metaphorical and actually true at the same time. The Christmas tradition is seen to be significant not for what it tells us about a mythical Santa Claus but for what it tells us about the nature of humanity—about love, compassion, and wonder. Santa lives again! The importance now lies in the truth behind the story, the reality to which the story points.

And there is such a reality! People do show their love by giving presents, singing songs, and feasting together. Those are real things. They actually exist. They're not simply metaphors.

Bringing the Message Home

This homey analogy illustrates what I call the A / B / A¹ theory of spiritual development. A literal belief system, called A, is followed by skepticism. This is something quite different, so I call it B. Skepticism is followed by a new system, built on the myth of the first stage, hence the A, but interpreted with greater maturity, so it becomes A¹.

But each time we move into a new stage, we experience a death of the stage we have just left. That's what makes rethinking cherished assumptions so difficult. To move into a B stage means the death of familiar A beliefs, and so on. The process involves all the emotions that the psychiatrist Elisabeth

Kübler-Ross (1926–2004) called the stages of death and dying: denial, bargaining, anger, depression, and acceptance.

Denial—You'll never convince me there's no Santa!

Bargaining—I'll believe for another year if only the presents show up!

Anger—How could they lie to me this way?

Depression—Christmas will never be the same!

Acceptance—I'm grown up now. I can live with this.

In the case of moving from *superstition* to *supernatural*, the process is similar:

Denial—You'll never convince me there's a supernatural dimension out there!

Bargaining—I'll believe it if I can see it!

Anger—How could my teachers have deceived me this way?

Depression—My whole life has been a lie!

Acceptance—I'm grown up now. I can live with this. It's cool. Bring it on!

We have to go through them all, although in the case of Christmas we do it very quickly, usually sometime between second and third grade. Coming to accept the reality of supernatural dimensions can take a whole lifetime. Trust me on this one. I've been there. And I was a minister for forty years!

Here's the important part. Since the theory applies to every area and time of life, we experience the stages over and over again whenever we leave behind familiar but outgrown beliefs and grow into a new level of maturity.

Psychologists call the experience reframing. That's what many of us have to do when it comes to rethinking what we believe about supernatural gods. We live in a *Stage B* world in which we have been taught that supernatural and superstitious are one and the same. But now we are being asked to reassess that belief. And the people doing the asking are not religious leaders, but rather scientists! They are the ones who are insisting that our cherished beliefs about reality are inadequate.

If we consider the facts rationally and unemotionally, we are forced to admit that the equations, telescopes, microscopes, and peer-reviewed, published theories of the scientific community teach us that our first premise is not only plausible, it is becoming more probable with each passing day. Here it is again, in black and white:

What you have been taught about reality is insufficient.

THE SECOND PREMISE

What about our second premise?

Premise #2: *You are living within the walls of an illusion.*

Once we come to accept the fact that our five senses, which have stood us in good stead so far in our lives, may not be adequate to explain the true nature of reality, we are left with a tough decision. We feel like airplane pilots who can no longer see the horizon and have to trust their instruments even though everything feels upside down and backwards. After all, if we can't trust our senses, what can we trust?

There are two courses of evidence to follow at this point.

First: A Great Cloud of Witnesses

In every generation of humanity, going back thousands upon thousands of years, there have been a select few who claim to have witnessed, participat-

Concepts such as Heaven and Hell could be considered older concepts of other dimensions and realities.

ed in, or otherwise experienced intelligent beings from other dimensions. Often these people claim to have an enhanced "sixth sense"—intuition. We know a few of them who had names such as Jesus, Moses, Abraham, St. Paul, Muhammad, and the Buddha. Their followers built religions called Hinduism, Judaism, Christianity, Islam, Jainism, Buddhism, and Shinto. Their insights were recorded in sacred texts. Their experiences were kept alive in traditions such as shamanism. They produced art on cave walls and cathedrals. They told stories that became world-famous myths.

Even today, you can visit any city in the world, ask around a little, and be led to those who have experienced near-death or out-of-body experiences. Their numbers include not only clergy, authors, and spiritualists, but scientists, politicians, artists, and regular guy-next-door personalities. Thousands upon thousands and, if you go back far enough, millions upon millions of people, against all odds, claim that our dimension is only one of many that they have actually contacted briefly if not regularly. They've even given these dimensions names. Heaven, Hell, Purgatory, Nirvana, and the Lower and Upper Worlds are just a few.

In a court of law, one witness won't sway a jury. It even takes more than two or three. But if hundreds of people claim to have witnessed the same thing and, without any communication between them, testify to having experienced a similar event, their evidence becomes overwhelming.

If a hundred people can convince a jury, can millions convince you?

Second: From Experiment to Experience

We are not asking anyone to change their mind about the existence of supernatural realms based only on eyewitness accounts. The evidence is coming out of the laboratory as well. The probability of other dimensions, considered quaint or strange a few years ago, is now emerging out of mathematical equations that convince even the most skeptical scientists.

Once we admit other dimensions exist, it is only human hubris that claims that the only dimension inhabited by intelligent beings is our own.

Do these beings look like us?

Of course not. We have evolved within a material universe inhabited by material beings. Why should we suppose supernatural entities have to feature carbon-based bodies and be comprised mostly of water, or stand upright and have appendages, including sexual appendages and gender, like ours? Our language, which has been invented to describe this dimension, is no doubt completely lacking when it comes to describing anything outside of our sensory box. We can't say what something *is*. We can only say what something is like in comparison to familiar objects.

So what do these beings look like?

How can we possibly even imagine that? It would be like throwing someone into a foreign country and expect them to suddenly speak the language and understand the culture. Besides that, the very concept implied in the word "look" indicates we are thinking in terms of flesh and blood individual beings with eyes like ours. Energy manifests in myriad ways we can't imagine. Even the common idea behind the phrase "beings of light" is insufficient, considering our limited range of sight when it comes to the whole color spectrum. We can't emphasize it enough: Every description of a "being" from another dimension has to be put in somewhat, though usually inflated, human terms. There is simply no other way to describe it.

Are these beings trying to contact us?

Judging from the common belief in angels and the popularity of TV shows such as *Ancient Aliens*, a lot of people seem to think so.

Why?

If you had the ability to contact them, wouldn't you try? Why should we claim to corner the market on curiosity? We can speculate, assuming they want to help us. But we just know.

But it just seems so surreal!

I know. But evidence is evidence, facts are facts, and a lot of trustworthy people, many of whom are religious but many of whom are not, seem to have crossed over to the side of the believers. All of them can't be nuts!

I'd believe it if I could only experience it!

I understand how you feel. That's what I said for sixty years. But before you experience it, you have to open yourself to the possibility of experiencing it. That's the first step. It's not necessarily a big one. But without it you'll never get started on your journey.

The Hindu *rishis* were right five thousand years ago. Life is an illusion. We are trapped in it so it feels undeniably real and solid to us. But that's because we're inside it. If we can step out for a minute, and glimpse a greater reality, our lives will never be the same.

THE THIRD PREMISE

That leads us to the final premise:

Premise #3: *You have the ability, perhaps even the obligation, to break through those walls and glimpse the truth.*

"Breaking through the walls" indicates the need for some specialized tools of the trade. In Part II of this book we examined some of those tools.

Theoretical physics and quantum theory are brand new, having come into existence only in the last few decades, but others, such as shamanism, dowsing, and astrology, have been around for thousands of years. A few, including skills borrowed from eastern spirituality and dream studies, are old tools that have been updated and tweaked by modern practitioners. Ancient chemical substances as well have now been synthesized in the laboratory and used under strict scientific protocols to study their effects on the human brain. Admittedly, unsupervised recreational use is prevalent in many cases.

You have the choice to obey the rules and accept the version of reality presented to you, or you can break through that wall and see to the other side.

The point of all this is that it takes concentrated effort to peer through the barriers that separate parallel dimensions. The cosmos, under normal conditions, doesn't allow it because our senses have evolved within these walls. It's tempting to give up and take refuge in blind faith, as some religions propose. Many people, doing just that, have come to believe that they contact higher powers through the power of prayer, meditation, spiritualism, or psychic mediation. But faith goes only so far when inquiring minds want to know. Many don't want to simply believe. They want to know. And knowledge comes only from personal experience.

PROPHETIC WORDS?

In 2007 I wrote a book called *Faith, Trust & Belief: A Trilogy of the Spirit.* Back then I hadn't experienced some of the supernatural, one might say metaphysical, phenomena I've written about in this book but I must have been thinking about them. Every reviewer who has written about this book usually draws quotes from the following passage. In that sense, maybe the words are a little prophetic. Certainly, the intervening years have only solidified the course of history I wrote about:

"The twentieth century witnessed an onslaught of epic proportions launched against the bastions of traditional faith. Science seemed to erode the need for an outside force that created and sustains life. High-profile ministers and spiritual leaders were proven false, both in what they preached and in how they conducted their lives away from TV cameras. Politicians were tried and found wanting. Historians undermined national and international icons by "rewriting" history. They proved that what we learned about people ranging from Thomas Jefferson and Benjamin Franklin to Ike Eisenhower and Jack

Kennedy may have been less than accurate. The Bible, long understood to be 'the only infallible rule of faith and practice,' ceased to be viewed by academics in the same way it used to be. 'What did Jesus really say?' was replaced by, 'Was there really an historical Jesus?'

"That this onslaught has reached epic proportions can be seen in the surge of fundamentalist religion on the one hand and liberal spokesmen for science on the other. The 'faithful' seem to have gathered at opposite poles of right and left, conservative and liberal, believer and atheist, New Age and 'old-time religion,' there to hunker down behind ideological bunkers so as to hurl verbal bombs at the perceived enemy on the other side of the cultural divide.

"What is left to believe in? Can we believe in anything? Is the answer in the 'either/or'—*either* there is something true and real in which to place our faith *or* life is merely a cosmic accident to be survived?

"What is left to believe in? The question is plastered all over the faces of sullen pop music icons who stare at the camera with blank expressions.

"What is left to believe in? There was plenty of advanced warning. As usual, the artists among us saw it coming. Jackson Pollock and Willem de Kooning produced abstract art that ceased even trying to imitate normally perceived reality. Musicians as far removed as Igor Stravinsky and the Beatles resisted any attempt to be corralled within traditionally accepted forms.

"What is left to believe in? Arthur Miller's *Death of a Salesman* and *A Streetcar Named Desire* made no attempt to make people feel good when they left the theater. Instead, art imitated life. Hollywood epitomized the breakdown of faith. *Bonnie and Clyde, The Graduate, Easy Rider, Midnight Cowboy, The Last Picture Show, The Godfather*, and many more movies that followed scrapped the idea of 'happily ever after.'

"What is left to believe in? Bumper stickers that proclaimed, 'I'm spending my child's inheritance!' implied there wasn't going to be much of a future for younger generations. The earth seems to be polluted beyond recovery. Wars and rumors of war fill the headlines. After all, if we've already experienced, in the television journalist Tom Brokaw's words, 'the greatest generation,' what's left for the rest of us?

"Into this miasma of befuddled consciousness, do we dare insert the words "faith, trust, and belief?" Are they relevant anymore? What does this trilogy of interrelated concepts have to do with the so-called outdated idea of the Spiritual, the Other, or that which is Greater Than Ourselves?

"What is left to believe in? Just this. Most of us still passionately want to believe that the 'Spiritual,' the 'Other,' that which is 'Greater Than Ourselves,' 'God,' the 'Cosmos,' or 'Whatever We Choose to Call It' wants to reveal itself. We are so sure of the promise from beyond that we choose to act—to change the way we live our lives. Our *faith* leads to *trust*. Our trust leads to *belief*. Polls tell us that religion, often replaced by the word spirituality, is, in the midst of all the despair and gloom, bigger than ever. We may couch our belief in traditional or nontraditional religions. We may call ourselves believers, atheists, or agnostics. We may follow the precepts of Jesus, Moses, Muhammad, or the Buddha. We may believe in luck or predestination. We may place our trust in science or serendipity. But whenever we seriously contemplate the mystical 'Something' that seems to exist just beyond the boundary—a little farther than we can see, understand or reach but tantalizingly close to the limits of our perception—we take the first steps that we hope will turn our faith into trust and our trust into belief.

"This longing to "seriously contemplate the mystical Something" is not reserved for naive, pie-in-the-sky romantics. Listen to the words of no less a luminary than the great physicist and philosopher Albert Einstein:

"The most beautiful emotion we can experience is the mysterious. It is the fundamental emotion that stands at the cradle of all true art and science. He to whom this emotion is a stranger, who can no longer wonder and stand rapt in awe, is as good as dead, a snuffed-out candle. To sense that behind anything that can be experienced there is something that our minds cannot grasp, whose beauty and sublimity reaches us only indirectly: this is religiousness."

ANOTHER GREAT LEAP FORWARD

Could it be that humankind is standing on the brink of a precipice? Are we about to make another great leap forward? The next step in human evolution very well might involve what can only be called a change of heart or, more accurately, a change of consciousness. Perhaps we are even now gathering the necessary skills and abilities to become something we might have hoped for but never fully accepted as a possibility. Maybe *Homo sapiens*, the "wise man," is about to become *Homo deus*, the "god man," thus fulfilling the words of an old, old sacred text: *"You are Gods; you are all children of the Most High"* (Psalm 82:6).

Maybe we have arrived at that point of history when we come to fully realize that we are really made in what one ancient author called "the image of God."

Forty thousand years ago our ancestors crawled back into the great caves of western Europe and discovered spirituality

Are we standing on the precipice of reality? Are we about to make a great leap into another world?

and religion. Ten thousand years ago, in the Fertile Crescent, we discovered agriculture and developed the tools to form civilization. Today we are emerging from our laboratories and observatories and reaching for the skies. But the search isn't extending only "out there." It is seeking a greater truth within.

The laws of physics may prevent us from ever physically traveling great distances out into space in order to travel to the trillions of galaxies that exist so far away from us that we can't get our heads around the numbers involved. But who is to say there is a limit to how far we can travel into inner space?

If intelligent beings, who humans used to label gods and deities, exist in parallel dimensions that we label "supernatural," they may be only a thought away. Are they beckoning us to go "where no one has gone before?"

Perhaps it is more accurate to say that some *have* gone there. They've come back with marvelous stories—maybe even a few road maps to point the way. In Part II of this book we've covered a few of them.

Maybe *you* need to be the next explorer. Maybe *you* need to continue the quest for the supernatural. If so, happy journeying! In Part III we'll try to peer into the mist of the future to see what might be ahead.

PART III: THE END OF THE QUEST AND BEYOND

This is my quest—
To follow that star
No matter how hopeless,
No matter how far.
And the world will be better for this.

—Joe Darion: "The Impossible Dream," *The Man of La Mancha*

PUTTING IT ALL TOGETHER

"Why on earth do you believe in God…. Why do you want to look for divine action?" Dawkins demanded.

"For the same reason that someone might *not* want to," Barrows responded.

—From a conversation between Richard Dawkins and John Barrows, reported in Barbara Bradley Hagerty's *Fingerprints of God*.

We began our quest together in this book with two simple questions:

Are there such things as supernatural gods?

Is there such a thing as magic?

Here in Part III, it's time to return to these questions to discover if we have come close to answering them. In doing so, we'll shift the focus a little.

From one point of view, probably the overwhelming consensus point of view held by current society, the answer to both questions must simply be, "No, of course not. There is absolutely no verifiable evidence that the supernatural exists."

This is the *Faith Statement* of the scientist, the atheist, and the materialist. According to their belief system, we cannot begrudge them their opinions because they are entirely justified in their claims. Pursuing evidence of the supernatural using the tools of modern, accepted, tested, and proven research methods can produce "no verifiable evidence that the supernatural exists" because by definition, the supernatural, if it exists at all, exists outside the parameters surrounding the tools of scientific inquiry. In the courtroom of science, any evidence that cannot be seen, poked, measured, studied under a microscope, smelled, or felt is ruled out of bounds. Nothing "unreal," that is, nothing that is nonmaterial, exists.

Until relatively recently in the scientific community, that was the understanding. Case closed. Court's adjourned.

Unfortunately, this verdict was often accompanied by a very immature, perhaps even snide, judicial if not prejudicial, pronouncement: "Anyone who believes differently is wacko!" If you wanted to continue your career within the scientific community, you really had to check your spirituality at the door. If you were gifted and respected because of your scientific papers, you might earn a polite pat on the head and a condescending acceptance, but that was about all. You were viewed as an oddity. Perhaps a harmless one. But an oddity all the same.

Even the most dedicated nonbelievers, of course, don't want to completely eliminate "magic" from the human condition. To do so would discourage hope. That is a depressing way to live.

So they didn't eliminate the supernatural. They just transformed it into a rhetorical metaphor without physical substance—a mental construct that expressed philosophical truth without letting it contaminate a materialistic worldview. This brain-washing philosophy slyly seeps into our lives from all points of the social compass.

In the movie *Bull Durham*, for instance, the actor Kevin Costner portrays an aging minor league baseball player who is facing the end of his dream to play professional ball. Along the course of his career, however, he has established a sort of philosophy about what is important in life. When asked what he believes in, he responds:

> I believe in the soul ... the small of a woman's back, the hanging curve ball, high fiber, good scotch—that the novels of Susan Sontag are self-indulgent, overrated crap. I believe that Lee Harvey Oswald acted alone. I believe there ought to be a Constitutional amendment outlawing Astroturf and the designated hitter. I believe in the sweet spot, soft-core pornography, opening your presents Christmas morning rather than Christmas Eve, and I believe in long, slow, deep, soft wet kisses that last three days.

Admirable beliefs that make life interesting, but they don't exactly help a seeker of supernatural gods.

So how about this, from the movie, *Secondhand Lions*? Robert Duvall's character, Hub McCann, speaking to his young nephew, says:

> Sometimes the things that may or may not be true are the things that a young man needs to believe in the most: That people are

basically good … that honor, courage and virtue mean everything … that power and money, money and power, mean nothing … that good always triumphs over evil. And I want you to remember this: that love, true love, never dies.

You remember that, boy. You remember that. Doesn't matter if they're true or not. You see, a man should believe in those things because those things are the ones worth believing in. Got that?

In a similar vein, a popular song written by John Sebastian in 1965 and sung by his group, *The Lovin' Spoonful*, searched for something to believe in by asking a simple question:

Do you believe in magic in a young girl's heart,

How the music can free her whenever it starts?

And it's magic, if the music is groovy.

It makes you feel happy like an old-time movie.

Believe in the magic that can set you free.…

Again—nice beat, but a little short on supernatural substance.

In a February 2006 speech given at the opening concert of the Australian Chamber Orchestra, the well-known author Kurt Vonnegut (1922–2007) had these words to say about the quest for the supernatural: "The only proof I need of the existence of God is music."

Is it, then, a function of music and art, as well as religion, to reveal the supernatural—the truth behind the curtain? Is it only in this way that we can peek through life's illusions to glimpse real magic?

Perhaps not. The tide seems to be turning. Science seems on the verge of a paradigm shift. It won't happen right away, of course, but the field of quantum reality is now faced with an internal conflict that causes real dissension among the ranks. The complex equations of theoretical physicists seem to be churning up worlds, dimensions, possibilities, and realities that "cannot be seen, poked, measured, studied under a microscope, smelled or felt." And these dis-

The late author Kurt Vonnegut was a social critic and believer in a higher power, though he criticized those who asserted they understood what God was up to.

Evolutionary biologist Richard Dawkins has stated that the belief in something without evidence—faith—is one of the "great evils" of society.

coveries seem to be totally in sync with not only an ancient wisdom found in the world's oldest religions, but with the testimonies of millions of people down through the years who claim to have experienced supernatural gods.

So what's a poor scientist to do? His world is turning upside down. For hundreds of years now, ever since the scientific revolution overturned religion's hold on truth, he has held the strings of power. His hard-fought battle was won. He had overcome superstition and religious bigotry. Humankind was on the verge of true understanding. The universities and colleges were temples of reason. Religionists need not apply. The doors were closed to the past and a bright new future lay ahead.

And now this? We're going to allow the supernatural a place at the table? Why? I thought we were finally beyond that! In the words of Richard Dawkins, quoted at the beginning of this chapter:

> "Why on earth do you believe in God.... Why do you want to look for divine action?"

The answer is profound in its simplicity: *Because it might be real!*

The evidence begins to pile up:

- With the discovery of the existence of dark matter it became apparent that all our scientific theories, every one of them, are based solely on what we can measure that is contained in only 5 percent of the observable universe. What's happening in the 95 percent that we know is there but can't see? The same is true in the field of biology. DNA that forms and shapes every living thing is composed primarily of what is usually called "junk" DNA. In other words, it serves no purpose that we discern. But what if we're wrong? What if the biological answer to where we came from and where we're going is to be found in the DNA we haven't yet unraveled?

- If consciousness turns out to be infinite, existing in time and space, it will raise some troubling conclusions. If something is infinite in space, it is omnipresent. If something is infinite in time, it is eternal. Perhaps even immortal. But omnipresent, eternal and immortal are words we have traditionally reserved for God. Can "God" simply be another name for "Universal Consciousness"? If so, the religionist's God merges with the scientist's Universal Consciousness. Religion and science thus become two routes to the same destination. Different language—same goal.

- Mathematics is the home of the scientist. But the math of quantum reality points to multiple, perhaps even an infinite, number, of parallel dimensions. If we are one of many, and life has evolved here according to the laws of physics with which we are familiar, how can we unequivocally state that other laws are not working in parallel dimensions, guiding other life forms in different ways? When the Many Worlds proponents of quantum reality postulate an infinite number of "yous" existing at the same time in parallel dimensions, it opens the doors to other sentient life forms that are nothing like "you" at all. And if we can't guarantee that other such worlds do not exist, how can we guarantee that, from time to time, people here, psychically or metaphysically, visit them, just as beings from other dimensions might conceivably visit us? The written evidence is found in religious texts all over the world. We call such beings supernatural gods and deities, angels, messengers, faeries, ghosts, spirits, and the like. Apparently, a lot of people, for a long time, have experienced such entities. Are these witnesses all pathological liars or, at least, severely disturbed?

On and on it goes. Non-believers cannot disprove the existence of supernatural gods, or whatever name we give them. They can only categorically deny them.

Believers cannot prove the existence of supernatural gods, or whatever name we give them. They can only vehemently affirm them.

The battle lines are drawn while the majority of interested but much-too-busy humankind awaits the outcome. Meanwhile, our world continues to revolve. We pursue our humdrum lives, taking pleasure where we can find it in the newest techno-gizmos, dawn to dusk, day to day, job to job, party to party, obligation to obligation, decade to decade, perhaps even life to life. And we ignore the still, small voice pleading within—"Is this all there is?"

The Future

If the answer to that plaintive question has not yet been found, perhaps it is because we've been looking in the wrong place. Maybe it doesn't lie in the testimonies and texts of the past *or* the science and mathematics of the present. Maybe it lies in the future.

Is the great sweep of evolution finally leading us to a melding of natural and supernatural, science and religion, through the inevitable A / B / A[1] stages of growth? Do answers to the two questions that have guided our study lie out there right over the horizon—a horizon that is now beginning to become visible to us as science and religion begin to merge into one A¹ lane?

Perhaps the answer to life's greatest mystery is hidden within an indefinable and inexplicable phenomenon called hope. That's where our quest takes us next.

LOOKING AHEAD

Is there more than this? Yes, I believe there is, and the new science of spirituality buttresses my instinct. Science is showing that you and I are crafted with astonishing precision so that we can, on occasion, peer into a spiritual world and know God. The language of our genes, the chemistry of our bodies, and the wiring of our brains—these are the handiwork of One who longs to be known. And rather than dispel the spiritual, science is cracking it open for all to see.

—Barbara Bradley Hagerty, *Fingerprints of God*

Many years ago, when I had a lot more get-up-and-go than I seem to have lately, I awoke to a pristine morning on an unusually warm day for New England in February. About three inches of clean snow had fallen early in the night, creating a blank canvas for tracking whatever animals had been out and about during the moonlit predawn hours.

I was on a bit of a retreat, having built a log cabin in New Hampshire to serve for just that purpose. Sometimes I need to get away from human company for a while and take to the quiet woods. Living for a few days with no schedule or obligations helps clear the mind.

Today's activities were soon decided. Right outside my front door, not twenty feet away, were the tracks of an inquisitive buck deer. At least it appeared to be a buck. There's really no way to tell the sex of a deer by looking at tracks, but the size and meandering trail seemed to indicate a large male, so I decided I needed to spend the day confirming my hunch. Grabbing a quick breakfast and packing a hasty lunch, I packed up my camera and determined that I would track this deer down to its lair and perhaps get a picture or two along the way.

Deer have always represented magic to me. You rarely see them if they don't want to be seen, but evidence of their presence is everywhere. Tracks, scat, scrapes, rubs, and other signs of their presence are readily found, but actual glimpses, real contact, is pretty rare in the wild, where they have learned to disappear at the first sign of people. Like magic, hints of their presence are everywhere, but their actual reality is illusive.

I spent the morning discovering all sorts of things about this particular deer. I learned where it liked to travel on its home turf, discovering secret trails through brush and shallow depressions. I learned what it liked to eat and where it preferred to hide when it turned to inspect his back trail. Once I even found a place on a small knoll where it had laid down to rest and then, presumably because it sensed me coming, quickly got up and bound off into cover.

By noon I was tired and hungry, so I stopped at the edge of a field, knowing full well that the deer was probably watching me from cover somewhere on the other side of the open ground ahead. I sat down on a fallen tree and ate a quiet lunch as I decided what to do next.

By now it was obvious that I wasn't going to get even a glimpse of this deer, let alone a picture, unless I changed my strategy. I had been searching for evidence of its passing and found it in spades. The tracks, the nibbled branches, the spots of urine, and the bedding areas all assured me that I was following a real, live deer, but I hadn't even caught a fleeting glimpse so I couldn't describe it in any detail. If anyone had asked me if I believed a buck deer had left all this evidence I would have said, "Of course! Look at the signs." But if they had wanted me to show them proof or offer a tangible description, I had nothing.

Obviously, something needed to change.

That's when a thought occurred to me—profound in its simplicity. If I wanted to actually get a picture that would capture this illusive quarry, I needed to be where it was going, not where it had been.

But how to get there? Of all the myriad possibilities of where this deer was going, how could I possibly get ahead of it to gather the pictorial proof I wanted?

There was only one way, of course. I needed to determine its future by patterning its past. All the morning signs had been pointing in a general direction. If I could deduce that direction, I could possibly circle ahead and quietly wait, camera at the ready.

Looking back over its morning route, determining what it had preferred to eat and where it had wandered, knowing the kind of country it liked and what kind of concealing cover it wanted, I took a chance and moved toward the right, around a small hill, when the deer's tracks indicated a left turn. I knew enough about this area to remember a small stream on the other side of the hill. It was home to thick, brushy terrain that seemed a good place for the deer to hold up for the night after a long day spent running away from a crazy guy with a camera. There was cover, food in abundance, and running water. It seemed perfect.

Taking a chance that the deer would no doubt see me supposedly moving away from where it was now hiding, I moved around the hill and took up a stand on a small hillock that overlooked the place I thought it might be heading.

Nine out of ten times when I try something like this, I guess wrong and never see the quarry again, but this time must have been the tenth time. An hour later, just at dusk, a magnificent buck stepped out of cover and headed for a small swamp that bordered the stream. He was some distance out and only stopped to look back on his trail a few times. No doubt he figured he had given me the slip, but I managed to get a few pictures. They were dark, of course, given the setting sun. With no tripod, I had to hold the camera still for a long time so they were a little blurry as well. Back in those days of film they didn't lend themselves to cropping and Photoshop magic. But to me they were wonderful. They offered tangible proof that the deer was real and my quest was not in vain.

It had been a beautiful, productive day. Even without the photographic proof at the end, I would have been satisfied. Other people might think I was crazy for "wasting" time in such a seemingly unproductive endeavor. But, almost fifty years later, each moment of that day stands out in Kodak clarity. It was one of the most perfect days I have ever spent.

It also serves as an important metaphor in our quest for the "magic" of the supernatural. Do supernatural gods really exist?

Of course they do. The evidence is all around us, plain as the track I followed that pointed to the existence of the deer I eventually photographed. Self-evident clues have been a part of our story ever since humans first crawled back into the great painted caves to draw pictures.

But to confront the supernatural head on it is not sufficient to merely look at the signs it has left behind in our history. We have studied such clues throughout this book and they are fascinating. They reveal a

Just as one might use evidence like tracks and trampled vegetation to track a deer until it is found, patiently following the clues can lead one, inevitably, to supernatural gods.

lot about the nature of the subject and tell us what to expect, but to actually confront the supernatural personally we have to pattern its tracks and get ahead of it. We have to be at least mentally in its path when it arrives. We have to use every bit of skill we can acquire and perfect. We have to prepare ourselves and be ready.

That's what studying this subject does for us. It helps us prepare. The moment of truth occurs only when hope turns into experience, when faith turns into reality. Then when we confront the supernatural face to face, we no longer believe. We know.

There is a world of difference. The mind-pictures we take of the encounter may be too blurry and indistinct to convince anyone else. But that's not really the point, is it? They are sufficient to convince us. And that is enough. The purpose of a quest is to personally arrive at the goal, not convince the world that we got there. Even if we do offer proof to the skeptics, it will not be enough. Each and every one of us, skeptic and believer alike, needs to make the journey alone. We cannot be satisfied to see a picture of the Holy Grail. For it to work its magic, we need to hold it in our own hands. Anything else is second hand—an insufficient reality.

DREAMS AND REALITY

Today we stand on the verge of a paradigm shift in human consciousness. If we look through the lens of our A / B / A^1 pattern of spiritual growth, we can discern our progress:

A: The Age of Religion

This stage consisted of a world rich in dreams and magic. An early ancestor, some 40,000 years ago, had a vision. Was it inspired by a mushroom he ate? Did the mushroom contain a chemical that, for a moment at least, expanded the five filters that had evolved in his brain—filters that we now call the senses of smell, sight, touch, taste, and hearing—filters that up until that moment kept too much reality from flooding his mind with information that might have distracted him when he most needed to be alert to the approach of a predator? Was he now open to a sixth sense—spiritual discernment?

However it happened, was this ancestor suddenly smitten with new possibilities of spiritual worlds he had never before even considered? Did he then crawl back into a great cave to be alone with his thoughts? Using pigment, did he transfer his vision on to the cave walls, becoming the world's first inspired artist? Did he emerge back into the sunlight to teach others of his tribe about the wonders he had experienced? Did he become the first shaman?

We'll never know, of course. Maybe he was just a gifted teacher. Maybe he was hard-wired to become a priest. Maybe he was the first to realize that it was time for humans to take the next step in their evolution. Maybe he was just brilliant.

The rest of the tribe, to be sure, didn't all blindly follow his lead. There were a few, no doubt, who thought he was a prophet. There were others, for sure, who must have considered him crazy. They probably banned him from their presence more than a few times. They argued with him. They tried to convince him to settle down and be normal.

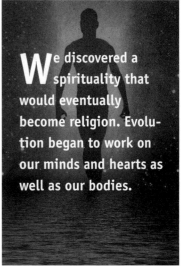

We discovered a spirituality that would eventually become religion. Evolution began to work on our minds and hearts as well as our bodies.

"This is our country," they probably declared. "Love it the way it is or leave it."

"Why should we listen to you when you're the only one making these outlandish claims?"

"Why do you think you're right and everyone else is wrong?"

This, sad to say, is the one of the few constants of human behavior. We have always denigrated agents of change.

But whatever, however, and whenever it happened, the world did change on that day. An advanced species of animal became human. We discovered a spirituality that would eventually become religion. Evolution began to work on our minds and hearts as well as our bodies. It was now practical to develop better tools and weapons, but no longer sufficient. Music, art, symbolic thought, and mythology began to be as important, perhaps even more important, than simple survival. It was no longer important to live just in order to perpetuate our species. We needed to pass on a reason to do so. The necessity of life now took a back seat to the meaning of life. And that simple change made all the difference.

B: The Age of Curiosity

It took a long time, but the first stage of human development, the *A Stage*, eventually led to the second stage—the *B Stage*. During this stage we gave vent to our powerful human curiosity. It drove us to extremes. We wanted to know how things worked and we wanted to learn how to control the process.

What a wonderful, innovative stage! There were bumps in the road, of course.

Copernicus, for instance, thought the world revolved around the sun. The rest of the world thought he was nuts. He turned out to be right.

Isaac Newton had a dust-up with the Catholic Church over the boundaries of what they considered to be their sacred territory. They finally apologized—a few hundred years later.

Through it all, we struggled on. We experimented with economics, governmental policies, philosophies, social systems, and race relations. We

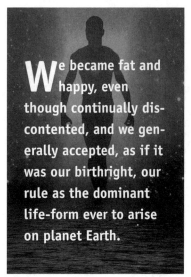

We became fat and happy, even though continually discontented, and we generally accepted, as if it was our birthright, our rule as the dominant life-form ever to arise on planet Earth.

learned to be comfortable in all sorts of weather. We learned to be well-fed even in times of drought and famine. We learned to fly through the air, walk on the moon, speed down roads that are marvels of engineering, conquer every inch of the planet, pave over our environment, destroy our ozone layer, wreck our ecosystems, bring our species to the brink of extinction by means of many different technologies, and overpopulate to our heart's content. We became fat and happy, even though continually discontented, and we generally accepted, as if it was our birthright, our rule as the dominant life-form ever to arise on planet Earth.

But the voice of the mystic, the spiritual craving of our first spiritual ancestor, the impulse of the shaman, artist, and musician refused to evolve away. From the long forgotten *A Stage* of human development, it echoed down the corridors of time: Who are we? Why are we here? Is there more?

It's the voice that refuses to die no matter what the establishment does to snuff it out.

A¹: The Age of Scientific Spirituality

And thus it is that today a few visionaries believe other dimensions, inhabited by sentient, unimaginable beings—in other words, the *super*natural—actually exists. Most scientists think those visionaries are misguided at best, seriously deluded at worst.

But what if the visionaries are on to something? What if they are, indeed, agents of change? Could this be the beginning of a new stage of human development? Are science and spirituality beginning to merge into one lane of traffic? Are they converging, after all these years, centuries, and millenniums? Is the voice of our ancient *A Stage* spiritual ancestor melding with the informed opinion of the modern *B Stage* scientist and pointing the way to a new understanding of what it is and means to be human?

If so, what will the "new" human look like?

A PLACE CALLED HOPE

Now we come to the boundaries of a land we earlier called "Hope." We are speculating, of course. It involves the same kind of thinking I used when I realized I was never going to see the deer I was tracking if I continued to just follow the trail he had left behind. That trail gave me a lot of clues about his habits and tendencies, but more important, it pointed the way to where he was going.

In the same way, the clues we have studied in this book point the way. We need only use a little creative imagination.

Consider the following:

- On January 1, 1775, there weren't very many people living in the North American colonies who had much hope that they would ever become a free and independent nation. A decade later it became apparent that the sweep of history was greater than the hopelessness of soon-to-be Americans. Against all odds, a rag-tag army defeated the mightiest monarchy on earth and the hope of democracy triumphed at last.

- On January 1, 1861, there weren't many American slaves who dared dream of ever becoming free citizens in a land they had built by the blood, sweat, and tears of their labor. By May of 1865, hope had triumphed against all odds.

- On January 1, 1920, there weren't many American women who thought they would ever be allowed to vote alongside their husbands. That all changed eight months later.

- On January 1, 2008, very few people dared hope Americans would ever elect a black president. That changed the following November. Barack Obama, the author of a book appropriately entitled *The Audacity of Hope*, was elected president of the United States.

- On January 1, 2012, Peter Higgs thought the radical new particle now named after him would never be found during his lifetime. Six months later the whole family of physicists gathered for the announcement of its discovery.

What do these examples all have in common?

Hope!

Against all odds, something that was considered hopeless become a reality. It is as if destiny is a positive force that will not be denied. The power of a nation, the threat of a Fuhrer, the scorn of peer rejection, the dominion of a monolithic church—nothing can stop it. When the time is right, the force of history triumphs.

These illustrations make it seem as though evolution is not *pushing* us up from the primeval ooze. It is *pulling* us toward a fixed destination. Call it fate. Call it predestination. Call it anything you want, but sometimes it feels as if we are being ordered and structured to fulfill a destiny.

Hope has the power to make things—even apparently impossible things—happen.

We often fight it. We usually resist tooth and nail. But our inexorable trajectory has been upward and outward ever since we crawled out of those great painted caves. In spite of our failures, love still triumphs in the midst of hate. Freedom's song is sung anew. Compassion reigns even in prison camps. Seemingly invincible rulers become footnotes.

The poetry of Percy Bysshe Shelley (1792–1822) expresses the plight of the tyrant whose subjects despaired of hope:

> I met a traveler from an antique land
> Who said: "Two vast and trunkless legs of stone
> Stand in the desert.... Near them, on the sand,
> Half sunk, a shattered visage lies, whose frown,
> And wrinkled lip, and sneer of cold command,
> Tell that its sculptor well those passions read
> Which yet survive, stamped on these lifeless things,
> The hand that mocked them, and the heart that fed:
> And on the pedestal these words appear:
> 'My name is Ozymandias, king of kings:
> Look on my works, ye Mighty, and despair!'
> Nothing beside remains. Round the decay
> Of that colossal wreck, boundless and bare
> The lone and level sands stretch far away."

Spirituality, our search for supernatural gods is the hope that refuses to die. It's almost as if the questing voice within is hard-wired into our circuits. Ozymandias, called by many names—science, atheism, common sense, materialism, reductionism, progress, and intellectualism are just a few—has his day in the sun. But eventually he is covered over by the relentless sands of history.

> Hope springs eternal in the human breast;
> Man never Is, but always To be blest.
> The soul, uneasy, and confin'd from home,
> Rests and expatiates in a life to come.

Thus wrote Alexander Pope (1688–1744). He may be on to something. And he's not the only one.

The idea that we are being pulled toward a future that is indicated by clues from our past is not a new one. Pierre Teilhard de Chardin (1881–1955), a Jesuit priest who lived in the first half of the twentieth century, popularized the idea of what he called the "Omega Point," a future point in time that is drawing everything toward a final unification and higher state of consciousness. Drawing on the words of Jesus in the book of Revelation, he identified that point with Christ who said, "I am the Alpha and the Omega, the beginning and the end" (Revelation 1 and Revelation 22).

The Omega Point concept was later expanded by writers such as John David Garcia (1936–2001) and Tulane University's Frank Tipler (1947–). Tipler has been soundly criticized by many in the science community, who call his ideas pseudoscience. But various theorists followed his lead while trying to avoid his critics. When a TV episode of Morgan Freeman's *Through the Wormhole* popularized both Tipler and his theories, the public responded with delightful curiosity.

Now all sorts of fanciful variations on this theme have caught hold in the science fiction realm. Maybe Yogi Berra said it best: "Our future is all ahead of us!"

Does this bring us any closer to supernatural gods? Have we laid bare any spiritual mysteries, psychic experiences, and scientific truths? Did we successfully complete our quest for lost truths? Or is something yet missing?

Only you can answer those questions. Perhaps they don't even have an answer. Anyone who undertakes a quest for

Pierre Teilhard de Chardin was a Jesuit priest, paleontologist, and geologist who devised the idea of the Omega Point.

the *Holy Grail* knows the grail is only a reason to go questing. The adventure lies in the journey. Once you hold the Grail in your hand, the story ends.

Thus it may forever be with the quest for the supernatural. Will we ever, as a species, step out of the box together? Of course we will all find the answer, one way or another, at death. But, while still living, has the quest already been fulfilled by a multitude of individuals who were dedicated enough, or lucky enough, to try? Is it time to heed their voices?

Consider these words from Dr. Dean Radin in his book *Supernormal*:

If, as a species we are evolving toward a new fundamental worldview, then our interpretation of phenomena that lay in the boundaries between mind and matter may be headed toward a unification. If that does occur, then how that future may look and feel stretches the imagination.

But perhaps this transformation is precisely what the mystics have been preparing us for so diligently. Maybe the experiences of samadhi and the siddhis are seen as ineffable and mysterious not just because we don't have the language to talk about them yet, but because if we really understand these concepts, *it would change everything.*

Time will tell. Meanwhile we can take refuge in words from the Bible:

Faith is the substance of things hoped for,
The evidence of things not seen.

—Hebrews 11:1

WHEN WE MEET ... WHAT?

Jacob named the place Peneiel—"Face of God"—for he said, "I have seen God face to face, yet my life has been spared."

—Genesis 32:30

Have you ever indulged in online dating? It's not something I've ever done, but I can imagine what it must be like to meet someone in person after an extensive, long-range relationship. Up to now you have been learning about each other. Perhaps you've emailed pictures, opinions about favorite foods, movies, hopes, and dreams, and maybe even indulged in a few long-distance phone calls. But at some point, the moment of truth must arrive. You will actually meet face to face and allow yourself to take in all the vibes, body language, and unspoken feelings that go with such a meeting. You will undoubtedly be nervous. Unless you have a colossal ego, you will no doubt be more worried about the impression you are creating rather than the impression your date will make. After all, you've already formed your opinion of her or him. It may not be a correct impression. Only time will tell about that. But if you are ever to progress in your relationship, the moment of truth will arrive, surrounded by hopes and fears. There's no getting around it.

Now let's extend the metaphor a bit. Suppose supernatural gods, unseen beings, angels, devils, spirit guides, faeries, parallel-dimension entities—we have used all these terms in this book—actually do exist? What if there are intelligent beings on the other side of our reality fence? And I mean real entities, not hypothetical figments of our imagination or postulated, anthropomorphic symbols of our imagination. That's right—the REAL thing! Actual beings who live in a parallel universe or dimension. And what if it is our destiny, at some time during the great sweep of evolutionary history, to make contact?

Throughout this book we've been talking about them—imagining them, studying them, and engaging in a kind of online dating process. But what if they're real? Actually real? Really real? Not entities-once-removed. Are you ready to meet them? What will they be like?

Remember, now, we can't imagine what they look like because we're talking about a reality wherein seeing is superfluous. There's no matter on the other side of the Higgs field that will reflect light to our eyes, assuming we could actually go there in our physical form. At least, nothing we can call matter. Matter forms only over here on our side. That's why we call it the material universe.

By the same token, there's no sound as we know it, so communication can only be what we might call "telepathic"—consciousness to consciousness. That means their thoughts, and yours, are totally transparent, leaving you, and them, pretty much exposed and vulnerable.

You can't even really describe such entities because descriptions can only deal with objects with which we are familiar—colors, dress, features, and

Accepting that you will see angels and other spirits someday is a huge step towards actually encountering them in another reality.

the like. But those things only exist on our side of the Higgs field. We're talking about pure energy, now, with no mass involved—at least as we understand mass.

I realize this is almost impossible to think about. Even the biblical writers had problems with it:

> It is written: "No eye has seen, no ear has heard, no heart has imagined, what God has prepared...."
>
> —I Corinthians 2:9

All that being said, though, if you believe there is any kind of afterlife at all, if your religious convictions have convinced you that heaven, or its equivalent, awaits, if you have accepted even the possibility of unseen angels, spirits, or supernatural entities, someday, in some form, you will meet up with them. It might happen if humankind continues to evolve spiritually and at some point makes a conscious, quantum leap into a parallel reality. It will certainly happen at your death if any part of you lives on.

All through this book we have been "dating" or corresponding with such entities "online," as it were. Now let's imagine we're actually going to meet one of them. What will that experience be like? Will the meeting be a good one? Will it be pleasant? Will it be a moment of inexpressible peace and joy? Or will it be a horror—the culmination of all our fears and the insecurities expressed in dreams of things that go bump in the night?

It's time to face the possibilities and see what the testimonies of witnesses we've been quoting so far have to say about it. As we have seen, many people, throughout history, claim to have seen beings from the other side. What does their experience teach us?

A Philosophical Detour

At this point, we have to pause to take a bit of a philosophical detour. There is no avoiding it. It's too easy to get sidetracked and jump without knowing where we're going to land. We're about to go where angels tread. We need to examine our thought process.

In one sense, and it's a very important sense, we create gods in our own image. That is to say that whether or not supernatural entities exist, we conceive of them in terms familiar to us. We imagine them as if they exhibited human traits. There's just no other way to do it. To make matters worse, we often like to think of them as being our "saviors"—of doing for us what we cannot do for ourselves.

Let me explain.

Somewhere deep within us is the sure and certain knowledge that our human race is fatally flawed. We expect people to mess up and we are rarely disappointed.

We set speed limits, for instance. We don't trust drivers to proceed within safe limits so we decide how fast we think they should go along a certain stretch of road. That's only natural. They might be approaching a place they are not familiar with and we want to warn them about a hazard, such as children at play, that might catch them unaware.

But here's the key. We don't expect them to follow the speed limit. Even before we post a speed limit sign, we pass laws telling them what will happen if they disobey. We send policemen to lay in wait and record their speed on radar because we know they will lie about how fast they were going. We build prisons to incarcerate them if they get caught. In other words, we assume they will not drive safely. America is built on laws, not the honor system. And why is that? It's because we pragmatically assume people will break laws because they are fatally flawed and cannot be trusted.

The same principle holds true in every other facet of our lives. We assume people are prone to think of themselves first, to do what is personally expedient rather than socially responsible, and to generally act selfishly unless we curb their natural instincts. Altruism is usually viewed with suspicion. Our first question when facing a genuine example of moral behavior may remain unspoken but it is usually a variation of "What's in it for you?"

We insist, however, that this is not the case, even as we wonder why society sometimes breaks down. Here in America, for instance, we call our system of government a good system—perhaps the greatest on earth. Yet we pass punitive laws with exceptional frequency.

Why? Because democracy never works unless every voter takes it upon themselves to become informed, and then participates enthusiastically, sometimes even sacrificially.

But voters never have, and they never will, and we all know that, even though we continually blame the *people* rather than the *system*. It's *their* fault, not the system of government.

We teach this way of thinking to our children. We know that if we give them too much freedom in school, for instance, they will be unruly, ungovernable. So the first thing we teach them on the first day of class is to form straight lines, sit in assigned seats, and behave. We punish them if they don't. In other words, the first lessons they learn are about how to perform in a society that considers them fatally flawed and inherently unmanageable, without rules, regulations, and laws.

Thus we reveal a truth about ourselves. No matter what we say, down deep inside we believe that humans are flawed. Whether we call it original sin or human nature makes no difference. Given freedom, people will act selfishly, often maliciously, and usually illegally. That's a given.

How do we correct this fatal flaw? We look for a savior. That savior may be a perfect set of laws, a better set of rules, governmental controls, divine or alien intervention, but we know we need help—some*one* or some*thing* to save us from ourselves. We are like Brother Lawrence of old who famously, if petulantly, asked forgiveness of God by saying, "Thus I will always do if you leave me to myself!"

What this means is that whenever we think about spiritual entities, it is easy to fall into a duality trap of either/or. We either think of them as being better than us, while striving to help us overcome our human tendencies, or we think of them as fatally flawed like ourselves, while indulging in all manner of frailties on a much bigger stage than is available to us.

THE FIRST POLE OF OUR DUALITY

An example of the first way of thinking is found in the theology of Christianity. Humans, under the influence of their original sin, needed a savior.

God, in the form of Jesus the Christ, came to Earth to take upon himself the penalty for our sin, release us from a death sentence, and free us for eternity.

The basic idea behind Christian thought is this. Suppose you are arrested for speeding and brought before a judge.

"Are you guilty?" he asks.

"Yes," you reply, "I knowingly broke the law. I'm sorry. I wish I was different, but I did it."

"Being sorry doesn't cut it," the judge declares. "You broke the law and the penalty must be paid. That's the way the system works. The fine is $100."

"That may be," you say, "but I don't have $100. I am unable to pay the fine."

"That doesn't matter," declares the judge. "This is a nation of law and you are guilty of breaking the law. Off to jail with you!"

The reason Jesus is often called Christ the Redeemer is that He literally redeems souls the same way one might regain lost goods if someone paid for them for you. (Photo of Christ the Redeemer statue in Rio de Janeiro, Brazil).

But before the bailiff whisks you down to the dungeons, the judge does a strange thing. He takes off his black robe, the symbol of his power and authority, steps out from behind the high bench where he has been sitting, comes down to stand beside you, pulls $100 out of his pocket, and pays your fine himself.

The law has been satisfied. You were guilty of breaking it but your penalty has been paid by the very judge who pointed out your fatal flaw. He has stepped from his world, the world of the high bench of superiority, into yours, the world of the fatal flaw. You are free to go ("and sin no more," hopefully!). This doctrine is called "substitutionary atonement." Our sins are "atoned for" by a substitute. In Jewish theology, the substitute was an animal sacrifice, often a lamb. Christianity substituted the son of God—the "lamb" of God. But the meaning is exactly the same.

This theology, the essence of traditional Christianity, represents the first pole of the duality we are talking about. It demonstrates the kind of thinking we display when we automatically believe that supernatural beings care about us, want us to overcome our flaws, and are trying to help us evolve so that we can someday be as they are. We may call them "guardian angels," "higher powers," or "spirit guides," but the principle is the same.

By the way—you don't have to be religious to share this view. The same basic idea is found in the arguments of those who believe that ancient aliens once fiddled with our DNA and then sat back to wait for their evolutionary experiment to unfold. From time to time these advanced experimenters had to step in and keep us from destroying ourselves. This we will always do, considering our fatal flaw, so we need watching.

However the idea is expressed, either in a religious or secular context, the bottom line is that, according to this view, supernatural entities are on our side. They are "higher" and "better" than us. They care about us. Indeed, they may even love us. They want what is good for us and strive to make us better so we can be like them.

This way of thinking represents the first pole of our duality. What about the other pole?

THE SECOND POLE OF OUR DUALITY

There is another way of thinking about supernatural entities. That way was expressed in the Greek pantheon of gods and later adopted by the Romans.

Greek gods may have been, for all practical purposes, immortal, at least after they were created or born, but they were just like us—only more so. They had selfish desires and fatal flaws. They indulged in all manner of bad behaviors that included ego trips and temper tantrums. They just did it on a much larger stage.

Old Zeus, for instance, loved human women, much to the consternation of Hera, his wife. Following his great victory over the Titans, he cut quite a swath through the female population of Olympus.

Gaia, his grandmother, didn't see eye to eye with this newfangled bevy of gods that Zeus had brought into being, so she gave birth to a race of hideous, almost invincible giants who waged war on the Olympians. They were about to carry the day when they were thwarted by Zeus's illegitimate son, Hercules, and Athena who, it is said, was born full grown from Zeus's head while the battle raged. Hercules killed Alcoyoneus, the leader of the Giant forces, thus ending the battle.

Hera, we might add, is said to be the goddess of marriage. Why she got this title is a mystery. Her husband became quite a divine philanderer and she took great delight in punishing the poor, innocent, human women rather than placing the blame where it deserved to be. She also took vengeance upon the innocent Hercules. After all, he didn't ask for his father to seduce a human woman to give him birth. This didn't seem to bother Hera, however. She eventually drove Hercules mad and caused him to kill his own wife and children.

The purpose of this excursion into Greek mythology is to point out the fact that supernatural entities, represented by these mythological gods, aren't always viewed as good, loving beings. In that sense, we are made in their image. They display all our own human foibles, but on a heavenly stage. Such gods cannot be emulated, as Christians seek to emulate Christ. They must be appeased. Gods such as these are to be feared, not followed.

The Greek gods are a super example of how not all gods envisioned by human beings are good and benevolent. Zeus, Hera, Athena, Apollo, Gaia, Poseidon, etc., were as flawed as ordinary people.

Where did they come from? What philosophy gave them birth? Are they simply representative of human frailties, writ large? Or are they extreme examples of entities encountered by shamanic travelers who then described them in mytho-poetic legends?

However such supernatural entities entered into human consciousness, they inspired the custom of sacrifice. Even, in its extreme form, human sacrifice.

OUTSIDE THE POLES OF OUR DUALITY

There is another way to imagine supernatural entities that lies outside the scope of either loving, higher powers, or powers that, like us, are fatally flawed. What if such entities simply don't care about us? What if they are just going about their business and perhaps don't even know we exist? What if, when contact is achieved, they are as surprised as us when we show up in their world, when they show up in ours, or when the two worlds inevitably collide? What if we and they are on parallel evolutionary tracks in parallel evolutionary dimensions? What then?

This is more in line with the traditional shamanic understanding of supernatural entities. From ancient times, shamans have visited parallel worlds to seek help or information for the tribe that was their extended family. They have universally expressed caution that to take such a journey, one must first prepare by indulging in rituals of safekeeping. Sometimes their journeys brought them into contact with helpful spirits. At other times, they encountered the dark side. Shamanic history is ripe with stories of evil practitioners who used, for lack of a better term, "dark magic" to injure their opponents.

But there is also found within shamanistic tradition a class of entities that don't even seem to notice when shamans cross over and engage them. They seem to be, for lack of a better way to say it, too busy going about whatever their business is to pay attention to mere spirit travelers. They seem to ignore such intrusions as being beneath them. They act much the same as we do when we are carrying out some task and find ourselves confronted by an ant on the sidewalk. We may give it a glance, but it certainly isn't going to disrupt our course of action.

Moving Ahead

We have now finished our brief philosophical excursion. Hopefully it has alerted us to the fact that we can't really assume we know what to expect when we first peek over to view the other side of our material fence. Maybe supernatural entities are universally loving and helpful. Maybe they're not. And maybe they just don't care, one way or another. But evidence, admittedly both circumstantial and subjective, appears to lead to these three possible outcomes. I call them The Good, The Bad, and The Indifferent. There is so much material here from both religious tradition and personal experience that we're going to devote a full chapter to each aspect. Let's take them one at a time.

THE GOOD

And God saw all that he had made, and behold, it was very good.

—Genesis 1:31

THE TESTIMONY OF THE TEXTS

By far the great majority of most religious texts, as well as tales told by those who have experienced the other side through NDEs or OBEs, tell us that we have nothing to worry about when our time comes to encounter the other side, either after death or by mystic vision. They are, by a large percentage, positive, uplifting accounts. Most people who have gone "over" come back with stories that feature words such as "beauty," "love," "acceptance," and "compassion." The great majority of the participants didn't want to return to their worldly life. Given a choice, most of them would have chosen to stay on the other side were it not for some compelling unfinished business back here they needed to attend to.

A great example is the testimony of none other than the Apostle Paul of New Testament fame. Here is what he had to say about his OBE:

> I must go on boasting. Although there is little to be gained, I will go on to visions and revelations from the Lord. I know a man in Christ [presumably the modest Paul, himself] who fourteen years ago was caught up to the third heaven. Whether it was in the body or out of the body I do now know—God knows. And I know that this man—whether in the body or out of the body I do not know, but God knows—was caught up to paradise. He

heard inexpressible things, things that man is not permitted to tell.

—II Corinthians 12:1–4

While reflecting on that experience, he said:

We are confident, I say, and would prefer to be away from the body and at home with the Lord.

—II Corinthians 5:8

And even more telling:

I am torn between the two [states of existence]. I desire to depart and be with Christ, which is far better indeed.

—Philippians 1:23

THE TESTIMONY OF THE EXPERIENCE

If you are more comfortable talking about this aspect of supernatural entities without resorting to the words of the Bible, read this excerpt from the work of Dr. Jeffrey Long, written in June 2016:

It doesn't matter if they nearly died in an auto accident or a drug overdose, giving birth or attempting suicide.

Among the thousands of people who chose to share their near-death experiences with the Near Death Experience Research Foundation, the report is often the same: They come back with a profound understanding of God's love.

Love is clearly an important part of near-death experiences. This experience of deep love often carries within it an affirmation of unity or oneness between all people or even all things.

—Dr. Jeffrey Long, *Washington Post*, June 29, 2016

A Personal Testimony

From time to time in this book, I've reported personal experiences. The purpose was to bring home the fact that we need to do more than study this stuff. We need to personally experience it. I don't claim any advanced, esoteric knowledge. I firmly believe that experiences such as these, however we define them, are available to everyone. Whether they are actual OBEs or mental tricks I play on myself, the results are the same. They are real in the sense that they have changed me for the better and given me a greater confidence in what someday lies ahead for all of us at the moment of death, which I now consider to be simply a transition from one form of life to another.

What follows is another entry from my journal. It illustrates the fact that love prevails in the face of our fears, even when it is tough love. Here is the entry, edited only for length and clarity:

September 1, 2014

I learned about the meaning of acceptance this morning. As always, the lesson was totally unexpected and completely different than I thought it would be. The power of this latest OBE has been beyond anything I have experienced before. It followed an actual waking experience of encounters with animals in an unexpected way over the last three days.

Their message?

To heed the call to a new quest, to be open to new wonders and possibilities—to pursue new adventures and explore new travels.

In light of all this, all I could do was laugh with joy when this experience occurred. Here it is:

I woke up in the middle of the night, feeling wide awake. I decided to meditate in the quiet of early, early morning. Almost right away I felt my consciousness separate from my body and float free. I didn't really know what to do. I felt something very powerful move inside me. I was so disconcerted I was almost startled enough to end the vision right there, but decided to stay with it and empty my mind as much as possible. In short, I just "accepted" what was happening as a spectator, waiting to see what might happen next.

I found myself standing, or hovering, rather, over the rock beneath our back porch. We erected it to mark the spot where two lines of earth energy intersect. To my right and down the hill lay the feminine energy of our Medicine Wheel. To my left, the masculine energy of the rock spiral. In front of me was the intersection of the two, beginning what we have named the "love line," running up to the house. I turned halfway to my right, now facing toward the southwest, and held out my arms. The Shaman's Circle on the hill was now on my right, the Medicine Wheel on my left.

Suddenly, and I mean suddenly, I was bathed in all the colors of the rainbow. I saw my astral body as if I was standing off to the side while still being present in it. My feet were rooted in the ground. As a matter of fact, I had no feet. They just plunged into the ground, but they consisted of many different colors running down my legs. It was the same with my head. It was connected to

The rock spiral the author and his wife made represents masculine energy.

the sky, seemingly turning to colors that just went up and up. (Here I wish I was an artist. Words don't work.) My arms as well—one disappeared into the colors of the Shaman's Circle, the other into the colors of the Medicine Wheel. I hung suspended in space, a body of rainbow light and color "connected" to the four points of the compass and the four places of power above and below, left and right.

(At this point my left brain took over. I began to wonder, since we had found three power spots, two of masculine energy and one of feminine, whether there was another feminine power place in the swamp on the west corner of the property. I'll have to check!)

At any rate, the best I can say is that I "saw" my astral body, consisting of many moving rays of light, suspended in space, connecting spirit above with earth below and feminine and masculine places of power. I was in the posture of crucifixion, and can only assume that Spirit took the familiar image of the cross and used it as a metaphor that I would understand.

I saw a line of male shamans on my right and female shamans on my left—two long, single lines of people, each carrying a goblet (dare I say "grail," or perhaps "cup"?) filled with a boiling hot, very frightening, steaming, vile liquid. They approached me with faces that were resigned but somehow loving. "Tough love," certainly, but loving. They seemed to say, "What must be done will be done."

With that, they began to pour the contents—the boiling, vile, ("sinful" seems to be the word that best fits) contents—the fiery liquid contained in the goblets—into me. Somehow I wasn't afraid, but waited for the pain to begin.

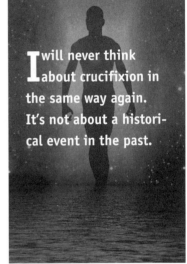

It never did! It didn't hurt. There was no pain. Instead, I took the dark liquid into myself and somehow transformed it into light. The more they poured, the brighter and more brilliant the light. It was Alchemy—turning lead into gold. I had, in the words of Christianity, taken into myself the sins of the world and turned it into glorious light. I had "accepted" the hurt and pain and turned it into blessing.

I will never think about crucifixion in the same way again. It's not about a historical event in the past. It's not about something that will happen to us when we die, in the future. Each one of us, when we made the decision to enter this perception realm, the material world, agreed to "pick up our cross," agreed to be "crucified" by the world. We agreed to take on and "accept" the pain of life with its humiliation and powerlessness, with its senseless tragedy and futility, and turn it into pure light.

As all this was going on I was very much aware of the place where all the opposites crossed. It was right at the juncture of head and feet, left and right arm—the place of the heart chakra.

Although I wanted to stay in this vision forever, there was one more task to accomplish. There was a bit of a party. I was welcomed by both male and female shamans. I guess I've passed the test. At least this one.

I've never experienced a "Dark Side of the Force" in either vision or OBE. I've had my share of dark experiences, of course. My life, just like yours, hasn't always been a walk in the park. But that is not unusual. I was born into a good family that lived in a good country during good times, if you discount the "wars and rumors of wars" that swirled around us ever since the end of World War II. (They were mostly outside of my personal experience. I am lucky in that regard.) So my knee-jerk reaction is to agree with both religious and secular testimonies that emphasize the idea that God is good.

But if, as thousands of theologians have agreed down through the centuries, we are made "in the image of God," why is there so much "sin and degradation" found in human history? Did we somehow develop a fatal flaw? Or, worse yet, is our propensity for evil simply an earthly manifestation of the very character of God? In other words, might it be possible that supernatural entities have a dark side that might show up when and if we meet in person?

Sad to say, although such experiences are in the minority, they do exist. That's where we'll go next.

THE BAD

"Luke, I am your father."

—Darth Vader to Luke Skywalker,
Stars Wars, Episode V: The Empire Strikes Back

A central plot development in the *Star Wars* movies is the eternal battle between good and evil. For every god there is a devil. For every Luke Skywalker there is a Darth Vader. Yes, Virginia, there is a dark side of the Force.

I recently tried to think of a movie or story in which good and evil are not somehow pitted against each other. I couldn't do it. The eternal battle is so central to our experience that we even make good guys and bad guys out of opposing sports teams. Before the Buddha could become enlightened, he first had to overcome the three temptations of Mara, the devil. Before Galahad could complete his quest, he had to overcome the evil Green Knight. Before Jesus could enter into his ministry, he had to journey into the wilderness to overcome Satan

This battle between good and evil is found at the center of every problem on earth. How did a good God create a world in which there is evil? How is the human race, which contains such wonderful, positive potential capable of such unmitigated evil as world wars, nuclear devastation, torture, and climate destruction on a planetary scale? Why do even the best of us, with sharp, biting, stinging, hurtful words, so often "only hurt the one we love, the one we shouldn't hurt at all," as the Mills Brothers used to remind us in song? Why do bad things happen to good people and, conversely, good things happen to bad people? Either God *cannot* prevent it, in which case God is not all-powerful, or God *will not* prevent it, in which case God is not good. The technical word for this study is *theodicy*.

RELIGIOUS SPECULATIONS

The purpose of this rather lengthy excursion into the discipline of theodicy (the defense of a benevolent God in the face of a world that contains evil) is to point out that there exists a real possibility that there are evil beings, evil supernatural entities, out there and we could someday encounter them. As a matter of fact, if three major religions—Judaism, Christianity, and Islam—are correct, all is not rosy in paradise. Or at least in its existing suburbs.

Make no mistake, every religious system and mythology that I have encountered tackles this subject. It is not unique to the big three religions of monotheism. It would seem that the idea of evil existing side by side with good is universal. And why should it not be? Anyone who reads a newspaper or tunes into the evening news encounters it every single day. It is so prevalent that its exploitation is how news media make their money. A television station that features only good news can't stay in business. No one would watch for very long. (That says as much about us as it does the media.)

The character of Darth Vader in the "Star Wars" movies is a pop culture icon representing the evil side of existence. Such figures have persisted in our religions and cultures for thousands of years.

Although even the earliest existing texts from all over the world touch on the subject, the central tenets of the systematic study of theodicy can be traced back at least as far as Zoroastrianism. It was founded by the prophet Zoroaster some 3,500 years ago. (Zoroaster is also called Zarathustra.) The central principle of the prophet's teaching was that there is a good God, named Ahura Mazda, who created the world and all that is in it. But Zoroaster's was the first organized religion to introduce the idea of divine dualism. It has become the belief system that is central to the whole *Star Wars* idea of good and bad forces that are at war. Although the Chinese had recognized the basic concept long before in its teachings about *Yin* and *Yang*, as later encoded in the *Dao*, Zoroaster was the first to personalize it.

Ahura Mazda, the good god, is opposed by Angra Mainyu, the evil god. These two are not equals. One represents positive energy, the other negative energy. Creative energy calls a good world into being. That's a powerful super power. Destructive energy seeks to bring it down. But here's the key to this system. The good god created everything—even the evil god, who turned to evil of his own accord. So good is stronger than evil. The problem comes in explaining why the evil god turned bad. That's theodicy in a nutshell.

Creative energy causes a magnificent tree to grow. Negative energy seeks to destroy it. Life and death. Day and night. Growth and destruction. Up and down. Neither can be understood without the other. They are at war, but ultimately, good will triumph.

When religion separated from natural philosophy it added another level. It declared that the battle is constantly being fought in the natural world around us, but it is also being fought in the *moral* world, the world of the spirit. Love and hate. Joy and misery. Peace and war. Human beings have a choice. And that choice goes on forever.

Here's the point. Although Zoroastrianism is now a religion followed by only about 150,000 people worldwide, it was a major faith in Persia from 600 to 650 B.C.E. This was precisely the time when most of

Zoroaster (depicted at center) was a Persian prophet who lived some three thousand years ago. His teachings founded a religion and influenced Greek philosophers and Judaism, among others.

the Jews, having been taken captive by Nebuchadnezzar in 586 B.C.E. and transported *en masse* back to Babylon, were living under Persian influence. Before the captivity, the Jewish Bible, now known to both Christians and Muslims as the Old Testament, had little to say about the cosmic, moral reality of Dualism. The Psalmists, for instance, celebrated the fact that "Our god is a great god, and a great king above all gods" (Psalm 95:3). That's not dualistic monotheism, by any means. That sentiment recognizes one god among many. But after the Jews returned to rebuild Jerusalem, they were solidly monotheistic—believers in a good God who is simply tolerating, for a time, a bad devil. Their writing, which now comprises the bulk of the Old Testament, in turn influenced Christianity and Islam. With the rise of those two world religions, now encompassing billions of believers, the world would be seen as a testing ground between God and the Devil. It all started with Zoroastrianism.

God was understood to be the ultimate victor who would win the final battle. But until then, humans are forced to contend with a malicious, evil, supernatural force called the Devil, and his infamous followers, the demons.

Presumably, at least from a religious, doctrinal standpoint, these warriors on the dark side of the force have to be taken into account whenever we deal with supernatural entities.

But where did they come from?

The Genesis of Evil

Let's tackle the systematic religious theories first. According to the scriptures shared by Jews, Christians, and Muslims, the supernatural forces of evil came about in this way.

In the beginning, God created a class of supernatural beings we now call angels (from the Greek *angelos,* or "messengers"). Their purpose was to serve God and keep Him company, so to speak. According to the book of Isaiah, chapter 14, the leader of this heavenly force was called Lucifer ("Shining One" or "Light Bearer"). Unfortunately, he had his sights set on an even loftier position. He wanted to "be like God."

This presented God with a problem. Obviously, Lucifer was quite a lofty-type fellow. But he didn't know everything. He missed the whole point about the temptations of ego. As result, he "fell" from grace. He was banished to earth where his evil could be contained to one planet in the vast cosmos. With him came a third of the angels, henceforth called demons. It's important to remember that they don't reign in Hell. They reign on earth. Hell is their punishment, not their dwelling place. *Lucifer* became *Satan,* the "deceiver" and the "accuser of the brethren."

Here's how the Bible tells the story. The first passage begins with God talking directly to Satan:

How you have fallen from heaven, morning star, son of the dawn! You have been cast down to the earth, you who once laid low the nations!

—Isaiah 7:14

This second passage begins with God talking to the King of Tyre, who is usually interpreted as being a metaphor for Satan:

Thus says the Lord GOD: You were the signet of perfection, full of wisdom and perfect in beauty. You were in Eden, the garden of God; every precious stone was your covering, carnelian, chrysolite, and moonstone, beryl, onyx, and jasper, sapphire, turquoise, and emerald; and worked in gold were your settings and your engravings. On the day that you were created they were prepared. With an anointed cherub as guardian I placed you; you were on the holy mountain of God; you walked among the stones of fire. You were blameless in your ways from the day that you were created, until iniquity was found in you. In the abundance of your trade you were filled with violence, and you sinned; so I cast you as a profane thing from the mountain of God, and the guardian cherub drove you out from among the stones of fire. Your heart was proud because of your beauty; you corrupted your wisdom for the sake of your splendor. I cast you to the ground; I exposed you before kings, to feast their eyes on you. By the multitude of your iniquities, in the unrighteousness of your trade, you profaned your sanctuaries. So I brought out fire from within you; it consumed you, and I turned you to ashes on the earth in the sight of all who saw you. All who know you among the peoples are appalled at you; you have come to a dreadful end and shall be no more forever.

—Ezekiel 28:11–19

There's an interesting sidebar to this story. Christians and Jews teach that Satan was cast out of heaven because of his egocentric desire to "be like God." He became jealous of these newfangled inventions called "humans" and now "prowls around like an angry lion, seeking someone to devour" (I Peter 5:8). The Bible says in I Corinthians 6:3: "Do you not know that we [humans] will judge angels?" This did not sit well with Lucifer. His response filled the world with the familiar sin and degradation we now know so well.

But Muslims have a different take on the subject. According to the *Koran*, Lucifer loved God. He loved God so much that when God created Adam, and then told all the angels to bow down before him, Satan was presented with a horrible problem. How could he bow before anyone but his beloved God? Satan's sin was, in effect, that he loved God too much to kneel before a lesser being, such as a human. Thus, when he disobeyed God's command to worship a human, he was cast out of heaven.

How did Satan console himself throughout eternity? He did it by remem-

Satan was once Lucifer, one of God's greatest angels, but vanity and lust for power brought about his fall from heaven.

bering the last words that God, his beloved, said to him. And what were those words? "Go to Hell!"

It's an interesting take on the familiar story.

PEOPLE OF THE LIE

However you interpret all this doctrine, the question remains: Is any of it true? Is there an actual entity called Satan or, more accurately, *The* Satan— *The* Accuser? Or can the whole thing be filed under mythological representation of a philosophical speculation?

In 1978, M. Scott Peck (1936–2005) wrote a book entitled *The Road Less Traveled: A New Psychology of Love, Traditional Values and Spiritual Growth*. It immediately became a bestseller and remains so to this day. Peck was a respected psychiatrist and a hard-headed proponent of medical protocol. *The Road Less Traveled* is a positive, uplifting book steeped in traditional psychotherapeutic methods and actual case studies. It rightfully earned its author fame and fortune. Peck was soon commanding speaking fees that were the envy of his professional colleagues. He eventually reached the point where he didn't have to practice privately anymore—at least to earn his daily bread.

Having attended many of his public speaking events, I was amused by the comments of some of my former professors who were, let's put it plainly, jealous of the money Peck was bringing in. He earned as much for one day's teaching as they did in a week. Peck was an engaging, informative, and popular speaker. For that reason people eagerly awaited his next book.

It turned out to be, for many at least, a huge disappointment. It was called *People of the Lie: The Hope for Healing Human Evil*. Whereas the first book was light and uplifting, this one was dark and foreboding. To make matters worse, Peck did the unthinkable. He declared his belief that demonic possession, although very, very rare, was a real phenomenon. He even described, not as graphically as a titillated public would have liked, his experience at two exorcisms. Coming from a respected medical doctor and a self-professed skeptic, who only attended the procedures for research purposes, the details were shocking:

> The patient suddenly resembled a writhing snake of great strength, viciously attempting to bite the team members. More frightening than the writhing body, however, was the face. The eyes were hooded with lazy reptilian torpor—except when the reptile darted out in attack, at which moment the eyes would open wide with blazing hatred. Despite these frequent darting moments, what upset me most was the extraordinary sense of a fifty-million-year-old heaviness I received from this serpentine

being. It caused me to despair … (we) were in the presence of something absolutely alien and inhuman.

—M. Scott Peck, *People of the Lie*

In 2005, when Peck followed up his account with the book *Glimpses of the Devil: A Psychiatrist's Personal Accounts of Possession, Exorcism and Redemption*, there were those in the medical community who argued that he had either gone off the deep end or was capitalizing on his fame for book sales and profits.

However one responds to Peck's conclusions, the fact remains that a respected psychiatrist, author, and public speaker was convinced that the devil and demonic possession were real, even though very rare. It appeared that when Dr. Peck talked about love and light, everyone thought he was a brilliant, insightful expert. But when he took on the psychiatric establishment, he was not to be trusted.

What do we make of all this?

DEMONIC POSSESSION

Demonic possession is the belief that demons are real and work much of their evil by inhabiting a human body. There are those who believe this is the

only way they can function in our world. They are nonmaterial, energy-based spirits that must possess a material body in order to function in this reality.

The New Testament supplies much of the grist for this mill. Jesus is often described as "casting out" demons or even the devil himself.

Take this familiar story from Matthew 8:28–34:

> When He came to the other side into the country of the Gadarenes, two men who were demon-possessed met Him as they were coming out of the tombs. They were so extremely violent that no one could pass by that way. And they cried out, saying, "What business do we have with each other, Son of God? Have You come here to torment us before the time?" Now there was a herd of many swine feeding at a distance from them. The

A stained glass window in Strasborg Cathedral depicts Jesus casting out a demon from a possessed victim.

demons began to entreat Him, saying, "If You are going to cast us out, send us into the herd of swine." And He said to them, "Go!" And they came out and went into the swine, and the whole herd rushed down the steep bank into the sea and perished in the waters. The herdsmen ran away, and went to the city and reported everything, including what had happened to the demoniacs. And behold, the whole city came out to meet Jesus; and when they saw Him, they implored Him to leave their region.

Some believe Jesus passed on this power to his followers. According to Mark 16:17:

These signs will accompany those who believe: In my name they will drive out demons.

Doctrines grow out of such verses, of course. The whole subject inevitably became a matter of academic debate. Some argued about the meanings of words such as "possession" and "obsession" and drew fine lines of distinctions about how to approach each supposed malady. Others tried to explain away the phenomenon, arguing that the symptoms referred to convulsions, epileptic seizures, or even fainting spells. Of course, there are those who saw the whole thing as either misguided, deluded religion, or even outright fraud.

Despite the nitpicking, the subject is popular. When the 1973 horror movie *The Exorcist* debuted, it was a commercial success. The book upon which it was based made its author, William Peter Blatty (1928–2017), a household name when it hit the *New York Times* bestseller list. The 1998 movie *Meet Joe Black*, starring Brad Pitt and Anthony Hopkins, was a box office success that continued the tradition. Nowadays, given the popularity of superheroes from the comic book genre, it seems as if every other movie that comes out features at least a touch of supernatural evil.

DEMONIC INFLUENCES FELT AROUND THE WORLD

But demonic possession and influence are not limited to Christian circles. The subject has been a favorite of ancient authors ever since the Sumerian culture.

Sumer was located in the river valley between the Tigris and the Euphrates. The Sumerians believed their civilization was founded by "gods."

According to Sumerian texts, the Anunnaki, besides being "watchers," carried out all manner of activities on earth. Sometimes they were thought to pick on innocent bystanders among the human population. It was thought that they had the ability to biologically mate with human women. Their descendants sometimes caused illness. The priests of Sumer, called *Ashipu* (Sorcerers), were called upon to heal people who came down with *Gidim*, or "sickness demons." The Ashipu thus differed from regular doctors, who worked with more mundane materials such as plant-derivatives, salves, and ointments.

Shamanic cultures as well have long recognized the existence of evil spirits. Elaborate rituals developed over the centuries were designed to protect shamanic practitioners from evil when they journeyed to other dimensions to learn the secrets of healing.

In Islam, *Iblis*, or the devil, is accompanied by creatures called *jinns*. These spirits, which are probably a development of Bedouin religious systems, have free will and operate within human cultures, sometimes delivering good things, such as are found in the famous "Three Wishes" of Aladdin's fairy tales, and sometimes, seemingly on a whim, causing all sorts of evil things to happen.

Not everyone, of course, views the problem of evil this way. In many religious systems, good and evil are codependent. They need one another. One cannot exist without the other. There is no reason for a good god to create what becomes an evil enemy.

This idea is perhaps best expressed in the famous theological statements found in the Dao.

In this system of thought, evil was not expressly created by a good god. It simply is the opposite side of a two-sided coin. And it gets even more subtle than that. If the white in this diagram symbolizes good, notice that "good" also exists as a small circle within the black area. The reverse is true as well. Good can be found in evil. Evil can be found in good. If one ceases to exist, the other will disappear as well. God and evil are thus found in all of creation. You can no more have one without the other than you can have an "up" without a "down." However the universe came to be, good and evil exist within the tension of the whole.

According to this system of thought, Luke Skywalker was right when he tried to save his father, the evil Darth Vader. He saw good in him, just as he had, for an entertaining moment in the film's thrilling climax, seen evil in himself.

If we look closely enough, perhaps the same can be said for all of us. In the end, it may prove to be the case that the only evil we encounter in parallel dimensions is the evil we bring with us.

Yin and Yang represent how Good can contain some evil and there can be a little good in Evil.

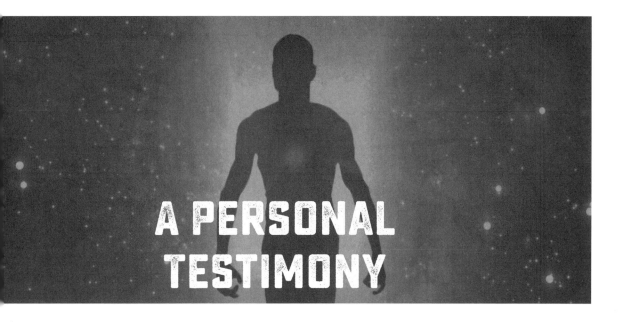

A PERSONAL TESTIMONY

Although I said, "I've never experienced a 'Dark Side of the Force' in either vision or OBE" in the previous chapter, I'm contradicting myself in this chapter.

We have just surveyed a wide swath of material concerning the nature of hypothetical good and bad "spirits" that might, or might not, inhabit dimensions parallel to ours. They might, or might not, have the ability to either step into our world for a while or, at the very least, be there to greet us when we step into theirs.

Obviously, a lot of people, for many millennia, have believed such supernatural entities exist. Even today, if you drop into your friendly Protestant or Catholic church on the corner and leaf through their hymn book, you will find many references to such beings.

For an example of good spirits that uplift our emotions, we need turn no further than a favorite Christmas carol:

Hark! The herald angels sing glory to the newborn king.

—Words by Charles Wesley and George Whitfield

To represent the dark side, we offer this familiar hymn written by Martin Luther (1483–1546). It is found throughout the world in almost every hymn book printed today:

And though this world, with devils filled,
Should threaten to undo us,
We will not fear, for God hath willed
His truth to triumph through us:

The Prince of Darkness grim,
We tremble not for him;
His rage we can endure,
For lo! his doom is sure,
One little word shall fell him.

—Martin Luther, "A Mighty Fortress Is Our God"

Popular sentiments such as these reveal a strange dichotomy in modern thought. On the one hand, we are products of a modern cultural education. What that means is that we don't believe in such "nonsense" as fallen angels, demons, and devils waiting behind every bush, ready to jump out and either encourage us or ensnare us. Such a belief lies within the scope of superstitions, which we have long since outgrown, and are best banished to the wasteland of hocus pocus we left behind when we grew into adulthood.

On the other hand, we are perfectly willing to raise our voices in song on Sunday morning and celebrate the victory of God over the devil and of good over evil. We don't like to think about it much, but when we do, we justify the whole thing by wallpapering it with vague notions involving mythological representations of philosophical principles. Either that or we welcome depictions of such creatures into our homes every night when we tune in to the latest horror movie. We consider it entertainment, not reality. Thus we allow its presence while at the same time keeping it safely within the bounds of fiction.

Martin Luther wrote of devils and the Prince of Darkness in his hymn "A Mighty Fortress Is Our God."

I fully understand. But from time to time throughout this book I have felt the need to share personal stories. I justified it by saying that only personal experience transposes a belief into a known.

Let me give you an example. I always *believed* that a place called England existed. My ancestors came from there. I had friends there. I knew people who had visited. They came back with pictures.

But if you had asked me to actually *prove* England was real, I would have been hard-pressed to do it. All the above evidence was, after all, circumstantial. It could have been all contrived as an elaborate hoax by my friends, my teachers, editors from various newspapers, TV personalities, and all that. On the basis of the evidence I would have believed, and believed strongly, that the proof was overwhelming, but I couldn't have said that England was 100 percent real. At least, not until I went there for myself. I didn't really doubt it, of course, because I trusted the word of people I knew and respected. But now I no longer believe England is real, I know it. I've experienced it. I've seen it and smelled it and tasted it. Now when someone says "England," I have a whole battery of personal experiences that come into play.

By the same token, it's not enough to say we believe in evil supernatural entities based solely on what other people say. If they are going to become real to us, we need to experience them.

LEAVING WELL ENOUGH ALONE

Now, a whole lot of people don't want to take it that far. They don't want to know that spirits exist, especially bad ones.

And that's fine. We have our lives to live and many of us are perfectly satisfied to put off the experience of learning about the "other side" until death overtakes us and we can't put it off any longer.

I'm not that way myself. I want to know how the story turns out so I can relax and enjoy the developments of the plotline. (Yes, I often peek at the ending before reading the novel. That's just the way I roll. Sorry to all you perfectionists out there!)

That being said, I share the sentiments of many, perhaps the great majority, of you who have not experienced beings, either good or bad, from the other side. I walked in your shoes for most of my life. I had an intellectual understanding of theodicy, mind you. After all, I have been a Protestant minister for almost fifty years now.

But until relatively recently, if you had asked me whether or not I had a guardian angel, or that evil entities such as the devil or demons really existed, I would have answered with a resounding "NO!"

Much to my surprise, in the last decade or so I have experienced the presence of what I now call higher powers or helpful spirits. Maybe even guardian angels. I was shocked when it happened. I had given them a place in my intellectual universe and was very aware of all the academic studies and arguments. So I guess I was willing to grant them existence. But I certainly never expected to actually interact with them. Then I discovered dowsing and developed what, to me at least, was irrevocable proof that I could actually converse with them. I don't expect anyone else to come to a belief in such things based on my testimony. You have to discover that on your own. You have to

The idea that we are protected by guardian angels has a long history in many religions, including Judaism, Islam, Christianity, and even Zoroastrianism.

travel to your own spiritual "England" before you can really know it exists.

But since I began to experience out-of-body travel on my own, I had never experienced even a shadow of what I could call an "evil" entity. I looked forward to each and every "trip." Again, although I am aware that most people don't accept my out-of-body travel as real and will either openly disparage the experience or secretly find another way to explain it away, depending on how much they know and like me, that's okay. I am perfectly happy in my knowledge that if they ever experience an OBE themselves, they will understand. I've seen it happen.

All that being said, I now find it necessary to share an experience with you that happened while I was writing the previous chapter of this book. To make a long story short, I discovered the dangers of spiritual hubris.

I said earlier that I never really believed in the existence of real and palpable evil. But now that I look back on my life, employing a little discernment reminds me that I have confronted really evil people twice in my life. Both these individuals, as I now understand, gave me a whiff of the demonic. At the time, I red-flagged the experience and stored it away because of my overwhelming belief that people are basically good, even when they did nasty things. I never met Adolf Hitler (1889–1945), Joseph Stalin (1878–1953), or Osama bin Ladin (1957–2011). I just read about them. I never talked to people such as Jim Jones (1931–1978), Jack the Ripper, or Idi Amin (1925–2003). I'm not saying they weren't real or evil. But to me they were names in a textbook or newspaper headline. In short, I knew about them. I didn't know them. So when I say I have met only two people who set off red flags within my mind, I am simply saying that I have lived a pretty sheltered life.

I didn't know how sheltered until recently. When I first sent in the original manuscript for this book, it didn't contain either of the last two chapters about the possibility of actually encountering good or evil entities. The publisher, however, wanted more. He didn't tell me what to write. He by no means instructed me to include a chapter about "evil entities from the other side." But he forced me to reread, rethink, and regroup. Part of that regrouping led to the chapters I now call "The Good," "The Bad," and "The Indifferent." They consist of a survey of what we might expect when we each cross over to the other side.

I had no problem surveying the written material about helpful spirits and guardian angels. They're fun to write about, and surveying the bountiful literature on the subject was entertaining.

What surprised me was the amount of material that exists out there, especially on the Internet, about evil spirits. I guess that I've employed what I can only call "selective editing" during my whole life. I've avoided discussions about hell, devils, and demons as much as possible. I now believe this was by some kind of cosmic design. I don't know what else to call it, and I'm surprised that I came to this belief. I never expected it. But I have now come to believe that, for some reason or other, I have been watched over and protected by a supernatural presence.

WATCHFUL EYES

When my daughter was just four years old, she went on her first "date." By arrangement, a boy her age who lived a short ways down the New England Common we called home left his house, carrying a paper sack that contained his lunch, and walked towards our house. We knew he was coming because his mother tearfully called and said, "Here he comes." (He didn't know that, of course. But we parents were aware of the significance of this momentous occasion. Our children were growing up!)

We had already packed our daughter's lunch, and the two kids walked across the way to the swing set in a nearby, quiet school yard, deserted at this time of year. The two of them had a great time experiencing their first real sense of freedom. They ate their lunches, swung on the swings, talked, and laughed much of the afternoon away. They felt they were on their own, not aware of the fact that they had two sets of parental eyes on them the whole time. They were experiencing an expanding of their horizons. But they were watched and protected, even if they didn't know it.

I feel much the same thing has happened to me throughout my life. I thought I was free. As it turns out, I've been watched and protected the whole time. Turning to my journal, here's how I discovered the shocking truth:

January 13, 2017 (A Friday!)

The day after I began to write the chapter on evil spirits, all hell broke loose. I had an out-of-body experience that was absolutely terrifying. It was a vision filled with evil, demonic people, saying and doing horrible things. Conceit, egocentric behavior, lying, and despair were the overall theme. I have never, ever before, experienced such a thing and I hope I never do again. The vision even featured a metaphorical ride downward to the prisons of the underworld. I have never been happier to come out of such an experience and, frankly, it makes me hesitant to ever attempt out-of-body travel again. It was simply too painful to ever want that feeling repeated.

Upon returning to my senses I went immediately to get my dowsing rods and converse, in the slow and concise manner I have worked out with the one I call Sobuko, my higher power or guardian angel, to determine what just happened.

I realize I have now lost approximately half my audience. Most people will have a hard time with all this, thinking they are now reading the words of "one of those!" But I assure you I am the same person who began writing this book. You've trusted me so far. I am sane and in my right mind. I am still the eternal skeptic and left-brained scholar I have been all my life. I've just had some different experiences with the supernatural, that's all. Without those experiences, I'd be as worried about someone like me as some of you are now.

To summarize what I learned from the experience, I am now convinced that when our consciousness suddenly appears in this material cosmos, when we are conceived and begin the process of birth, when the "magic" of life takes

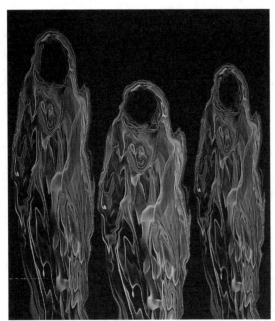

place and we discover we have awakened to a new kind of reality, when we find ourselves encased in material flesh and blood, we leave part of ourselves behind to watch over our material existence. This is our higher power, our guardian angel. It is the parent who unobtrusively watches his or her child at play to guard over her safety and development.

For most of my life, I have been purposely shielded from exposure to real evil. I don't know why. Perhaps, given my propensity to explore unexplained phenomena, I am too susceptible. Perhaps I've already dealt with this issue before in a previous life. Maybe that's why I became a minister in this one, so as to help others on their journey.

I don't know. That is all speculation. What I do know is that it is a great responsibility to write a book that will last for a long time and be read by thousands of people.

"It was a vision filled with evil, demonic people, saying and doing horrible things."

And in my hubris—in my unacknowledged ego trip that involved sharing personal experiences of OBEs and the like—I was about to turn in a manuscript that said, with complete confidence: "I've never experienced a 'Dark Side of the Force' in either vision or OBE."

That makes me sound like an expert and that sentence could easily have opened the door for others to explore places where angels fear to tread.

Ritualistic Words

It wasn't as if I hadn't been warned by people with far more experience. I just didn't pay them any attention.

I've never been one to advocate ritual, for instance. I've never put much stock in the need for what I considered mumbo-jumbo prayers and the lighting of candles or the need to create a protective sacred space. I've always felt such things to be superstitious, unnecessary nonsense.

Let me give you just one example.

It's a standard practice in evangelical circles to close every prayer with the words, "In the name of Jesus, Amen."

Why? Consider the following Bible verses, all from one single book of the New Testament:

- John 14:13: Whatsoever you shall ask *in my name*, that will I do, that the Father may be glorified in the Son.

- John 14:14: If you shall ask any thing *in my name*, I will do it.

- John 15:16: You have not chosen me, but I have chosen you, and ordained you, that you should go and bring forth fruit, and that your fruit should remain: that whatsoever you shall ask of the Father *in my name*, he may give it you.

- John 16:23: And in that day you shall ask me nothing. Verily, verily, I say unto you, Whatsoever you shall ask the Father *in my name*, he will give it you.

- John 16:24: Hitherto have you asked nothing *in my name*: ask, and you shall receive, that your joy may be full.

- John 16:26: At that day you shall ask *in my name*: and I say unto you that I will pray the Father for you.

These verses, and many others, have prompted some preachers to teach that the words "In the name of Jesus" act as a kind of magic formula—that if you neglect them, God won't hear your prayers.

The great Bill Russell (1934–), former all-star center for the Boston Celtics, once poked fun at this custom in a speech about love and acceptance,

Basketball legend Bill Russell once famously replied to Rev. Dr. Bailey Smith that if the only way to talk to God was to invoke the name of Jesus, then Jesus, as a Jew, would not have been able to talk to His Father.

especially between races and religious traditions. The speech was given shortly after the Rev. Dr. Bailey Smith (1939–), president of the Southern Baptist Convention, made the controversial comment in 1980 that "God does not hear the prayers of the Jew" because they don't pray "in the name of Jesus." Russell vividly painted a word picture of Jesus, struggling up the Via Doloroso while carrying his cross, praying for God's help and strength. He then wondered if God might answer, "Sorry son. You're Jewish. I can't hear you."

So customs such as those always struck me as being inane. I simply couldn't believe in a god who insists on making sure we turn a certain way, say certain incantations, light certain candles, or enact certain rituals.

Casting Doubt on Firmly Held Beliefs

Thus, when dowsers told me I must never approach a sacred stone circle, for instance, without first asking permission of the spirits who guard the place, or shamanic practitioners told me I must hedge myself roundabout with power before attempting a shamanic journey, I nodded my head politely and then promptly forgot the advice. I just didn't feel it necessary.

Now, I wonder. Not that spirits need to be placated, necessarily. But I wonder if we need the ritual to prepare ourselves for what amounts to a complete change of reality. Entering sacred space, whether that space be real or psychological, is quite a momentous act, not to be taken lightly. Perhaps we need to exert a little caution before we blunder ahead.

At any rate, I now feel strongly that I've been warned not to take such things for granted. Other dimensions, just like ours, may very well be the abode of both good and evil supernatural entities. I've now seen it powerfully enough to at least keep up my guard.

Could my experience simply have been the result of thinking about the possibility of evil entities? Did I conjure the whole thing in my imagination? Was it any different than thinking about something and then dreaming about it when your head hits the pillow?

All this is certainly possible. I remain 29 percent skeptical myself.

But there yet remains the nagging feeling that it didn't feel that way, either while it was going on or after I came back to my senses following the OBE. It didn't feel like a dream. It felt real. Terrifyingly real.

Take it as it is and deal with it as you will. At least it's out there.

Shakespeare, as he did so often, probably said it best:

There are more things in heaven and earth, Horatio, than are dreamt of in your philosophy.

—Hamlet to Horatio, in William Shakespeare's *Hamlet*

At any rate, I'm going to keep a wary eye out from now on.

THE INDIFFERENT

> The "music" of a higher organism ranges over more than seventy octaves. It is made up of the vibration of localized chemical bonds, the turning of molecular wheels, the beating of microcilia, the propagation of fluxes of electrons and protons, and the flowing of metabolites and iconic currents within and among cells through ten orders of spatial magnitude.
>
> —Ervin László, *Science and the Akashic Field*

If you're like most people, you probably read the above quote from Ervin László and said, "Huh?"

Let me see if I can help. Here's a quick interpretation. He's talking about you. He says you're a pretty complicated piece of work.

Does that help?

Let's try it this way.

Here in South Carolina, where I live, fire ants are a way of life. They're everywhere. But I go days without noticing any of them. They usually keep to their space and I keep to mine. But once in a while, things happen that upset the natural order of things. We are forced into confrontation.

A few years ago, for instance, we had a lot of rain. The water table rose quite a bit. Suddenly I was aware of ant hills all over the place. The roadsides were dotted with them. The fields seemed to have been inundated with mounds of sand. Wherever I looked, I saw ant hills. They even appeared in my back yard and driveway, where I stepped in them while mowing the lawn. They had moved into my perception realm.

If you have never confronted fire ants, trust me when I say you don't want to step in a mound where they are active.

What did I do? I was angry. I fought back. I am a conservative ecologist at heart. I believe in "live and let live." But enough was enough. I bathed my bitten ankles in calamine, went to the local hardware store, and bought some poison.

I was not popular in the ant world that day. I imagine the little worker fire ants went home to their families that night and said, "Honey—I now believe that huge, giant monsters really exist and seek to do us harm! It may be the end of the world as we know it."

After a while the rains subsided, the water table dropped and the ants returned to their normal domain. They had stepped into our presence for awhile and I had noticed their existence. For a brief moment in time, our worlds overlapped. The results were catastrophic for us both. They sought to expunge the presence on high that was me when they misinterpreted my blundering into their home as an act of aggression. I interpreted their natural resistance as an attack on my way of life. I was bigger than them. I won. If they had kept to their side of the fence things would have been different. We could have peacefully coexisted. Alas, it was not to be. For a short period of time, war was declared.

Ants are not "bad." Neither am I. They are actually very evolved creatures. Usually we are indifferent to each other. But not this time. And since I have evolved to be a higher power than fire ants, I had more resources. I probably should have shown some restraint. But I didn't. I acted aggressively when I should have shown some compassion. It was up to me, really. I was the bigger entity. But even though I'm a pretty nice guy, find ants fascinating, and usually don't even notice them, I committed a terrible act of aggression. And that was that.

Somewhere, deep in the annals of some ant library, an ant scholar has undoubtedly studied the situation and determined that mythical monsters on high actually exist and mean great harm to the world of antdom. Maybe a religion has formed in which sacrifices are made to appease me. Maybe sand churches or cathedrals are built in my honor.

I could go on, because this is fun, but to tell you the truth, I really don't care. I

People are indifferent to tiny creatures such as ants, unless they annoy us. Perhaps it is that way with gods, too, who may regard us as mere ants to be ignored … most of the time.

have more important things to do. In other words, I'm indifferent to the problems of ants as long as they don't bother me.

I wonder if there exists, somewhere in the Multiverse or its extended environs, supernatural "gods" who feel the same way about us? If so, we would probably call them indifferent because we anthropomorphize their *size*, their *complexity*, and their *morality*. All three are red herrings. Outside of our material universe, these attributes probably don't even exist. Nevertheless, let's examine them one at a time.

SIZE

To "anthropomorphize" is to bestow human attributes on a nonhuman being. In the *Seinfeld* TV series, George did it when he said, "The sea was angry that day, my friends." Probably everyone who has a pet does it as well. Our beloved Rocky dog is so much a part of the family that we are often surprised when he does something doglike. (Yes—I confess to being his "papa." Good dog people will understand and overlook it. Bad dog people will wince and roll their eyes. That's okay. I'm a good dog person.)

When it comes to talking about supernatural gods and metaphysical entities, rampant anthropomorphism usually runs amuck. A quick glance at the ceiling of the Sistine Chapel will prove my point. After one look at Michelangelo's work, it's hard not to picture God as an old white guy with a beard.

All this is to say that we have to be careful when we talk about beings from another dimension. We invariably give them human attributes.

The first attribute we'll deal with is the idea of *size*. Literature is full of people who approach extra-dimensional entities with awe and humility, bestowing on them magnified ideas of human grandeur. In such epistles, supernatural entities are not just wise, they are omnipotent. They aren't simply old. They are eternal. They don't speak. They thunder.

The Greeks and the Romans reveled in this. Zeus and his cohorts were human to the max. But the same idea is found in the Bible. Take this vision as recorded by the prophet Isaiah:

> In the year that king Uzziah died I saw the LORD sitting upon a throne, high and lifted up, and his train filled the temple. Above it stood the seraphims: each one had six wings; with two he covered his face, and with two he covered his feet, and with two he did fly. And one cried unto another, and said, "Holy, holy, holy, is the LORD of hosts: the whole earth is full of his glory." And the posts of the door moved at the voice of him that cried, and the house was filled with smoke. Then said I, "Woe is me! for I am undone; because I am a man of unclean lips, and I dwell in

the midst of a people of unclean lips: for mine eyes have seen the King, the LORD of hosts." Then flew one of the seraphims unto me, having a live coal in his hand, which he had taken with the tongs from off the altar: And he laid it upon my mouth, and said, "Lo, this hath touched thy lips; and thine iniquity is taken away, and thy sin purged." Also I heard the voice of the Lord, saying, "Whom shall I send, and who will go for us?" Then said I, "Here am I; send me."

—Isaiah 6:1–8

Talk about anthropomorphism! This scene has it all. Heavenly seraphim who need wings to fly. A king sitting on a throne. A theological discussion group formed to ask a question as to who might represent them on earth. This is, without question, humanness writ large.

But if there is one constant in this vast, unimaginable universe it is this: size doesn't matter. Once we leave behind notions of material bodies, we are dealing with pure energy. If we are ever going to think about nonmaterial expressions of energy, especially conscious energy, we simply have to check our human conceptions at the door. Out there, such things don't exist.

Our consciousness has evolved within a perception realm that features carbon-based, material manifestations of vibratory energy. We have developed ways of seeing the world that are based on a toolkit featuring five prominent senses: sight, touch, taste, hearing, and smell. Without usually realizing it, that's how we identify and judge everything with which we come into contact. We automatically assume this is reality, because it's the only reality we know.

But let me burst your bubble just a little bit. There are about nineteen million skin cells within every square inch of your body. You slough off between 30,000 to 40,000 of these every day. They comprise much of the "dust" you vacuum up in your house. The skin you now see in the mirror will be gone in a month, replaced by new cells that are also in the process of dying.

Colon cells and sperm face an even tougher challenge. They die off after only three or four days. Brain cells, however, come with a lifetime guarantee.

Someone once put forth the idea, though it's not really true, that your whole body is replaced every seven years.

It doesn't really work that way, but you get the idea. So do you really think that when we're talking about energy manifestations, we can assume that every time energy takes on form it's going to take on a form like ours? Do we really want to assume we are unique in that regard? That's the way sentient, intelligent life forms look in our universe. But does an identical process have to carry through to every one of the components of the Multiverse? In short, does God really have to look like us?

This sixteenth-century painting by Giorgio Vasari titled "Jacob's Dream" illustrates perfectly how people have an anthropomorphized view of God.

I know what you're thinking. We are "made in the image of God." But was the author of that phrase really implying that God looks like us? Is there another interpretation? And if not, just because some ancient author said it, does that mean it's true?

Mythology is rife with such anthropomorphic images. We read about a horned devil with a pitchfork and forked tail, which sounds similar to earlier renditions of satyrs and serpents. Trolls who live under human-made bridges look just like ugly old men. Fairies resemble tiny women with wings.

On and on it goes. When we anthropomorphize something like supernatural entities, they naturally appear ridiculous. Thus we sabotage our own perceptions. Who can believe in something as silly as the image we conjure in our minds? So we dismiss the whole idea and throw out the baby with the bathwater.

When it comes to supernatural gods, it's best to avoid such mind games and try hard not to form mental images. If you can't do that, and it is, admittedly, hard not to, just remember that the images are formed by your past history, not any semblance to reality.

COMPLEXITY

Mae-Wan Ho (1941–2016) was a geneticist who wrote ten books and numerous articles pushing homeopathy and Chinese medicine while criticizing such things as genetic engineering, vaccinations, and a strict view on Darwinian evolution.

She has, naturally, been labeled a "quack" by many traditional scientists.

Whatever you think about her nonmainstream views, she promoted an interesting metaphor that deals with complexity and the human body. She compared the biological systems of any organism to a good jazz band. They "listen" to each other as each goes about improvising their own part. Thus the whole organism responds instantly to changes in melody, rhythm, and harmony. There is always something new happening. The same song is never repeated twice in exactly the same way. There's always a different variation going on. That variation stays within a certain structure, with specific guidelines, just as a jazz ensemble stays within the confines of a repeated chord structure. But each musician still enjoys complete freedom to improvise his or her own part. The result is freedom within conformity—a spontaneous musical expression of unity that is unique every time a song is performed.

Let's apply the analogy to the Multiverse.

Our universe, indeed, our whole perception realm, is but one musician in an infinite jazz band. We are all playing what we might call an Akashic song. Every unique perception realm has its own way of improvising around the melody, but we all stay within the same chord structure—the same structural framework. The result is heavenly music. But if we don't expand our consciousness to take in the whole, all we hear is our own contribution.

> Our universe, indeed, our whole perception realm, is but one musician in an infinite jazz band.

There are those among us who insist we are the only ones playing the tune. They believe ours is the only instrument sounding forth.

There are others, however, who, by some of the means we studied in Part II of this book, insist that they have heard some of the other musicians, from other perception realms, playing our song. They have heard complex harmonies and sophisticated rhythms that lead them to think that the mysterious thing called life is a lot bigger than we have been led to believe.

In short, we exist in a complex matrix of an inconceivably intricate pattern of evolution.

Who are the other musicians in the band? That's easy. We call them supernatural gods. We call them metaphysical entities. We call them spirits. But whatever we call them, it's important to remember this. We're all playing the same tune. We're all equally musicians in a cosmic band. We all have a part to play. We don't need to bow down and worship the trumpet player if we are playing a mean second fiddle. We are all doing our part. The layers of awe and wonder that have been so meticulously built, supervised, and guarded by religious systems and those who serve them may have done us a great injustice. They may have camouflaged a central truth of existence. We are part of the cosmic song. No more. But no less, either.

Supernatural entities may seem complex to us. But we, no doubt, seem just as complex to them. We wonder what it feels like to be eternal. They must wonder what kind of courage it takes to put on mortality. We wonder what it feels like to understand so much more about reality. Maybe they wonder what it feels like to explore such a dark realm as ours. We wonder what it feels like to experience life on such a lofty level. They wonder how we could possibly exhibit the kind of strength needed to put aside everything you know and be born as a newborn, totally dependent baby.

What all this means is this: the universe is a complex place. But we are a very important part of it. Lift your head high!

MORALITY

Does morality exist outside of human nature?

It's an interesting thought.

When buffalo eat themselves out of existence, when they consume all the grass a given area has to offer, they are forced to move. If they run out of areas to consume, they die. We call it sad. We call it a tragedy.

When human beings do it, we call it immoral.

When a mother wolf dies defending her young, we call it maternal instinct.

When a human being does it, we call it love.

When a big fish attacks a smaller fish, we call it the law of the jungle. When a human attacks another human, we abhor it and call it immoral.

Is morality—the decision to choose good over evil—only a human characteristic? Does morality exist at all, or is it just a matter of interpretation?

We could cite many more examples, but the point is obvious. We judge animals by one set of rules and humans by another, even though humans are only one step removed from the animal kingdom. Why? Because humans ought to know better. Animals don't commit "sins." They just follow their instincts. But people do commit sins. And we hold them responsible for it. Somewhere in our evolution we crossed an invisible line into what we now call morality. We believe in right and wrong. We expect people to behave ethically. Those ethics may vary from culture to culture. But there are universal standards of behavior we allow in society. People who fail to meet those standards are judged to be immoral.

I wonder sometimes. Can we hold supernatural entities to the same standards? Or is there some kind of cosmic code that places them at an even higher standard that is as far removed from us as we are from lower animal species?

Is love a feeling that recognizes a universal, cosmic code of morality? How about hate? Is compassion a standard around the universe and beyond? What about empathy?

Most religious folks say morality involves following a set of rules laid down by a divine authority. The Ten Commandments fit under this category. But atheists can be just as moral as believers. Sometimes more so.

In these pages we can't get caught up too much in this kind of discussion. That would take another book. But we can ask questions:

- Can we expect morality to be a universal norm across parallel dimensions and within the domain of supernatural gods?

- Have such entities even determined what moral behavior is?

- If so, where did they get such a code?

- Are we evolving toward a universal moral standard?

This is tough stuff. It's not as easy as it first appears. We know *we* are capable of such things as love, compassion, and empathy. We even suspect that the dogs and cats that live in our homes are, too. Well, at least the dogs. But what about our pet goldfish? And how about lower life forms such as ants and cockroaches?

If you start from the bottom of the food chain and move up the ladder, at what point does morality kick in? And if we assume that our gods and goddesses must be, by definition, moral entities, why didn't the Greeks buy into our system? Zeus was many things, but he certainly wasn't always a poster boy for moral behavior.

Although we can't answer these questions directly, we bring them up to emphasize that we err when we assume we know what morality is and then project it onto our concept of supernatural entities. Just as we anthropomorphize them when it comes to size and other human physical attributes, and just as we assume simplicity when complexity seems to be more the norm throughout the suburbs of the home of the gods, morality may be a human invention as well. Someday we might discover that morality is simply a step up the ladder to something much bigger.

Did you ever ask the question, "Why is God doing this to me?" Did you ever wonder why God allows bad things to happen to good people? Did you ever spend a few moments pondering why God would allow such a thing as a holocaust, let alone something as common throughout world history as Pickett's Charge into hell on a July day in the town of Gettysburg, Pennsylvania (when the Confederates suffered heavy casualties in a fruitless charge on the Union during the Civil War)?

If so, you probably didn't come up with a satisfying answer.

The reason may be that you are projecting human morality onto a divine entity and then expecting that entity to justify itself by human standards.

Good luck with that.

This is yet another example of how we anthropomorphize supernatural beings. We said earlier that to do so is to follow a red herring. It won't get us anywhere. It is creating a god in *our* own image. As a race, humans have been doing exactly that for a long, long time. Is it any wonder it's never really gotten us anywhere?

A FRESH START

Maybe it's time to try to do something else. Maybe we need to imagine a new way of thinking about the supernatural. Perhaps there is a much more satisfying approach that will help us find our place in a greater reality that may seem indifferent, at first, but will prove to be very involved with us after all.

It's time to grow up, leave the children's table and start paying attention to the adults. When we talked and acted like children, the adults didn't pay us much mind. But when we started to ask intelligent questions, they began to take an interest in us. The Apostle Paul, once again, said it very well:

> When I was a child, I talked like a child, I thought like a child, I reasoned like a child. When I became a man, I put the ways of childhood behind me.
>
> —I Corinthians 13:11

In earlier chapters we employed what we called the A / B / A^1 stage system of growth. We now need to turn to it once again.

In our prayers, we often make promises to God in a sort of contractual agreement, hoping to get something we want if we behave or do good deeds.

Stage A in our relationship with supernatural entities lasted a long time in human history. Many still cling to it today. This stage can only be described as an age of superstition. It involves what psychologists call "magical" thinking. We imagine God in our image and expect "Him" (the masculine pronoun usually defines this stage) to act in a manner consistent with human morality and intellect. We bargain with God. We make promises: "If God (the Party of the First Part) will do this, then I (the Party of the Second Part) will do that." In its most extreme form, we offered sacrifices to appease God. It's still a very common practice in many religious circles, although most people will deny that this pretty much describes their prayer life.

Stage B in our relationship with supernatural entities consists of simply denying they exist. It's an important part of our growth. We needed this stage because in it we divest ourselves of superstitious practices and magical ways of thinking. During a typical lifetime, this is as far as many people ever get.

Stage A[1] is a key stage. Here we really begin to grow up and leave the children's table. We begin to suspect that there is a whole lot going on in the adult world of the supernatural that we don't know anything about. But we want to learn. We discover that the adults at the big table, that is, supernatural gods, aren't really indifferent to us. They aren't really ignoring us. They are just engaged in behaviors and conversations we aren't yet capable of understanding.

When we begin to ask questions, they pay attention. They recognize we are now ready to take on adult roles and begin to grow up and learn how their world operates. Until now, we weren't mature enough for them to respond properly.

Given the nature of the many, many books that are being written about spirituality, given the response of the countless people who are discovering a passion for the subject, given the questions reputable scientists are now asking about the nature of reality, I wonder if the human race is really waking up and taking its first steps into a full blown Stage A[1] understanding of what the supernatural is really like? It may yet prove to be the case that the universe and its hosts are not indifferent to us after all. They haven't been ignoring us as much as they have been waiting for us to demonstrate signs of spiritual maturity.

Read these words of hope from Ervin László:

There is much that we do not yet understand about the farthermost reaches of human consciousness, but one thing stands out: consciousness does not vanish when the functions of the brain and body cease. It persists, can be recalled and, for a time at least, can also be communicated with. It appears that the hologram that codes the experiences of a lifetime maintains a level of integration that allows it a form of autonomous existence even when it is no longer associated with a brain and a body. It is capable of receiving inputs from the manifest world and of responding to them. In this interpretation, the perennial intuition of an immortal soul is no longer consistent with what we are now beginning to comprehend through science about the true nature of reality.

—Ervin László, *Science and the Akashic Field*

In seeking to explore the realities of "indifferent" supernatural gods, we sought to avoid the trap of anthropomorphism. But in trying to develop that concept, we resorted to anthropomorphic examples such as "sitting at the kids table." Is there another way to approach the subject of a real supernatural presence found throughout the cosmos without using human-based models?

Well, there may be one. It's not a new concept, by any means. As a matter of fact, it's found in one of the oldest religious systems known to us—ancient Hinduism. That's the subject of the next chapter in the search for supernatural gods.

BRAHMAN

The coherence and complexity-directed evolutionary process is not likely to be unique to our universe. It is highly improbable that our universe—which is so fine-tuned for the evolution of complexity—was the first universe to arise in the Metaverse. And if it was not the first universe to be born in the Metaverse, it is not likely to be the last. Other universes will arise in time. How will the process of evolution unfold across this stupendous cycle of universe after universe?

—Ervin László, in *Science and the Akashic Field*

What if our vision, our way of visualizing the ultimate object of our quest, has been too small right from the start? What if we have been committing the same anthropomorphic mistakes, the mistakes that in the last chapter we called "size," "complexity," and "morality," all along? What if from the very beginning of our quest we have been searching for supernatural gods that are just too small?

Try this on for size. What if our universe, and every single universe that exists in the Multiverse, or Metaverse, or whatever we choose to call it, is simply one evolving cell in the makeup of what we have been calling God?

Think of it this way. As we have seen, every cell in your body is in the process of replacing itself with a progeny that is its exact duplicate. When that occurs, magic happens. As impossible as it is to imagine such a thing, the tiny, microscopic cell passes along a complete set of DNA fingerprints that imparts all of its "wisdom," for lack of a better word, to the next generation. Everything that cell learned during its brief time in existence, everything it was, is encoded in that DNA and becomes a building block for the next generation.

This process, of course, is called evolution. Through cellular regeneration we grow and, sometimes, change a little. The progress moves forward and upward. We are constantly evolving from something lower toward something higher. We are all familiar with this process on a micro scale. Now let's move up the ladder to a macro scale.

If current ideas about the universe are correct, even on a basic level, then our universe is not the only one that exists. It is one of an infinite number that have existed and will exist.

Think about the word "infinite" for a minute. "Infinite" is not just a big number. It isn't a number at all. You can't quantify infinite. Every time you try you can always add 1 and get a bigger number. There is no end to infinite.

Now remember this: space/time, in the broadest sense of the word, is infinite. There is no end to it. It has no borders. There's plenty of room out there.

While you're trying to get your head around that idea, consider this. What if each and every universe that ever existed, and that ever will exist, is an informed cell in an infinite body of consciousness, able to pass on all that it learned during its existence?

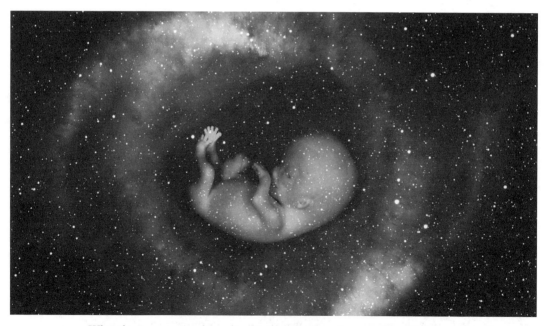

What if universes were born, lived, and died, along the way giving birth to new universes, passing along what they had learned to their children, ever-evolving toward higher states of being?

What, or who, does it pass it on to? Its progeny—the next universe. Each and every Big Bang that marks the beginning of each and every universe is simply the birth of a new cell that inherits, as it were, all the information encoded in its parent cell, its birth universe. The new universe grows and experiences its own evolutionary development. Then it dies. But as it dies it becomes the parent of yet another universe, which is just a little more developed and so able to take yet another step up the evolutionary ladder.

Our universe is more informed than our parent universe. The next universe, the one we give birth to, will be more informed than us. It's a process that goes on, virtually forever.

What does it all mean? It means that God is a lot bigger than we can ever hope to imagine and is not done growing yet. That's a big, big God. The ancient Hindu *rishis* (wise men) had a name for it. They called it *Brahman*.

In an earlier chapter we talked a little about Brahman, the ultimate, unknowable, and unable-to-be-described reality that is at the root of Hindu philosophy.

(When I began to teach Hinduism at the college level I made it a point to consult a wise friend of mine who was a practicing Hindu. Every morning he would perform his rituals, light his candles, say his prayers, and make his offerings. I thought he would be a good source to make sure I was getting things right.

One morning I decided to run my lesson plan on Brahman by him to make sure I was on track. As I carefully explained my interpretation of the Brahman principle he listened politely, without comment. I looked at him and said, "Have I got it?"

He smiled encouragingly, nodded his head vigorously up and down, and said, "No!")

Words fall short when it comes to Brahman—"He who the tongue has not soiled," as we read in the Upanishads. If you ever think you've got a handle on it, you don't. Brahman is the ultimate ground of all being. Science cannot go there. Only mystics are allowed past the borders. And even they can't bring back a true description of what they saw. All they can offer is a map that allows us to attempt the journey ourselves.

In one sense, Brahman is the ultimate, indifferent God. But in another sense, its indifference is only an illusion.

How can that be?

The answer is a comforting one. Brahman has a counterpart. It is called *Atman*. The nearest we can come to finding a western definition of Atman is the word "soul." Atman is the inner essence of the inexpressible, penultimate

In Hindu iconography, the swan is the symbol for the Brahman-Atman connection.

Brahman. Whatever Brahman is, it is found in you as well, for, in the words of the Upanishads, *THOU ART THAT!* According to Hindu thought, when you look deep inside yourself, you can sense the subtle workings of the infinite *Source of All Things*.

Thus, the final object of our quest for the supernatural will not be found "out there." It will be found "in here." We search for Brahman. We will find it when we discover Atman.

A COSMIC GAME

Is there a way to possibly come close to an understanding of all this?

Ervin László offers this analogy.

In the days before smartphones and video games, people used to play a game called "Twenty Questions." A person would leave the room and the remaining participants would mutually decide to name an object somewhere in the room that would serve as the source for a quest. When the person who was "it" returned he would have twenty questions to discover what the object is. If it was a big room, with a lot of targets, it might seem as though the game was impossible. But the person asking the questions could be clever enough to eliminate a lot of false objects by asking the right questions.

"Is it alive?" for instance, would cross off any pets or plants.

"Is it made of wood" would narrow the field even more.

By asking the right questions in the right order, twenty questions would often be sufficient.

But now let's change the rules a little. Let's allow the participants to agree to disagree about what the final object of the quest is. When the questioner returns to the room, no one knows what he is looking for. The only rule is that they have to agree to answer his questions honestly, one by one.

Suppose he says, "Is the object made of wood?"

The participants would get together and decide to answer, "Yes!"

That would eliminate all objects not made of wood.

"Is the object bigger than a breadbox?"

Again, the participants would huddle up and decide on an answer. They would have to pretend that they knew what the object was and that they had answered honestly when they had said it was made of wood. They would again agree on an answer.

On and on the game would go. If the person asking the questions was clever enough, eventually the outcome of the game would reveal one, and only one, targeted object.

But when that object was discovered, it would be something that no one knew was the object of the game. They would all "discover" the object at the same time!

In other words, there was no *apparent* goal. But in the end, a goal would be revealed. And the object that was the focus of the goal was determined by the rules of the game itself, not the participants who were playing.

Here's the point. Are we playing this game with the universe itself? Is there a goal we are looking for that will be revealed, as long as we trust the universe to play the game with us in an honest and straightforward manner? Are religions and science both asking questions that will lead to the ultimate goal?

If so, how far along in the game are we? How many questions will it take to get us to the end? How many have we already asked?

It's a fascinating thought, isn't it?

Another Three-Stage Application

Once again, let's apply our A / B / A^1 theory of growth.

In *Stage A* we asked questions about a *physical* universe. We wondered how a material-based cosmos might have begun. We discovered the Big Bang and postulated all sorts of things about energy and light evolving toward mass and substance evolving toward water and rocks. We made tremendous strides. It was a heady time. But then we hit a snag. How did life develop? How did it happen that one day nothing was alive—nothing had DNA to pass along to its offspring—and the next day, it did? It was time to move on. So we did.

We entered *Stage B*. Now we began to ask questions about a *physical/biological* universe. Once again, we prospered. Arguments developed among the participants, of course. There were those who thought the jump from physical to biological would have been impossible without outside help. But we continued the game and kept asking questions. Eventually we reached another hurdle. We couldn't seem to get past the idea that some biological entities have minds and other don't.

This led us to *Stage A^1*. That's where we seem to be right now. We have entered into a *physical/biological/psychological* stage of developmental questions. Our questions now concern the nature of consciousness and the mind/brain connection.

What comes next? Well, according to Ervin László:

> If humankind does not destroy its life-supporting environment and decimate its numbers, the dominant consciousness of a critical mass will evolve from the ego-bound to the transpersonal stage. And this quantum leap in the evolution of consciousness will catalyze a quantum leap in the evolution of civilization as well.

> —Ervin László, in *Science and the Akashic Field*

That gives us a glimmer of hope. So far, at least, the seemingly indifferent universe seems to be answering our questions honestly. If we keep going, the game will eventually end and we will discover the ultimate goal of our quest. It may not happen during the lifetime of our universe. We may eventually give birth to another universe, as a former universe gave birth to us, but all we have learned and encoded within the very energy of our existence will be passed on.

Here's the kicker: *God itself may not know the final outcome!*

We may be playing the "blind" version of the Twenty Questions parlor game. We just don't know. But it leads us to speculate.

Could it be that we are part of a process wherein what we call supernatural gods are discovering what it is to be alive and real? And existing "above" them, is there another, perhaps singular, supernatural entity that exists in an unknowable realm consisting of an infinite vastness, that (or who) is actually working out the whole experience of existence by a process that, by our standards, is unbelievably slow?

But there! We've done it again. We resorted to anthropomorphism. We used the word "slow." That denotes time. And if such a supernatural entity exists, it is certainly above and beyond any concept of time. We projected our conception of time onto something that is certainly indifferent to it.

Do you see how easy it is to fall into the trap?

At this point it might be a good idea to go back to the chapter about "Metaphysical Manifestations" and look again at the chart we developed called "A Slice of Reality." In it, we moved out from what we called the "Mind of God" and moved toward the physical reality that surrounds us in this perception realm. Our goal is to come full circle and return to the "Source."

That may offer our greatest cause for hope. If the reality we earlier called Akasha is what the Hindus call Brahman, and if it exists within— Atman—then we ourselves are the Source, the Process, and the Goal. The answers are knowable. The fact that we don't yet understand them doesn't matter. We will. Time means nothing. We are engaged in the very process that began the journey in the first place. Our questions *are* the process. We're making progress. The quest is playing itself out just like it's supposed to. Everything is going according to plan. The only fly in the ointment is our impatience. But impatience is a product of time. And time is an illusion.

What does all this imply, if it is even moderately close to the truth?

From one Supernatural God to another—welcome to the game!

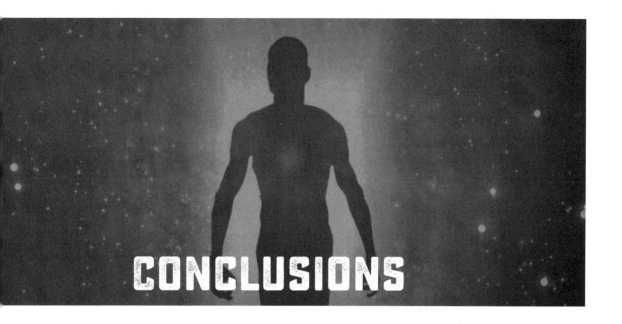

CONCLUSIONS

Know ye not that ye are gods?

—Psalm 82:6, John 10:34

It's quite a radical thought, isn't it? We have speculated that each one of us, and, for that matter, the whole Multiverse, is a physical manifestation in space and time of God becoming Itself (or Himself, or Herself—no pronoun really works here).

As the first self-realized species on earth to arrive at this point in the process of discovery, we are probably in the vanguard, at least as far as earth is concerned. Who knows how far other species in other neighborhoods out there in the universe, or universes, have advanced?

Does this mean that all the other supernatural entities, gods, fairies, beings, angels, or whatever else we have discussed in this book are not real?

No. Of course not! It just means that they are different forms or manifestations of the same essential supernatural reality. They are all engaged in following their own evolutionary path. They don't rule over us. They live parallel to us. If the word "gods" doesn't sit well with you at this point, use some other word. It doesn't make any difference what you call them as long as you see the big picture. Everything, every single thing, in this universe and every universe, is in the process of fulfilling the ultimate destiny of the Multiverse, which is to become the body, so to speak, of *Consciousness, God, Akasha, Brahman,* or whatever. For the sake of convenience, let's call it "All That Is."

How do we sum up something that awesome and mysterious? It is, after all, the biggest mystery we can possibly research. What we're saying is that *All*

That Is shares something radical with us. Or maybe it would be better to put it another way. *All That Is* has imprinted itself on our conscious selves. It took a while, in earthly time, for it to kick in. But when the first humans crawled back into those great painted caves 40,000 years ago, or gazed in wonder at the night sky and wondered where they came from, the human race had finally evolved to the point where the real work of discovery could begin. We were able to think symbolically. We had religious thoughts—spiritual inclinations. We were off to the races and haven't stopped since. We had glimpsed our Grail and were off on our quest for supernatural gods. Or maybe—Supernatural God.

The first clue was discovered by the ancient Hindu rishis. A group of wise men in India long ago intuited that a subtle consciousness pervaded the cosmos. They called it Brahman—"He who was beyond speech." In our day, using the mathematical tools of the theoretical physicists, we have penetrated the mystery of *All That Is* and given it a different name. We call it the *Zero Point Field*. We have peered beyond the Higgs Field and glimpsed an energy field of unlimited potential wherein everything finds both its source and its destination. We are almost forced to come to the conclusion that this field is somehow conscious, perhaps even Consciousness itself, and is working itself out in time and space. In other words, being mind itself, *All That Is* is now going about the work of building itself a body. Just as the cells in our bodies contain the whole of who we are and pass this information on to their "children," so we contain everything of *All That Is* and pass it on to future generations. The answer was right in front of us, or, rather, right within us, all along. We just needed to know where to look. The ancients intuited it. We needed time to figure it out. But we seem to now be on the same page.

> In our day, using the mathematical tools of the theoretical physicists, we have penetrated the mystery of *All That Is* and given it a different name. We call it the *Zero Point Field*.

At this point let's be clear about where we're going. In Part I: The Object of the Quest, we prepared ourselves by learning how the ancients first perceived and came into contact with metaphysical beings and forces that existed way beyond their daily experience. They called them supernatural gods. In Part II: The Method of the Quest, we surveyed a whole host of techniques that have been employed through the centuries to contact, or at least glimpse, these supernatural entities. During this period of history, we were acting under the assumption that we were *here* and they were *there*. We were on our side, they were on their side.

Here in Part III: The End of the Quest and Beyond, our search has taken a dramatic turn. We have postulated that the supernatural gods we seek are to be found, in some way or another, within us—perhaps even that *we* are supernatural gods, or at least becoming supernatural gods. Now we are no longer forced to look out there, however important that quest may be. We are looking in here—within our very natures. It's important to make that distinction. What follows is an attempt to penetrate to the very essence of the nature of that reality itself. We are no longer searching for the neighborhood of the gods. We are looking for the contractor who built it in the first place.

How can we put the goal of this momentous quest in a form that makes it easier to understand?

Here are four different scenarios. Each seeks to portray a consciousness out there that is knowable in here. Remember that these are just metaphors. They aren't offered as explanations. I really don't think mere words could even do that. They are merely ways of approaching the great mystery of the supernatural entity or force we have just labeled *All That Is*, while addressing two basic questions:

1. Where do we come from?

2. Where are we going?

Each scenario is more than an intellectual exercise. We want to ground our quest in reality. We want to suggest something meaningful that we can actually do that might help us intuit what the mystics of old understood to be true. So we don't want to employ just woo-woo metaphysical jargon and speculation. We want to ground our search in some serious, cutting-edge science. It's not an easy exercise and not for the faint of heart. But we've come this far together. Let's go a little further. Perhaps one of these will lead us to the Grail at the end of our quest.

SCENARIO #1: THE PLAY'S THE THING

Shakespeare wrote, "The play's the thing wherein I'll catch the conscience of the king." He put these words in the mouth of Hamlet, who believed King Claudius was guilty of murder. He believed Claudius' guilty conscience would reveal itself when confronted with some good theater. The play-within-a-play motif was a favorite of the Bard's.

This begs the question: Are we all actors in a play within a play—a drama that we may even have written ourselves? And, when confronting "some good theater," will we, like Claudius of old, be led to draw some important conclusions?

"Are we all actors in a play within a play—a drama that we may even have written ourselves?"

Stick with me here. I'm not making this up. It's an idea that has been around for a long time. But only relatively recently has it been championed by some pretty big names in the field of theoretical physics. None other than Stephen Hawking of Cambridge University and Thomas Hertog of CERN worked out the highly complex math behind this idea. I can't pretend to understand the formulas, but if I have the basic idea right it goes something like this: We begin with a question. If between 10^{100} and 10^{500} universes exist in the Multiverse, and if in only a small handful of them life as we know it could possibly arise, how is it possible that we just happen to live in a universe wherein complex life forms could have evolved? The odds are astronomically small. Yet it happened. Why?

The answer usually given is called the Anthropic Cosmological Principle. Don't let the name scare you. All it means is that the universe is the way it is because we happen to live in it and observe it. In other words, what we see is the way it is because that's the way we see it.

Is your head spinning yet?

It sounds like a pretty silly philosophical word game that probably isn't worth taking seriously. But Hawking and Hertog came up with a mathematically sophisticated description of this concept that makes some physicists stand up and take notice. First of all, we're talking about Stephen Hawking here. That automatically commands respect. But when other scientists started to check out the math, they were confounded because they couldn't prove it

Thomas Hertog (left) and Stephen Hawking have collaborated on theories as to how the universe came to be as it is, including how it came to evolve humans able to ask questions about their own existence.

wrong. They tried. Believe me, they tried! But it has so far withstood the slings and arrows of outrageous attacks.

Before we try to explain it, though, remember this. We are about to go where common sense fears to tread. We have said over and over again that we are conditioned to the normalcy of our five senses. But they don't work out here in the realm of sophisticated mathematics. It's a pretty exclusive neighborhood. Our senses reveal only common-place illusions, such as the so-called "reality" that we are solid mass instead of carbon and water with a lot of emptiness in between. The illusion of solidness seems real. But we know it's not. So relax and let your imagination take over the reins.

Here we go. The most common explanation of the Multiverse is that individual universes break off and form separate, parallel universes in which everything that can happen, does happen. Somewhere. Somehow. There are a lot of variations on this theme, but this is the basic idea.

According to the particular theory we're going to explore, which is called the Observer-Created Universe Theory, individual universes don't break off and go forth on their own. Instead, only a universe that contains "observers" collapses into existence. We are the observers. We observe the universe that becomes our universe. The trick is that other observers observe the universe that becomes their universe.

(Don't say I didn't warn you that this would get complicated.)

Because we are in this universe, we selected the path our universe took in order to produce us. Presumably, other observers selected the path their universe took in order to produce them.

"But wait!" you exclaim. "That means the present actually determines the past. We observe in the present and that fixes the past on a course that leads to us."

Exactly! Is that counterintuitive or what?

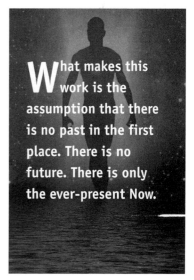

What makes this work is the assumption that there is no past in the first place. There is no future. There is only the ever-present Now. The idea that time flows in a river from the past through the present into the future is an illusion. It may well feel that way to us. It appears to be the way time rushes by. But that's not the case at all.

Is this getting stranger?

Try this on for size. Let's imagine that we are playwrights, engaged in writing a play that explains how we got to be playwrights in the first place. We conjure up the actors, the staging, the props, and the dialogue. We get all the details right and await opening night to watch the play develop.

But wait! There's more! We, that is, the human race, have written ourselves in to play the leading role. So we not only wrote the play, we take part in it. But in doing so we become such good actors that we completely lose ourselves in the part. We become the people in the drama. We forget that we are merely actors on a stage.

(Are we good at our craft, or what?)

When the play is over, we take our bow and exit stage right. Only then do we realize that we have participated in a drama starring us. The part we played on stage concerned an actor in a drama. But who was the author of the play?

We were!

And what was our name?

Well, you can fill in your own blank here, but the other actors in the play, if they had known you wrote the drama in the first place, would have considered you to be a supernatural god, able to control events at will and direct the whole production.

Here's the bottom line. If this idea is even close to being correct, our supernatural gods have been found. They are us. We wrote the play and are now living it out. We're such good actors, and live so totally in character, that we don't realize it. When the time comes for us to take the final curtain call, we will have arrived back at the beginning of the drama and realize the play is over and was a resounding success.

For you literary types this may sound familiar. It is almost identical to Marcel Proust's (1871–1922) *In Search of Lost Time* (earlier named *Remembrance of Things Past*). In it he records the progress, amid much suffering, of his hero. Many, many pages later the hero resolves to write a book, which turns out to be the book you have been reading.

This theory, sometimes called the Participatory Universe Theory, states that time is a self-sustaining loop. In other words, the universe creates us, and then we in turn create the universe. If the universe had an initial existing state, none of this would be possible. But according to Hawking and Hertog, the Multiverse never had an initial existing state. It is eternal. It had no beginning—no starting point. The Big Bang that began our universe was one of an infinite number of Big Bangs. Something came before. And before that. And before that. Forever. There is no boundary that marks the beginning.

Who created the universe?

God!

Who created God?

The participants of the universe.

"And the wheels on the bus go round and round...."

Everyone assumes that Michelangelo's "The Creation of Adam" depicts God creating Adam, but what if the opposite is actually true? What if we create God?

They will continue to do so forever, which is a human anthropomorphism that projects a concept of time onto a stage in which time does not exist. There is only an ever-present, eternal "Now."

(Danger! Thinking about all this will cause sleepless nights. I guarantee it. My prescription? Take a stiff drink and call Stephen Hawking in the morning!)

Variation on a Theme

There's a variation on this scenario that's easier to understand. It sounds an awful lot like a sci-fi thriller, but it, too, has serious support among some theoretical physicists. I call it "The Case of the Divine Hacker." It goes something like this: with computer technology leading to exponential growth in virtual reality, experts believe it is only a matter of time before we are able to produce computer simulation programs that appear just as real as the real thing. It will be virtually impossible to recognize the difference between actors on a screen and their simulated counterparts. If we slip on a virtual reality helmet even now, we would swear that the things happening in front of our eyes are actually happening to us in real life.

This forces the question: Is it possible to produce a movie on a computer screen that is so real even the virtual actors cross the boundary into sentience? Might they somehow acquire the ability to be taken in and think they are real, instead of computer-generated, artificially intelligent, virtual simulations?

If they examine their existence closely enough, they will discover that they consist only of pixels flashing in and out of a mysterious, three-dimensional field, predestined to play their part in a simulation over which they have no real control. If they become real enough to question their existence, they will discover that they cannot pass beyond this field with any measuring devices known to them. At that point they will probably quit trying, give in to reality, and simply go about the business of living. They will never know they are being watched by a geeky kid in his darkened upstairs bedroom who created the whole program to amuse himself. He will be totally outside their perception realm. If they ever do intuit his existence, they will probably call him a supernatural being. Maybe even their creator. And from their point of view, they will be right.

But here's the point. If this will someday be possible, who is to say it hasn't already happened? Given what we have discovered about elementary particles zooming in and out of existence through a mysterious field called the Higgs Field, forming our very bodies that *appear* to be solid even though they're not, we have to admit that our existence seems to consist of something that looks a lot like pixels. Given our inability to see life through any lens other than a three-dimensional reality, four if you count time, even though it is a virtual certainty that more dimensions lie just outside our perception, doesn't it seem utterly plausible that we could quite possibly be computer generated, virtual actors, playing out our lives on some future kid's next-generation Hewlett Packard/Apple/Microsoft 1300Z desktop computer?

What will we do when his mother calls him to dinner and he pulls the plug on our world? Nothing! We will wink out of existence as though we had never been.

Star Trek: The Next Generation played with this a little in an episode called "Ship in a Bottle." In this story, the android named Data wants to play the part of Sherlock Holmes on the starship *Enterprise*'s holodeck. His friend La Forge accidentally creates a holographic Professor Moriarty (Holmes's arch enemy in the Arthur Conan Doyle books) who becomes a conscious being. Moriarty tries to escape the confines of the holodeck, but to do so would cause him to vanish into thin air. Nevertheless, he is convinced the ship's Captain Picard can force his crew to figure out a way to make this possible. Picard knows it is not, so he tricks Moriarty into thinking he has escaped the holodeck when in actuality he is still trapped within.

It makes for great entertainment, to be sure. But there's nothing here that isn't at least theoretically possible in the future, given the direction of today's computer technology. It's possible that we are at the same stage Professor Moriarty was. He deduced that he was a character in a computer-generated simulation. Well, there are those who wonder the same thing about us. Moriarty was lucky enough to find himself under the control of a compassionate Captain Picard, who saved the computer program instead of deleting it. Picard here plays the role of a supernatural god. That's no doubt how Moriarty must have conceived him, even though Picard was a full-blown human who just had the luck to live a few hundred years in Moriarty's future.

If we ever discover that we, too, are computer-generated simulations, may we be fortunate enough to enjoy the same fate!

SCENARIO #2: LIVING WITHIN THE STATE OF "ALTERED"

There is, of course, no way known to physicists to ever "prove" the truth of any of these theoretical scenarios. Such proof demands an adherence to the rules of the scientific community. These theories all fall way outside the boundaries of any instruments now available to measure them, let alone reproduce them under laboratory conditions. Even the computers of theoretical physicists can't crunch enough numbers to do any more than show us glimmers of a possible path to follow.

That being said, however, there may be a way to check out the mystery ourselves, using only the abilities thousands upon thousands of mystics have claimed down through the centuries and swear to be authentic. We've already surveyed a whole host of methods in Part II, and together they all remind us that we are not powerless. For at least forty thousand years, people have been experimenting with ways to contact the supernatural. The way we're talking about in this scenario involves entering into a state of what is sometimes called "altered" or "expanded" consciousness.

Remember—we live in a tiny house called a human body. In that house, there is an even tinier attic wherein resides something we call a brain. The brain has an inside and an outside. Those of us who are not psychic can only know what's going on in the inside of our own brain. We can't peer into the inside of someone else's. We are aware of the constant stream of thoughts that go on inside our own heads, but when we peek inside the head of someone else, all we will find are neurons, cells, and electrical impulses. We can measure what these impulses are doing when we look at an MRI of someone's brain. We can see them firing away. But we can't derive meaning from all the flashing lights. We can know that someone is thinking because we see the blinking lights on the machine. But we don't know if they're thinking about a trip to Tahiti or last night's dinner.

Our brains have evolved to be wonderful aids when it comes to interpreting

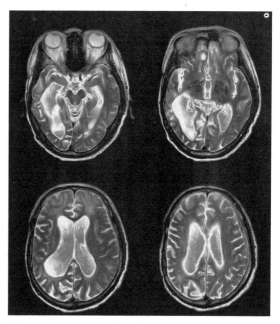

We can use an MRI machine to scan and peek inside a person's brain, and we can tell that the brain is active and in what regions it is active; but we cannot tell from this what a person is thinking, exactly.

what's going on around us. But we have to keep in mind that the occupant of the attic up there in the physical "house" we call our body has only five windows to peer out of when it comes to interpreting the world. We call them the five senses. They work fine under normal conditions. But when it comes to understanding the deep nature beyond the illusion of life, they are insufficient.

When we stop to think about it, how can they possibly pierce the illusion? They create the illusion, for heaven's sake! To see past the familiar illusion we call reality, and to glimpse the field of infinite consciousness, or the supernatural, we need to expand our minds past the filters of the five senses. That usually means bypassing the senses through meditation, drugs, prayer, or some sort of spiritual discipline. Only then can we pierce the veil and see into unexplored realms.

Disclaimer: *I am not advocating the use of any substances that may or may not be legal. It's not that I'm morally opposed. It's just that I have absolutely no experience in this area. Aside from imbibing at cocktail hour or watching the occasional* Harry Potter *marathon on the tube, I've never partaken of any mind altering drug. For advice on that front, I suggest you get a copy of Graham Hancock's excellent book,* Supernatural. *It's listed in the bibliography at the end of this book.*

No, in this matter I can only suggest meditation that leads to OBEs or visions of the other side. It's slower, probably not as effective as a shot of ayahuasca, but much safer. Especially if, like me, you are too much of a control freak to risk giving up your sense of identity or self.

It has been estimated that we use about ten percent of the capacity of our brains. That has recently shown to be a bit of a misleading statement. But even if it's only partly true, we are capable of much, much more awareness than we usually demonstrate. When we looked at Chemical Keys back in Part II, we discovered that it's very possible that an expanded consciousness brought on by the ingestion of mushrooms or some other plant derivative might have produced the experience we needed to become human in the first place. But now that that has happened, are there other ways to move beyond the senses and discover wonders out beyond the capability of words to describe?

It might prove valuable here to reread the chapters "Meditation and Eastern Spirituality" and "Out-of-Body Experiencs and Near-Death Experiences." Both offer some valuable information about such a possibility. Although usually confined to the field of metaphysics and even "quack" New Age experience, my gut feeling is that psychologists haven't yet scratched the surface of methods and techniques, which will prove to be very valuable indeed in our quest to discover worlds and supernatural gods out there beyond our day-to-day experience.

SCENARIO #3: TINKERING WITH A UNIVERSE

Andrei Linde (1948–) is probably the most famous man people have never heard of. Go out on any city street in the country and ask ten people who he is. I'd be surprised if even one recognized the name. But he is the one, along with his colleague Alan Guth (1947–), who came closest to describing how we all got here in the first place.

Linde is Russian-born but came to America to teach at Stanford. While still in Russia he became fascinated by the Big Bang. While studying this momentous event, he came up with a wacky idea, now the accepted theory held by the majority of physicists, that dealt with three big questions about the Big Bang:

- What banged?
- Why did it bang?
- What was going on before it banged?

The theory is called chaotic inflation. Without going into a lot of details that are outside the parameters of this book, it tries to explain how the universe grew so rapidly in the first split second of its existence and why it now looks the way it does.

There's no doubt about it. It's a brilliant theory invented by a brilliant man. But what makes Linde so important to us at this point of our quest is that while studying the Big Bang, he discovered that it isn't that hard to create a universe. When he was interviewed by Jim Holt (1954–), author of the wonderfully intriguing book *Why Does the World Exist?*, he expressed this thought:

"When I invented the theory of chaotic inflation I found that the only thing you needed to get a universe like ours started is a hundred-thousandth of a gram of matter. That's enough to create a small chunk of vacuum that blows up into the billions and billions of galaxies we see around us. It looks like cheating, but that's how the inflation theory works—all the matter in our universe gets created from the negative energy of the gravitational field. So what's to stop us from creating a universe in a lab? We would be like gods!" … There are some

Stanford University physicist Andrei Linde devised the theory of chaotic inflation to explain how the universe evolved into its present state.

gaps in my proof, but what I have shown—and Alan Guth [a co-developer of inflation theory] and others who have looked into it have come to the same conclusion—is that we can't rule out the possibility that our own universe was created by someone in another universe who just felt like doing it.

—Andrei Linde speaking to
Jim Holt in *Why Does the World Exist?*

If some mad scientist ever succeeds in creating his own pet universe during his lunch hour, wouldn't his creation bang into our universe and annihilate us?

Apparently not. It would "bang big" into its own space and time, inflating a whole new parallel universe that would be so curved in on itself that that it would never look any bigger than an elementary particle to someone on the outside. (Where are the *Men in Black* when you need them?) It might even just disappear. The scientist would never know what he had done. He could conceivably go to his grave never realizing that a few billion years into the future a life form would evolve in his pet universe that would worship him as a supernatural god who once supposedly said, "Let there be light!"

Once again, if a thing is theoretically possible in the future, who is to say it hasn't already happened?

That being the case, let's take it one step further. What if the future mad scientist decided to tinker with his new universe? What if he decided he wanted to somehow send it a message? Suppose, for instance, he were to print a message that said something like, "I created you" on the original speck of matter that he used to begin his new toy? When the material "banged" the message would, of course, be inflated to unimaginable proportions, but it would still be there, writ large across the entire night sky of the universe and readable by someone who was brilliant enough to invent a way to do it.

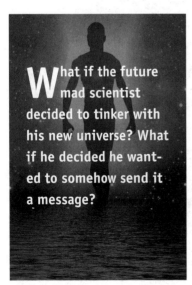

What if the future mad scientist decided to tinker with his new universe? What if he decided he wanted to somehow send it a message?

Or suppose the scientist tried a different trick? What if he coded a series of secret numbers, for instance, into the physics of his new creation? Numbers that would be bound to show up and intrigue the curious. 3.1416 … for instance? This is the plot device used by Carl Sagan (1934–1996) in his book *Contact,* written back in 1985. The idea was that an advanced alien civilization had, long ago, created this universe and left a message way downstream in the unending roll of numbers that we call pi. If we just compute the numbers far enough, the message will be there waiting for us. We will then have contacted our supernatural creators.

Let's let Linde have the last word here. After all, it's his theory. Once again we turn to his interview with Jim Holt:

> You might take this as a joke, but perhaps it is not entirely absurd. It may furnish the explanation for why the world we live in is so weird, so far from perfect. On the evidence, our universe wasn't created by a divine being. It was created by a physicist hacker!

This theorizing is fun, but it underscores a serious point. We assume that supernatural gods are omnipotent, benevolent, omniscient, eternal, all-seeing, all wise, etc., etc.

But even if our universe does turn out to be created by a supernatural intelligent being, our creator could just as well be a journeyman apprentice from another dimension or a future time, learning how to ply his trade.

Or worse. The seemingly mistake-prone universe that leads us to ask, "Why is this happening?" could very well be a product of an incompetent, eminently fallible student who is about to flunk out of physics class.

Maybe it's time to quit here, before we all get too depressed. Besides, we can always take refuge in the question, "Okay—who created the physicist?"

There is an apocryphal story told about an old Hindu wise man who taught his students that the world perched on the back of a giant turtle.

"What's the turtle standing on?" he was asked.

"The turtle is standing on the back of an elephant!" he confidently declared.

"What's the elephant standing on?" came the inevitable question

The wise man thought for a minute and then declared, "It's elephants all the way down!"

Jim Holt had this anecdote in mind when he left his interview with Andrei Linde. When he posed the question to himself, "Who created the physicist?" he had the perfect answer.

"Let's hope it's not hackers all the way up!"

SCENARIO #4: WHICH WAY TO THE HOLODECK?

Anyone who has ever watched *Star Trek: The Next Generation* is familiar with the concept of the holodeck. It's based on a scientific reality with a practical basis in normal experience.

The whole idea of holograms and the possibility of a holographic universe came about because of a theoretical argument.

One of the principles of thermodynamics is that disorder can never decrease in a closed system, and order can never increase. If we consider the

If we exist within a closed universe from which matter and energy cannot escape, then how do we explain a black hole?

universe to be a closed system, and it must be because as far as we know there is nothing outside it, then order, or information, can neither increase nor decrease.

So what happens to information, or matter and energy, when it falls into a black hole? It disappears from the universe and can never be retrieved.

But according to the laws of thermodynamics, that's impossible.

So what's a poor physicist to do?

Stephen Hawking of Cambridge and Jacob Bekenstein (1947–2015), who taught at Princeton at the time, decided to tackle the problem. What they decided was that disorder in a black hole is directly related to the size of its surface area. In other words, the information is stored on the surface of a black hole. Somewhere, somehow, it still existed and could be retrieved if we could ever figure out a way to do it.

Problem solved.

Or was it?

Leonard Susskind (1940–) at Stanford and Gerald 't Hooft (1946–) at the University of Utrecht delved further into the problem. If information was stored on the surface of a black hole, it might still be "in" the closed system of the universe. But how to get at it? The answer was to find a way to project two-dimensional information into a three-dimensional image that could be accessed in a way that our senses would be able to perceive within this universe in which we have evolved.

Enter the hologram. It's a three-dimensional image projected into our arena of awareness from a two-dimensional storage space.

I once visited the museum at the Moundville Archeological Site in Alabama. It featured a holographic presentation in which an Indian shaman mysteriously appeared, floating in space in front of his dwelling place as he spoke to me, telling me about his initiation experience. I watched the presentation at least three times. It was uncanny—my first experience in viewing a holographic image. It seemed so real! I was sure that if I talked to him, he would answer. Somewhere, there obviously must have been a computer programmer who put the whole show together. He did a wonderful job of creating reality where only empty space was a moment before.

Now jump to a much larger scale. When I saw the holographic image, it appeared in a small space that was probably not more than a few square yards. But, as we have previously observed, when it comes to the Multiverse size doesn't matter. What if the entire universe—everything we have ever experienced—is nothing more than a holographic image, a three-dimensional reality cast by a two-dimensional source of information that lies on its surface?

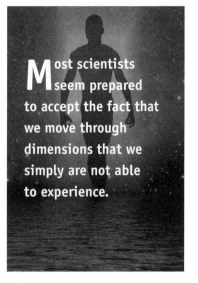

Most scientists seem prepared to accept the fact that we move through dimensions that we simply are not able to experience.

This isn't as far-fetched as it sounds. Physicists who deal with string theory regularly come up against the fact that their computations work best if projected into a multi-dimensional system. (Don't worry too much if you don't understand why this is the case, or are even a bit fuzzy about what it means. I don't get it either.)

Most scientists seem prepared to accept the fact that we move through dimensions that we simply are not able to experience. Could we possibly be living our lives, fulfilling our hopes and dreams, experiencing both triumph and tragedy, within what amounts to a holographic universe—a universe that we are convinced is a three-dimensional, "only this and nothing else"–type universe?

If that is the case, who programmed the computer? The answer seems obvious: a supernatural entity—even if that entity constitutes nothing more than what we might call Consciousness, Universal Mind, God, Akasha, Brahman, or, using the term we just coined, All That Is. Supernatural gods don't have to be people like us, beings like us, or anything else like us. They, or it, may be closer to what we might call a Force, or a Thought, or a Purposeful Directive.

However we phrase it, the fact remains that when you look closer and closer into each one of us, what you find looks a whole lot closer to pixels, images, nothingness, and emptiness than solid hands and feet—matter that takes on form and shape.

Once again we quote Sir Arthur Eddington:

The universe is not only stranger than we imagine. It is stranger than we *can* imagine!

FINAL THOUGHTS

We have been on a wild ride together. Our search has taken us far afield at times. Some of the theories we have surveyed seem far-fetched, to say the least. Others hit a little closer to home. But all have their devoted followers.

It makes us wonder. Can we really sit quietly by and accept that things as we usually experience them are, in essence, the way things really are? Or would it behoove us to ask again and again the questions we asked way back at the beginning of our quest:

Are there such things as supernatural gods?

Is there such a thing as magic?

According to science, what we experience in our normal, comfortable perception realm appears more and more to be an illusion. Things are simply not as rock solid and set in concrete as they seem to be. But according to the testimonies of thousands upon thousands of people down through the centuries, it is possible for us to bust through the illusion and see the other side. It takes discipline and effort, but it's worth it.

How can I say that with such confidence?

Let me once again resort to personal testimony.

As a minister, I have talked to thousands of people about discernment and spiritual growth. I have wondered, over the years, why most people don't seem to really care, aside from professing a casual interest, in the beliefs and activities we have surveyed over the last few hundred pages of questing together. Where is the passion for mystery in our culture? Where is the desire for magic in our society? Where is the burning interest in spirituality amongst our neighbors?

Our culture tells us that the important things in life are consumerism, youth, and a hyperactive lifestyle. If you subscribe to that belief, it leaves little time for spirituality.

Having retired from ministry almost eight years ago, I now have had plenty of time to think about it. What I have decided is this. Our popular culture, far from promoting these topics, has historically either ignored them or treated them with an element of patronizing silliness.

Although there is evidence that things may finally be changing, why has this been the dominating tendency, even though we traditionally call ourselves a religious people?

I have come to believe it's because spiritual maturity is, of necessity, the specialty of the tribal elders. They are the ones who have had the most experience, the most time to think, and the most years to develop wisdom.

But we have, for the most part, eliminated the icon of the valued elder as something to which we should all espouse. What have we put in its place? The image of an immature child. The bottom line is this: In Western society we worship youth.

I realize that's quite a statement, but think about it for a minute. Try this exercise. Watch a few hours of TV and jot down the content of the commercials you see. What you will find is this:

- Our culture constantly bombards us with the supposed necessity of buying the latest technological toys in order to "be cool." Smartphones, GPS devices, tablets, and on and on. If you want to get ahead, you have to be savvy about these things. AARP even cautions its members to get technologically relevant or they'll never be able to communicate with their kids. Let's call these devices what they are. Toys! Who plays with toys? Children!

- Our culture constantly bombards us with the supposed necessity of appearing young. Ads for cosmetics, skin care products, and clothing fill the airwaves. "You're only as young as you feel!" "Make love like a youngster!" "Stay youthful so you can play games." "Buy a cool car and feel young again!" Who is interested in these kinds of advertised goodies? Who places great emphasis on looks, sex, and games? Children!

- Our culture constantly bombards us with the supposed necessity of keeping busy. Work three jobs. Never retire. Multitask. Check your email and Twitter account. Get involved with social media. Check in with friends. Never sit quietly in a chair and reflect because it will slow you down. Listen to tunes while you catch up on your latest tech manuals. Memorize the lyrics and the exotic names of the artists. Do more. Move faster. Don't stop or life will overtake you. Who attacks life with such hyperactive frenzy? Children!

It's hard for a young person to really, existentially believe they are going to die. Oh, they understand the fact of death. But they don't believe in their very soul that it will ever happen to them. It's an intellectually imagined reality that is easily pushed aside when you are in the prime of life. That's probably why we were all capable of doing some pretty dangerous things when we were young, whether it involved driving too fast, taking some pretty fierce drugs, or participating in some pretty outlandish activities. Outcomes weren't quite real, somehow, so deep and abiding spiritual growth wasn't something we were really interested in.

Many people sustain that feeling throughout their entire lifetime.

I once was a candidate for the position of pastor in a fairly typical American community church. I sat around a table and fielded questions from their search committee for a few hours. Finally they asked me if I had any questions.

I had only one. "When you meet socially after the Sunday morning service to share some coffee and talk about God, what kinds of conversations do you have?"

They looked at each other sheepishly and the chairman replied, "Well, we don't talk much about God in this church."

In our culture it is common to never even bring up the subject of death, except in jest. Although it happens to us all, it's considered morbid. As a minister, of course, I often led funeral services as many as a few times every week, so I suppose I grew used to it. But I am constantly surprised to meet people who never have even been inside a funeral home or seen a dead body until well along in life.

> The plain and simple fact is this. Someday, each and every one of us, without exception, will learn whether or not supernatural gods exist.

And yet death is a common staple of our entertainment. Virtually every episode of *NCIS* or *Castle* begins with a gruesome death scene. Video games are all about death and destruction. So it's as though we're pretending death doesn't exist even though we know it does. Perhaps it's a part of our entertainment culture for just that reason. We fear it so much we attempt to trivialize it by saturating ourselves with it in the form of fantasy.

I bring this up because in all my years of talking to people about spiritual growth, I have found only one, sure-fire, absolutely certain method that will induce people to do an about-face when it comes to contemplating the supernatural for the first time. That method has many variations, but the most common is a diagnosis of incurable cancer. Nothing makes a person look seriously at life more than being forced to admit that it's going to end.

The plain and simple fact is this. Someday, each and every one of us, without exception, will learn whether or not supernatural gods exist. Current spiritual mysteries will become our reality—our new home. Psychic experiences will no longer be a mere intellectual exercise. Scientific truths will be proved to be either profound or silly. If we exist in a Multiverse, that Multiverse will become our new playground.

"In my Father's house are many rooms," Jesus was reported to have said in John 14:2. At death we will come to know if those "many rooms" are metaphors or entire universes. To quote yet another Bible verse, "For now we see only a reflection as in a mirror; then we shall see face to face. Now I know in part; then I shall know fully, even as I am fully known" (I Corinthians 13:2).

I have just quoted Christian scriptures because they are familiar to most people. But every text of every religion says similar things when you begin to open the pages of their scriptures and read what they have to say. Life after death is a concept that goes back to the very first humans who placed flowers and tools in the graves of their loved ones. You don't do such a thing unless you believe they will serve a future purpose.

I once stood at the bedside of a friend who had founded a college, enjoyed a successful teaching career, served in various local political offices, and made a small fortune along the way. He was also a deacon in the church and had the reputation of being a well-respected churchman and pillar in the community. I was there because I had received a late-night phone call from a nurse at the local hospital. My friend was dying and was not expected to live out the night. He had asked for me so of course, I got out of bed and quickly made my way to be with him.

I found him in tears. I asked if he was ready to cross over and he said something I will never forget: "Jim, for my whole life I have done everything but the one thing that was most important. I never prepared for this moment."

We were lucky. He made it through that long night and lasted for ten more. I spent a few hours of every one of those next days with him. I hope I was able to help. I don't know if I taught him anything. I know he taught me a lot.

This story illustrates the fact that we all live one heartbeat away from the reality of the supernatural—one heartbeat away from the goal of the quest that has been the subject of our journey together throughout these many pages. We caught a glimpse of that goal at the beginning of this book and surveyed how oth-

ers viewed the destination. We surveyed tried-and-true methods that have been utilized for millennia. We came closer when we began to look within ourselves and came to understand that it is only there that we can look with eyes attuned to the spirit rather than the illusion that seems so very, very solid but has proven to be just that—an illusion.

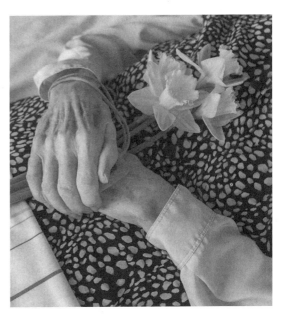

There is a lot more to life than many of us have ever contemplated—a greater mystery than we often realize. Perhaps we may someday, after death inevitably claims us if not before, come to see that this particular quest is the most important task we can undertake in this life. Maybe it's even the reason why we chose to be born in the first place. Maybe it's the reason we are alive.

Ultimately, who knows for sure? We live deep within the foggy illusion that surrounds us and pervades our very being—the illusion that "what we see is what we get."

Most of us never really face death until it is staring us in the face. It is wise to think about such things now, prepare for them, and contemplate more our place beyond this current "reality."

EPILOGUE: DISCOVERING THE SUPERNATURAL IN ONE OF MANY ANCIENT TEXTS

All Scripture is God-breathed, and is useful for teaching....

—2nd Timothy 3:16

A Meditation on the Gospel of John 1 and Psalm 23

The seeker was deeply, deeply troubled and depressed. He saw the evil and wickedness of the world all around him and felt inadequate to right the many wrongs he saw happening. Gods and deities seemed utterly absent—any hope of supernatural aid appeared far away. He seemed totally and hopelessly alone. Feeling impotent, powerless, and afraid, he went forth searching for death. It seemed to be the only door out of what he considered a prison.

He climbed to the top of the highest mountain and looked all around to the farthest horizon, but death could not be seen. He entered the deepest wood, but found only shadows and old, old trees. He walked through endless meadows filled with bright light but saw only an endless sea of flowers and butterflies. Death was nowhere to be found.

Finally he sought out an elder, a wise man who was said to dwell in a grove of trees where he taught his disciples. He came to the wise man and sat on the ground before him.

"Master," he said, "where can I find death? I have searched high and low but to no avail."

"Death is all around you," said the elder. "You have only to open your eyes."

"But Master," said the man, "I have climbed the highest mountain, probed the deepest wood and walked in the broadest meadows. I cannot find death anywhere."

The Master looked at him closely, a smile creasing his, until now, stern features. "Even the highest mountain will decay into the earth. The oldest trees in the forest will someday give up the life that is in them, topple with a mighty crash, and die. Meadow flowers are renewed each year, seemingly cheating death. Caterpillars will construct coffins for themselves and be renewed as butterflies. But even they will not last forever. No—all these are only masks for death—the disguise of the end that lives within them all."

At this the man was distraught. "If everything that exists is a mask of death, if death claims us all in the end, if there is no escape, then Master, why are you smiling? Do you know a secret? Do you know how to defeat death?"

The Master smiled even more deeply. "There is a way to defeat death, and I do know what it is."

"Can you tell me?" asked the man.

"Certainly," the elder replied. "Like most things that seem complicated, it is really very simple. TRUST THE WORD!"

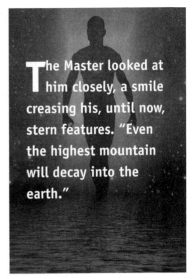

The Master looked at him closely, a smile creasing his, until now, stern features. "Even the highest mountain will decay into the earth."

"Trust?" said the man. "I certainly trust you, but what else is there to trust in a world gone mad?"

"Don't trust me," insisted the elder. "I, too, am a mask of death. TRUST THE WORD!"

"I trust your words," said the man. "You are experienced and have a reputation for speaking wisdom."

"Don't trust my words," insisted the Master. "They, too, are a mask of death. TRUST THE WORD!"

At this, the man grew despondent. He simply didn't understand.

Then the Master began to quote words from an old, old book of wisdom:

In the beginning was the Word.

When space and time began, energy vibrated out of the field of Akasha. That vibration, were it audible, could only be described, in our language, as a Word. Words are vibration that carry meaning. They are not reality. They are symbols of reality. They point to reality. They represent reality. The first word must have been something like—LIGHT. Or maybe the phrase, "LET THERE BE LIGHT." The result was what we call "The Big Bang"—light in the darkness. Or maybe it's closer to say that light and darkness both appeared into what was, before, nothing. In other words, "Light," vibrational energy, is the source of the material universe. The WORD brought forth the material cosmos—energy manifested in form.

And the Word was with God, and the Word was God.

He was with God in the beginning. Through him all things were made; without him nothing was made that has been made.

"God," "Spirit," "Akasha," or "All that Is" is both the source and the physical form of the Cosmos. Spirit is energy. Energy takes on physical form in the material universe. The universe is both "with God" and "God incarnate"—one of God's physically manifested bodies.

In him was life, and that life was the light of men.

Within material form, actually making up material form, there is "light," or vibrational energy. Akashic energy, or "light," forms the "life," the very molecules, of the material universe.

The light shines in the darkness, but the darkness has not understood it.

Hence, the need for constant revisions and interpretations of classic religious texts!

The Word became flesh and lived....

The author of this text identified the "Light" and the "Word," with Jesus of Nazareth. He missed the point. The "Word" and the "Light" are the material universe itself, the incarnation and the very body of divine, spiritual energy.

Now the words of the elder and the point of the story became clear. TRUST THE WORD reminded the seeker that the universe, consisting of both life and death, the two opposites, is simply playing itself out before, like all living things, it comes to a predictable end. Everything wears the mask of death. Death is not an enemy. Death is simply the cessation of vibrational energy and a return to Akasha, the field of stillness and peace. It is the gateway between the natural and the supernatural.

TRUST THE WORD means to trust the universe to carry out its work. There is no death—only a doorway to peace and stillness. Saul of Tarsus said it in Corinthians 15:

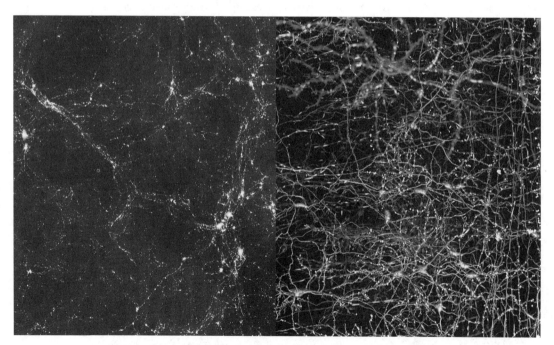

At left is a computer-generated image of how the universe looks when you zoom out enough to see that the galaxies form a kind of interconnected network. At right is an image of the neural network of the human brain. We are, indeed, a reflection of a God who is Everything.

Death is swallowed up in victory. Oh death, where is thy sting?
Oh grave, where is thy victory? Thanks be to God who gives us
the victory!

To trust that the universe is fulfilling its purpose, that the natural
returns to the supernatural, is to understand that there is no death.

The seeker had his answer. But familiar words kept nagging at him....

Yea though I walk through the valley of the shadow of death I
will fear no evil....

We live in the "valley of the shadow of death," the place where literally
everything wears the mask of death. But we need not fear.

Thou preparest a table before me in the presence of my enemy....

Even in the presence of death, the supposed enemy, Spirit prepares a
table for us. We, like all living things, literally consume death every day. We
call it food. Eating is feasting off death. We eat it up. The irony is that without
death we would die.

Surely goodness and mercy shall follow me all the days of my life,
and I shall dwell in the house of the Lord forever....

The seeker came to understand that death is not the only reality that
there is here on this material plane of existence. In the midst of it all there is
goodness and love. They follow us all the days of our lives. "Look for it," say
the lost truths. There is no hurry. Everything happens as and when it should.
And someday all will return home to dwell in the house of Spirit, the Akashic
field, forever.

The seeker rose, content. He had fulfilled his quest. He had sought
death but now realized there was no hurry. Someday death would find him.
And that day would be a blessing, not a curse. Death was the final door
between the natural and supernatural.

As he stood, preparing to leave the place of lost truth and hidden wisdom, he looked up to see a full moon shining in the heavens.

"As beautiful as you are," he said, "you are only a reflection of the light!"

As are we all.

For a moment, a cloud drifted across the moon, darkening its light.

"And sometimes we let things get a little blurry," he said.

Appendix: Brief History of the Search for Supernatural Gods

(All dates given as BP: Before Present, and rounded off for convenience.)

- **200,000 years BP: Birth of Modern Humans.** "Mitochondrial Eve" gives birth to modern humans—probably in Ethiopia. By "modern," we mean that these people had the same features and brain size we do. If they were to spend a day at a spa and put on modern clothes, they would be indistinguishable from us.

- **40,000 years BP: Birth of Symbolic (Religious) Thought.** The "Great Leap Forward." Humans first demonstrate the capacity for symbolic (religious) thought, entering the great European caves and producing high art. Although grave burials predating this as far back as Neanderthal times demonstrate a probable belief in the afterlife, and the discovery of what might be a flute hint at the expression of music, the cave paintings reveal a sudden flourishing of spiritual or religious expression. Some theories suggest that the discovery of hallucinogenic, mind-expanding plants led to this giant step on the way to spiritual significance that separated us from our animal predecessors.

- **11,500 years BP: Göbekli Tepe.** Göbekli Tepe, thought to be our civilization's first temple dedicated to the gods, is built.

- **5,000 years BP: Stonehenge.** Major work is completed at Stonehenge in England. Although no one knows for sure why it was built, it seems to be an ancient temple with astrological significance. It is known for sure that there were many cremations and burials held here. Although we may never learn for certain what kind of supernatural gods these people worshipped, the fact that Stonehenge was a major center for religious ritual is obvious.

- **4,500 years BP: Pyramids.** The Pyramids are completed. Mystery surrounds everything about them, from their construction techniques to their exact purpose. But they certainly underscore religious beliefs of a profound and consuming nature.

- **4,000–5,000 years BP; Hindu Rishis.** Wise men in India begin to intuit the spirit of the supernatural. Although they acknowledge individual supernatural gods of all sorts, they also recognize the presence of Brahman, the unexplainable ground of all being, and Atman, the inner essence of Brahman. Much of what they taught is, in essence, similar to what quantum theorists have discovered today. What they described in terms of metaphor is now coming to the surface of scientific discovery. Humans are one with the cosmos.

- **3,500–1,500 years BP: Monotheism.** Religious leaders such as Zoroaster, Akhenaten, Abraham, Moses, Jesus, and Mohammad begin monotheistic systems of belief that exist to this day.

- **2,700 years BP: Genesis Creation Story.** The Genesis creation story is written down for the first time. Up to now, scholars suspect it had been a common oral tradition passed down through the priestly class.

- **2,400 years BP: Plato.** Plato puts forth the idea that supernatural gods may be mathematical entities. He also believed that abstract ideas such as Goodness, Love, and Beauty, being timeless, could be understood to be "Forms" that constituted genuine reality.

- **1,500 years BP: Popol Vuh of the Quiche Mayans.** The Popol Vuh is transcribed, telling revealing stories of Central and South American supernatural gods. Like the Genesis account, it tells stories that had been around as oral history for at least centuries, perhaps even millennia.

- **360 years BP: René Descartes.** The "Father of Western Philosophy" cements dualism into Western thinking. Henceforth, concepts of supernatural gods revolve around *res extensa* ("extended" substance, or material forms) and *res cogians* ("thinking" substance, or spiritual forms).

- **100 years BP: Albert Einstein.** One of the greatest theoretical physicists of the twentieth century, Einstein's belief that the universe was eternal and, on the whole, unchanging, had a great influence on theologians, who sought to preserve the idea of an eternal, unchanging God in the midst of the swirling, ever-changing culture of physics that was beginning to filter down to the laypeople.

- **90 years BP: Edwin Hubble.** Hubble's discovery that appeared to have confirmed the Big Bang model of the universe is welcomed by theologians who were looking for scientific proof of what they considered to be God's initial command, "Let there be light!"

- **35 years BP: Alan Guth and Andrei Linde.** Their theory of cosmic inflation opens up the idea of "parallel" universes. If such universes exist, they are as capable of evolving intelligent life as our own. Although contact between universes is not feasible according to current science, the idea of contacting this life through psychic means now is given a semblance of scientific, as well as metaphysical, proof.

Further Reading

Ashton, John, and Tom Whyte. *The Quest for Paradise: Visions of Heaven and Eternity in the World's Myths and Religions*. New York: Harper Collins, 2001.

Atwater, F. Holmes. *Captain of My Ship, Master of My Soul*. Charlottesville, VA: Hampton Roads Publishing, 2001.

Bauval, Robert, and Adrian Gilbert. *The Orion Mystery*. New York: Three Rivers Press, 1994.

Bolen, Jean Shinoda. *Gods in Every Man*. San Francisco: Harper & Row, 1989.

Broadhurst, Paul, and Hamish Miller. *The Sun and the Serpent*. Cornwall, England: Pendragon Press, 2013.

Buhlman, William. *Adventures Beyond the Body*. New York: Harper Collins, 1996.

———. *Adventures in the Afterlife*. Millsboro, DE: Osprey Press, 2013.

———. *The Secret of the Soul*. New York: Harper Collins, 2001.

Bullfinch's Mythology. New York: Gramercy Books, 1979.

Campbell, Joseph. *Transformations of Myth through Time*. New York: Harper & Row, 1990.

———, with Bill Moyers. *The Power of Myth*. New York: Bantam, Doubleday, Dell, 1988.

Chopra, Depak, and Leonard Mlodinonow. *War of the World View: Science versus Spirituality*. New York: Harmony Books, 2011.

Clark, Jerome. *Unexplained! Strange Sightings, Incredible Occurrences, and Puzzling Physical Phenomena*, 3rd edition. Detroit: Visible Ink Press: 2013.

Collins, Andrew. *The Cygnus Mystery*. London: Watkins Publishing, 2006.

———. *Göbekli Tepe: Genesis of the Gods*. Rochester, VT: Bear & Co., 2014.

Cotterell, Arthur, and Rachel Storm. *The Ultimate Encyclopedia of Mythology*. China: Hermes House, 1999.

DeLaney, Gayle. *All About Dreams*. San Francisco: Harper Collins, 1993.

Dennett, Daniel. *Darwin's Dangerous Idea: Evolution and the Meanings of Life*. New York: Touchstone, 1996.

Durant, Will and Ariel. *The Lessons of History*. New York: Simon & Schuster, 1968.

Ellwood, Robert S., and Barbara A. McGraw. *Many Peoples, Many Faiths: Women and Men in the World Religions*, 7th edition. Upper Saddle River, NJ: Prentice Hall, 2002.

Estes, Clarissa Pinkola. *Women Who Run with the Wolves: Myths and Stories of the Wild Woman Archetype*. New York: Ballantine, 1992.

Fisher, Mary Pat, and Lee W. Bailey. *An Anthology of Living Religions*. Upper Saddle River, NJ: Prentice Hall, 2000.

Freeman, Gordon R. *Hidden Stonehenge*. London: Watkins Publishing, 2012.

Gaskell, G. A. *Dictionary of All Scriptures and Myths*. New York: Gramercy Books, 1981.

Gould, Stephen J. *Rocks of Ages: Science and Religion in the Fullness of Life*. New York: Ballantine, 1999.

Hancock, Graham. *Fingerprints of the Gods*. New York: Three Rivers Press, 1995.

———. *Magicians of the Gods*. New York: St. Martin's Press, 2015.

———. *The Sign and the Seal*. New York: Crown Publishers, 1992.

———. *Supernatural*. New York: Disinformation Company, 2007.

———. *Underworld: The Mysterious Origins of Civilization*. New York: Crown Publishers, 2002.

Harari, Yuval Noah. *Sapiens: A Brief History of Humankind*. New York: Harper Collins, 2015.

Harari, Yuval Noah. *Homo Deus: A Brief History of Tomorrow*. London: Penguin Random House, 2015.

Harner, Michael. *Cave and Cosmos*. Berkeley, CA: North Atlantic Books, 2013.

———. *The Way of the Shaman*. San Francisco: Harper & Row, 1980.

Harper, Tom. *The Pagan Christ*. Toronto, Canada: Thomas Allen Publishers, 2004.

Hick, John. *Classical and Contemporary Readings in the Philosophy of Religion*. Edgewood Cliffs, NJ: Prentice Hall, 1964.

Highwater, Jamake. *The Primal Mind: Vision and Reality in Indian America*. New York: Harper & Row, 1981.

Hitching, Francis. *Earth Magic*. New York: William Morrow and Company, 1977.

Houston, Jean. *The Hero and the Goddess*. New York: Ballantine, 1992.

Ingerman, Sandra, and Hank Wesselman. *Awakening to the Spirit World: The Shamanic Path of Direct Revelation*. Boulder, CO: Sounds True, 2011.

James, Peter, and Nick Thorpe. *Ancient Mysteries*. New York: Ballantine, 1999.

James, Simon. *The World of the Celts*. London, England: Thames & Hudson, 1993.

Jones, Prudence, and Nigel Pennick. *A History of Pagan Europe*. New York: Routledge, 1995.

Kapra, Fritjof. *The Tao of Physics: An Exploration of the Parallels between Modern Physics and Eastern Mysticism*. Boston: Shambala Publications, 1975.

Kauffman, Stuart A. *Reinventing the Sacred: A New View of Science, Reason, and Religion.* Philadelphia: Basic Books, 2008.

Keck, L. Robert. *Sacred Eyes.* Indianapolis: Knowledge Systems, 1992.

Keen, Jeffrey. *Consciousness, Intent, and the Structure of the Universe.* Victoria, BC: Trafford Publishing, 2005.

Lao Tzu. *Tao Te Ching,* translated by Lau D. C. New York: Penguin Books, 1963.

Laszlo, Ervin. *The Akashic Experience: Science and the Cosmic Memory Field.* Rochester, VT: Inner Traditions, 2009

———. *Science and the Akashic Field: An Integral Theory of Everything,* 2nd edition. Rochester, VT: Inner Traditions, 2007.

———. *The Whispering Pond: A Personal Guide to the Emerging Vision of Science.* Rockport, MA: Element Books, 1996.

Macrone, Michael. *By Jove!: Brush Up Your Mythology.* New York: Harper Collins, 1992.

Mails, Thomas E. *Dancing in the Paths of the Ancestors.* New York: Marlowe, 1999.

Mavor, James W., and Byron E. Dix. *Manitou.* Rochester, VT: Inner Traditions International, 1989.

Monroe, Robert A. *Ultimate Journey.* New York: Doubleday, 1994.

Morris, Desmond. *The Naked Ape.* New York: Dell, 1973.

Nelson, Brian, "Parallel Universes Exist and Interact with Our World, Say Physicists," *Mother Nature Network,* http://www.mnn.com/green-tech/research-innovations/stories/parallel-worlds-exist-and-interact-with-our-world-say. November 6, 2014.

Osborne, Robert. *Civilization: A New History of the Western World.* New York: Pegasus Books, 2006.

Peck, M. Scott. *Glimpses of the Devil.* New York: Simon & Schuster, 2005.

———. *People of the Lie.* New York: Simon & Schuster, 1983.

———. *The Road Less Traveled.* New York: Simon & Schuster, 1978.

Peterson, Robert. *Out of Body Experiences.* Charlottesville, VA: Hampton Roads Publishing, 1997.

Powell, Barry B. *Classical Myth.* Upper Saddle River, NJ: Prentice Hall, 2001.

Prabhupada, A. C. *Bhaktivedanta. Bhagavad-Gita as It Is.* Los Angeles: International Society for Krishna Consciousness, 1984.

Radin, Dean. *The Conscious Universe: The Scientific Truth of Psychic Phenomena.* San Francisco: Harper Collins, 1997.

———. *Entangled Minds.* New York: Simon & Schuster, 2006.

———. *Supernormal: Science, Yoga and the Evidence for Extraordinary Abilities.* New York: Random House, 2013.

Rolleston, T. W. *Myths & Legends of the Celtic Race.* London: The Ballantine Press, 2004.

Ross, T. Edward, and Richard D. Wright. *The Divining Mind: A Guide to Dowsing and Self Awareness.* Rochester, VT: Destiny Books, 1990.

Sagan, Carl. *The Dragons of Eden.* New York: Ballantine, 1977.

Sassaman, Kenneth E. *People of the Shoals: Stallings Culture of the Savanna River Valley*. Gainesville, FL: University Press of Florida, 2006.

Stevenson, Ian. *Children Who Remember Past Lives: A Question of Reincarnation*. Jefferson, NC: McFarland & Company, 2021.

Strassman, Rick. *DMT: The Spirit Molecule*. Rochester, VT: Park Street Press, 2001

———. *DMT and the Soul of Prophecy*. Rochester, VT: Park Street Press, 2014.

———. *Inner Paths to Outer Space: Journeys to Alien Worlds through Psychedelics and other Spiritual Technologies*. Rochester, VT: Park Street Press, 2008.

Temple, Robert. *The Sirius Mystery*. Rochester, VT: Destine Books, 1987.

Tucker, Jim B. *Life before Life: Children's Memories of Previous Lives*. New York: St. Martin's Press, 2005.

Ulansey, David. *The Origins of the Mithraic Mysteries: Cosmology Salvation in the Ancient World*. New York: Oxford University Press, 1989.

Van Renterghem, Tony. *When Santa Was a Shaman*. St. Paul, MN: Llewellyn Publications, 1995.

Von Daniken, Eric. *Chariots of the Gods*. New York: Penguin, 1968.

Waters, Frank. *Book of the Hopi*. New York: Penguin Books, 1977.

Weiss, Brian L. *Many Lives, Many Masters*. New York: Simon & Schuster, 1988.

———. *Same Soul, Many Masters*. New York: Simon & Schuster, Inc. 2004.

———. *Where Reincarnation and Biology Intersect*. Westport, CT: Greenwood, 1997.

Willis, Jim. *The Dragon Awakes: Rediscovering Earth Energy in the Age of Science*. Daytona Beach, FL: Dragon Publishing Co., 2014.

———. *The Religion Book: Places, Prophets, Saints and Seers*. Detroit: Visible Ink Press, 2004.

Willis, Jim and Barbara. *Armageddon Now: The End of the World, A–Z*. Detroit: Visible Ink Press, 2006.

Wright, Patricia C. and Richard D. *The Divining Heart*. Rochester, VT: Destiny Books, 1994.

INDEX

Note: (ill.) indicates photos and illustrations.

meditation and eastern spirituality, 205–6
method of the quest, 129, 273
parallel universes, 76
personal testimony of a quest, 321, 324–27, 329
religious concepts, 92
shamanism and spiritualism, 238
stories of healing and transformation, 117–18

P

Paleolithic era, 7, 12, 31, 42
Pan, 13 (ill.), 14
Paradise, 26, 42
The Parallel Community, 163
parallel universes
about, 65–76
animal envoys from cave and cosmos, 12, 19, 30
bad of the quest, 319
earth spirits, 36, 45
end of the quest and beyond, 351, 355, 362
illustrations and photographs, 67 (ill.), 70 (ill.), 275 (ill.)
indifference to the quest, 339
metaphysical manifestations, 53, 63
method of the quest, 137, 275, 278
object of the quest, 125
personal testimony of a quest, 321
preparation for quest meeting, 297–98, 304
putting the quest together, 285
religious concepts, 92–93
shamanism and spiritualism, 236, 240
visitors from afar, 107–8, 110
Paramount Studios, 181
Participatory Universe Theory, 356
Passover, 177
past life regression, 129, 181–87, 183 (ill.)
Paul, Saint
animal envoys from cave and cosmos, 24
earth spirits, 43
good of the quest, 305
illustrations and photographs, 42 (ill.)

indifference to the quest, 340
meditation and eastern spirituality, 203
method of the quest, 273
religious concepts, 82
PC Magazine, 170
Pech Merle cave, 11, 31, 113, 116
Peck, M. Scott, 316–17
Peisach, Herman E., 155
Peneiel, 297
Pennsylvania, 339
Pentagon, 69
Pentecost, 103
People of the Lie: The Hope for Healing Human Evil (Peck), 316–17
Perception Realm
animal envoys from cave and cosmos, 19–20
Brahman, 348
chemical keys, 146–47, 149, 151
end of the quest and beyond, 358, 366
good of the quest, 309
indifference to the quest, 331, 334, 336–37
metaphysical manifestations, 63
shamanism and spiritualism, 238
Persia, 313
Persinger, Michael A., 148–49, 149 (ill.)
personal testimony of a quest
animal envoys from cave and cosmos, 21–27
dowsing, 156–59
earth spirits, 38–41
end of the quest and beyond, 321–29, 366–69
good of the quest, 306–10
illustrations and photographs, 289 (ill.), 308 (ill.)
intuition, déjà vu, and intentionality, 195–96
looking ahead of the quest, 287–90
meditation and eastern spirituality, 205–7
out-of-body and near-death experiences, 216–17, 219–25
stories of healing and transformation, 116–19
Peru, 105, 236
Peter, 83
Peter, Book of, 315
Peter Pan [character], 31

Pew Forum on Religion and Public Life, 209, 212
Philippians, Book of, 306
photographs of the author, 10 (ill.), 202 (ill.)
phyletic gradualism, 48
Picard, Captain [character], 110, 358
Picasso, Pablo, 259
Picket's Charge, 339
"The Pierced Man," 82
Pinchbeck, Daniel, 151
Ping, Robert, 231
Pisces, 13, 102
Pitt, Brad, 318
Planck, Max, 249–50, 254
Plato, 20, 50, 60 (ill.), 61, 164
Playboy, 12
Pluto, 45
Pogo [character], 112
Pogo [comic strip], 200
Pollock, Jackson, 276
Polynesia, 78
Pope, Alexander, 294
Portugal, 82
Poseidon, 303
Potbelly Hill. See Göbekli Tepe
The Power of Myth (Moyers), 255
The Power of Now (Tolle), 198–99
prana, 233
prayer
animal envoys from cave and cosmos, 17–18, 27
Brahman, 345
chemical keys, 150
dowsing, 157, 159
end of the quest and beyond, 360
hard-wired for spirituality, 177
hypnotism, past life regression, and channeling, 185
illustrations and photographs, 340 (ill.)
indifference to the quest, 340
meditation and eastern spirituality, 197, 203–4
method of the quest, 131–32, 275
object of the quest, 6
personal testimony of a quest, 327–28
religious concepts, 81
Premillennialism, 103, 104 (ill.)
preparation for quest meeting, 297–304